Working with Walter Benjamin

My father remained fascinated by the fact that there was a philosopher with 'our name'. To which I always added, 'another philosopher!' It is perhaps in the space opened by the possibility of being 'another philosopher' that most of the work I have done has itself taken place. It seems fitting therefore to dedicate this book to the memory of my father's fascination.

Working with Walter Benjamin

Recovering a Political Philosophy

Andrew Benjamin

EDINBURGH
University Press

© Andrew Benjamin, 2013

Edinburgh University Press Ltd
22 George Square, Edinburgh EH8 9LF

www.euppublishing.com

Typeset in 10.5/13 pt Sabon by
Servis Filmsetting Ltd, Stockport, Cheshire,
and printed and bound in Great Britain by
CPI Group (UK) Ltd, Croydon CR0 4YY

A CIP record for this book is available from the British Library

ISBN 978 0 7486 3434 7 (hardback)
ISBN 978 0 7486 4898 6 (paperback)
ISBN 978 0 7486 3435 4 (webready PDF)
ISBN 978 0 7486 9160 9 (epub)

Contents

Acknowledgements

Work arises from contexts. This final form of this book was developed in a seminar at the London Graduate School at Kingston University and then in a graduate seminar in the Department of Philosophy at De Paul University in Chicago. The members of both seminars worked to provide an exemplary context in which to develop this project.

I also want to thank friends, colleagues and students with whom I have discussed the detail of Benjamin's work. This took place in seminars, supervisions, private discussions (face-to-face as well as on Skype) and email exchanges. I have learnt a great deal. The limits are of my own making. In particular I would like to thank Peg Birmingham, Howard Caygill, Michael Fagenblat, David Ferris, Heidrun Freise, Joanna Hodge, John Lechte, Lucie Mercier, James Muldoon, Peter Osborne, Tony Phelan, Eleina Steikou, Uwe Steiner, Gerhard Richter, Elizabeth Rottenberg, Dimitris Vardoulakis, Henrik Wilberg, Christopher Wallace and Jess Whyte. I would also like to thank Keren Shlezinger and Samuel Cuff Snow for their assistance with the preparation of the manuscript.

The Appendices are rewritten versions of papers that have appeared earlier. They have been modified to a greater or lesser degree in order to accommodate being placed within this larger project. They initially appeared as:

'Boredom and Distraction: The Moods of Modernity', in Andrew Benjamin (ed.), *Walter Benjamin and History* (New York: Continuum Books, 2005), pp. 156–70.

'Benjamin and the Baroque: Posing the Question of Historical Time', in Helen Hills (ed.), *Reframing the Baroque* (London: Ashgate Press, 2011), pp. 161–79.

'The Illusion of The Future: Notes on Benjamin and Freud', in Andrew Milner, Matthew Ryan and Robert Savage (eds), *Imagining the Future: Utopia and Dystopia, Arena* 25–26 (2006): 193–204.

Introduction

All philosophical knowledge has its unique expression in
language.

Walter Benjamin

These are the days when no one should rely on his 'competence'. Strength
lies in improvisation. All the decisive blows [*Alle entscheidenden Schläge*] are
struck left-handed.[1]

So wrote Benjamin in *One-Way Street*. To introduce a work that is
orientated around the possibility of Benjamin's philosophical project
having an effective afterlife is an undertaking that is marked by a
number of inherent difficulties. The difficulties do not stem from the
presence or absence of 'competence'. On the contrary these difficulties
become clear once there is an attempt to avoid subordinating Benjamin's
work to moral or political frameworks where the latter are based on a
refusal to allow the complexities and the nuances within his own work
to emerge. What has to be maintained is the 'left-handed blow'.[2] In this
context the act of 'introduction' has a specific meaning. To introduce
is to stage. Rather than an Introduction assuming that what is brought
into existence appears as though it were either untouched or already
completed, here other hands have been at work. Benjamin's work has
received specific forms of direction.

With Walter Benjamin there had been a prevailing supposition. The
choice had always been clear: Marxist rabbi or merely Marxist. As
with all clear choices the clarity of both the structure and its content is
merely apparent. What should in fact be at work is a radically different
philosophical project, one which will have already received another
type of direction. The latter – the other direction – might be described
as proceeding within the 'diversion' (*Umweg*) that Benjamin names as
'method'. If theology remains – and it is the presence of theology that

in certain instances allows for the bridge bringing elements of Judaism into his work – then it stands opposed to religion.[3] Benjamin's work introduces a specific thinking of the opposition between theology and religion. Theology continues as an effective presence structuring his philosophical project. Introducing Benjamin therefore must stage this opposition as integral to its own Introduction.

It should be noted at the beginning therefore that the nature of the opposition between theology and religion demands detailed clarification in its own right. Hence, it is essential to be clear as to what a critical engagement and thus a genuine counter to religion is like (and in addition the figure of religion that such a counter maintains). In general terms what is meant here by an effective and thus genuine counter – what will be identified henceforth as a *counter-measure* and which needs to be understood as a form of critique – has a two-fold designation. (The term – *counter-measure* – will continue to be deployed throughout the chapters to come.) In the first instance the *counter-measure* is a counter-movement that retains the centrality of measure. However, what is measured and the nature of the measure will have a different quality. The second is that it involves the repositioning of the object of critique in terms of that which has a determining effect on the object in question. What this then means is that it is possible to generate an effective counter to the assumption of continuity. Within that setting – the setting created by the opposition of religion and theology – there are failed attempts to think the limit of religion. They become failed counters that signal no more than mere revolt. Perhaps the most banal form that an opposition to religion might take is atheism. Atheism entails the identification of religion with a claim about knowledge and in which the knowledge of a deity forms the basis of religion. Consequently, if religion were to be identified as defined in purely epistemological terms, then it would indeed follow that the introduction of any form of epistemological uncertainty could then be taken as having brought the force of religion into question. However, central to Benjamin's project is that such an approach to religion fails to grasp the effect of religion and thus what religion actually is. Moreover, the attempt to counter religion with the assertion of atheism is equally premised on a failure to grasp the way in which religion is deployed within the political. Taken generally religion is a force within conservative politics not because it maintains a deity at its centre but because, as Benjamin suggests, it is from the outset 'practical'.[4] Practicality here is the way in which religion structures every aspect of life and thus every subject position, even that subject position that defines itself as 'irreligious'. Hence the response to religion has to be a political one and not the evocation of the critical paucity of atheism.

Atheism is an inherently apolitical position – hence it will be more closely allied to a conservative political position than to one that seeks a transformation of structures of normativity and relations of power. What is clear – and this is a position that can be linked to thinkers as diverse as Marx, Weber and Tawney – is that there is an important symbiosis between religion and the structure of capitalism.[5] The futility of atheism as a response to religion is that it conflates a set of personal beliefs – what might be described as the religious – with the presence of a political order. If atheism were thought to be the *counter-measure* to religion then such a move would be premised on a radical misunderstanding of the nature of religion.

The investigation of the ways religion and theology differ – a difference in which undoing the imposed continuity of the former is what theology allows – is a topic to which repeated returns are to be made in this particular encounter with the work of Walter Benjamin. If there is an element that might deflect the centrality of the relation between theology and religion as an uncritical presence while providing the means by which it can be reconsidered then it can be located in 'life'. Indeed, part of the contention to be made throughout the following chapters is that 'life' is one of the key terms in Benjamin's work. Life of course has to be differentiated from that which would have been taken at the time Benjamin was writing as a *Lebensphilosophie*.[6] Equally, life, in Benjamin's renewal of the term, has to be stripped of its connection to both neutrality and any determination that would have been derived from biology. The question then is how is that rethinking of life to be understood? This question – as will come to be seen – continues to introduce Benjamin's work. Informing any answer to that question – the question of how life is to be understood – is the conjecture that 'life' as the term is present within Benjamin's thought is not simply human life as though the latter were a given. Rather, it pertains to the possibilities and the potentialities already inherent in that life. Life brings with it a life to come. Given this formulation the project that then arises concerns the recovery of that other possibility for life. The key point here is that it is a possibility within life. The future is a condition of the present. The future cedes its place therefore to the present as a site of potentiality.[7]

Once the assumption is that there is a potentiality within the life that is already there, then it is clear that what is involved is not a claim about either 'mere life' or that life which is at hand. Rather, it is a claim made about the being of being human.[8] (Potentiality and life define human existence.) Potentiality is a possibility within being. And precisely because it is a possibility within being, what is then of significance is how there can be an account of the move from potentiality to actuality.

Part of the argument to be developed in the chapters to come is that this move is staged by Benjamin in terms of different modalities of destruction. That move is there both within and as existence, once existence has a more complex description than that which would have been furnished by having taken the given as an end in itself. The complexity is there in what will be called henceforth *the fabric of existence*. The latter is a term that identifies human being in terms of modes of relationality rather than isolated subjectivity, a position that is consistent with the modalities of subjectivity developed by Benjamin in a number of the texts that are central to this overall project,[9] and which finds precise expression in *Fate and Character* when he argues that:

> No definition of the external world can disregard the limits set by the concept of the active human being. Between the active man and the external world, all is interaction [*Wechselwirkung*]; their spheres of action interpenetrate.[10]

While a return will be made to this passage in the context of Chapter 3, it has to be understood as undoing any separation of the human from the world, a separation that then brings with it the related position in which questions of correlation are deemed to be necessary. Staged by passages of this nature is the recognition that human being is already worldly.

Within *the fabric of existence* there is a potentiality for an eventual identification of life with the just life. The eventual, however, will necessitate that event that enables the possibility of this identification. The acknowledgement therefore of the just life as inherent (as a potentiality) in life necessitates what Benjamin identifies as the infinite postponement of the Last Judgement. This is a postponement that involves the maintained opening of a space. That space, a spacing that allows, will be developed in the argument to come in terms of what will be called a *caesura of allowing*. The caesura is the term that links destruction and spacing.

As part of the attempt to understand the difference between religion and theology as terms within Benjamin's writings, the formulation *the fabric of existence* has to be understood as the creation of a sense of place that stands as a *counter-measure* to a conception of place as determined by religion. Central to both capitalism and religion, which for Benjamin are defined in terms of each other, is their domination of spaces of experience and the creation of subject positions. Within capitalism as religion, and thus within that conception of religion which is the functioning of capitalism, 'each day commands the utter fealty of the worshipper'.[11] What this means is that if there is a conception of another life within that setting – a setting in which every day is a 'feast day' – then it is not there as a potentiality within life as it lived out. Another life, a life that is other, would have to be defined in terms of what might be described as a literal 'afterlife'. This is the life that demands the Last Judgement: the life that is the afterlife. The question of religion's *counter-measure* returns, and in so doing it returns as the question of life. As an opening, the first element of a response is going to be that if there is a term within Benjamin's writings that identifies the way that potentiality within life is to be understood – and thus the potentiality whose presence is already a distancing of religion – then it can be found, at the outset, in the differing permutations of the term *Glück*.[12]

At the outset *Glück* can be translated as either 'luck' or 'fortune' or 'happiness'. As a term, however, its interest is twofold. In the first – though this is a position that will be developed in Chapter 1 – its interest can be located in the way it stages destruction. That staging means that it is to be understood as marking potentiality's actualisation. Secondly – and this is the point to be noted here as part of an Introduction – that interest resides in the way it recalls elements central to Ancient Greek thought.[13] Indeed, it is possible to go further and suggest that what is at stake in Benjamin's evocations of life – life as separate from life as a given or life as biology – has a clear point of reference in Sophocles' *Antigone*. To be more precise, the reference is to the last speech by the Chorus. This is a speech in which the Chorus advances the *counter-measure* to the conceptions of law, and thus the subject positions that such conceptions of law demand, that is at work within the positions that establish the conflict between Creon and Antigone. If that conflict is the tragedy then its resolution and thus the project of delimiting the hold of the tragic is to be found in this *counter-measure*.[14]

The first line of the last speech by the Chorus in Sophocles' *Antigone* reads as follows:

πολλῷ τὸ φρονεῖν εὐδαιμονίας
πρῶτον ὑπάρχει[15]

A direct translation is the following: 'The greatest part of happiness is wisdom.'[16] Within that translation 'happiness' translates *eudaimonia* and 'wisdom' is the translation of *to phronein*. However, if the translations were into German rather than English, then the former, *eudaimonia*, could be translated as *des Glücks* or even *der Glückseligkeit*. (Ezio Sevino's Italian translation translates *eudaimonia* as *buona vita*.)[17] If 'wisdom' is indeed linked to 'happiness' (*eudaimonia*) then wisdom allows for the actualisation of a potentiality in life. Wisdom allows for the move from mere life to the good life (or perhaps more accurately the just life). The fundamental point is that life cannot be taken as an end in itself. Moreover, there needs to be the possibility for the actualisation of that which endures in life as a potentiality.

Within the framework of Sophocles' *Antigone*, 'wisdom' (*to phronein*) functions almost as the *sine qua non* for the actualisation of the good life. It could be viewed as its trigger. Moreover, the counter indicates that what both Creon and Antigone lack is 'wisdom'. This should not be understood as a point made only in relation to the play's closure. Indeed, it is essential to the play's structure and overall development that the evocation of the centrality of *to phronein* has occurred at an earlier stage in the play. The last speech by the Chorus has to be understood therefore as recalling and reinforcing the earlier evocation of 'wisdom'. The positioning is deliberate. At the play's centre, Haemon, as part of a heated exchange with his father Creon, says the following:

> If you were not my father [μη πατερ], I would say that you had no wisdom [ουκ φρονειν].[18]

The significance of this line is twofold. In the first instance it locates the centrality of *to phronein* within the play as a whole. In the second it means that any possible attribution of centrality *to phronein* locates *to phronein* as standing in opposition to the law on the condition that the law is defined in terms of immediacy. Immediacy stands opposed to mediation. Mediation involves deliberation and thus judgement. (The latter will always have the form of a contestable decision.) Both deliberation and judgement involve a conception of time that is radically distinct from the temporality of immediacy. Judgement has wisdom as its necessary correlate. Present therefore is a form of definition that, on the one hand, notes the radical difference between the conceptions of law evoked by Creon and Antigone and yet, on the other, elides that difference insofar as both conceptions of law are defined in terms of immediacy.[19]

Moving to mediacy, and as a result countering the exigency of immediacy, holds open the possibility of another relation to the law. Creon and Antigone remain the 'same' insofar as both hold to conceptions of law defined by immediacy. What this means is that the *counter-measure* has a twofold presence. In the first instance it involves the identification of immediacy as being the determining element within law and then secondly opening up the move to mediacy as its counter. Law does come to an end. There isn't an opening to the measureless. There is a *counter-measure*. In this context it amounts to a possible reworking of the law such that the law is then of necessity interarticulated, from the very start, with the possibility of judgement (where judgement marks the inescapability of mediacy). In other words, what both Haemon's intervention and the last speech by the Chorus open up as a possibility is a critique of law in the name of law. This is the staging of Walter Benjamin's project. It is a critique, however, that takes the potentiality for the just life as its point of departure. The modernity in which Benjamin's critique of law is advanced recalls fundamental aspects of Greek heritage; however, that recall is also a moment of differentiation from that heritage, since fundamental to Benjamin's position – and this is a position shared by Heidegger – is that access to a founding sense of propriety necessitates the destruction of the given.[20] Both Ancient Greek philosophy as well as Ancient Greek tragedy have a different relation to the undoing of both law and fate's definition in terms of immediacy. Oedipus' revolt in *Oedipus Tyrannous* – revolt as the refusal of fate – on the one hand, and Athena's undoing of the law in the *Eumenides* on the other, are profoundly different activities. Athena undoes fate. Oedipus' revolt maintains it. That they cannot be assimilated marks modernity's separation from the Greeks (while of course underscoring their contemporary relevance).

The evocation of the domain of Ancient Greek tragedy occurs at a distance from Benjamin. And yet there is also a proximity. Distance and proximity are the terms that mark the necessity within Benjamin's work for a relationship between destruction and life (a relationship whose presence is one of the predominating concerns of Chapter 1). This is the force of the distinction between theology and religion. The latter holds fate in play, holding it while refusing to name fate as fate and thus normalising its presence. As a result, within that process what will have become impossible is the possibility of its yielding an opening in which the potentiality for a world that is other is actualised. Theology is that which occasions just this possibility. Theology names the 'decisive blows'. Theology is 'left-handed'. If further evidence is needed for the division between religion and theology – recognising that the latter is inextricably bound up with what Benjamin identifies as 'profane illumination' – then it can be found in his identification of the limits of hashish. The limit is located at the divide and in the need for a divide between religion and theology. Benjamin writes:

> But the true, creative overcoming of religious illumination certainly does not lie in narcotics. It resides in a profane illumination, a materialist, anthropological inspiration, to which hashish, opium or whatever else can only give an introductory lesson.[21]

'Profane illumination', while named as a 'creative overcoming', needs to be understood as another modality of the 'blow'.

It is important at this point, as these particular 'blows' can also be understood as the *counter-measure*, to return to aspects of the latter's detail. While the specificity of the *counter-measure* will continue to return and be developed in the following chapters, it is nonetheless still possible to recall two of its fundamental characteristics. The first pertains to the ubiquity of measure. Countering occurs in the name of another sense of measure. The *counter-measure* identifies what is being countered such that a limit is established and an opening emerges. In the case of religion the limit that arises is established by the identification of religion as a structured interdependency located between a specific modality of historical time and the subject position demanded by it. (This will be pursued, for example, by Benjamin in *Fate and Character* in terms of the relationship between 'fate' and 'guilt'.) The limit provides the opening in which time and subjectivity are able to be reconfigured. It is, of course, the opening that is the second aspect of the *counter-measure*. However, before turning to it, it is essential to note the way the ubiquity of measure figures. If what is being countered is one measure then the emergence of another cannot be arbitrary. What this opens up is one of the most difficult aspects of a project defined by the recovery of a political philosophy for which to advance a sustained and unequivocal argument. The position to be presented here is that what is countered is one conception of life. Moreover, the other measure, thus the *counter-measure*, is provided by the potentiality for the 'just life' that inheres in 'mere life'. It is the possibility that has already been noted in relation to Sophocles and which comes to the fore when mediacy counters immediacy, and thus when justice counters the law. The *counter-measure* stages therefore the possibilities afforded by the interconnection of justice, judgement and mediacy.

The second aspect of the *counter-measure* that needs to be noted pertains to the opening established by the process of countering. While the details of that opening will be developed in Chapter 1 in terms of the relationship between 'destruction' and a *caesura of allowing*, it can still be noted that if what is countered is a form of determination, countering occurs in the name of a necessary indetermination. Determination is a form that already inheres, for example, in the reiteration of immediacy, within which the naturalisation of historical time works to determine in advance what counts as historical as the measure that will have already been set, or where 'fate' determines subjectivity such that subjectivity is immediately given.

Indetermination allows for measure since what is retained is the opening provided by the non-identification of 'mere life' and the just life, a non-identification that inheres in the distinction between actuality and potentiality. The reason why there is an indetermination is that what is not provided in advance is the form to be taken by the actualisation of a potentiality. It is a form that will be the result of work and therefore has to be understood as an activity. Indetermination is such that it provides an opening in which activity will be the finding of form, a finding that is orientated by the possibility of the interplay between justice, mediacy and judgement rather than one provided by the severity of the connection between immediacy and what Benjamin will refer to in *Fate and Character* as the 'order of law'.

The distancing of law – which has to be understood as that which determines life but is not integrated into life – can be found in Benjamin's evocation of 'doctrine'. He argues, for example, in *The Origin of German Tragic Drama* that:

> In its finished form philosophy will, it is true, assume the quality of doctrine, but it does not lie within the power of mere thought to confer on it such a form. Philosophical doctrine is based on historical codification [*historische Kodifikation*].[22]

If Scholem is right in his suggestion that the term 'doctrine' needs to be understood in the context of a link between Torah and 'instruction', then it would appear that what is at work here is a return of an externality in control of law, a position dependent upon the subsequent identification of Torah with law.[23] The resolution to this problem inheres in the differing ways 'historical codification' can be understood. On one level it evokes law in its separation from life, and yet while that will always be there as a possibility, the formulation 'historical codification' has a doubled presence. On the one hand, therefore, it is a fated presence and as a consequence the historical is present as the already determined nature of law. And yet, on the other, harboured within any 'historical codification' is the move from what is there – where its being 'there' has to be understood as its already being at hand – to the possibilities that are demanded by the potentiality of the move from 'mere' existence to a 'just' existence. In other words, rather than read the evocation of doctrine as the assumption of pure fate, which here would be law in its radical separation from life such that in its coming to be connected to life its presence would be immediate rather than mediate, it can be understood as the provision of a 'guideline' (*Richtsnur*). While a return will need to be made to the presence of 'guidelines' – a term evoked by Benjamin in *Towards a Critique of Violence* as part of the distancing and eventual 'depositioning' of law – what the evocation of the link between 'doctrine' and history opens up are intimations of that which takes place with the abeyance of the 'order of law'. Not only will there have been a transformation of the relationship between subject and law, it will also be the case that the attendant conception of subjectivity and thus being a subject will themselves have been the site of a radical reconfiguration. The interplay between the two – history and subjectivity – reinforces the general argument that the fundamental repositioning of conceptions of historical time are accompanied by transformations on the level of the subject. The subject is not opposed to the work of historical time such that it is the op-position that allows it to become historical. (A positioning that assumed what might be described as the initial ahistoricality of subjectivity.) Rather, subject positions are interarticulated, *ab initio*, with the different conceptions of historical time that are being worked through in Benjamin's writings.

If there is a final word that needs to be added in relation to the way the recourse to 'history' can be understood, as the recourse to that which undoes the already determined, then reference should be made to the argument in *Towards a Critique of Violence* in which Benjamin argues that a critique of law – where the latter is defined simply in terms of an oscillation between 'positive law' and 'natural law' – has to break with the enforced continuity of that movement. Critique demands that which stands 'outside' (*außerhalb*) both. For Benjamin this will result from a 'philosophico-historical view of law'.[24] If 'doctrine' emerges then it will be the presence of philosophy taking place after the work of destruction.

Notes

1. All references to Benjamin's writings here and in the chapters to come will be to the English edition followed by the German, that is, to Walter Benjamin, *Selected Writings, Volume 1: 1913–1926*, ed. Marcus Bullock and Michael Jennings, trans. Rodney Livingstone et al. (Cambridge, MA: Harvard University Press, 1996); *Selected Writings, Volume 2: 1927–1934* (Cambridge, MA: Harvard University Press, 1999); *Selected Writings, Volume 3: 1935–1938* (Cambridge, MA: Harvard University Press, 2002); or *Selected Writings, Volume 4: 1938–1940* (Cambridge, MA: Harvard University Press, 2003); followed by reference to *Gesammelte Schriften*, 7 vols, ed. Rolf Tiedemann and Herman Schweppengäuser (Frankfurt: Suhrkamp Verlag, 1980).

Other references to English translations will be to Walter Benjamin, *The Origin of German Tragic Drama*, trans. John Osborne (London: New Left Books, 1977); and *The Arcades Project*, ed. Rolf Tiedemann, trans. Howard Eiland and Kevin McLaughlin (Cambridge, MA: Harvard University Press, 1999).

For the most part, the published translations have been used. Where adaptations have taken place this has been done in order to sustain consistency of argumentation, and modifications have not been signalled. The reference in this case is Benjamin, *Selected Writings* 1, p. 447; *Gesammelte Schriften* IV.1, p. 89.

2. Highlighting the centrality of the 'blow' (*Schlag*) is indebted to the work of David Ferris. See Ferris, 'Politics of the Useless: The Art of Work in Heidegger and Benjamin', in Dimitris Vardoulakis and Andrew Benjamin (eds), *'Sparks will Fly': Benjamin and Heidegger* (New York: SUNY Press, 2014).

3. The relationship between Benjamin's work and Judaism has at least two registers. In the first there are moments at which direct reference is made to elements within Judaism. These occur as much in relation to figures and historical themes as in relation to liturgy or prayer. The other register concerns the compatibility between aspects of Benjamin's work and elements within Jewish theological and philosophical thought. It is often the case that Benjamin's thinking is informed by Judaic sources. However, it is precisely these sources which at times can be used to think the opposition between religion and theology and in which they inform – informing by forming – theology's opposition to religion. In other instances the opposite may be the case. The lack of clarity here attests to the fact that 'religion' for Benjamin has nothing to do with religious belief. Rather it has everything to do with the creation of a relationship between a specific modality of historical time and its attendant subject position. The relationship between Benjamin and Judaism has to be investigated on many levels. The only sustained reference made to it here concerns deploying those elements of Judaism that play a fundamental role in a Benjaminian critique of religion. It should be added, however, that ignorance of Benjamin's relation to Judaism is ignorance of his project in general. In terms of writings on Benjamin's work that explore directly Benjamin's relation to Judaism see Brian Britt, *Walter Benjamin and the Bible* (Lewiston, NY: Edwin Mellen Press, 2003); Eric Jacobson, *Metaphysics of the Profane: The Political Theology of Walter Benjamin and Gershom Scholem* (New York: Columbia University Press, 2003); Bram Mertens, *Dark Images, Secret Hints: Benjamin, Scholem, Molitor and the Jewish Tradition* (Berlin: Peter Lang, 2007); and Stéphane Moses, *L'ange de l'histoire* (Paris: Editions du Seuil, 1992).

4. Benjamin, *Selected Writings* 1, p. 289; *Gesammelte Schriften* VI, p. 101.

5. Despite the differences in their positions both Tawney and Weber note the interarticulation of capitalism's development with Protestantism. Indeed Benjamin's own analysis of Protestantism in his study of *Trauerspiel* – that is, *The Origin of German Tragic Drama* – can be understood as a contribution to that overall analysis. See R. H. Tawney, *Religion and the Rise of Capitalism* (London: Penguin Books, 1969); and Max Weber, *The Protestant Ethic and the Spirit of Capitalism*, trans. Stephen Kalbe (Oxford: Oxford University Press, 2010).

6. In terms of the relationship between Benjamin and *Lebensphilosophie* see Nitzan Lebovic, 'The Beauty and the Terror of *Lebensphilosophie*: Ludwig Klages, Walter Benjamin and Alfred Bauemular', *South Central Review* 23.1 (Spring 2006), pp. 23–39. Lebovic's superb analysis locates

the complexities within *Lebensphilosophie* as it is understood at the time in which Benjamin is writing. It therefore allows genuine philosophical acuity.

7. It is interesting here to compare this point to a position held by Leibniz. As a part of his treatment of the Monad he argued – both in the *Monadology* (§22) and in the *Theodicy* (§360) – that the present state of the Monad, and the presence of its movement between successive states, is such that 'le present y est gros de l'avenir'. This can be read as maintaining a position in which the future is always a condition of the present. The difference in regard to Benjamin is not the doubled nature of the present but that this doubling is to be explicated in Benjamin's work both in terms of potentiality that yields a conception of the present as a site of conflict and the possibility of that potentiality's actualisation. Potentiality within Benjamin's work demands a form of 'destruction' that 'will enable its actualisation'. Leibniz's position is fundamentally different. There are, however, a number of recent attempts – most of which take up other aspects of Leibniz's work – to locate a greater proximity between Benjamin and Leibniz. See, for example, Paula L. Schwebel, 'Intensive Infinity: Walter Benjamin's Reception of Leibniz and its Sources', *MLN* 127 (2012), pp. 589–610.

8. 'Mere life' (*bloßes Leben*) is a formulation that is intrinsic to Benjamin's rethinking of life. The formulation marks the reductive identification of life with biological life. 'Mere life' is the latter. Equally, 'mere life' is the life that is subject to and subjects itself to 'fate'. The interruption of these identifications – their destruction – occurs in the name of another possibility for life. This is a position that will continue to be developed in the chapters to come.

9. In this regard see my *The Fabric of Existence: Placed Relationality as the Ground of Ethics* (forthcoming).

10. Benjamin, *Selected Writings* 1, p. 202; *Gesammelte Schriften* II.1, p. 180.

11. Benjamin, *Selected Writings* 1, p. 288; *Gesammelte* Schriften II.1, p. 173.

12. For a detailed discussion of Benjamin's work in this area and its relation to both Hölderlin and Sophocles see my *Leben und Glück* (forthcoming).

13. There have been other philosophical engagements with Walter Benjamin that have highlighted what might be described as the Greek dimension of his thought. See in particular both Antonia Birnbaum, *Bonheur Justice: Walter Benjamin* (Paris: Payot, 2009); and Martin Blumenthal-Barby, 'Pernicious Bastardizations: Benjamin's Ethics of Pure Violence', *MLN* 124.3 (April 2009), pp. 728–51.

14. I have developed this interpretation of the Antigone and its consequences for a more general interpretation of the actuality of Greek tragedy in my *Place, Commonality and Judgment* (London: Continuum, 2010).

15. Sophocles, *Antigone, Woman of Trachis, Philoctetes, Oedipus at Colonus*, ed. and trans. Hugh Lloyd Jones (Cambridge, MA: Harvard University Press, 1994), l. 1348.

16. Other contemporary translations are: 'Of happiness far the greatest part / Is Wisdom', in *Sophocles' Three Tragedies*, l. 1348, p. 45; and 'Besinnung ist von den Gütern des Glücks / bei weitem das höchste', in Sophokles, Antigona *in Dramen*, ll. 1348, p. 261. What is important in all of these

instances is a form of complementarity in regard to the nature of the relationship between 'happiness' and 'wisdom'.

17. Sofocle, *Antigone*, trans. Ezio Savino (Milano: Garzanti, 1989), p. 309.
18. Sophocles, *Antigone*, p. 755.
19. The *Antigone* will always mark as much a clash between family and the *polis* as it does between female and male. There is an obviously gendered dimension to the play. And yet the recourse made to law's immediacy – the twofold recourse in terms of Antigone and Creon – while involving gender is not explicable in gendered terms. Were that to be the case then gender would be linked to the immediacy of the law and thus relations between the genders would be inevitably tragic. The play can be read as suggesting that the relationship between genders – a relationship that allows for conflict but resists tragedy – is a relationship that is always already mediated in advance by the complex operation(s) of judgement. Hence, while a concern with either kinship or with slavery is a fundamental element of the play, their presence cannot be thought outside the clash between the immediacy of the law and its mediation (and transformation) by judgement. Positions which differ from this argument but which in the end need not be incompatible with it can be found in the work of both Butler and Chanter. See Judith Butler, *Antigone's Children: Kinship Between Literature and Death* (New York: Columbia University Press, 2000); and Tina Chanter, *Whose Antigone? The Tragic Marginalization of Slavery* (Albany, NY: SUNY Press, 2011).
20. Heidegger in *Being and Time*, for example, argues that the need for a destruction (*Destruktion*) of 'tradition' lies in the effect of its givenness and thus the assumption that it is already at hand; see Heidegger, *Being and Time*, trans. John Macquarrie and Edward Robinson (Oxford: Basil Blackwell, 1962).

> Tradition takes what has come down to us and delivers it over to self-evidence; it blocks our access to those primordial 'sources' from which the categories and concepts handed down to us have been in part quite genuinely drawn. (Ibid., p. 43)

Overcoming that 'block' demands a destruction of the given if the given is taken as an end itself. Benjamin will differ from Heidegger in relation to what it is that is opened up by the process of destruction. However, as will be suggested in the chapters to come, 'destruction' is a defining motif within a great deal of 'modern philosophy'. In fact, it can be argued that one of the dominant tendencies within 'modern philosophy' is defined by the presence of different modalities of destruction as well as destruction's necessity.

21. Benjamin, *Selected Writings* 2, p. 209; *Gesammelte Schriften* II.1, p. 297.
22. Benjamin, *Origin of German Tragic Drama*, p. 27; *Gesammelte Schriften* I.1, p. 207.
23. There is an important discussion of the question of 'doctrine' that is situated in relation to these passages in Eli Friedlander, *Walter Benjamin: A Philosophical Portrait* (Cambridge, MA: Harvard University Press, 2012), pp. 31–3. Friedlander also connects this passage from Benjamin to Scholem. While the direction of this interpretation is different it should be noted that

Friedlander underscores the centrality of these references to 'doctrine'. It might be added here that the discussion of doctrine as it occurs here, if Scholem is correct in linking it to Torah, can be viewed as reoccurring in the exchange between Rosenzweig and Buber known as *The Builders*. See Franz Rosenzweig, *On Jewish Learning* (New York: Schocken Books, 1955).

24. Benjamin, *Selected Writings* 1, p. 238; *Gesammelte Schriften* II.1, p. 182.

Chapter 1

Opening

Natural history does not extend to mankind, any more than
does universal history; it knows only the individual. Man is
neither a phenomenon nor an effect, but a created being.

Walter Benjamin

1

Dates may reveal very little. Attributing a productive centrality to
specific dates therefore could only ever have force if these dates had
already become the site of a form of attribution rather than an origin.
In other words, dates have force, and can only have force, retroactively.
And yet, within the parameters created by such a setting dates retain a
type of exigency. Almost directly after the Russian revolution and in
the aftermath of what could be described as the 'failure' of the German
revolution, Walter Benjamin wrote a number of highly significant texts.[1]
They are all positioned in relation to – and are thus positioned by – a set
of key terms, for example 'law', 'justice', 'life', 'destruction', 'violence',
'fate', 'theology', 'religion'. The list is tentative and could be either supplemented or clarified. The contention of this project – one defined by
working with the writings of Walter Benjamin – is that this constellation
of terms when articulated together form the basis of an exacting and
highly significant contribution to political philosophy, one in which, as
has been intimated, life is central.

  With the arrival of a specific form of philosophical thinking the
temporality of dates is left to one side and another thinking of time
has to emerge. Time within this setting and the thinking it occasions
can be connected to a form of retroactive productivity. Moreover,
once the range of possibilities marked out by the terms noted above is
connected to what may have been Benjamin's final text, namely 'On

the Concept of History', then the case for the presence of a singular contribution to a philosophical thinking of the political becomes even more compelling. At stake here is philosophy and thus a thinking of the political. Even Benjamin's own engagement with forms of political activity – for example, the actions of the Social Democrats in the Germany of the 1930s – incorporates a philosophical measure. Integral to the understanding of that measure is the way the apparently neutral status of 'interpretation' comes undone. The practice of 'interpretation' gives way to a mode of thinking in which all the elements of that relation, that is subject, object as well as the process of interpretation, are in fact transformed in the process. Within that context interpretation will be taken as assuming a type of neutrality in relation to both subject and object insofar as neither will have been transformed by the process, and thus the elements that figure within it take on a normative status. 'Interpretation' as a process encounters a limit. As will be suggested, transformation in this context has to be explained in terms of its effect on both the subject and the object.

Precisely because what is at work within the chapters to come is neither straightforwardly philological let alone synoptic, this project can be best understood as strategic if not projective.[2] The conceit organising this work is nonetheless quite clear: either there are elements of Benjamin's writings that are useful in their own right for the development of a philosophical thinking of the political, or there are not. If they are useful for that development then what will be important is how those elements work both within and for a philosophical thinking of the political. Utility will not be explicit. It will have to be recovered. The process of recovering is in part connected to the form in which certain texts both work and moreover can be made to work. What matters, in other words, is the possibility of Walter Benjamin's writings working beyond the date at which they were written. Hence this particular project – *Working with Walter Benjamin* – is concerned with that work's afterlife, where work is not a given but rather the site of work's recovery. This means that work will have already envisaged a form of afterlife. Living on demands recovery.[3] This accords with Benjamin's own understanding of quotation, namely 'quoting a text implies interrupting its context' (*seinen Zusammenhang unterbrechen*).[4] Moreover, this is a position that is reinforced in *Literary History and the Study of Literature* when he writes that there is within such study a transformation of what would have counted as the original. What this means, as he goes on to write, is that 'what is at stake is not to portray literary works in the context of their age, but to represent the age that perceives them – our age – in the age during which they arose.'[5] The claim that has to be made here to this positioning of the 'literary work' is that it is true of works in general and not just literary works. Indeed, because as a claim it pertains to that which occurs as a result of a work's afterlife, there is no reason to suppose that it will not be equally true of philosophical texts as it will be of works of art. Once this position is accepted then there is no reason to suppose that such a claim about the literary in its capacity to be extended to the philosophical cannot then be applied to Benjamin's works themselves. Hence there is an opening that while deferring to context allows equally the determining hold of context to be deferred. This opening occasions another approach. Within it the argument is that to allow Benjamin's work to be productive is to maintain it as philosophical. The viability of his work is not found therefore in its instrumentality, other than as what both forms and informs a philosophical thinking of the present.[6] However, it should not be thought that even these writings, let alone Benjamin's writings in general, have an indifferent relation to the political – even a philosophical thinking of the political. Indeed, references to the political and the actuality of what for Benjamin counted as contemporary political events abound. What matters is how that relation is to be thought. In other words, references to the actuality of the political are not to be identified with a thinking of the political. With the philosophical the latter is central. Moreover, the insistence of politics' actuality can only be understood in light of that thinking if the primacy of the philosophical is to be retained. The question of what is involved in a philosophical thinking of the actuality of the political remains a genuine philosophical problem. What will be argued throughout the chapters to come, though specifically in regard to the eventual engagement with Benjamin's text *On the Concept of History*, is that the actual can be approached in terms of a philosophical thinking of the political as a *politics of time*.[7]

There is no easy answer to the question of the political in the work of Walter Benjamin. Even when his work is taken as a whole the reference to other modes of political thought are beset by problems. How, for example, would it be possible to reconcile the range of incompatible – and perhaps in the end irreconcilable – names and references? The names of Marx and Brecht are invoked with what may appear to be the same force as the names and concepts of Klages and Schmitt.[8] Rather than attempt to resolve the complexities that would stem from any attempt to establish a rapprochement between these names by operating merely on the level of the proper names – a level on which the presence of written texts will always have been subordinated to the proper name – the only way of engaging with Benjamin's work, if it is to be the site of philosophical thinking, demands a twofold move. In the first instance, and as a reiteration of the above, there needs to be a loosening of the hold of the proper name and thus the modes of compatibility and consistency that the insistence of proper names may demand and therefore, in the second, it must be able to recover – recovery and retroactivity working together – a project whose potentiality is necessarily already there within a range of different texts. In this instance this range consists of the texts that are defined by a determined period of Benjamin's thinking but which are of course to be supplemented by a more extended range of texts. What matters here is the development of a consistent project. The contention is that, for the most part, it first emerges in texts written between 1919 and 1921 and which can then be supplemented by other texts located outside that defined period.[9] Each of the texts deemed central to this project will be taken up in the course of this book, and individual chapters will be devoted to each one of them.

This means that there is a procedure that will be followed here. There is a way forward.[10] Rather than mere speculation, the path ahead involves working closely through Benjamin's texts. As has already been noted this will reach a productive end point in a discussion of his text *On the Concept of History*. (A text that is of course a set of fragments with their own fragmentary supplements.) The steps leading towards it will be provided by an engagement with the following texts: *The Meaning of Time in the Moral World* (1921), *Fate and Character* (1919–21), *Towards a Critique of Violence* (1921) and the *Theological Political Fragment* (1920).[11] Taking these texts up will also necessitate allowing for the noted registration of another text written during the same period, namely *Capitalism as Religion* (1921).[12] The significance of the latter text – as was suggested in the Introduction – can be derived for the most part from the clear necessity of understanding what is involved in the systematic way in which Benjamin distinguishes between theology and religion.[13]

Benjamin's writings are too quickly either praised for their evocation of the theological or condemned for precisely that same evocation. For the most part, and in both instances – praise or blame – this is due to a conflation of the theological with religion. Care in interpretation will avoid this conflation. Equally, it will make clear that the division between the theological and religion is a fundamental point of his project. And yet, even if their difference is assumed and thus the conflation avoided, as has been mentioned, it is not as though the question of how the difference between theology and religion is to be understood has become redundant. Indeed, understanding their difference remains a central task in any interpretation of Benjamin's work. As part of an answer to that question it needs to be noted that integral to their difference is the possibility of locating in Benjamin's work a fundamental difference between modalities of historical time. One pertains to theology and the other to religion. (The latter ties religion and capitalism together as evincing the same sense of historical time.) However, while there is a type of opposition at work here it is not as though what is opposed does not occupy the same historical period – where periodisation is defined by dates – either as a potentiality or as an eventual difference. Differences and potentialities are the articulation of modalities of the political. What this means is that Benjamin's work needs to be understood as occurring within what has already been described as a more generalised politics of time. It will be essential to turn to a clarification of what is meant by such a politics at the end of this chapter.

2

If it were necessary to state in advance the way in which the texts named above cohere, then reference could be made to Benjamin's famous allusion to the way in which 'fragments' of a now broken vessel cohere. The allusion occurs in his work on translation. The 'vessel' here could be understood as Benjamin's work when taken as an entity to be recovered. The 'fragments' on the other hand would then refer to the presence of published, unpublished, complete and incomplete texts. Benjamin writes in *The Task of the Translator* that:

> Fragments of a broken vessel that are to be glued together must match one another in the smallest details, although they need not be like one another.[14]

The point being made here is that these texts do not appear to be the same. And yet, within them there is a singularity of project. The nature of the texts in question – texts as either literal fragments or fragments of a yet to be completed project – demands a specific interpretive strategy, namely one grounded in an approach that links the presence of a productive abstraction, namely the emergence of a political philosophy, to particulars. Abstraction arises, indeed can only arise, from close attention to detail. The ensuing philosophical thinking – Benjamin's – will of course have had to incorporate from the start its own productive fissuring. This is a possibility that is already present, firstly, in the significance of allegory and the subsequent displacing of the symbol – a move in which mediacy is then privileged over the appearance of immediacy (and in which immediacy has to be understood as mere appearance). And then secondly, it inheres in the necessity that the image be rethought.

Benjamin's preoccupation with the image – a preoccupation that results in what will come to be termed 'the dialectical image' – is premised on a refusal of the giveness of the image. The 'dialectical image' is the reiteration of the mediate as opposed to the immediate. This is the image that sides with allegory.[15]

Detail, however, is not an end in itself. Consequently, a stated beginning to this project is essential. What is needed is a frame of reference, created in order to allow for the recovery of Benjamin's thinking of the political to be presented (*albeit* a frame that will always stand in need of greater elaboration and continual adaptation). That initial frame will be constructed as the development of two moments that will be taken as defining what is central to Benjamin's thinking. They provide a setting whose clarification will emerge from the run of texts to be considered. The first is the evocation of 'destruction', which while given a precise formulation in his 1931 text *The Destructive Character* is nonetheless a decisive motif whose renamed presence continues to appear throughout his writings. Destruction is named and renamed. The second is comprised of two lines that define with stark clarity the nature of the project being worked out in *Towards a Critique of Violence*,[16] a project that concerns a concept of value that is intrinsic to human being. These two moments do not exist on their own. This must be the case as singularity is bound up with relationality. There is therefore more than mere contingency at work here. While the detail of the argument needs to be developed, it can still be suggested that when taken together these two texts stage the way destruction and value have an original interarticulation within Benjamin's work. Precisely because of that founding interconnection – and thus the retention of the original insistence of value within Benjamin's work – his *Towards a Critique of Violence* would be misunderstood were it to be assumed that it is about violence. The 'violence' of that text (which after all is not violence but *Gewalt*), while not the same, is much closer to what Arendt means by power.[17] While it will be taken up at a later stage it is worth stating in advance the way Arendt distinguishes between power and violence. She writes:

> Power and violence are opposites: where the one rules absolutely the other is absent. Violence appears where power is in jeopardy, but left to its own course it ends in power's disappearance.[18]

On the other hand, *Gewalt* as a term in Benjamin's argument will move between Arendt's 'power' and some of the senses inherent in the English word 'violence'. The position that has to arise is that there will always be different modalities of *Gewalt*, rather than its equation with 'violence', as though the latter had a single literal presence. *Gewalt* has different determinations. It cannot be generalised or simplified. Hence as a term it marks the site of a conflict: a conflict that concerns both the nature of the political and the necessity that the political has an ineliminable relation to *operability*. (As will emerge in the context of Chapter 4 this latter term – *operability* – captures what is essential to *Gewalt*.) It should be added that the differing modalities of *Gewalt* account for the existence of the present as a site of conflict and for the way in which destruction becomes a possible response to the present defined in these terms. What has to emerge is the thinking that is compatible with the claim that conflict 'is not the exception but the rule'.

There is an important link to *operability* (*Gewalt*) that is located in Benjamin's evocation of 'destruction', and while what is meant by 'destruction' comprises a project to which it will be necessary to return, it suffices to note at this stage that it has two aspects which identify its concerns. The first one is more general, namely that 'destruction' as a defining element in Benjamin's work is a further instance of a motif that will highlight the centrality of destruction within modernity (where the latter is understood as a specific form of philosophical development). This is a motif that arises with dramatic clarity in Descartes' opening to the *Meditations* (to be taken up in Chapter 2) and which when given greater extension becomes the *sine qua non* for forms of inauguration.[19] The second element is that destruction – the process of destruction – while identifying another beginning demands that the question to be addressed is how that beginning is in fact other. Part of an answer to that question is that such a beginning – a beginning understood as an inauguration – in order that it be other, cannot be thought as variety within continuity. Difference when linked to destruction is inextricably bound up with the possibility that what is other must be more than a form of variation, development as 'eternal return' or even as progress within continuity.[20] The presence of that which is 'other' has to be understood as possible. Moreover, its projected possibility is the basis of Benjamin's entire politico-philosophical project. Here the naming of that which is 'other' indicates an opening that occurs with and as destruction.[21] That which is 'other', the possibility of there being an 'other' possibility, breaks the link between destruction and nihilism in the first instance, while eschewing the incorporation of the 'other' into a movement from an *arché* towards a *telos* in the second. In addition, what is opened up is the possibility that 'being other' also defers both the temporality of 'eternal return' and the temporality of the Last Judgement (the latter position is given a precise formulation by Benjamin in *The Meaning of Time in the Moral World*).[22] Moreover, and to gesture towards the primacy of value within Benjamin's philosophical project, it is the deferral of the temporality of the Last Judgement that opens up the place for justice rather than defining justice in terms of either immediacy or as that which is only possible as the Last Judgement.

Even though destruction may be a motif within modernity, and that motif may have a certain ubiquity, differentiating one modality of destruction from another has to occur in terms of how the processes of inauguration, beginnings and the subsequent presence of that which is other are themselves understood.[23] Destruction does not have an essential nature. And this may be true due to the way destruction actually works as an operative presence within thought. This other beginning that is staged in Benjamin's work – and its being other is fundamental here even if the question of how it is present as that which is 'other' is yet to be clarified – necessitates the creation of an opening marked by the necessary interplay of continuity and discontinuity. Indeed, the question of continuity as linked to destruction will be a continual refrain within this book.

In a famous story that Benjamin tells Bloch, the concerns of continuity and discontinuity are staged. What matters, however, is that the staging of the discontinuous occurs in a way that has profound implications for any attempt to understand what is stake in Benjamin's conception of both interruption and discontinuity. The passage is the following:

> The Hassidim tell a story about the world to come. Everything there will be arranged just as it is with us [*bei uns*]. The room we have now will be just the same in the world to come, where our baby sleeps now, there it will sleep in the world to come. The clothes we are wearing we shall also wear in the world to come. Everything will be as it is now just a little different. [*Alles wird sein wie hier – nur ein klein wenig anders.*][24]

Understanding the way destruction is linked to creation and then to the relationship between discontinuity and continuity will depend upon understanding what is at stake in the formulation 'a little different'. This is a formulation that also appears in a more problematic context as a 'slight adjustment' when Benjamin writes on Kafka.[25] While the inflection may be marginally different what occurs in both these contexts is the description of a world to come. This is a future defined in terms of its presence as other and which would not have the form necessitated by the Last Judgement, let alone a form appearing as that which is the result of that Judgement. (In addition, the subject position linked to the Last Judgement – that is, the subject as originally guilty – would not apply.) However, at this point in the development of this position, the image of the future is not what is of primary concern. What is of significance in both instances is that the possibility of that which will be 'a little different', and that which will have comprised 'a slight adjustment', exists as yet to be actualised possibility at the present. Destruction endures therefore as the central concern.[26]

Taken more generally, however, it can be suggested that Benjamin uses a number of interrelated terms – e.g. *destruktiv*, *Zerstörung* – to generate a specific understanding of destruction. Within the context of his text on Karl Krauss, for example, and as part of his attempt to underscore the significance of Loos, Scheerbart and Klee, Benjamin argues that in responding to the singularity of their differing projects it becomes possible 'to understand a humanity that proves itself by destruction'.[27] The destruction in question is specific. Destruction here involves attempts to break open the hold of that which would identify a given event (creative work, human actions, etc.) in terms of universalising tendencies – e.g. creativity – or reposition them in a way that effaced their material particularity. (The latter would concern, for example, what Benjamin identifies as Loos' 'battles' (*Kämpfe*) with ornament.) Destruction therefore, as has already been suggested, is an opening. As an opening it brings contingency into play. And yet destruction is a necessity. There is a necessity for destruction. Part of that necessity lies in the fact that for Benjamin concurrent with destruction is the emergence of *the actual quality of things*, where that quality cannot be identified with what Benjamin will describe as 'what lies nearest to hand'. Staged here is both a conceptual as well as an experiential position. It is essential that the latter – that is, the experiential – figures, since with 'destruction' Benjamin needs to be understood as thinking his distance from the conception of experience developed by Kant. In other words, while experience has its conditions of possibility – and it should be added these conditions are not themselves experiential – those conditions are both external to the subject and construct the subject as their after-effect. Space and time are now – within modernity – marked by both complexity and conflict. This is the distancing of the Kantian 'transcendental aesthetic'. While what is meant here by the expression 'the actual quality of things' will be taken up below, it is still possible to suggest that destruction is linked, at least in outline, to a specific form of realism (one in which the real can never be at hand as itself and is therefore shown as itself as a consequence of destruction).[28] Benjamin has, of course, already referred to this possibility and in a similar language.

> The less a man is imprisoned in the binds of fate, the less he is determined by what *lies nearest at hand* [*das Nächste*], whether it be a people or circumstances.[29]

Precisely because of the location of the given – that which is already there – destruction brings with it a twofold necessity. In the first instance that necessity refers to a sense of opening and, in the second, to a conception of the real that emerges within and as part of the process of destruction. The work of these two elements – which allow for a summation in terms of the interplay between an opening to the real and an opening for the real – can be identified in Benjamin's text *The Destructive Character*.

The first element – which can be defined as concern with the creation of openings – is clear from the way the text itself begins. In this regard Benjamin writes:

> The destructive character knows only one watchword: make room [*Platz schaffen*]. And only one activity: spacing [*räumen*].[30]

There is a necessity built into the creation of openings understood as space making. However, such acts do not simply occur. They have a connection to what is already there. In addition, the act of destruction does not envisage an already determined connection to an imagined future. Hence there cannot be a determination coming from an already established image. Benjamin is unequivocal on this point. He writes in the same text that the 'destructive character sees no image [*kein Bild*] hovering before him'.[31] What the latter formulation entails is the impossibility of identifying a connection between Benjamin's thinking of destruction – a thinking that will have its own methodological enactment in a number of the texts under consideration here – and utopianism if the latter is defined in terms of the hoped for presentation of a pre-existing image. Moreover, in Benjamin's writings the word utopia cannot be attributed a simply positive quality. Indeed the opposite is the case. In his *Origin of German Tragic Drama*, for example, he notes the following:

> The function of the tyrant is the restoration of order in the state of emergency: a dictatorship whose utopian goal will always be to replace the unpredictability of historical accidents with the iron constitution of the laws of nature.[32]

Here a dictatorship – Schmittian in orientation and explication – is identified as having a goal that is clearly named as 'utopian'. Dictatorship is the effacing of contingency in the name of fated nature. However, what matters in this context is not the presence or absence of the word 'utopia' – all the word's reiteration indicates is that projects of the future are as much the province of 'tyrants' as they are of their opposite – hence what is of actual significance is the structure of thought within which that word is positioned. Rather than the evocation of the utopian

– which is a term that may be irredeemably mired in the problems of projected images and forms of political action in which that image is then enforced – what is essential to the absence of a determining image is both the creation of the future and a conception of the present as that which brings with it as a potentiality the possibility for the future to be made (underscoring thereby the centrality, once again, of the concept of potentiality in Benjamin's work).[33] Within such a setting the future would be a condition of the present. Praxis, as linked to the actualisation of already present potentialities, needs to be thought therefore in terms of that break with images that works to construct other possibilities. To which it can be added that precisely because the activity of work is central it has to follow that activity cannot be reduced to the presence of that other image. Hence Benjamin writes of Proust that his 'method is actualisation [*Vergegenwärtigung*] not reflection'.[34]

The creation of the future therefore does not occur *ex nihilo*. It is defined in relation to a potentiality for the future. However, Benjamin's sense of destruction is not determined by an image. Nor, moreover, does it take place for the sake of an image. On the contrary, that destruction is inextricably bound up with 'spacing' understood as place creation, and consequently opens up the question of determination recast as the to-be-determined. Another project emerges if a different question is posed. The answer would concern what comes to figure within the place opened by destruction. That question refers to what can figure and thus it also refers to what is able to figure. It is not as though these possibilities are just tentative. Equally, it is not as though they had faltered in advance. The recovery of the presence of an original inscription of value precludes such possibilities. Rather, the point is that what occurs in the space opened by destruction – 'spacing' as premised on destruction (and it should be recalled that is Benjamin's exact formulation) – is not determined in advance. Indetermination becoming determinant – more generally finitude as the after-effect of that which is originally in-finite – is a process that is best captured here by the term 'allow'.[35] To allow is to let happen and thus to occasion without that happening or the nature of the event being determined in advance. The interconnection of destruction and allowing – drawing on Benjamin's own vocabulary – will continue to be reformulated throughout the chapters making up this book in terms of a *caesura of allowing*. The *caesura* as an opening is only a form of freedom if freedom is understood as premised on the destruction of the already given – which will then appear, for example, as 'fate' or 'guilt', and finally as 'mythic violence'.

With the presence of the real there is the creation of an opening. Freedom within such a setting would not therefore be the province of a subject. Rather, freedom would be what *allowing* brings with it and moreover that which *allowing* releases. As a result, freedom needs to be repositioned in terms of releasing and spacing (where both are predicated upon modes of destruction and neither is a predicate of an individual). There is a further element involved here, i.e. activity. Benjamin has already alluded to the same creative process in his identification of 'spacing' as an activity. Activity is central. Though it should be added in this regard – even if this an argument whose adumbration awaits – that the activities taking place within the *caesura of allowing* are to be defined in terms of creativity linked to a reworked conception of life. As will be seen, 'life' – life in its differentiation from both 'natural life' and 'mere life' and therefore as a repositioning of 'life' in terms of a concern for the 'living' – holds the original relationship between Benjaminian destruction and value in place. Life names value. Value is there in the recovery of life.

The presence of destruction as creative – as a creative power – continues throughout Benjamin's writing. Indeed, it brings with it a range of names. Destruction is named and renamed. These names stage possibilities that the usual source of creativity – for example, the imagination – does not. Hence Benjamin writes that:

> Pure imagination is concerned exclusively with nature. It creates no new nature. Pure imagination, therefore, is not an inventive power.[36]

What is of course clear is that what is present with the 'caesura' as it forms part of that specific engagement of Benjamin's with Hölderlin – an engagement located in Benjamin's study of Goethe's *Elective Affinities* – is the centrality of productivity. Again, it is productivity without determination. There the caesura is the 'pure word'. The 'caesura' is also a term that reappears, however, in the *Arcades Project*, where it is linked to the work of the materialist historian.[37] The caesura names, or perhaps the complex relation between destruction and creation which is captured in the formulation *caesura of allowing* is named, in addition, in the interruption that is also present in the work of 'fortune' (*Glück*) in both *Fate and Character* and the *Theological Political Fragment*. (There has already been a hint of this possibility in the Introduction.)

'Fortune' is a form of destruction. In the first of these texts – again it is one to which a return will be made in later chapters in order to take it up in detail – Benjamin argues in relation to the hold of fate that:

> It was not in law rather in tragedy [*Nicht das Recht, sondern die Tragödie war es*] that the head of genius lifted itself [*sich . . . erhob*] for the first time

from the mist of guilt, for in tragedy demonic fate was breached [*wird das dämonische Schicksal durchbrochen*].[38]

The two significant moments here are the lifting of the head and the presence of a breach. It should be added here that destruction present as a 'breach' is linked, as will be seen in *Towards a Critique of Violence*, to 'the suspension [*die Entsetzung*] of the law'. Equally, it is that which allows for an undoing of the hold of fate. Fate – defined in the *Origin of German Tragic Drama* as 'entelechy of events within the field of guilt' – is the force of continuity that while positioning subjects comes to be breached.[39] In the specific context of *Fate and Character*, however, both lifting in the first instance and the breach in the second need to be understood as figures of interruption and thus of destruction. The *caesura of allowing* is repositioned continually. The process of destruction is named and renamed throughout Benjamin's work. While the detail will of course appear in the presentation to come of the argumentative strategies of Benjamin's actual texts it is nonetheless, still permissible to allow for a degree of generalisation. In terms of that generality it is possible to attribute to destruction, where its presence is understood both as a term though equally as a process in Benjamin's writings, four important aspects or qualities.

In the first instance the interruption stands for nothing other than itself. Present as the interruption. It has a founding purity. The term 'pure' here, though only as a beginning and as noted above, is a citation from Hölderlin's actual text. In the latter's *Remarks on Oedipus*, as quoted by Benjamin, the 'caesura' is 'the pure word'. That purity, of course, has to be thought within that context, though it also has to be thought beyond it. As such the term, in being tied to the 'caesura', has force because it is the possibility of a presence that is outside the usual determinations of continuity for its own sake. Equally, it is outside modes of thought structured by what will become an untenable oscillation between ends and means. Moreover, this evocation of the 'pure' as a figure within Benjamin's work is the distancing of utility. To which it should be added that it will be in terms of that distancing that this singularity will already have had inscribed into it an implicit structure of value. And this will be the case even if this inscription remains unannounced. While value will be addressed explicitly, there is an already present suggestion of its presence in the 'breaching of fate' as an opening. Hence, even as a singularity the 'pure' contains an original form of plurality. Interruption as a singularity – a singularity whose anoriginal plurality will come to figure – is formulated in the essay on Goethe's *Elective Affinities* in terms of the 'expressionless'. In that context Benjamin writes that the 'expressionless is a critical violence' and then, in a discussion of Hölderlin's conception of 'sobriety' in the same text, writes of the 'expressionless':

> It is only another name for that caesura, in which along with harmony every expression simultaneously comes to a standstill in order to give free expression to an expressionless power [*ausdruckslosen Gewalt*] inside all artistic media.[40]

The 'standstill' within 'harmony' is the undoing of an already determined logic of continuation. There is a 'halt' in which the 'power' for a form of transformation comes to presence by its having become the actualisation of expression's possibility. It comes to be expressed. That expression, however, takes the 'expressionless' as its condition of possibility. Destruction inaugurates. There will not have been an image to be followed.

The second quality is that destruction occasions the continuity of spaces of allowing. In other words, the creation – through acts of destruction – of openings is defined by what is best understood as a founding sense of indetermination. Present here therefore is an indetermination that brings with it the capacity for determination. The presence of the move from this indetermination to determination as defined in terms of a capacity needs to be understood as another inscription of potentiality at the centre of Benjamin's philosophical project. The latter – creation through destruction as involving an actualisation of potentiality – provides the basis of a possible set of actions arising from destruction. As will be seen, Benjamin will name this in *Towards a Critique of Violence* as a type of 'anarchism'. The 'anarchism' in question does not have a direct lineage to the history of anarchism. Rather, here the term needs to be situated within a setting created by the interplay of creation and indetermination. As such Benjamin's invocation of the term 'anarchism' can be taken as referring to the presence of an *an-arché*. The latter needs to be understood as a moment or point of origination that is not structured by an already determined relation between an *arché* and a *telos*. Reference has of course already been made to this possibility. It occurred in the passage from *The Destructive Character* noted above in which destruction is defined both in terms of place creating but as importantly as marked by the absence of an already determining 'image'. Creation pertains therefore to both a place to be determined and a place where determinations occur. Place – as that which occurs with the *caesura of allowing* – has this originally doubled quality. The end therefore is given not as a reality that is at hand and thus it cannot be provided by either an image (for example, the world of the 'Last Judgement') or as that which would be there in an image. While this may seem to privilege negative definitions, more is at stake. What such an end awaits is an image and thus there is the necessity that its image be created. (The correlate is of course underscoring the pointlessness in understanding its creation – the actualisation of a potentiality – in purely imagistic terms.) Given the impossibility, for Benjamin, of a conception of an end as already determined, the end can only be there as that which is to be created. That creation is the realisation of what is allowed. Destruction and inauguration work together. This is the work of 'genius'. The end in question therefore – and here this is an end that could never have been a *telos* – can no longer be thought with the structures provided by means/ends on the one hand and *arché/telos* on the other. Given this setting it is not difficult to envisage a philosophical connection between the 'expressionless' and what has been designated above as the *an-arché*.

The third quality of destruction is that what interrupts and thus what destruction reveals is the way in which what is – what is taken to be real – is in fact an imposed sense of order. Hence the problematic status of that which is at hand. Equally, the naturalisation of the imposition of order provides the force of the opposition that Benjamin will draw a number of times between the 'order of law' (*die Ordnung des Rechts*) and 'justice' (*Gerechtigkeit*). The reason why this is the case is that it is the effect of the destruction undertaken in the name of the latter ('justice') that identifies both the ground of their conflation and equally their naturalisation and thus the posited immutability of law, and therefore their destruction provides the opening to justice. This is another formulation of the critique of law in the name of law. What it opens up is the setting in which law would take justice as its condition of possibility. This set-up is an opening occasioned by the work of the *caesura of allowing*.

The presence of order as imposed – an instance of which is named above as the 'order of law' (*die Ordnung des Rechts*) – occurs in different ways. Another form in which it is present is as an imposed conception of time as a form of continuity (fate on the way to becoming historicism) or the identification (which will be of course a misidentification) of human being with natural being. In the case of the latter this is what Benjamin will continue to identify as 'mere life' (*bloßes Leben*) and thus not what is possible for life in its differentiation from its reduction to 'mere life'. The trap of this reduction, a trap in which 'fate' takes on the quality of history and the subject as originally guilty, is captured by Benjamin in the following terms:

> Fate leads to death. Death is not punishment but atonement, an expression of the subjection of guilty life to the law of natural life.[41]

This is the process by which 'mere life' – noting from the start the confluence between 'natural life' and 'mere life' – is created. Interrupting the hold of fate transforms the conception of subjectivity, since the latter was defined in terms of original guilt. Guilt's presence as original emerges within this act of destruction as always having been an after-effect. 'Mere life' will have been marked in advance by the processes within which life would have come to be equated with what is in fact no more than 'natural life'. In those instances in which that equation takes place what is occurring is a process of naturalisation. Within it 'nature' loses its quality as artifice. Recovering nature from its presence as artifice demands that it be de-natured – here there is a reiteration of acts of destruction. The de-naturing of nature (in the name of nature, and thus in the name of another nature) is a further description of destruction. However, it also indicates that what acts of destruction show is the way in which what had been thought to have had the surety of nature or the security of the already given, and thus of that which is there already at hand, are themselves constructions. This is the twofold sense of the real within Benjaminian destruction. What had been constructed is not innocent. Moreover, Benjamin's provocative suggestion made in *On the Concept of History* that documents of culture are themselves already documents of a form of barbarism should stand as a constant reminder both of the impossibility of innocence and, more abstractly, of the related impossibility of a purely singular event.[42]

Constructions which come to be naturalised, and thus constructions which become the object of destruction, involve as integral to the process of construction the revealing and thus possible effacing of a founding disequilibrium of relations of power. Those relations are effaced and retained (either as effaced or as linked to a 'natural' order). This is what destruction shows. Their retention had always involved their naturalisation. They came to exist as a norm. As natural and as norm, what cannot be envisaged – within the setting in which these relations are normalised – is the possibility of their own self-overcoming. This is of course central to the analysis of Protestantism developed by Benjamin in *The Origin of German Tragic Drama*.[43] While it may be that an apparently modern sensibility sees itself as distanced from the world of *Trauerspiel*, it remains the case that, to the extent that what cannot be thought is the possibility of forms of self-overcoming – what will emerge at a later stage in this study as a possible 'othering' of the world – the modern inadvertently clings to the world of *Trauerspiel*. Benjamin's study of the seventeenth century endures as relevant. What that means of course is that the determinations of that world – the presence of time as natural and the contemporary as a site of already enacted completion – inhabit modernity as a pervasive and still effective presence. As has already been indicated, this is the world analysed by Benjamin in terms of the oscillation between religion and capitalism. Both religion and capitalism permeate the world – they are both 'cults' – and their destruction cannot be thought from within the setting created by the apparent necessity of (and for) their own continuity. Again this is to be understood as an opening towards a politics of time.

While Benjamin's claims made in relation to both the history and the practice of German Protestantism are specific, there is, as the position sketched above indicates, an important type of generality at work within them. Revealed by what endures as operative within German Protestantism as analysed in *The Origin of German Tragic Drama*, and indeed this could be understood as a general concern of Benjamin's, is that despite the appearance of the self-contained and the self-enclosed, such set-ups are only ever appearances. What will always continue is the possibility of an awakening. Within the dream, within the naturalisation of fate, or within its affirmation – the latter is of course the counter Promethean element within both philosophy and politics – norms that efface power in order to retain power, cannot think their own undoing. Within such a setting all that can ever be envisaged are modes of amelioration within which this disequilibrium is retained within the constancy of its modification. Disequilibria of power endure therefore after the process – a process only there in its having been effaced – as natural and as such take on the quality of norms. To which it should be added, though this is a point that will be developed, that the presence of norms to be undone – or nature to be de-natured – is not nihilism in any sense at all. What occurs is a critique of norms in the name of norms. Hence the reference, that has already been made, to the co-presence of continuity and discontinuity.

The second sense of 'norm' is of course that which occurs after the destruction of normativity as naturalised and unchanging. Destruction occasions the truth of nature as a construction – construction in which what 'is' is then identified with the work of nature – and thus as a form of after-effect, to be made present (and as a consequence to be experienced as such). Again this is Benjaminian realism. Benjamin's references, for example, to the language of dreaming, enchantment and even the experience of boredom must be understood as part of the creation of a setting that in being destroyed is then revealed to have been held in place by dreams, magic and the tyranny of specific moods (e.g. boredom).[44] Destruction results in a form of exposure. Moreover, the real demands it. Indeed, it is possible to move further here and note Benjamin's citation of Brecht's critique of an equation of the real with its purported image. Brecht, quoted by Benjamin, writes that 'less than ever does the mere reflection of reality reveal anything about reality.'[45] To which Brecht goes on to add: 'The authentic reality [*Die eigentliche Realität*] has slipped into the functional.'[46] While both are comments made in the context of an engagement with photography, the position made in relation to the real allows for a form of generality; namely, that the real cannot be identified with what is at hand. What is real emerges within acts of destruction. Again, the premise of such a position is that the 'at hand' is a form of semblance rather than the real.

All of the terms noted above – 'dreams', 'magic', 'moods', etc. – define the process in which experience and experience's conditions of possibility are given a location in the present and thus have the possibility of being attributed historical specificity. The way they exert their hold is in part through the determination of experience. This means, firstly, that experience always has a setting in which it is occasioned as experience. And secondly, that the subject within experience exists and can only come to exist within a similar set of constraints. In each instance there is a process of subject creation in which both instances can only be understood as what they are through processes of destruction. Of course, precisely because magic, dreaming and the hold of moods are experiential, what is occasioned – and thus what will have been allowed – are other modalities of experience.[47] Destruction has to be thought in relation to 'other' experiences and thus the possibility of 'othering' as an experience. Spaces of allowing are spaces of experience. Othering is therefore not simply conceptual. (The emergence of 'othering' forms the basis of the argumentation set out in Chapter 2 and which arises from an analysis of the final thesis of Marx's *Theses on the Philosophy of Feuerbach*. An analysis which not only allows for the emergence of othering, it will also position othering as linked to a form of inauguration. The contrast is of course open to interpretation. The latter remains acts in which what is remains the same. All that shifts is their interpretation.)

The fourth quality of destruction needs to be understood as an original form of inscription that breaks the link between destruction and the unproductive oscillation between ends and means. This quality has already been noted, namely in terms of an already present inscription of value. It is this latter position that can be identified in *Towards a Critique of Violence* and defines with exemplary clarity the concerns of that text. While *Towards a Critique of Violence* is a text that will be discussed in much greater detail at a later stage (Chapter 4), and it needs to be noted that it is a text that brings its own complications, it is worth noting in advance the way the link between value and destruction occurs within it and, further, why that link has a determining effect on

Benjamin's entire project. (The project whose recovery is being staged here.) What needs to be added is that this link is not contingent. There is a pervasive and fundamental form of necessity at work. Destruction, through its connection to both life in the first instance and creation in the second, is marked in advance by the ineliminability of value. Life takes on value in its separation from both 'mere life' and life as 'natural' life. The being of being human – the ontology of human being – is life. Moreover, what also exists, as a possibility, is an identification of what life will have become with the just life. A form of becoming, intimations of which are already present within the fabric of existence.

In *Towards a Critique of Violence* the reality of an already present relation between destruction and value can be identified at two specific moments in the development of the text's own argumentation. In the first instance it involves aspects of the project that allows for the distinction between 'mythic' and 'divine' violence to be both drawn and clarified, while at the same noting one of the most significant consequences to which this distinction gives rise. If it can be assumed that the 'mythic' names the temporality of fate, that is imposed continuity – a temporality that will be reworked as Benjamin's writings develop such that it comes to name in addition the temporality of historicism, while 'divine violence' is the act of destruction that undoes the hold of fate and thus interrupts its naturalised continuity (or the presence of its continuity as natural) – the development of the position which differentiates the 'mythic' from the 'divine' links destruction and value. This occurs as a result of the inscription of different modalities of life into the way in which they come to be differentiated.[48] In this regard Benjamin writes that:

> Mythic violence is bloody power over mere life for its own sake; divine violence is pure power over all life for the sake of the living [*um des Lebendigen willen*].[49]

A return will be made to the detail of this passage. However, at this stage the exigency dictated by the claim that 'divine violence' occurs for the sake of the living (*um des Lebendigen willen*) – and Benjamin's formulation is precise – still needs to be noted. However, no matter how 'divine violence' is understood once the setting of this passage is noted, this modality of *Gewalt* cannot be thought as though the presence of its relation to life – and here life is life in its necessary differentiation from 'mere life' – was simply an arbitrary relation. Holding 'life' apart from 'mere life' – linked to the recognition of 'mere life' as 'mere life' and thus not as life – is a defining aspect of Benjamin's project.

3

The second moment that needs to be noted in this regard occurs after Benjamin's argument that 'existence' (*Dasein*) cannot be thought to have a greater quality than a 'just existence' (*gerechtes Dasein*). Indeed, he suggests that holding to the primacy of the former, that is existence taken as an end itself, as though human existence were nothing other than mere existence, is described as 'false' and 'ignoble'. Moreover, that latter position would need to be contrasted to a more complex positioning of human being (where the expression 'human being' is to be understood as ontological and thus pertaining to the being of being human and thus not as a simple form of abstraction from the given-ness of human beings). While it is clear that for Benjamin human being cannot coincide with 'mere life', the counter-position to this conception of human being is not given in an understanding of life in which life is equated with what is already there; that is, life with the semblance of life, or in the equation of life with the life of an individual, or the apparently redemptive claim that human life – the life of human beings – derives its value from a mimetic relation to God in which the human would figure as the image of God. For Benjamin, in this instance, life opens beyond its own semblance and equally beyond the individual subject as the locus of a concern. The identifications of the individual as either the locus of life or the locus of the political are overcome in the name of life. The move beyond both these identifications – a movement to be understood as the *counter-measure* – is the significant point. In this instance the *counter-measure* can only exist as a potentiality, a potentiality there within the fabric of existence – a fabric of which the individual will only ever be there as an after-effect.[50] A potentiality, moreover, that demands 'destruction' as the condition for its actualisation. At work here is not a counter that is simply imaginary, let alone utopian. Here there is a *counter-measure* that works to open up – an opening that is equally a maintaining – a type of counter-realism. Countering the real can only ever take place in the name of the real (a real that is always the other real – where the latter equates the real with that which is at hand). This position, defined as it is by the necessity of potentiality, is described by Benjamin as the 'not-yet-attained condition of the just man' (*Nochnichtsein des gerechten Menschen*).[51]

The passage in which this line occurs brings with it a range of attendant interpretive difficulties. However, at this stage, when read in conjunction with the earlier passage connecting 'divine violence' as that which occurs for 'the living', it signals two of the key elements at work in Benjamin's philosophical project. Namely, in the first place, the primacy of potentiality is present here in the formulation 'not-yet-attained'. And then secondly, it establishes a link between potentiality and the articulation of an original positioning of value. A claim about the 'just man' has to be understood as that which presents a mode of human being. In other words, what is present here is a specific formulation of the being of being human, one where what the interconnection of potentiality and value presents is a thinking of the ontology of human being in which the ethical cannot be separated from the ontological. In sum, being and the potentiality linked to the 'just man' cannot be separated. They are defined in terms of each other. The fundamental point here is that, as a consequence of this reciprocity of definition, not only is value inscribed as an original condition of both history and work undertaken in relation to it, it is also the case that the basis of value is ontological. This accounts for why Benjamin argues in his study of Goethe's' *Elective Affinities* that 'characters in fiction can never be subject to ethical judgement [*der sittlichen Beurteilung*]'.[52] To do so would be to forget that character in that context was defined in terms of its relation to fated being, which if taken in its own terms is being without potentiality. Ethical judgements are linked to the lives of human beings. (As he writes in the text, 'nur an Menschen'.) The ethical, in other words, cannot be separated from life. Fictional characters are different in that they are 'entirely rooted in nature' (*daß sie völlig der Natur verhaftet sind*).[53] Life in its separation from the semblance of life is life that has overcome any identification with natural life.

As noted above, if there is an ethics then it has its ground in that which constructs the ontology of human being. As such it is no longer defined either by a historical naturalisation of civil society, and then thought in terms of normativity, or by a relation to the law and the 'supersensible', deferring the hold of claims concerning normativity – a position structured by the envisaged impossibility of destruction in which the police will become the extra-moral enforcers of norms, on the one hand, and on the other, the Kantian insistence on a relation to law as delimited by the supersensible. The positions to be deferred and the connection between ontology and value are already present in the first of the passages from *Towards a Critique of Violence* noted above. At this stage the most important component of these lines comprises the claim that 'divine violence' is concerned with a relation to 'all life' (*alles Leben*) and, moreover, that it occurs 'for the sake of the living' (*um des Lebendigen willen*).[54] There is also an important point here that will gesture towards the way in which the relationship between theology and religion will come to play a pivotal role.

The project of the positioning of what has been identified as 'the just man' as that which has not yet attained a form of presence could be seen as having a correlate within Judaism in terms of the conception of *Tikkun Olam* (which means the repair or the mending of the world). And yet the position is more complex that it seems. The term appears in aspects of liturgy linked to the *Aleinu*. However, it is given an inflection that indicates how the 'world' is to be understood. The entire line in which it occurs reads as follows: *takken olamn b'malkhut Shaddai.* What this means is that there is a link to the repairing of the world in which its directionality comes from God. In other words, the world will come to be other as a result of its relation to God and God's relation to the world. What is excluded is the world's becoming other as the result of the actualisation of a potentiality that can be located purely in the world. This is a location that yields a subject position defined by its already present integration within the fabric of existence (an integration that has to be thought in relation to the division between potentiality and actuality). The force of Benjamin's claim concerning the potentiality for justice, a claim that has to be understood as the move from religion to theology, might be described as the move from the sovereignty of God towards the sovereignty of justice. Benjamin's project therefore involves the mending of the world. This is a project that, while linked to life, has to be understood in its differentiation from the conception of *Tikkun Olam* as defined liturgically. Justice is a potentiality within life itself. To think this possibility is not to think within the confines of religion. Rather, for Benjamin, it is to think theologically.[55] Again the 'left-handed' blow has to endure as decisive.

The final point to note in this opening consideration of these two passages from *Towards a Critique of Violence* is that in the contrast between the 'mythic' and 'divine', as ways of differentiating between two different modalities of 'violence' (*Gewalt*), the former involves the perpetuation of the identification of life with 'mere life', which is not only that conception of life subjected to the immediacy of the 'the order of law', it is equally a life in which whatever justice may be, justice is necessarily extrinsic to life; as such it is not there as part of the fabric of existence. (The possibility of justice as intrinsic to life is of course the position that has already been noted in relation to Benjamin's formulation of the 'not-yet-attained condition of the just man'.) Whereas the latter – that is, 'divine violence' – has a thoroughly different relation both to time and to life. The force of this other relation means that not only is 'divine violence' envisaged as the interruption of the continuity of the mythic – a position, the mythic, whose repetition is present as naturalised – it envisages a relation in which what is held open is the possibility of there being a conception of justice that pertains to the 'living' – and thus to life – where the latter is taken as a totality (life that will always be more than the life that could be reduced to a simple anthropocentrism[56]). In other words, and even though the full details of the distinction between 'mythic' and 'divine violence' have yet to be spelt out, what is at work within it is twofold. In the first instance, there are two radically distinct relations to time: time thought in terms of continuity, which unfolds as 'fate' or 'historicist chronology'; and time linked to 'destruction', which is staged in terms of the *caesura of allowing*. And in the second, there are two fundamentally different conceptions of life. It must be noted that that this latter element is not two different relations to life. Rather, it is two different configurations of life, both of which pertain at the same time. The interrelation between time and modalities of life provides the basis for beginning to account for what has already been identified as a politics of time.

The significant element that marks out the political nature of time is that the present is created by the co-presence of at least two different modalities of time and therefore two different conceptions of life. While it will always be the case that the present is in fact more complex, what has to be conceded is that the present is a site of conflict precisely because what can always be envisaged is the present as that which could be other than itself. This is a position that is, of course, co-present with one that is constrained both to disavow and to resist this possibility. What this means is that the possibility of the dynamic creative force contained within destruction is unimaginable. There is a significant point here in which the link to destruction and creation involves a reworked conception of the imagination – it would be the imagination without a directing image – as opposed to the sublime. While sublimity may involve an emphatic opening which may be thought as destructive insofar as it is an experience for which the subject is unprepared, the sublime nonetheless creates a limit. This is the case at least in the way the sublime occurs in Kant's *Critique of the Power of Judgment*. Within the argumentation of this text, the sublime's disruptive possibilities are recuperated. The sublime becomes the affirmation of the work of reason. More accurately, the determinations of reason establish both the limit and its borders. It does not occasion. On the contrary, it occasions the demand that becomes the reimposition of limit conditions. These conditions can be found in the way the 'displeasure' to which the sublime gives rise results in the eventual 'pleasure' that accompanies the recognition that the subject is the subject of reason and thus of that which will have already been delimited in advance. The process of being other – which, as has been indicated, is formulated as 'othering' (a position developed in much greater detail in Chapter 2) in order to underscore the presence of activity – is not just a formal possibility, it is also an experiential one. In addition, it stems from the ways in which there is an already present interconnection between destruction and value.

A politics of time therefore names a philosophical thinking of the political that takes the present as defined as much by a potentiality for its being other as it is defined by the effacing of that potentiality in the name of an order that prevails. The latter is naturalised and thus identified with the norms that sustain it. Holding to a politics of time draws together what has already been identified as the interarticulation of destruction and value (the latter understood as the locus of the living). The political becomes the way in which that potentiality is actualised or its actualisation resisted. The political therefore is given by the recognition of the construction of the present in terms of a founding irreducibility. Thinking the political is to think though the determinations of the way that this irreducibility entails conflict's ineliminability. This is the reason why Benjamin can claim in *On the Concept of History* that the 'tradition of the oppressed teaches us that the "state of emergency" in which we live is not the exception but the rule'.[57] Ineliminability, if Benjamin's project is followed, is not apparent. Benjamin's concerns are delimited by the becoming apparent of that setting. The site in which this irreducibility occurs is the present. Once the present is no longer defined within the continuity of historicism then it becomes the site in which the irreducibility – the irreducibility that defines a politics of time – can be said to be always already at work. The irreducibility therefore equates to a founding disequilibria of power. While it is founding its significance can be located in what can be described as the anoriginality of its presence.[58] That is, it is present without there being a moment prior to the presence of power relations. The disequilibria of power are therefore constitutive. They open up the possibility of their own radical transformation.

Notes

1. For a general history of this period see A. J. Ryder, *The German Revolution 1918–19* (London: Routledge, 1958). What stands opposed to the insistence of inauguration as the result of destruction are arguments throughout the history of philosophy that hold to the impossibility of modalities of inauguration linked to destruction avoiding actual violence and the interruption of order, which if not natural cannot be overturned without the overturning debasing those involved. There is a range of different positions that can be united under the heading. It can be found as much in Burke's writings on the French Revolution as it can in Popper's response to the actual violence of revolution. In regard to the latter, see Karl Popper, *The*

Unended Quest (London: Fontana, 1982). Equally as important here are Hume's writings. In his case particular attention should be paid to his examination of the execution of Charles I. In regard to those participating in such activities Hume wrote:

> The grievances which tended chiefly to inflame the parliament and nation, especially the latter, were the surplice, the rails placed about the alter, the bows exacted on approaching it, the liturgy, the breach of the Sabbath ... On account of these were the popular leaders content to throw the government into such violent convulsions; and to the disgrace of that age and of this island, it must be acknowledged that the disorders in Scotland entirely, and those in England mostly, proceed from so mean and contemptible an origin. (Hume, *History of England*, Vol. 5 (Indianapolis: Liberty Fund Press, 1983), p. 145)

For a detailed investigation of Hume's relation to Jacobitism see F. J. McLynn, 'Jacobitism and David Hume: The Ideological Backlash Foiled', *Hume Studies* IX.2 (1983), pp. 171–99.

2. There are, however, a number of outstanding introductions to Benjamin's work that intend to provide a more wide-ranging account. The best of these at the moment is David Ferris, *Walter Benjamin* (Cambridge: Cambridge University Press, 2008).

3. An important affinity can be drawn here between the conception of the 'after-life' of a work, taken up by Benjamin in a number of contexts, and the conception of 'survivre' that forms an integral part of Derrida's reading of Blanchot. I have discussed the former in 'The Decline of Art: Benjamin's Aura', in Andrew Benjamin, *Art Mimesis and the Avant-Garde* (London: Routledge, 1991). See also Jacques Derrida's 'Survivre', in Derrida, *Parages* (Paris: Galilée, 2003), pp. 111–203.

4. Benjamin, *Selected Writings* 4, p. 305; *Gesammelte Schriften* II.2, p. 536.

5. Benjamin, *Selected Writings* 2, p. 464; *Gesammelte Schriften* III, p. 290.

6. To this end see my 'Time and Task: Benjamin and Heidegger Showing the Present', in Dimitris Vardoulakis and Andrew Benjamin (eds), *'Sparks Will Fly': Benjamin and Heidegger* (New York: SUNY Press, 2014).

7. This term originates in the work of Peter Osborne; see Osborne, *The Politics of Time: Modernity and Avant-Garde* (London: Verso, 1995). While the acuity of Osborne's insight concerning the relationship between politics and differing conceptions of historical time cannot be faulted, the point of contention, in relationship to Benjamin, concerns Osborne's argument that the movement of time can be understood in terms of narrative. As will be argued, the caesura cannot be understood as a device that stages the end of narrative from within the confines of narrative itself. In regard to the latter point see Osborne (1995: 157). In sum, interruption demands a more complex conception of internality and externality that is captured by restricting the argument to the structure of narrative.

8. In this regard it should not be thought that there aren't important texts that seek to rework the relationship between Benjamin and Schmitt. See, for example, Marc de Wilde, 'Meeting Opposites: The Political Theologies of Walter Benjamin and Carl Schmitt', *Philosophy and Rhetoric* 44. 4 (2011);

and Christoph Schmidt, 'Zeit und Speil: Gesitergespräche zwischen Walter Benjamin und Carl Schmitt über Ästhetik und Politik', in Jen Mattern, Gabriel Motzkin and Shimon Sandbank (eds), *Jüdisches Denken in einer Welt ohne Gott. Festschrift für Stéphane Moses* (Berlin: Verlag Vorwek, 2001).

9. For an invaluable contextualisation of a number of the texts to be taken up within this project see Michael Jennings, 'Towards Eschatology: The Development of Walter Benjamin's Theological Politics in the Early 1920s', in Carolin Duttlinger, Ben Morgan and Anthony Phelan (eds), *Walter Benjamins Anthropologisches Denken* (Freiburg im Breisgau: Rombach Verlag, 2012), pp. 41–58.

10. Benjamin's now famous description of method has already been noted. His formulation is: 'Method is a digression [*Umweg*].' For a discussion of the formulation see Howard Caygill, *Colour of Experience* (London: Routledge, 1998), p. 58. Caygill describes this formulation as 'lapidary'.

11. For the sake of accuracy, even fidelity, the titles of texts have been translated directly from the German. Hence, for example, *Zur Kritik der Gewalt* becomes *Towards a Critique of Violence*. Whatever quality the *Zur* introduces cannot be avoided. Hence there has been the attempt to retain its meaning by the use of the *Towards*.

12. See Daniel Weidner, 'Thinking Beyond Secularization: Walter Benjamin, the "Religious Turn" and the Poetics of Theory', *New German Critique* 37.3 111 (Fall 2010), pp. 131–48.

13. There is an extensive range of attempts to establish the nature of this distinction. It is interesting to note in this regard that Joshua Robert Gold identifies it in strictly political terms when he writes that 'Benjamin regards it as a means of distinguishing historical materialism from social democracy to the extent that theory is capable of dispelling the hold that the myth of progress has over working class politics.' Joshua Robert Gold, 'The Dwarf in the Machine: A Theological Figure and its Sources', *MLN* 121 (2006), p. 1232.

14. Benjamin, *Selected Writings* 1, p. 260; *Gesammelte Schriften* IV, p. 20.

15. For a systematic overview of Benjamin's theory of allegory see Bainard Cowan, 'Walter Benjamin's Theory of Allegory', *New German Critique* 22 (Winter, 1981), pp. 109–22; and Michael Schmidt, 'L'allégorie entre écriture et l'instant', in Heinz Wismann and Patricia Lavelle (eds), *Walter Benjamin: Le critique Européen* (Paris: PUS, 2012), pp. 199–213. The overall importance of allegory can be gleaned from Pierre Bouretz's description of Benjamin as 'réinventur de l'allegorie comme clé de la connaissance'; Pierre Bourtez, *Les Lumières du messianisme* (Paris: Herman éditeurs, 2008), p. 12. For an overview of the position of 'dialectical images' in Benjamin's work see Max Pensky 'Method and Time: Benjamin's Dialectical Images', in David Ferris (ed.), *Cambridge Companion to Walter Benjamin* (Cambridge: Cambridge University Press, 2004), pp. 177–98.

16. For an important reading of the first of these texts see Irving Wohlfarth, 'No-Man's-Land: On Walter Benjamin's "Destructive Character"', *Diacritics* 8.2 (Summer, 1978), pp. 47–65.

17. For a systematic overview of the use of the term *Gewalt* within German philosophical writing see Etienne Balibar, 'Gewalt', in Wolfgang-Fritz

Haug (ed.), *Historisch-Kritisches Wörterbuch des Marxismus*, Vol. 5 (Berlin and Hamburg: *Argument*, 2001). Another important contribution to understanding Benjamin's use of this term is Massimilano Tomba, 'Another Kind of *Gewalt*: Beyond Law Re-Reading Walter Benjamin', *Historical Materialism* 17.1 (2009), pp. 122–44.

18. Power for Arendt provides the essence of government. Moreover, power is linked to a conception of human being that is positioned within a founding sense of collectivity (Arendt's word will be 'concert'). That sense is already the site of a founding legitimacy. In this regard Arendt writes:

> Power springs up whenever people get together and act in concert, but it derives legitimacy from the initial getting together rather than from any action that then may follow. (Hannah Arendt, *On Violence* (New York: Harcourt, Brace & World, 1970), p. 52)

19. See the opening of Chapter 2 for a sustained account of the process of destruction in Descartes. Central to the overall argument is not the claim that 'destruction' in these settings can be essentialised. Rather the claim is that inauguration takes destruction as that which enables it to be possible.

20. Benjamin's own engagement with 'eternal return' has a number of different sources in his writings. One of the most germane for these concerns is his treatment in 'New Theses C', in *Paralipomena to 'On the Concept of History'*. There he writes: 'Thinking the idea of eternal recurrence once more in the nineteenth century, Nietzsche becomes the figure on whom mythic doom is now carried out.' (Benjamin, *Selected Writings* 4, pp. 403–4; *Gesammelte Schriften* I.3, p. 1241.)

21. Malevich writes the following in 1920, in the *Bulletin of the Executive Committee of Moscow State Art Workshops* 1 (3 October 1920) (quoted in *Kazimir Malevich: Suprematism* (New York: Guggenheim Museum Publication, 2003)):

> We should not resemble our fathers. Their faces, palaces and temples may be splendid a thousand times over but our new meaning will not inhabit them. We will build our own, our new world and thus will not wear the forms of Greece and Rome; we shall not be the peddlers of antiques.

The significance of this point is that it indicates the way in which a certain thread of modernist thinking – thinking deployed as much in the realm of art as it is in philosophy – locates inauguration as the result of destruction and discontinuity.

22. A detailed engagement with this paper forms the basis of Chapter 2.

23. Heidegger, specifically in §31 of his *Grundfragen der Philosophie*, is also concerned with endings and beginnings and the move to that which is other in relation to what pertains 'now'. As such it is a section that is not simply integral to the way in which he understands historical time; its ostensible concern is how continuities and discontinuities within it are constituted and, reciprocally, how they are inscribed in the process of historical time itself. Rather than a concern with philosophy's history that is articulated in

terms of simple continuity, Heidegger's project is not just with beginnings and endings, more significantly it is with the structure of decision that pertains to them. There are two senses of beginning and end in Heidegger's argument. The first sense of 'end' is articulated in the following:

> The greatness of the end consists not only in the essentiality of the closure of the great possibilities but also in the power to prepare [*der Kraft zur Vorbereitung*] a translation to something wholly other [*zu einem ganz Anderen*].

The important question here would be to begin to both link and thus distinguish between what Heidegger may mean by 'a translation to something wholly other' and that which is occasioned by the *caesura of allowing*. See Heidegger, *Grundfragen der Philosophie* (Frankfurt am Main: Vittorio Klostermann, 1992); the English translation is *Basic Questions of Philosophy: Selected 'Problems' of 'Logic'*, trans. Richard Rojcewicz and Andre Schuwer (Bloomington: Indiana University Press, 1994).

24. Benjamin, *Selected Writings* 2, p. 664; *Gesammelte Schriften* IV.1, p. 419. The passage has a complex history involving both Bloch and Scholem. In addition, it is cited by Giorgio Agamben in *The Coming Community*, trans. Michael Hardt (Minneapolis: University of Minnesota Press, 1993). Agamben asks in relation to this passage, identifying the 'a little bit different' with that which is 'otherwise': 'How is it possible that things be "otherwise" once everything is definitely finished?' (p. 54). The mistake that Agamben makes is twofold. Firstly, he interprets the passage literally rather than seeing it as folded into a process of inauguration through destruction. What is inaugurated is a process rather than that which is both complete and final. Secondly he ignores the subtlety of Benjamin's thought, which is staged around the interplay of discontinuity and continuity. Translation is a prime example. So is the project of *Towards a Critique of Violence*, which needs to be understood – as shall be argued in detail – as a critique of law in the name of law.

25. Benjamin, *Selected Writings* 2, p. 811; *Gesammelte Schriften* II.2, p. 432.

26. As Benjamin's writings develop over time, 'destruction' remains a motif, though one increasingly linked to historical materialism. Hence he argues in *Eduard Fuchs, Collector and Historian* that 'the task of the historical materialism [*die Aufgabe des historisches Materialismus*] is directed towards a consciousness of the present which explodes the continuum of history' (*Selected Writings* 3, p. 262; *Gesammelte Schriften* II.2, p. 268). Here the 'forcing open' (*aufsprengen*) names a modality of destruction.

27. Benjamin, *Selected Writings* 2, p. 456; *Gesammelte Schriften* II.1, p. 367.

28. See also in this regard the discussion of 'subversion' in James R. Martel, *Textual Conspiracies: Walter Benjamin, Idolatry and Political Theory* (Ann Arbor: University of Michigan Press, 2011), p. 61. In regard to Martel's work, his outlining of the importance of Benjamin as a 'political thinker' is developed in Martel, 'Taking Benjamin Seriously as a Political Thinker', *Philosophy and Rhetoric* 44.4 (2011), pp. 297–308.

29. Benjamin, *Selected Writings* 1, p. 398; *Gesammelte Schriften* VI, p. 84.

30. Benjamin, *Selected Writings* 2, p. 54; *Gesammelte Schriften* IV.1, p. 397.

31. Benjamin, *Selected Writings* 4, p. 541; *Gesammelte Schriften* IV, p. 396.
32. Benjamin, *Origin of German Tragic Drama*, p. 74; *Gesammelte Schriften* I.1, p. 253.
33. I first argued for the centrality of the concept of potentiality for understanding the work of Walter Benjamin in my 'Boredom and Distraction' (now Appendix A). I have developed that position in further recent writings on Benjamin. The way in which potentiality is used in this paper and elsewhere in my work on Benjamin concerns the presence of an unnamed though nonetheless indispensible concept at work in Benjamin's writings. It should be noted that a similar position, though argued for in an importantly different way, has also been advanced in Samuel Weber, *Benjamin's -abilities* (Cambridge, MA: Harvard University Press, 2008).
34. Benjamin, *Selected Writings* 2, p. 244; *Gesammelte Schriften* II.1, p. 320.
35. While the language is slightly different there is, nonetheless, an important correlation between the indeterminate as it is used here and the judgement drawn by both Benjamin and Brecht concerning Kafka. They agree that in terms of generic determinations his work has an 'undecidability'.
36. Benjamin, *Selected Writings* 1, p. 282; *Gesammelte Schriften* VI, p, 117.
37. Benjamin, *Arcades Project*, p. 475; *Gesammelte Schriften*, V.1, p. 595 [N, 10a3].
38. Benjamin *Selected Writings* 1, p. 203; *Gesammelte Schriften* II.1, p. 174. Though it will be necessary to return to this point – and this will occur in Chapter 3 – what has to be noted is that Benjamin writes of the 'the head of genius'. Why 'genius'? While the answer can in part be traced to the role of 'genius in Hölderlin' – a project that informs one of Benjamin's earliest papers – the conjecture here is that the term names the doubled force of destruction. In order to underscore the relationship between destruction and inauguration the term 'genius' is used. The 'genius' stands opposed to the endless repetition of 'demonic fate'. With that formulation what can also be heard is the presence of the Goethe of the *Urbild* with whom Benjamin engages on the final pages of his *The Concept of Criticism in German Romanticism*.
39. Benjamin, *Origin of German Tragic Drama*, p. 129; *Gesammelte Schriften* I.1, p. 308.
40. Benjamin, *Selected Writings* 1, p. 341; *Gesammelte Schriften* I.1, p. 181.
41. Benjamin, *Origin of German Tragic Drama*, p. 131; *Gesammelte Schriften* I.1, p. 310.
42. Benjamin writes in *Experience and Poverty*: 'This poverty of experience is not only poverty on the personal level, but also poverty of human experience in general. Hence a new kind of barbarism' (*Selected Writings* 2, p. 732; *Gesammelte Schriften* II.1, p. 215). For an important discussion of this point plus the complex connections between barbarism and what is named in this project as a *caesura of allowing*, see Kevin McLaughlin, 'Benjamin's Barbarism', *Germanic Review* 81.1 (Winter 2006), pp. 14–16.
43. See Appendix B. For a detailed discussion of Benjamin's relation to German Protestantism, see Jane Newman, '"Hamlet ist auch Saturnkind": Citationality, Lutheranism, and German Identity in Benjamin's *Ursprung des Deutschen Trauerspiels*', *Benjamin Studien* 1 (2008), pp. 175–95.
44. For a discussion of the complexities of magic, its relation to fate and its

role as determining the meaning of events – a project that will incorporate a concern with clairvoyance, and a theme that will occur in Chapter 6 in the context of a more general treatment of Benjamin's *On the Concept of History* – see Eric Downing, 'Divining Benjamin: Reading Fate, Graphology, Gambling', *MLN* 126 (2011), pp. 551–80.

45. Benjamin, *Selected Writings* 2, p. 526; *Gesammelte Schriften*, II.1, p. 384.
46. Benjamin, *Selected Writings* 2, p. 526; *Gesammelte Schriften* II.1, p. 384.
47. See the important discussion of the dream in Eli Friedlander, *Walter Benjamin: A Philosophical Portrait* (Cambridge, MA: Harvard University Press, 2012), pp. 90–112.
48. It is this context that will problematise arguments such as the one advanced by Sami Khatib that 'divine violence has a proto critico-ideological function rendering it impossible to justify and legitimize.' Whether Benjamin is successful in doing so is another question. However, the link between destruction and life provides precisely that possibility. See Sami Khatib, 'Towards a Politics of "Pure Means": Walter Benjamin and the Question of Violence', *Anthropological Materialism* <anthropologicalmaterialism.hypotheses.org>.
49. Benjamin, *Selected Writings* 1, p. 250; *Gesammelte Schriften* II.1, p. 201.
50. See also Benjamin, *Selected Writings* 3, p. 146; *Gesammelte Schriften*, II.2, p. 442:

> Counsel woven in to the fabric of the lived life [*gelebten Leben*] is wisdom. The art of storytelling is nearing its end because the epic side of truth – wisdom – is dying out.

51. Benjamin, *Selected Writing* 1, p. 251; *Gesammelte Schrift* II. 1, p. 201. There is a fundamentally important point at stake here. In writing of the question of the ethical in Benjamin – a question that is recalibrated in terms of 'ethical time' – Werner Hamacher, in 'Guilt History: Benjamin's Sketch "Capitalism as Religion"', trans. Kirk Wetters, *Diacritics* 32.3–4 (Fall–Winter 2002), pp. 81–106, writes the following:

> Ethical time does not flow in future but rather comes *ex futuro*. This reversed time, this counter time, moving against the linear time of development and against guilt time's indifference to time, is able to restrain the cause-effect sequence – breaking its nexus of guilt and punishment and even expunging the traces of the misdeeds – only because it is not thetic, or given time. It is rather a forgiving, an annulling, annihilating *coming* time. (p. 104)

The accuracy of this formulation cannot be doubted. If there is a qualification it concerns what is described as 'guilt time's indifference to time'. That 'indifference' is in fact the naturalisation of fated time. 'Indifference' needs to be understood as the staged refusal of the possibility of time and therefore the law being other than that which has already determined its being what it is. In the latter case being is having been fated.

52. Benjamin, *Selected Writings* 1, p. 304; *Gesammelte Schriften* I.1, p. 133.
53. Benjamin, *Selected Writings* 1, p. 304; *Gesammelte Schriften* I.1, p. 133.

54. Benjamin, *Selected Writings* 1, p. 250; *Gesammelte Schriften* II.1, p. 200.
55. For a treatment of the conception of *Tikkun Olam* as central to an aspect of Jewish philosophy see Emil L. Fackenheim, *To Mend the World: Foundations of Post-Holocaust Jewish Thought* (Indianapolis: Indiana University Press, 1994).
56. There may be intimations of this position in *The Story Teller* when Benjamin suggests that the 'righteous man [*der Gerechte*] is the advocate for all creatures and at the same time he is their embodiment' (Benjamin, *Selected Writings* 3, p. 158; *Gesammelte Schriften* II.2, p. 459). This is of course creatureliness beyond 'mere life'. In other words, it is the position in which the position of the Sovereign within *Trauerspeile*, who is the 'lord of creatures' while remaining 'a creature', is overcome (*er ist Herr der Kreaturen, aber er bleibt Kreatur*) (*Origin of German Tragic Drama*, p. 85; *Gesammelte Schriften* I.1, p. 264).
57. Benjamin, *Selected Writings* 4, p. 392; *Gesammelte Schriften* I.2, p. 697.
58. The term 'anoriginal' names a complex origin. An origin as a site of a founding irreducibility. This term has been and remains central to my work. For a sustained presentation of the term see my *The Plural Event* (London: Routledge, 1997) and my *Being-in-Relation* (forthcoming).

Chapter 2

The Meaning of Time in the Moral World

The brooder whose startled gaze falls upon the fragment in his hand becomes the allegorist.

Walter Benjamin

1

The first text to be taken up is an unpublished 'fragment' written in 1921. It will allow for the development of this project insofar as it will allow for a more systematic staging of the interconnection between destruction and morality. (The latter is what has already been referred to in terms of the presence of an implicit conception of value defined in terms of life and the 'not-yet-attained condition of the just man'.) This connection can be taken a stage further by noting that destruction is itself bound up with the process of critique. Indeed, it can be argued that this position has a certain generality within Benjamin's writings. Hence not only does he claim that Edward Fuchs breaks with the 'classicist conception of art', it is also the case that with Fuchs there is an instance of that which 'may prove destructive [*destruktiv*] to traditional conceptions of art'.[1] A critical engagement can be thought in terms of its being a modality of destruction. Both destruction and critique play a fundamental role within modern philosophy. They are in part constitutive of it. Critique involves an important divide between a concern, in the first instance, with conditions of existence – hence the Kantian heritage – and, in the second, philosophical strategies that cannot be separated from different modalities of interruption and beginning. While it is a divide that allows for possible and instructive moments of connection, it is the destructive dimension that is the point of focus here. A clear instance of such an understanding of the complex interconnection between critique and destruction occurs in the opening of the 'First Meditation' in Descartes'

Meditations on First Philosophy. Descartes defines his strategy in the following terms:

> I have withdrawn into a peaceful solitude and shall be able to apply myself seriously and with liberty to overturning/destroying all my former opinions.[2]

It is important to note here that Descartes, when writing in Latin – and the text was originally written in Latin – deploys the term *eversioni* (*eversio*), which has the twofold sense of an overturning as well as an act of destruction. The contemporary French translation of the Latin – the translation undertaken by the Duc de Luynes in 1647 and approved by Descartes – is the much more emphatic *à détruire*. It remains the case, however, that what is integral to Descartes' project is twofold. There is, in the first instance, cessation, thought as destruction, and, in the second, a beginning premised on that destruction. Tradition, philosophy (and its relation to science) and finally God were, for Descartes, not immune from the process of doubt. As such, Descartes was then able to stage a re-founding of the philosophical on the basis of the radical interruption that doubt establishes. If Descartes' position is essentially modern in that it brings together an end, understood as a form of interruption, and a beginning that ensures, or seeks to ensure, the effective nature of that interruption, then it is also equally pre-modern, as its thinking of interruption assumes neither a setting structured by a disequilibrium of power nor does it evince any understanding that interruption cannot operate simply on the level of the conceptual. Life in the sense in which it is being developed here has to remain untouched by Cartesian destruction. This is why it has to be argued – *pace* Descartes – that destruction once bound up to life necessitates a philosophy of history (and thus a conception of historical time) that has a threefold determination. In the first instance it would be one in which interruption can itself be thought. Secondly, this brings with it the attendant recognition that such a thinking of interruption is itself the work of power and is defined in relation to already present relations of power. And finally, in part because of power's intrinsic presence, inherent to destruction is the question of value (value and life, as has been noted, come to be defined in relation to each other). Implicit in this latter point is the supposition that value emerges when destruction involves continuity and discontinuity within life. Once the three points identified above, points whose interarticulation further reinforces the already outlined basis of the understanding of historical time that is integral to the recovery of Benjamin's political philosophy, are taken into consideration, they reveal further the limits of Cartesian destruction.

For Descartes destruction has to be thought in terms of its non-relation to life. Indeed it is possible to go further and argue that it is a separation that is effected by the movement of Cartesian philosophy itself. The distinction that Descartes attempts to establish in terms of that which is proper to the being of being human, thought in Cartesian terms as *res cogitans*, and the same subject having a body, locates any Cartesian thinking of life as that which pertains exclusively to bodily life (perhaps even animal life) and not therefore as what is proper to human being. This position could be reworked such that the body, while the source of what Benjamin identifies as 'mere life', is present in terms of an equation of animal being with bodily being, Descartes' identification of 'thinking' and the effective presence of the 'soul' are intended, *inter alia*, to identify that which this equation would (or perhaps should) make impossible. The subject is not its body. Of interest therefore is the question of the life of *res cogitans*. However, the impossibility of the latter functioning as a genuine question within the Cartesian system can be accounted for in terms of *res cogitans* having no activity other than thinking. Within the Cartesian philosophical system the nature of the distinction between a subject as *res cogitans* and what might be described as the subject's life – a life that involves a conception of sovereignty in which the body is subject to forms of externality over which it cannot exercise control – indicates firstly that for Descartes there is an important split within sovereignty. In the first instance, the locus of sovereignty is the subject as *res cogitans* and thus any sense of 'destruction' pertains uniquely to thought. Here the subject can subject itself to the interplay of destruction and creation. Cartesian doubt needs to be understood as the enactment of that position. Radical doubt is a form of subject-centred sovereignty. It is equally a form of creative destruction. However, in the second, the other sense of sovereignty that is at work here and which delimits Descartes is that thinking of destruction involves that which is external to the subject. Here, therefore, sovereignty is defined in terms of externality. The externality is the identification of worldly loci of what exerts sovereign power. The latter – which could be named simply, perhaps too simply, as the church and the monarch – are not subject to the conception of destruction that defines Cartesian thought. As such they cannot be subjected to either an actual or a philosophical conception of destruction. In sum, it can be argued that destruction maintained the disequilibria of power that characterised and defined the relationship between time and task in Descartes as developed in the project of the *Meditations*. Philosophy's separation from life, within which life is reduced to animal life, establishes a limit. A limit that would allow the question of philosophy's relation to human life – life in its separation from animal life – to emerge as an important question in its own right. What this means of course is that it is only the destruction of the identification of life with animal or bodily life that gives the question of life a philosophical future. Benjamin's distinction between 'mere life' and that which occurs 'for the sake of the living' needs to be understood in precisely this context. The distinction between them, where that distinction is understood as a possibility for thought, is premised on a form of destruction. Not only does it underscore the interconnection of destruction and critique, it also indicates that the truth of life necessitates the destruction of its already given, and thus naturalised, presence. The limitation of Descartes therefore is not found within the identification of a relationship between destruction and beginning. What matters is the destruction's structural presence within a given philosophical system.

Taken generally, destruction is an important motif within differing conceptions of the philosophical. While it would always enable a link to be established between, for example, Descartes, Heidegger and Walter Benjamin, insofar as all were concerned with the overcoming of tradition in the name of another philosophical inauguration, it also allows for the identification of genuine differences between their philosophical positions to be identified. The differences between their conceptions of the philosophical lie both in the ways that destruction is understood and inauguration is staged as well as in how the present, as the site of destruction and inauguration, is itself construed. Nonetheless, both the value and the limit of Descartes can be located in the insistence on destruction's necessity, hence there cannot be a beginning other than one premised on a mode of destruction. The limit, which is equally as instructive, concerns the interplay of what might be described as the relationship between power and time, which is then acted out in terms of the identification of different modalities of sovereignty and, importantly, conceptions of sovereignty that in certain fundamental instances cannot be subject to destruction. While the limits of Descartes are clear, those limits open up the significance of Benjamin's work, which can be located at that precise juncture: that is, at an intersection that is comprised of the nexus of destruction and inauguration on the one hand, and what can best be described as a politics of time on the other. This juncture provides the way destruction can be understood as integral to the reworked project of critique. And, in addition, it shows the way a concern with both value and life are integral to it once the move from a Cartesian thinking of destruction towards a Benjaminian one takes place.

In order to develop an understanding of the ways in which this juncture operates in Walter Benjamin's writings, rather than attempt to provide a synoptic account, emphasis will be given, as stated at the chapter's outset, to a specific text, that is *The Meaning of Time in the Moral World*. This text was written at the same time as Benjamin was beginning to work out the detail of his decisive text on the relationship between law and politics – his *Towards a Critique of Violence*. The former text remained unpublished at the time. However, it was written in 1921, the same year as *Towards a Critique of Violence* (the text to be taken up in Chapter 4). The reason for orientating the project of developing the connection between critique and destruction in relation to this text is that despite its brevity it stages elements fundamental to Walter Benjamin's political philosophy and thus to the conception of critique that can be seen to emerge from his writings. There are three elements that are central to his overall project and which find varying forms of expression in this short text. The first is the suspension of the law in the name of a relation to come between justice and morality. The second is the recognition that such a relation to the law involves the creation of an opening whose content cannot be determined in advance. As such it brings a sense of mediacy into play that is itself premised on the deferring of immediacy. (The latter will appear as the destruction of 'fate'.) The suspension of the law is the suspension of immediacy. The creation of both the spatial and temporal dimension of mediacy is a move fundamental to a politics of time. The third is that such an opening, and thus what it allows, has its conditions of possibility in an already present potentiality, within the already present complex of relations between the self and the world. The latter has already been identified as *the fabric of existence*. Hence, implicit in the last of these elements is that destruction's relation to a founding inauguration endures initially, and of necessity, as a potentiality awaiting actualisation.

As a prelude to taking up the detail of Benjamin's text, it is vital that greater attention be paid to the way in which 'destruction' can be reconceived as having a founding relation both to the possibility of a philosophical thinking of politics and equally to a conception of potentiality. While Benjamin does not refer to Marx in this regard (though as his writings go on references to Marx become more detailed as well as more nuanced), there is an important suggestion as to how a conception of destruction as inherently bound up with potentiality might be understood in terms similar to those occurring in Marx's own writings. It takes place in the final *Thesis* (*Thesis 11*) of his *Theses on the Philosophy of Feuerbach*. While on one level the language of the text is reasonably straightforward in its juxtaposition of interpretation and change, it can still be suggested that the language of the juxtaposition contains the very problem that its staging would always have necessitated. Marx wrote the following:

Die Philosophen haben die Welt nur verschieden interpretiert, es kommt aber darauf an, sie zu verändern.[3] (Emphasis in the original)

The traditional translation of this famous line which, while not incorrect, is constrained to exclude other possibilities harboured within the original, takes the following form:

> The philosophers have only *interpreted* the world in various ways, the point, however, is to *change* it.[4]

In its original handwritten form, the words *interpretiert* and *verändern* were underlined. Despite the traditional translation, it is not as though what is juxtaposed here is inaction and action. What the setting opens up, as a question, is what *verändern* means. Part of the answer is to be found in the incorporation within that term of *ändern* ('to other'). In addition, a further part of any answer is also to be located in the implicit sense of process that the term contains. (Hence, the always possible move from *verändern* to *Veränderung*.) Moreover, rather than suggest that all that is at stake within the *Thesis* is the possibility of change, where change and thus destruction might be assimilated to various forms of modification, as though change could be subsumed under the heading of 'adaptation' (*Anpassung*) or 'transformation' (*Verwandlung*), once centrality is attributed to the presence of *ändern* then the *Thesis* itself can be understood as juxtaposing 'interpretation' to the process of making the world other. And it should be noted that what is at stake here is a thinking of 'the world' (*die Welt*), the term that is there in both Benjamin and Marx. ('The world' (*die Welt*) is, after all, named in the title of Benjamin's text.) What has to be othered is the world. This is a position – the possibility of 'othering' – that will come to be linked to what Benjamin names in *Towards a Critique of Violence* as 'divine violence'. As construed by the *Thesis*, 'interpretation' accepts the givenness of the world. Interpretation therefore retains the modality of continuity. At its most exact it can be argued that 'interpretation' takes place within a historicist logic. As a consequence of that location 'interpretation' both as a process and in regard to the conception of the object – the object of interpretation – that it envisages, retain their already determined fate. The object remains untouched. Equally, the means of interpretation will not have been transformed in the process. The counter here – the *counter-measure* – to this set-up is the othering of the world. Hence the exigency of the question: what is meant by the othering of the world? Attempting to answer this question necessitates locating the domain of response.

As a beginning it has to be recognised that othering is a process. However, as a process it necessitates that moment at which the process is itself inaugurated. The inauguration is only possible if the potentiality for being other is already there. That potentiality would be already present within what can be described as the *there is* quality of the world. Interpretation, as it is used in its juxtaposition with othering within the *Thesis 11*, assumes that the *there is* quality of the world is actually coterminous with the world. 'Interpretation', as the term is being used here, is committed therefore both to a type of empiricism as well as to modalities of fate. In contradistinction to this position, it can be argued that Marx's understanding of othering assumes that the world's material presence brings with it, as an immaterial force, its capacity to be other. The resultant othering of the world is the continuity of process, a process demanding its form of inauguration, thus the staging of discontinuity, in which that potentiality continues to be realised. The othering of the world therefore takes the form of a complex event. It demands a sense of externality in which there is a type of continuity that cannot be predicated upon an actual logic of the world, if that logic is identified with what is at hand. What this means is that part of that event is the presence of a counter-strophe and which would thus be present as a productive catastrophe. The catastrophe has to be thought therefore in terms of the co-presence of continuity and discontinuity.[5] And therefore in terms of what has already been identified as the *caesura of allowing*. However, the catastrophe as an effective presence demands a specific conception of internality. The latter, internality, is there as a potentiality within the world, one entailing that the world will always have contained a capacity to be other (even if at a specific moment within history that capacity is not recognised or it may even have been refused). Othering, therefore, does not signal the presence of an event demanding a form of pure externality. On the contrary, othering necessitates forms of relationality. In addition, though this recalls a point already made, othering, understood as a form of destruction, brings value into play. Value, however, is not located within either a subject or within what could be extracted from abstract subjectivity. The locus of value will reside in the world (albeit as a potentiality). Here it is vital to add the additional though nonetheless implicit point that within modernity, as part of its self-definition, the presence of the world as a locus of value is grounded in the inescapable reality that the world (Marx's *die Welt*) is structured by the effective presence of the disequilibria of power relations. Thus worldly life is both the actual presence of a given set of power relations, though equally it is that which can be othered. Othering becomes another setting of those relations. What this would mean, in Benjamin's own terms, is that 'the world of law' (*die Welt des Rechts*) would cede its place to 'the moral world' (*die moralische Welt*).

2

Benjamin's short text *The Meaning of Time in the Moral World* opens with a consideration of the relationship between law and legal institutions and what he refers to as 'times long past'.[6] It had been thought, Benjamin suggests, that both law and legal institutions have an already given relationship to 'morality'. And yet, as he claims, this is not the case. He goes on to argue:

> What endows the law with this interest in the distant past and with power over it, however, is something very different indeed from the representation of the presence of morality in the past. The law [*Recht*] actually derives these features from a tendency that sets it off sharply from the moral world. This is the tendency for retribution [*Vergeltung*].[7]

What must be noted from the start is that at work here is the undoing of the assumption that there is an axiomatic relationship between law and morality. Once this assumption is undone – and this undoing has to be understood methodologically as a form of destruction – then, and only then, it is possible to pose the question of the relationship between law and morality as a genuine question. This question must be seen as implicitly always at work within the fragment.

Within the text itself the evocation of 'retribution' summons the domain of fate and thus the work of immediacy. Within *Fate and Character* (to be taken up in Chapter 3), written two years before the fragment on 'the moral world', 'fate' is inextricably bound up with an imposed and then naturalised form of continuity. There is an additional element which, in this context, is decisive. Fate also defines the realm of 'guilt', a realm in which 'guilt' is imposed on life. 'Guilt', for Benjamin, in part borrowing from Hermann Cohen's *Ethik des reinen Willen*, defines the subject position within the temporality of fate.[8] The interruption of the work of guilt occurs within a context, as argued in the line from *Fate and Character* already noted and in which the mistaken conflation of 'justice' (*Gerechtigkeit*) with the 'order of law' (*die Ordnung des Rechts*) has been identified – an identification that allows justice to be separated from law – and it is this identification that locates the possibility for the interruption of fate in forms of action. That interruption did not occur within law. It distances law in its occurring. Indeed its location was 'outside' the law (or at least that conception of law that can be differentiated from justice).

To return to the passage that has already been identified as staging these concerns – and it is a passage that will continue to prove central to the recovery of a political philosophy from Benjamin's writings – it should be noted that for Benjamin:

> It was not in law rather in tragedy [*Nicht das Recht, sondern die Tragödie war es*] that the head of genius lifted itself [*sich . . . erhob*] for the first time from the mist of guilt, for in tragedy demonic fate was breached [*wird das dämonische Schicksal durchbrochen*].[9]

Again, the two significant moments here are the lifting of the head and the presence of a breach. Both need to be understood as figures of interruption. Another name for the staging of this release is 'happiness' (*Glück*). In this regard Benjamin is explicit: 'Happiness is what releases [*herauslöst*] the fortunate man [*den Glücklichen*] from the chains of the fates and the nets of his own fate.'[10] In all three instances what is staged is an interruption that needs to be understood as an opening. The opening is generative. It occasions and thus allows.

This provides the setting in which it is possible to situate that against which retribution is pitted. What is opened up thereby is the space and possibility for the *counter-measure*. 'Retribution' as an act which in having been decreed in advance is the refusal of mediacy to the extent that the latter is understood as the spatio-temporal dimension of the decision and thus of judgement. The decision once understood as a judgement is marked in advance by its inherent contestability. (Contestability assumes both the mediate nature of the decision, though equally it assumes that contestation involves place – the locale of contestation.) While what is identified as 'retribution' is subject pragmatically to contemporary temporal limits within legal practice – for example, a statute of limitations – it remains the case that what Benjamin calls the 'power of retribution' (*vergeltende Gewalt*) can hold sway from one generation to the next; a fateful continuity. What is needed therefore is the presence of a form of *Gewalt* that will function as a *counter-measure*.

While it is not Benjamin's actual argument, it is possible, nonetheless, to suggest that a modern version of retribution appears in the apparent necessity to link law and punishment. For Benjamin, however, retribution as a structuring force is 'indifferent to time'. Moreover the 'Last Judgement' (*das jüngste Gericht*) is identified with the final moment of 'retribution', thus the end as the locus of a total and all-encompassing judgement and punishment. (One in which the subject's position defined in terms of guilt has its most insistent presence.) What is important here is that for Benjamin the link between the Last Judgement and the moment when retribution is allowed 'full rein' and thus where the domain of immediacy is opened up fails to understand what he describes as the 'immeasurable significance of the Last Judgement'. Prior to pursuing that 'significance' it is vital to note the distinction between immediacy and mediacy, since the terms themselves as well as the way they differ combine to play a fundamental role both in this text and then more generally in the recovery of Benjamin's philosophical project.

Immediacy operates within the relation between fate and law; moreover, it assumes a subject position that is structured by that relation. Immediacy also envisages, both in regard to that subject and to the conception of historical time in which that structure is located, that it yields, as has already been indicated, a subject position defined by a sense of what is identified in a number of different text as 'original guilt' (for example, of having been fated). Retribution, whether present in terms of law or a specific conception of justice, occurs within the structure generated by fate and guilt. Consequently, what is at work here needs to be understood as necessitating the presence of an already (pre-)determined response to an already given and determined subject. Given the structures of this setting justice (or what would count as justice) would come to be equated with retribution, a positioning that has an almost necessary reciprocity, since such an equation does, of course, obviate the possibility of the mediate. The mediate is precluded precisely because the operative presence of that which is always already determined in advance (for example, the work of fate and the structure of guilt) closes the frame in which mediation could have occurred. Mediacy brings a different setting into play. With mediacy the subject is no longer located in a set-up that is determined firstly by an original structure of guilt, and then secondly by a conception of justice in which justice is equated with retribution.

The project of 'morality', in the way the term is used in Benjamin's text, necessitates the freeing of justice from such a setting. In going beyond it – a going beyond that is the result of the setting's destruction – justice could no longer be equated with a single immediate act, if that act is understood as having a self-completing finality. This needs to be understood of course as a further opening up by Benjamin of the identification of an intrinsic sense of value as that which has already been identified as present in terms of the 'not-yet-attained condition of the just man'. In the context of this fragment, justice is that which is always and of necessity an ongoing concern. Justice brings with it therefore the inevitability of forms of contestation. As such, mediacy is not only the overcoming of the singular act; mediacy, as noted above, demands a sense of place, a spacing, in which justice as a process can then occur and be acted out. (Othering is a staged presence.) Within mediacy justice necessitates subject positions that are defined as much by commonality as they are by place. Immediacy involves the singular act of a God (or a monarch) while mediacy involves the temporality and thus the institutional presence of sites of deliberation. Immediate acts leave the sites in which they occur as always the same. Within the sites of deliberation the ontology of human being, the being of being human, would come to be defined in ways that made place a locus of the continuity of transformation. As such place and othering work together, and as a result the ontology of human being would have to incorporate, as part of its redefinition, the centrality of a relation to place and simultaneously to others. As a result, the being of being human can be recast as being-in-relation. (Again this can be read as part of the reply to Cartesian destruction. Within the latter the place of human being remains the same.)

Having begun to note part of the force of the distinction between immediacy and mediacy it now becomes possible to return to the way that distinction is at work, albeit implicitly, in Benjamin's attempt to distinguish between 'law' and the 'moral world'. Indeed, it is possible to go further and to suggest that both the centrality of process and thus the work of mediacy are already there in Benjamin's text. It occurs in the line that provides the text with its title. Benjamin is in fact concerned with the 'meaning of time in the economy of the moral world' (*in der Ökonomie der moralischen Welt*).[11] The evocation of the presence of an 'economy' is the underscoring of the ineliminability of process. Moreover, it needs to be understood as making the additional claim that relationality is a process. Being is an activity.

Returning to the question of the significance of the Last Judgement, it should be noted that it arises when its identification, thought in terms of 'retribution' and law, is undone, suspended, in the name of a quality that for Benjamin is unthinkable within the realm of law, namely 'forgiveness' (*Vergebung*). What this amounts to, of course, is immediacy ceding its place to mediacy, through what will emerge as the former's depositioning or suspension. Both terms signal the presence of a form of destruction. Indeed, this is the significance of the Last Judgement, though only when it is understood as the day that is 'constantly postponed'. With this shift from 'retribution' to 'forgiveness', and once the necessity of postponement or deferral is introduced, then what is staged is the move from the 'world of law' to the 'moral world'. The suspension of the law, the moment that can be understood as a form of destruction, is the inauguration of the 'moral world'. In other words the inauguration as recovery of the 'moral world' depends upon an act of destruction. The othering of the world is the condition of its becoming moral. It is at this point in the development of the overall argument of Benjamin's text that the figure of Até emerges.[12] The full passage from Benjamin's text is as follows:

> In order to struggle against retribution, forgiveness finds its powerful ally in time [*in der Zeit*]. For time, in which Até pursues the evildoer, is not the lonely calm of fear but the tempestuous storm of forgiveness which precedes the onrush of the Last Judgement and against which she cannot advance.[13]

Here is the crucial moment. There is a repositioning of time. Time is now placed and as such it is also present as part of the world, a presence that is an evocation of the essential placedness of human being. In time as placed, place, as a quality of the world, there is a contest in which what emerges is the site of the political and thus the political as involving a site. At one moment Até is at work, thus there is the work of fate; equally, however, it is also the domain in which forgiveness finds expression. Place therefore, in having a doubled quality, introduces the interconnection between being-in-relation – as involving place and thus being-in-place – and the politics of time. (The expression of forgiveness both accounts for the presence of fate while at the same time locating the potential undoing of fate's hegemony.) Forgiveness always defers retribution, a deferral which needs to be thought as an opening that stops Até's work.[14] It introduces, while defining, the possibility of the 'moral world'.

The question now concerns how this opening of the moral world is to be understood. In order to capture its force it is essential to draw upon a term to which reference has already been made, that is 'caesura'. The term continues to play a fundamental role within Benjamin's writings from the First Doctoral Dissertation (*The Concept of Criticism in German Romanticism*) until the *Arcades Project*.[15] The caesura is a form of radical interruption. Even though there is an interruption it occurs within a setting. The caesura is an awakening that can be assimilated to neither destruction as nihilism nor transformation as a form of negation. (Hence the refusal of an inherent amorality on the one hand and a distancing of a conception of transformation as that which could only have been driven by the power of the negative on the other.) As has already been suggested, what defines the caesura in this context is that it allows, in other words the caesura occasions and is the *caesura of allowing*. However, what it occasions, the form of the occasioned, is itself not given in advance. The caesura therefore can be thought as comprising a moment integral to the othering of the world. What is occasioned is not an extension of the world's already existing logic. The othering of the world therefore depends upon a *caesura of allowing*. What is central to this conception of the interruption is twofold. In the first instance it is the opening up of a space of activity. The second is that what is opened up is not determined by that which occasioned it. This is the force of the term 'allow'. The term is understood here as meaning *to occasion* or *to let happen*, when this now pertains exclusively to the world. The happening in question cannot be explicated either in terms of a cause or determined foundation (*arché*) or judged or evaluated in terms of a given end (*telos*). There is the opening up of a process and thus the inauguration of an 'economy' defined by the continuity of activity. The *caesura of allowing* is therefore an *anarché*.

The lines of the fragment's final paragraph are presented in dramatic terms. Benjamin is, of course, aware of this mode of procedure, since he will begin his last paragraph by noting his use of this type of language and by then going on to add that such thinking must be capable of being formulated 'clearly and distinctly in conceptual form' (*in Begriffen*). The storm 'drowns' the anxious cry of the 'criminal' (*Verbrecher*), it destroys 'traces' of 'misdeeds' (*Untat*) and this occurs even if the 'earth' (*Erde*) must be ravaged in the process. This storm precedes the Last Judgement; the preceding does not simply occur before the Last Judgement. Its occurrence defers the Last Judgement where the latter is understood as the coincidence of law, finality and retribution. It keeps Até at bay. This is the point at which Benjamin introduces an emphatic juxtaposition that demands careful reformulation. Forgiveness as a movement and a process is presented in terms of its being 'God's anger', which 'roars through history in the storm of forgiveness'. This happens in order to take away that which, were it not for this storm, would have been 'devoured by the lightning bolts of Godly wrath' (*den Blitzen des göttlichen Wetters*). Intimations of the process of deferral are compounded. The introduction of deferral needs to be set against immediacy. Immediacy, as noted above, is the work of fate and thus also the Gods. Retribution is not the result of a potentially contestable decision. Retribution is an enacted finality that occurs without mediation. Retribution is the result of the articulation of law as pure immediacy and correspondingly the interconnection of fate, law and guilt. History as chronology is interarticulated with a subject position in which the subject is produced as already guilty. The subject is thus fated while also being the subject of fate.

And then there is the *counter-measure*, the result of the counter-strophe, of mediacy. Integral to the process of mediacy is the proposition that 'God's fury' saves. It saves what would otherwise have been exposed to the finality of the Last Judgement, that is, finality as immediate. What awaits greater clarification is what this set-up stages, namely the 'meaning of time in the moral world'. What occurs within this 'time' is, as the final lines of the fragment make clear, the following: in the first instance, 'time' extinguishes the 'traces' of all 'misdeeds'; in the second, precisely because of its temporal duration, this process occurs 'beyond all remembering or forgetting' (*jenseits allen Gedenkens oder Vergessens*). In the third, this positioning is itself integral to the 'process of forgiveness' (*Vergebung*). (And it should be noted that 'forgiveness' is not just defined by the moment of its happening; it is, by definition, a 'process'.) Finally, what is not completed is the process of 'reconciliation' (*Versöhnung*).

Despite the complexity of these formulations, what is beginning to emerge is a way of understanding the nature of the distinction between 'law' and the 'moral world'. Two points with which to begin. The first is that rather than comprising two distinct domains, 'law' in the first instance and the 'moral world' in the second, they must be viewed as occurring together. They take place in relation to each other. And precisely because they are mutually exclusive it has to be the case that, were there to be a moral world, and thus forgiveness, there would have to be a necessary suspension of the law to the extent that law is identified with immediacy, thought within the temporality of fate and yielding a subject as already guilty. (What this opens up is the possibility of a critique of law in the name of law. This is the project to be taken up in Chapter 4.) Hence, as a beginning, though with its argumentative basis more securely established, it is now possible to reiterate the text's opening contention, namely that there is no a priori link between morality and law. Moreover, that necessity implies that any attempt to enact or sustain forgiveness – and there can only ever be attempts for the very reason that forgiveness occurs within and as a process and thus as mediacy – is equally to evoke the suspension of the law. The second point is that what is involved here is a contestation of times. The latter is a point that is already there in Benjamin's suggestion that forgiveness has its greatest ally 'in time'. There is an enacted conflict between the 'storm of forgiveness' and the 'onrush of the Last Judgement'.[16] Once the 'postponement' of the Last Judgement is taken as central, the Last Judgement as itself the site of a potentially infinite postponement, occurring in the move from retribution to forgiveness, what is then opened is the actual locus of forgiveness. A logic of postponement also figures in Benjamin's encounter with Kafka. He writes of Kafka's *The Trial* in a manner that repeats the argumentation here:

Postponement is the hope of the accused man only if the proceeding does not gradually turn into judgement.[17]

Judgement in this strict context would have the form of an immediate decision, immediate because of the refusal of the temporality and the place of contestability. The opening has to be maintained. Place becomes central. In other words, in both instances place is reconfigured. In the context of *The Meaning of Time in the Moral World*, rather than the earth being the place where fate exerts its control over human decisions and therefore where place is equally the locus of the Gods, place becomes the site both of the decision and the centrality of human actions. What this means is that in the move from law to forgiveness, what occurs is the opening of the space of the decision and of judgement (what will of course be another form of judgement, namely judgement as the decision within mediacy). Forgiveness depends upon the interrelationship between spacing and immediacy. This spacing, as the continuity of space's transformation, is the mark of the political. This is a point alluded to in Benjamin's own emphatic claim that in the storm of forgiveness traces of misdeeds will be erased and that this will occur 'even if it must ravage (*verwüsten*) the earth in the process'.

Given this description, what has to be pursued is how the reference to the 'earth' (*Erde*) – as in part a naming of place – is to be understood. As a beginning the ravaging of the earth is the 'erasure of the trace of misdeeds'. However, this is not simple destruction; the latter would be the form of destruction demanded by guilt and enacted within differing forms of finality. Rather, here it is the destruction of forgiveness. The 'earth', as a term within Benjamin's text, can only be understood adequately when it is viewed as designating what has already been described as the placedness of human being. The earth becomes, as a consequence, that which continues within the continuity of forgiveness, continuing though 'slightly altered'. Forgiveness, precisely because it does not pertain to the complex interplay between fate, law and retribution, a set-up defined in terms of immediacy, indeed it demands the suspension of immediacy, is always in place. Forgiveness is an already present potentiality. A potentiality once thought within the sphere of the moral that opens up the connection between the process of forgiveness and the coming into being of the 'just man'. The 'earth' therefore is held in place by its having become the site of morality; morality emerges with the continuity of the mediate. Morality, as has already been indicated, depends on the suspension of the law and, as a consequence, is positioned beyond destruction as a form of nihilism. At work within the opening of morality, at work within it precisely because it becomes morality's precondition, is a suspension that will always have to be reconfigured in terms of the *caesura of allowing*, precisely because what is allowed is the identification of the earth as the space of mediacy.

While 'forgiveness' necessitates moments of completion – there must be forgiveness, decisions are made – a further element remains. For, as Benjamin suggests, what is not brought to an end is the process of 'reconciliation'. The latter is the continual living out of the consequences of having forgiven. Forgiving does not occur once. While what Benjamin may have meant by 'reconciliation' is open to debate, it is nonetheless still possible to link the incomplete nature of reconciliation, as demanded by forgiveness as a process, to the continual deferral of the Last Judgement and then to place as the site of the mortal (human) activity of forgiveness.[18] (Within this setting the Last Judgement is understood in the restricted sense of that which is demanded by the relationship between law and retribution.) Forgiveness is an instance of the operative presence of mediacy and thus the 'economy of the moral world'. As such the incomplete nature of reconciliation names the locus of the decision and reiterates the already identified relationship between spacing and mediacy. The latter is of course the place of the political. What this means is that the connection between the political and the moral is allowed for by the suspension of the relationship between law and fate. This has to be understood as involving that which is inherently incomplete, where incompletion and mediacy have a necessary co-presence insofar as the incomplete refers both to the opening of time in the move from the immediate to the mediate, an opening that can also be named as 'postponement', as well as to the continuous holding open of the place of mediacy and thus of the judgement within and as finitude. When taken together what the set of relations – relations that are as much temporal as they are spatial – names are processes and thus a moral economy. This refines further the initial formulation of the juncture where the structure of critique and its necessary imbrication with destruction takes place – an imbrication that can be reworked in terms of the sense of realism that defines Benjamin's understanding of destruction as an act that reveals.

3

Benjamin, in a text written a few years before this fragment and which was preserved by Gershom Scholem in his *Tagebücher*, that is *Notizen zu einer Arbeit über die Kategorie der Gerechtigkeit*, noted the following in relation to justice:

> *Gerechtigkeit scheint sich nicht auf den guten Willen des Subjekts zu beziehen, sondern macht einen Zustand der Welt aus, Gerechtigkeit bezeichnet die ethische Kategorie des Existenten, Tugend die ethische Kategorie des Geforderten. Tugend kann gefordert werden, Gerechtigkeit letzten Endes nur sein, als Zustand der Welt oder als Zustand Gottes.*[19]

(Justice does not appear to relate to the good will of a subject, rather it is part of the condition of the world. Justice designates the ethical category of existing, virtue the ethical category of the required. Virtue can be required; justice can in the end only exist as a condition of the world, or as a condition of God.)

Central here is the twofold insistence on the 'world' and 'existence'. Slightly earlier in the text, as transcribed by Scholem, the relationship between 'justice' and 'the world' is formulated in the following terms: *Gerechtigkeit ist das Streben, die Welt zum höchsten Gut zu machen* ('Justice is the striving to make the world the highest good').[20] The world is not as it is given; if the given equates both the world that is at hand and that world will be as it is in perpetuity.[21] Both the world and a concern with existence can only come into consideration with the suspension of the effective presence of fate and guilt, the realm of the gods, thus the world as already determined in advance, and finally what will emerge later in Benjamin's writings as the world of historicism, namely a conserving world of the always the same. Hence, contextually, this accounts for the importance of Benjamin's reference to Até. In order to draw together some of the themes already noted, a return will be made to the figure of Até. While a number of contexts are possible, the presence of Até in both Homer and Aeschylus underscores what is at play.

In the *Iliad*, in defence of his actions, after having been reproached by the Achaeans for stealing from Achilles, Agamemnon responds that he is not at fault. He was not the cause of what befell him. His sight had been blinded. As such he was unable to discern, at the time of those actions, the distinction between right and wrong. Ends are not the work of humans (mortals). On the contrary – as the *Iliad* makes clear – 'It is the Gods that bring all things to their end.'[22] Agamemnon continues in his defence by locating the actual cause in Até: 'Eldest daughter of Zeus Até who blinds all – accursed one.'[23] In Aeschylus it is possible to locate a similar fateful impulse. In the *Agamemnon*, in order to present Até and therefore the interplay of time and subjectivity that is staged in relation to that name, the Chorus recounts a story of an 'infant lion' brought up in a 'home' (δομος). Despite this separation there is a reversion. The 'domus' as a place cedes its place to the sense of place that defines the lion. The animal reverts to the 'character' (ηθος) to which it is fated. The ensuing destruction – though it is the destruction that is inherent in fate, and thus the modes of destruction which in Benjamin's language is the destructive force of 'mythic violence' – is accounted for by the Chorus in the following terms:

> What a god had cause to be raised as an inmate of the house was a priest of Até.[24]

In the same speech by the Chorus Até is further described as the 'deity with whom none can war or fight'.[25] Precisely because of that limitation, and thus what would appear to be the possibility of stopping her work or restricting her presence, the question of the possibility of a *counter-measure* emerges. While in the case of the *Oresteia* Athena will appear as the figure of 'divine violence' and suspend – bloodlessly – the hold of the Gods, a process that has the Furies led from the stage in the Underworld, the *counter-measure*, present as a form of destruction, is equally a critique of fate by which what becomes the object of critique is the understanding of historical time as well as the conception of subjectivity that fate demands.[26]

In both instances the figure of Até shows emphatically that the world of mortals, that is the world, the 'earth' and thus the place of the decision, can only emerge to the extent that the world of the Gods no longer defines the locus of the decision. In such a move, the decision as an immediate response yields its place to the decision as that which emerges from the inherent mediacy of judgement. In other words, it is only the suspension of that conception of the world that allows for the emergence of a world defined as the locus of being-in-place – again this is what is provided by what was referred to earlier in terms of the sense of realism that is the result of the Benjaminian destruction. This is a potentiality that inheres in the fact of worldly existence. (That fact has already been noted in the citation from Benjamin that 'judgement' 'exists as a condition of the world'. In addition, this is Marx's othering of the world.) In the same passage from the *Iliad*, the causal relation that results in occurrences in the world is always removed from the human domain. The determining role in what are taken to be human actions and thus assumed to be the result of decisions, where the decision itself structures the domain in which responsibility and judgement would be at work, is given to Fate (*Moira*). Fate is present both in a personified form and as a form of time. With regard to the latter, the time of Fate is that in which human actions occur. However, it is equally the time over which humans cannot exert control. They are subject to Fate. Thus while present they are not only fated as subjects, they are positioned within a structure of original guilt.

What is introduced here within the world opened by the figure of Até as it occurs in both the *Iliad* and Aeschylus' *Agamemnon* is a temporal distinction between, on the one hand, the eternality of fate, an eternality within which particulars occur, one in which history as the history of events takes place and, on the other, a domain of activity and thus of history (another conception of history) that can only occur with the suspension or depositioning of the former. In other words, the distinction on the level of the world is between the fateful world and the 'moral world'. However, it needs to be noted that this suspension does not reduce human actions to the pragmatic (that which would be dealt with in the context of a concern with the judgement of human actions under the heading of 'positive law').[27] Rather, it necessitates a rethinking of that which grounds judgement, responsibility and thus the decision. And in so doing it brings with it the inevitability of what has already been described as the placedness of human being, that is human being as being-in-place. It has to be recognised in addition that the domain of the relationship between fate and particularity will always need to be suspended. Suspending becomes an activity precisely because it involves the continuity of action – the continuity of discontinuity – and therefore cannot be understood in terms of a logic of negation. Equally, though from the other perspective, it stands opposed to the temporality of eternal recurrence. There is, as a consequence, the continual possibility of a form of return. Such a return would not occur in the name of the Gods; rather what continues to endure is, on the one hand, the interplay between fate as a conception of historical and political time and the conception of law that stems from it and, on the other, the continuous creation of that which occurs within the space opened by the *caesura of allowing*. (An instance of the latter is the already noted 'process of forgiving'.) What is opened, in moving from the immediate to the space of mediacy, is not just the 'moral world', it is also the possibility of critique. What this means is that critique becomes possible to the extent that there is the othering of the world. However, precisely because the othering of the world is the re-creation of the world as the 'moral world', or as a world in which justice, rather than being linked either to an ought or to the transcendent, is a 'condition of the world', it is not established as a single event. On the contrary, it has to be understood as the continuity of practice. A continuity in which the locus of critique, and this will equally be the case with justice, is the world in the continuity of its being othered. Othering becomes the assertion that justice is an affirmed quality of the world. Why? Because existing and existing justly have the potentiality of being synonymous. Hence the continual recourse to the force of the distinction between 'existence' and the potentiality to exist justly that has already been noted in Benjamin. This is a distinction which has a transformative capacity, precisely because of its link to an affirmation of the moral world which in turn depends upon destruction.

To reinforce the contention that this potentiality is an already present quality within the world and which can be recovered from the world given the suspension or depositioning of the law – this is after all the juncture in which the structure of critique is to be located – is a position held by Benjamin. This can be noted in a suggestion made almost in passing in *Towards a Critique of Violence*. Benjamin's contention is that what he terms 'educative power' (*erzieherische Gewalt*) has the 'power to annihilate through the destruction of all law making'.[28] The force of this passage is twofold. In the first instance it can be located as an identification of a form of 'power' (*Gewalt*) that has the potential to bring about a suspension of the work of immediacy, where the power is located within a setting that brings with it the possibility, and thus the potentiality, not to have been always and inevitably – thus fatefully – structured by the actual logic of the world. The second is the link that this conception of 'power' has to forms of agreement that have their base within 'sympathy' and 'trust'. In other words, there is within the fabric of existence an ineliminable potential that, given the suspension of the law (where the latter is understood in terms of immediacy), there are other forms of relationality. They have to be allowed.

The complex relation between critique and destruction names the juncture within which the *caesura of allowing* comes to be linked as much to an encounter with the philosophical and the work of art as it does to social relations. Once the world is longer reducible either to the merely conceptual or taken to be explicable in terms of the assumption of its *there is* quality – a quality that unfolds as much in relation to the positing of the immutability of structure as it would in relation to its reduction to the merely empirical – then the relationship between destruction and critique is inextricably bound up with the affirmation of the world's potentiality to be other.

Notes

1. Benjamin, *Selected Writings* 3, p. 269; *Gesammelte Schriften* II.1, p. 480.
2. See René Descartes, *Oeuvres de Descartes*, ed. Charles Adam and Paul Tannery (Paris: Librairie Philosophique J. Vrin, 1996). For the Latin, see Tome VII, p. 18; and for the French Tome IX, p. 13. For an examination of this *eversio/destruction* within the terms of Descartes' own project, see

Denis Kamboucher, *Les Méditations métaphysiques de Descartes* (Paris: PUF, 2005), pp. 191–201. It is interesting to note that the most recent significant translation of the *Meditations* into English – that is Descartes, *Meditations on First Philosophy*, trans. Michael Moriarty (Oxford: Oxford University Press, 2008) – opts for 'destroying' rather than 'overturning' (p. 13). For a further and importantly different interpretation of this act of 'destruction' see Descartes, *Meditations on First Philosophy*, trans. Michael Moriarty (Oxford: Oxford University Press, 2008). There are, of course, interpretations of Descartes' overall philosophical project which, while noting the role of 'destruction', do not attribute it a central role within any subsequent interpretation. For an instance of such an approach see John Cottingham, *Cartesian Reflections: Essays on Descartes's Philosophy* (Oxford: Oxford University Press, 2008), pp. 53–7.

3. For the German text *Thesen über Feuerbach*, as well as a facsimile of the original manuscript, see <http://www.mlwerke.de/me/me03/me03_533.htm>.

4. Karl Marx, 'Theses on Feuerbach' [1845], in *Karl Marx: Selected Writings*, ed. with an Introduction by Lawrence H. Simmon (Indianapolis: Hackett, 1994), p. 101.

5. The catastrophe is a counter-strophe and, as shall be seen, has the structure of a caesura. This point is developed in detail in the argument to come.

6. This text has not attracted a great deal of critical commentary. Without doubt the most important discussion of it occurs in Ashraf Noor, 'Walter Benjamin: Time and Justice', *Naharaim. Zeitschrift für deutsch-jüdische Literatur und Kulturgeschichte* 1 (2007), pp. 38–74. The importance of Noor's discussion of Benjamin's text is located generally in the way he insists rightly that any understanding of Benjamin's work on justice necessitates locating it within a philosophy of historical time. And more specifically in the way he connects it to Scholem's own concerns at the time and thus how Benjamin's text needs to be explicated both in relation to Scholem's commentary on the Book of Jonah (see Scholem, *Tagebücher 1917–23*, ed. Karlfried Grunder, Herbert Kopp-Oberstebrink and Friedrich Niewöhner (Frankfurt: Jüdisher Verlag, 2000)) and in Scholem's incorporation of a text by Benjamin – *Notizen zu einer Arbeit über die Kategorie der Gerechtigkeit* – in the first volume of the published *Tagebücher*, that is Scholem, *Tagebücher 1913–17*, pp. 401–2. My own discussion of Benjamin is indebted to Noor's perspicuous analysis.

7. Benjamin, *Selected Writings* 1, p. 286; *Gesammelte Schriften* VI, p. 97.

8. Hermann Cohen, *Ethik des reinen Willens* (Berlin: Cassirer, 1921), p. 343. For an important overview of the relationship between Cohen and Benjamin see Rochelle Tobias, 'Irreconcilable: Ethics and Aesthetics for Hermann Cohen and Walter Benjamin', *MLN* 127 (2012), pp. 665–80.

9. Benjamin, *Selected Writings* 1, p. 203; *Gesammelte Schriften* II.1, p. 174.

10. Benjamin, *Selected Writings* 1, p. 203; *Gesammelte Schriften* II.1, p. 174.

11. Benjamin, *Selected Writings* 1, p. 287; *Gesammelte Schriften* VI, p. 99.

12. The reference in Benjamin is taken to be to the *Iliad*. There are, however, a range of possible sources. Another possible reference is Nonnos, who in the *Dionysica* describes her as 'the death bringing spirit of Delusion' (XI, p. 113). The passage goes on to describe her as using 'coaxing deceitful speech' (XI, p. 117). See Nonnos, *Dionysiaca 1–15*, trans. W. H. D. Rouse

(Cambridge, MA: Harvard University Press, 1940). Equally, Até plays an important role in a number of central moments in Aeschylus' *Oresteia*.

13. Benjamin, *Selected Writings* 1, p. 286; *Gesammelte Schriften* VI, p. 97.
14. While it will be necessary to return to the figure of Até, it is nonetheless still possible to suggest that, in Aeschylus' *Libation-Bearers*, integral to the reformulation of justice, and this is the overcoming of acts determined by fate, and therefore with the emergence of what is called 'fresh acts of justice' (ll. 805), there is concomitant distancing of the threat of Até (ll. 824–5). See Aeschylus, *Libation-Bearers*, in Burian and Shapiro (eds), *The Complete Aeschylus* 1.
15. I have discussed the varying uses by Benjamin of the term caesura in my 'Benjamin's Modernity', in *Style and Time Essays on the Politics of Appearance* (Evanston: Northwestern University Press, 2006), pp. 5–24.
16. This almost chiasmic play of forces reiterates the position announced by Benjamin in the *Theological-Political Fragment* that:

> The secular order should be erected on the idea of happiness. The relation of this order to the messianic is one of the essential teachings of the philosophy of history. It is the precondition of a mystical conception of history, encompassing a problem that can be represented figuratively. If one arrow points to the goal toward which the secular dynamic acts, and another marks the direction of messianic intensity, then certainly the quest of free humanity for happiness runs counter to the messianic direction. But just as a force, by virtue of the path it is moving along, can augment another force on the opposite path, so the secular order because of its nature as secular promotes the coming of the Messianic Kingdom. (*Selected Writings* 3, p. 305; *Gesammelte Schriften* II.1, p. 203)

This play of forces will be discussed in much greater detail in Chapter 5.
17. Benjamin, *Selected Writings* 2, p. 807; *Gesammelte Schriften* II.2, p. 427.
18. The language of 'forgiveness' is of course also the language of a certain Christianity. In Benjamin, however, it can be argued that the deferral of reconciliation is linked to the refusal of immediate forgiveness. Immediate forgiveness is of course the position that Hegel attributes to Christ. Hegel's comment on *Luke* VII: 48 is decisive in this regard. Hegel writes:

> This expression is no objective cancellation of punishment, no destruction of the still subsisting fate [*kein Zerstören des nicht bestehenden Schicksals*] but the confidence which recognised in the faith of the woman who touched him, recognised in her a heart like his own, read in her faith her heart's elevation above law and fate [*Gesetz und Schicksal*] and declared to her the forgiveness of her sins [*Vergebung der Sünden*]. (*The Spirit of Christianity*, in G. W. F. Hegel, *Early Theological Writings*, trans. T. M. Knox (Philadelphia: University of Philadelphia Press, 1975), p. 239; *Der Geist des Christentums*, in G. W. F Hegel, *Werke*, vol. 1, *Frühe Schriften* (Frankfurt am Main: Suhrkamp, 1986), p. 354)

What is at work here is complex. 'Law and fate' are only overcome through an act of counter-immediacy. Moreover, the conception of law that is in play in Hegel's formulation is the production of law as immediate. This can be described as the literalisation of the law. I have tried to show that this literalisation marks a separation between law and justice that first occurs in Paul and in so doing undoes an identification of law and justice that occurs throughout Greek thought. Benjamin's suspension of the law is the suspension of the law as immediate in order to create a repositioning of the law as inherently mediate. Were that to be possible it would allow for a rearticulation of the relationship between law and justice. See my *Place, Commonality and Judgment: Continental Philosophy and the Ancient Greeks* (London: Continuum Books, 2010).

19. Scholem, *Tagebücher 1913–17*, p. 401.
20. Ibid., p. 401. It also needs to be noted that the term 'striving' – a term bound up with the inscription of an anoriginal sense of force within the work of 'concepts', also plays a fundamental role in the *Theological-Political Fragment*.
21. Scott McCracken, 'The Completion of Old Work: Walter Benjamin and the Everyday', *Cultural Critique 52, Everyday Life* (Autumn 2002), pp. 145–66. I would argue that this opens up a way to appreciate the everyday as the threshold between the ordinary and the extraordinary, between what is and what might be. The extraordinary is never the 'truth' of the everyday, but neither is it its untruth.
22. Homer, *Iliad*, 19, 90ff.
23. Ibid., 19, 91–2ff.
24. Aeschylus, *Agamemnon*, in *The Complete Aeschylus* 1, ll. 735–6.
25. Ibid., l. 769.
26. On the role of Athena in the *Oresteia* see my *Place, Commonality and Judgment*.
27. Here Benjamin's own critical engagement with the tradition of both natural law and positive law, as outlined in the opening pages of *Towards a Critique of Violence* and which will be taken up in Chapter 4, is crucial.
28. Benjamin, *Selected Writings* 1, p. 247; *Gesammelte Schriften* II.1, p. 196.

Chapter 3

Fate and Character

Friendliness . . . does not abolish the distance between people but brings it to life.

Walter Benjamin

1

With the setting created by the way in which the *caesura of allowing* emerges within the framework created by Benjamin's short fragmentary text *The Meaning of Time in the Moral World*, it becomes possible to turn to another central text written at more or less the same time, namely *Fate and Character (Schicksal und Charakter)*.[1] That the terms 'fate' and 'character' will have already had their own historical registration is true by definition. Were that registration both to continue and their meanings to continue to be determined in advance, it would then be the case that as terms their field of operation would have been fated. In other words, they would have been fated to mean whatever it is that these primary forms of registration and determination demand. 'Fate's' fate, however, is not simply semantic. 'Fate' names a specific conception of historical time. As such 'fate', once taken as naming a modality of historical time, is bound up firstly with an already present determination and then secondly with that determination's unimpeded repetition. The latter becomes a form of eternal return while the former is an effacing of the future as a result of the present having been presented – or conceived – as complete. The presence of this conception of the present, the present as self-completing, has to be understood therefore in terms of a temporality that is both self-determined and self-enclosed, and therefore equally a conception of place as a locus defined by the continuity of its form as already determined. What is – 'is' in the sense of what exists – will continue and continue through its maintaining the form that it already has. Such a setting can either refuse the possibility of a future, in the first place, or, in the second, imagine a future that oscillated between a projected image and the return of what has already been – as such either the future would be known or the future would have an imaginary relation to the present. In the case of the latter it would be a projection that was unrelated to the present. In that particular instance a lack of relation would not refer to the positioning of a determining externality, rather its significance lies in its having assumed in advance the absence of an already present potentiality within the present. This means that such a conception of the future joined with a reciprocal conception of the present could not be thought in terms of an opening created by the *caesura of allowing*. The limitation has to be understood as occurring because this specific opening, the one staged by the *caesura of allowing*, and it is an opening in which the future happens, is itself the result of an already present interconnection between destruction and value which in turn depends upon the productive force of potentiality. In regard to the question of value as it has emerged in the preceding chapter, it has been named by Benjamin – and this will only be one possible name among others – as taking place within and as the 'moral world'.

In *One Way Street*, in a poignant yet nonetheless charged reference to Andrea de Pisano's *Spes* (*Hope*), Benjamin wrote, presumably after the seeing the work in the Baptistery in Florence:

> On the portal, the *Spes* [*Hope*] by Andre de Pisano. Sitting, she helplessly extends her arms towards a fruit that remains beyond her reach. And yet, she is winged. Nothing is more true. [*Dennoch ist sie geflügelt. Nichts ist wahrer.*][2]

That she is winged is already significant. Wings and winged angels will be recalled in the description of the Angel in Klee's *Angelus Novus*, to which reference is made in *On the Concept of History*.[3] Here the presence of wings – and note the formulation 'And yet she is winged' (*Dennoch ist sie geflügelt*) – complicates her relation to a named goal. The goal is not in her grasp. More dramatically, it endures 'beyond her reach'. Indeed, it may be the solidity of the object, its presence as a work, that reinforces the impossibility of movement. An impossibility that allows the question of movement's becoming possible to be posed. Moreover, it may be that she struggles against, though equally within, her material presence. While this might be taken as a sign of despair engendering a melancholic longing – where the longing may become an unending end in itself – the state of being 'winged' introduces an important ambivalence. Either the goal is unattainable despite the presence of wings or it is attainable precisely because of their presence. The former would be the basis of despair's continuity while the latter writes the potentiality for othering into the very fabric of her presence.[4] Her helplessness is there to be overcome. Hence hope takes as its precondition the appearance of hopelessness. Hope therefore is inextricably bound up with a potentiality for the radically other. Hope demands the activity of othering. Hope is a potentiality whose actualisation involves activity. Andrea de Pisano's work stages a fated presence that introduces within it the sign of fate's potential undoing, an undoing that is not enacted within the image. Rather, it attends it. Here is an image of that which sets the precondition for its being enacted. Hope is a possibility that inheres – if it is to inhere at all – in the fact that she is 'winged'. The helplessness or hopelessness staged by fate – staged in its vanishing as fate and appearing as natural – calls on the setting of fate's undoing. There is no image of the future. Rather there is the image of the future's possibility. A possibility, given the deferral of the Last Judgement, for which there cannot be an image.

Benjamin's text *Fate and Character* makes a specific set of demands. The setting in which those demands can be situated is in part structured by the strategy of the text's opening concerns. Undoing the fate of 'fate' is not only part of the text's methodological trajectory, it is a trajectory that is repeated, as will be suggested, in the opening of *Towards a Critique of Violence*, in Benjamin's attempt to show the impasse of defining law both in terms of the opposition between means/ends on the one hand and then in terms of the opposition between natural and positive law on the other. The impasse, in its marking the place of destruction, is established in order then to move beyond both of these oppositions and in so doing inaugurate another thinking of law. In other words, it is only by moving beyond them that it becomes possible to allow the question of law to be reposed. In *Fate and Character* the terms 'fate' and 'character' are defined in part by an attempt to rethink what is designated by them, which are, of course, definitions to be understood as their 'fate'. As a result the opening interpretive question needs to pertain to the implicit necessity at work within Benjamin's text. Hence the question: why is it important to rework what is intended – perhaps meant – by 'fate' and 'character'? Even though this latter question does not contain the answer in any direct sense, what it does is stage that which forms the question. Undoing the predetermined meaning of both 'fate' and 'character' is of course to free them from their fate. To free terms – what Benjamin will continue to refer to as 'concepts' – from their fate is both to concede the ineliminability of time, of concepts having been fated, and thus of having allowed fate, within the framework provided by the presence of fated meanings, to have a twofold designation.

In the first instance it identifies a conception of time as determined sequence. This is a conception of time, moreover, that is naturalised such that in its undoing it then becomes possible to understand time as a site of what has already been identified as anoriginal complexity, where that complexity evidences the presence, at the present, of irreducible and thus conflicting modes of historical time. As has been argued in relation to this irreducibility, it needs to be understood as marking the presence of a politics of time because that irreducibility evidences different positions in relation to 'life', and thus different conceptions of life and value and therefore of their relationship. When taken together, what this indicates is that both time and life are themselves articulated within (and as) a founding disequilibrium of power. Value and power are interconnected insofar as specific conceptions of value, if they are not mere abstraction, are linked to the continuation of their presence or the possibility of destruction and inauguration. Possibilities that are already present in the distinction between 'mere life' and the possibility of a just life. Not only is this the politics of time, it also means that since that disequilibrium structures the presence of life that disequilibrium has to be recognised as integral to a philosophical thinking of life.

The second element at work within 'fate' understood as a modality of historical time is that the undoing of fate's fate is to hold to the possibility of a productive destruction as an already present possibility which is present at the present. A possibility held in play by time and which when understood in abstract terms becomes possible because of the complex set of relations sustaining a politics of time. A complexity effaced through processes of naturalisation but exposed within the recognition that, as mentioned above, the presence of the political is that which works both with and within different modalities of time. That recognition yields a relationship within which what is recognised is both naturalisation as semblance and the potentiality for othering. One way of understanding what is opened up by both this recognition and the attendant affirmation of potentiality would be in terms of the move to allegory. This is a move – an allegorisation of the world – that occurs in the face of the appearance of immediacy, continuity and unity. A position stated by Benjamin with stark clarity in *Central Park*, when he wrote: 'Majesty of the allegorical intention: to destroy the organic and the living – to eradicate semblance (*Zerstörung des Organischen und Lebendigen – Auslöschung des Scheins*).[5] Equally, of course, this is the possibility that is enacted within the 'dialectical image' where the latter involves the presence of a disruption within time.

In the context of the text *Fate and Character*, time – understood in the first instance as identified with the temporality of 'fate' – yields a subject position that is defined in terms of 'guilt' (*Schuld*). Historical time, and it needs to be remembered that within a politics of time there are different modalities of time, always creates subject positions. As a general claim therefore historical time and its capacity to create subject positions work together. The process of subject creation is fundamental to the role of 'fate'. Historical time binds subjects to it. To refuse to allow 'fate' to have this designation and thus to undo 'fate's' fated position must again be seen as an intervention within time and thus as a form of destruction. It is an intervention that has a twofold designation. There is both the interruption and what this recognition then affords. That recognition needs to be understood as an opening, one whose necessity is announced throughout Benjamin's work. One of its more emphatic presentations of that process occurs in *The Arcades Project* in terms of the reiteration of the word *erwachen*.[6] Awakening from a dream is to discover having dreamt and that which this wakeful discovery then holds open. Equally, it is present in Benjamin's critical engagement with what he terms 'cultural history' and of which he writes that:

> [It] lacks the destructive element which authenticates both dialectical thought and the experience of the dialectical thinker.[7]

It should be noted that what is at work in this formulation is both the conceptual and the experiential. What this underscores is not just the role of experience, nor just the centrality of activity; it also highlights the point noted above concerning the relationship between historical time and the creation of subject positions.

As a beginning what needs to be worked through is the opening in which 'fate' is freed both from its own fate and then with what this destruction then stages. Given this setting the point of departure stems from the already determined position in which the concepts of 'fate' and 'character', as they are traditionally understood, are located. Within that location there is a type of interpretative interconnection with the resultant consequence, or at least this is the supposition that attends the way both 'fate' and 'character' are conventionally understood, which is that the knowledge of 'character' would yield the knowledge of a specific 'fate'. Moreover, there is a form or reciprocity at work within their relation. In the end, for Benjamin, both 'fate' and 'character' are not just defined in terms of each other, it is equally the case that within the context of that traditional understanding it has become impossible to separate them. As a consequence Benjamin's first interpretive move, noting that this move has as its aim ridding these terms of their already determined nature and thus opening them up, is not just to open another form of thinking but also to allow, through the destruction of the already determined, for what is at work within the reiterated presence of 'fate' and 'character' to emerge. Present here is, of course, another gesture to the mode of realism that attends Benjamin's project. It is a realism to which reference has already been made, a realism in which what counts as the real emerges from the destruction of that which is 'at hand' and thus with its non-identification with that which is at hand. (The real is only at hand after a 'left-handed blow'.)

What matters in the first instance is that the causal connection that determines both the relationship between 'fate' and 'character' and equally the attendant appearances – the 'system of signs' – through which their presence is understood can itself be distanced. With that distancing there is another setting. In this regard Benjamin, in relation to his own project, writes that:

> The inquiry that follows is not concerned with what such a system of signs [*Zeichensystem*] for character and fate is like but merely with what it signifies [*die Bezeichneten*].[8]

In other words, the concern moves from accepting an already present system of signs as the locus of investigation, an acceptance in which that setting would then have been defined by both the naturalisation of the system and the impossibility within it of effecting a sustained separation of 'fate' and 'character', to one in which their separation and redefinition will have become possible. That separation is not a counter-view within the realm of opinion. Rather, separation will be the denaturalisation of an already determined setting and therefore equally the undoing of its constituent elements. In sum, this amounts to the projected undoing of 'fate's' fate, in other words a *counter-measure*.

As a way forward, the next step in the argument being developed in Benjamin's text – a step that begins with the move in which 'fate' and 'character' are to be interpreted as 'wholly divergent' – is to begin to develop an understanding of the setting in which they occur and of which they are the result. This is what is meant by concentrating on what they signify rather than with the attribution to them of an inherent truth defined by already given determinations. (The interpretive link here is to 'fate's' imposition even though this is a location that will in the end become more complex.) The setting in which these terms were initially fixed identifies 'character' with the 'ethical' or the 'moral', and then 'fate' with 'religion'. These identifications are, however, for the position being developed by Benjamin, made in 'error' (*Irrtum*). This 'error', however, is not mere happenstance. The 'error' will be revealing.

In regard to the relationship between 'fate' and 'religion', part of noting Benjamin's actual argument is that what it shows is that central to the development of this position is the way 'religion' figures within it and thus what has to be taken up is the thinking of religion that occasions it. Attending this analysis is the question to which reference has been made, a question that framed an integral part of the Introduction to the project of recovery, namely: what is religion? A question that once posed brings into play the more demanding question – again one already noted – of the relationship between religion and theology. In any attempt to engage this question it is always essential to be precise. Here this means being attentive to the difficulties that Benjamin's own argumentation will encounter.

2

The 'error' that linked fate and religion is a connection that was established to 'guilt' (*Schuld*). In regard to the Ancient Greek world – and this is Benjamin's example – the existence of what is described as 'fate-inspired misfortune' (*das schicksalhafte Unglück*) stems, for Benjamin, from the Gods, and is described as the result of a 'religious offence' (*religiöse Verschuldung*). The viability of the link between fate and religion – and this despite appearances – and which in turn is premised on the connection to 'guilt' (*Schuld*) is for Benjamin called into question because of the absence of any connection, in the Greek world, between 'fate' and 'innocence' (*Unschuld*) (though perhaps it is better to cast this as the opposition between 'fate' and 'unguilt'). In the Greek world, again for Benjamin, 'fortune' (*Glück*) is not the result of a blameless life – of a life of 'unguilt' – rather it is there as that which may prompt *hubris*. There is an interesting, albeit implicit, point made here insofar as *hubris*, while its point of orientation is the individual (and there were laws against it), it was also taken as working against the community. As Aristotle makes clear in both the *Rhetoric* and the *Politics*, acts of *hubris* are not just abuses of power, they also take on the quality of events demanding communal judgement.[9] The extension beyond the individual, within which the individual subject becomes the sovereign subject, opens up what will be fundamental to an understanding of the operation of 'fortune' (*Glück*) in Benjamin's writings: namely, the way in which the eliding of an original singular subject reworks the relationship between the subject as a pure singularity, a set-up that becomes impossible once the subject is always already in relation both to other subjects and to the 'moral world'. In part this will become the Benjaminian refusal of a thinking of the political where the thinking in question takes the singular subject – either the subject within liberalism or the subject as positioned in its necessary separation from the world – as both its point of departure and orientation. That refusal has extension insofar as the subject in question could no longer be the locus of either the moral or 'fortune'. As should be clear, this creates a set-up that seeks to overcome the definition of both the political and the moral in terms of a founding and thus original singular subject. (A singularity that can only ever be posited after the event.) There is a further consequence, as will be seen in his *Theological Political Fragment* (and as will be developed in Chapter 6), namely that the search for 'fortune', if the latter is thought to be the province of an individual and as a consequence only to be attained by an individual, creates a state of affairs that will only ever lead to 'misfortune'. The individual loses its position as an end and in so doing the structure of means/ends comes to be displaced further. The reason for this being the case is that, for Benjamin, rather than a singular subject being the locus of hope, there is a relational subject. What comes to matter is life. Life – the life of the living – as that which forms an intrinsic part of the world. Indeed, this is a position concerning the interconnection of the human and the world that is presented by Benjamin in *Fate and Character* when he argues that:

> No definition of the external world can disregard the limits set by the concept of the active human being. Between the active man and the external world, all is interaction [*Wechselwirkung*]; their spheres of action interpenetrate.[10]

In fact, in Benjamin, as can be argued for example on the basis of this 'interaction' (*Wechselwirkung*), a process that positions an already present relation between subject and world thus opens up the possibility of a similar sense of relation between subjects. The already present 'interaction' between subjects and world – a setting in which relationality *is*, that is, it is what it is in its being acted out – can be described more generally as *being-in-relation*. In the Benjaminian context, however, *being-in-relation* is to be renamed as life. (To which it should be added that this is 'life' in its necessary differentiation from both 'mere life' and 'natural life'.)

For Benjamin, as the argument within *Fate and Character* develops, there is no inherent connection at all between 'fate' and 'unguilt'. Hence there is the reciprocal question – given the presence of this non-relation – of how then the relationship between 'fate' and 'fortune' (*Glück*) is to be understood. Having allowed this setting to emerge through the destruction of pre-existing positions, positions which contained already present identifications and connections – this is of course 'fate's' undoing – not only are the question of what 'fortune' is and the related question of how it is connected to 'fate' able to emerge, both questions arise in such a way as to indicate defining elements fundamental to 'fate'. Here, in lines that in being recalled can now be read as setting the tone for Benjamin's entire thinking of 'fortune' (*das Glück*), he writes that:

> Fortune [*Das Glück*] is rather what releases [*herauslöst*] the fortunate man [*den Glücklichen*] from the embroilment of the Fates and from the net of his own fate.[11]

While there may still be some distance to be travelled in order to understand fully what is meant here by 'fortune', it is not difficult, even at this early stage, to note its productive force. 'Fortune' (*das Glück*) is a mode of destruction and as such has operability. In part that productivity is located in 'fortune' naming a modality of 'destruction' which is present here in terms of a form of allowing – named in the passage noted above as a 'releasing' – and thus as the movement that has already been identified by the word caesura. Destruction here involves inauguration. (This is the operability of destruction.) That movement in this context involves forms of separation and thus a type of liberation. Both possibilities captured under the heading of a 'release' (*herauslösen*). Here, then, what occurs with the registration of fate's having been overcome is the recognition of having been trapped in fate's 'net', though equally what is opened up is what has already been identified as a 'space of allowing'. This movement of release and separation is reasserted a few lines later. However, the way towards it must be prepared.

Having separated 'fortune' from 'fate' – indeed the relation between them has in some sense now been inverted – Benjamin's next move is to inquire where 'fate' is then to be located. With the asking of this question, 'fate' can no longer be thought as providing a form of naturalised immutability. The latter – that is, naturalised immutability – once retained, however, can only be stemmed by a hubristic revolt against it, or this would be the supposition. (Note here the return, now under a slightly different heading, of *hubris*.) *Hubris* – if the example of Oedipus is retained – is in this context a response to 'fate' that normalises 'fate'. It is the revolt that maintains fate. Oedipus accepts fate's reality in the attempt to circumvent it. It is no longer an externality that determines the will. Fate is present within such a setting as that which is taken – *albeit* spuriously – either to be inescapable or refusable and thus as that which is always already given. At work here is a specific configuration of the logic of the gift.

There are two questions staged by the presence of such a logic. The first concerns how to understand fate's having been taken over and its presence as that which is already present. Secondly, and clearly relatedly, what is then brought into play are questions pertaining to what is involved in the *othering* of fate, given the limitation set by Oedipus. (Here *othering* names the *counter-measure*.) What this means of course is that the refusal of fate – even the revolt that maintains it – cannot comprise a *counter-measure*. Both refusal and passivity lack what has already been identified in the context of Benjamin's paper on Fuchs as 'the destructive element'. Countering, which has to be understood as the *counter-measure* present as a mode of destruction, is an undoing and thus a 'depositioning'. Hence, and to evoke two specific examples which would seem to stand opposed to fate, a *counter-measure* is provided neither by Oedipus' revolt nor, moreover, is it provided by Bartleby's passive nihilism.[12] Rather, the *counter-measure* is the doubled process that was noted earlier. It will involve therefore acts of separation and remains unthinkable outside of its having opened a space of allowing. Bartleby's passivity, like Oedipus' revolt, is no more than the appearance of a *caesura*, that is a form of feigned interruption that does not have the quality of a *caesura of allowing*. What is absent from both revolt and nihilism is any sense of measure that would bring another conception of value into play. In the case of passive nihilism what this means is that it is no more than a gesture oscillating between quietism and acquiescence. It is not the overcoming of any form of sovereignty precisely because Bartleby's passivity fails to address the actual locus of potentiality, name the world's potentiality to be other. Moreover, the question that would need to be addressed is why – perhaps for whom – would Bartleby 'prefer not to'. (The suspicion has to be that this is a position that is uniquely Bartleby's. It is thus merely aesthetic.) It is not just that it is too early for Bartleby's 'I would prefer not to', it is rather that Bartleby, like Oedipus, maintains fate in the failure to counter it. Any *counter-measure* has to involve the interplay of an awakening and a form of destruction. They work together.

Passivity is not the refusal of determination. On the contrary, it is the denial of activity. Or rather it is denial as activity. Passivity stands opposed to the combination of elements that underscores Benjamin's thinking, namely the relationship between destruction and what that destruction allows. Finally, Oedipus' revolt and Bartleby's passive nihilism mark the failure of knowledge. They fail to know what it is that continuity – and here it will be fated continuity – actually is. That failure is evidenced in the presence of a sham or mock-heroics that need to be viewed as the failure to have understood what political agency involves and the particularity of the relationship between potentiality and activity as it occurs within a domain delimited by the already present interplay between time and the creation of subject positions.

3

Precisely because 'fortune' stages the destruction of fate as a naturalised entity, what then has to arise as a site of investigation has as a consequence to be determined by the question of the setting in which fate is to be understood. (An understanding that is of course premised upon the destruction of what has already been described in the context of Benjamin's text as 'fate's' fate.) As a prelude to any answer to this question it must be recalled that what is at work here is a setting created by the interarticulation of modalities of historical time taken in conjunction with the construction of subject positions. Time and the construction of subject positions – and hence subjectivity – work together. This is how the connection between 'fate', 'unfortune' and 'guilt' is to be understood. And it is here that Benjamin adds:

> Such an order cannot be religious no matter how the misunderstood concept of guilt appears to suggest the contrary.[13]

Hence the question: what does the term 'religious' mean in this precise context? The order of 'fate' involves 'unfortune' and 'guilt'. Within them – within the strictures they set and strictly within that setting – there is no path of 'liberation'. However, here it should be noted that this is not religion if religion is understood as a domain of belief on the one hand and that which forms a site of either direct or indirect moral rectitude on the other. Guilt here would not be religious because it does not pertain to an individual subject who has become guilty as a result of innocence ('unguilt') having been betrayed. Guilt is of a different order. It pertains to history and as a term it is – on one important level – inherently amoral. Hence Benjamin's formulation of the connection between guilt and life that is developed in his essay on Goethe's *Elective Affinities* in which he argues that:

> Fate . . . does not affect the life of plants. Nothing is more foreign to it. On the contrary, fate unfolds inexorably in the culpable life. Fate is the nexus of guilt among the living.[14]

The amorality of 'guilt' means that an account of guilt cannot be given with the framework of religion. Rather, both guilt and religion have to be accounted for in terms of the relationship – as will be seen – between law and subject positions within history. These are of course the subject positions that are the after-effect of the presence – more emphatically the co-presence – of guilt and religion. If there is a connection between guilt and religion then it has to do with the work of time and the conventions of religious belief. Perhaps, in this context, a distinction needs to drawn between the religious and religion. If religion is involved it is no longer the religion of private, non-universalisable belief. This would be the domain of the religious. If religion is to figure in this context at all then it is the conception of religion developed in *Capitalism as Religion* and which, as has already been noted, names a particular modality of historical time. This is the 'religion' that is present within and as capitalism. In other words, religion, as the term is used in this specific context, is not that which appears within the history of religion – if the latter is understood in terms of having doctrine that positions belief – it is rather that conception of religion which is present as a specific modality of historical time. Fate and religion are modalities of time and the creation of subject positions.

In regard to both 'fate' and religion, historical time figures both in terms of the inevitability of continuity and the naturalisation of that continuity, hence its compatibility with 'fate', while at the same time refusing the incorporation within it of any intimation of the possibility of its own self-overcoming. The separation of guilt and religion, while perhaps not expressed within Benjamin's text with the concision that is necessary, is premised nonetheless on the fact that the overcoming of guilt is not a return to innocence. That return could only have been a genuine possibility within religion. (Occurring at the end of time and only for the 'few'. The implausibility of this proposition strikes once again against the claim that the 'now' of writing occurs now at the 'end of days'.) With religion, as the term is employed here, the return to innocence is a possibility that, because it takes the individual as the locus of both guilt and innocence, has to have left the world untouched. Any worldly engagement therefore necessitates a reciprocal transformation of the subject, in which the individual cedes its place to a conception of subjectivity that takes *being-in-relation* as original.

Central to the development of the argument that attempts to break the link between fate and a 'religious context' is the emergence of a non-identification of fate with the opposition between guilt and innocence. Therefore, fate gives rise both to a different conception of historical time though, more importantly in this context, a different conception of subject. Indeed, what now emerges is a subject position in which being a subject means being subject to the law. This subject is the legal subject. Here it is important to note that what Benjamin means by the term 'law' has taken on the temporality of fate. Here he writes that 'all legal guilt is nothing other than unfortune'.[15] To reiterate the point, 'legal guilt' is a subject position in which law takes on the quality of 'fate' – where quality stands for its identification with a specific conception of historical time. Within this structure Benjamin suggests that the 'order of law' (*die Ordnung des Rechts*) has become conflated with 'justice' (*Gerechtigkeit*). (It should be clear that, within German, one sounds within the other.) The question to which this setting gives rise concerns the possibility of a counter-measure to that conflation. While that possibility is introduced by Benjamin – noting from the start that it takes place in a passage that has already been cited – in terms of different modalities of destruction, what it opens up is the need to rethink 'justice' in its separation from its conflation with the 'order of law'. This will occur later on in terms of a critique of law in the name of law, which is an overcoming of the 'order of law' in an opening towards justice. More pragmatically, what the conflation brings into play is the possibility – once there is this undoing – of positioning law as grounded in justice rather than having to assume that a law in virtue of being a law is automatically just.

At this point in *Fate and Character*, what the text introduces is a way of undoing the hold of that conflation. It takes the following form:

> It was not in law rather in tragedy [*Nicht das Recht, sondern die Tragödie war es*] that the head of genius lifted itself [*sich . . . erhob*] for the first time from the mist of guilt, for in tragedy demonic fate was breached [*wird das dämonische Schicksal durchbrochen*].[16]

This 'lifting', 'raising' and 'breaching'– activities that recall the already noted 'releasing' – reveal the 'mists of guilt' as the 'guilt context'. They are part of a process that involves connecting destruction to the denaturing of nature and thus to the non-identity between 'mere life' and life (where the latter is understood as the province of 'the living'). Here there is the emergence of a subject that for Benjamin remains 'silent' and 'immature' (*unmündig*); the subject occurs within the world of Ancient Greek theatre. While there may be a form of what Benjamin refers to as 'moral speechlessness' attached to this position, silence cannot be thought to have an all-encompassing presence.[17] Benjamin's position therefore needs to be nuanced.

If there is an argument for the centrality of fate then it has to involve the following. In the 'demonic' – that is, in the realm of the majority of Greek tragedy, the domain of fate – being human was determined by a relation to the Gods and to Fate (the Moirai being the three goddesses of fate). Therefore, if there is an anthropology in the work of Ancient Greek theatre, then for Benjamin it needs to be defined exclusively in terms of fate. Here it should be added that there is an individualising tendency within fate – a tendency in which each person has their own *moira*. For example, in the *Antigone* – Antigone (the character) says of herself that she has the same 'fate' as the 'daughter of Tantalus'.[18] Fate pertains to individuals who are then individually fated. Hence the attempt by Oedipus to escape his own fate. While Benjamin adds at this point that 'pagan man becomes aware that he is better than his god, but the realisation robs him of speech remains unspoken',[19] it is important to be aware that this is neither a complete nor an exact formulation. There are important moments that complicate it. Indeed, Benjamin's own reference to the figure of Prometheus in *Towards a Critique of Violence* already indicates that this is the case. Moreover, while Benjamin does not discuss Aeschylus in any systematic way in his overall writings, it is still clear that if there is a figure of 'divine violence' in the Greek world, a figure whose project is to bring to an end the temporality of fate as that which organises both law and subjectivity and thus who has the presence of 'genius', it is Athena in the *Oresteia*. Her undoing of the 'order of law' in the name of justice is the redemption of justice. Moreover, the displacing of the Erinyes at the end of the *Eumenides* enacts the 'bloodless' *counter-measure* – the *counter-measure* as a form of destruction – that in the context of *Towards a Critique of Violence* marks 'divine violence'. Furthermore, in the fragmentary remains of Aeschylus' *Niobe* in which Niobe speaks, both the act of speaking and her occupying the place in which speaking is possible have to be understood as that which ends the hold of fate, an ending that is an opening – hence, in the context of that place, speaking is the *caesura of allowing*. Speaking is creating. Indeed, it is the presence of speech that is the presence as the *counter-measure* to that which should have been impossible, an impossibility that would have been the staged presence of fate. Finally, and even though questions of authorship endure, Aeschylus' *Prometheus Unbound* can also be read in terms of its performing – performing by voicing – what in the context of *Fate and Character* has to be understood as the work of the 'genius'. Within the context of Aeschylus' own project there would have been a transformation of Zeus. An undoing in which immediacy would have given way to mediation.

Even though the overall position concerning the relationship between the Gods and fate is more complex than Benjamin may have allowed, what is important to note is that he argues that, even with the recognition of a possible suspension of the Gods and the interruption of guilt's pervasive hold, there can still be no return to the 'moral world order' (*die sittliche Weltordnung*). This formulation along with a number of permutations plays an important role within German philosophy and theology. There are three instances that are instructive here. In the first instance, a version of the term can be found in Fichte's *Über den Grund unseres Glaubens an eine göttliche Weltregierung*. In the context of a work that is concerned with repositioning the relation between God and the locus of human activity – a repositioning that will result in the accusation of atheism – Fichte constructs the relationship between God, law and what here is a *moralische Ordnung* in the following terms:

> *Dies ist der wahre Glaube; diese moralische Ordnung ist das Göttliche, das wir annehmen. Er wird construirt durch das Rechttun.* (This is the true faith, this moral order is the divine, that we accept. It [the true faith] is constructed by the law making.)[20]

What is important about this formulation is that the separation Benjamin is working towards between law and fate is refused. His use of the term indicates what is being undone and thus the opening that such an undoing would then yield.

The term also occurs in an important passage of Nietzsche's *The Birth of Tragedy*. The setting is created by the possibility that, through the destruction wrought by the Dionysian, it might be possible to sense 'the highest artistic primal joy'. After which Nietzsche then adds, in relation to a pervasive yet restricted response to the productive co-presence of the Apollonian and the Dionysian, that:

> Of course our aestheticians have nothing to say about this return to the primordial home, or the fraternal union of the two art-deities, nor of the excitement of the hearer which is Apollinian as well as Dionysian; but they never tire of characterizing the struggle of the hero with fate [*den Kampf des Helden mit dem Schicksal*], the triumph of the moral world order [*den Sieg der sittlichen Weltordnung*], or the purgation of the emotions through tragedy, as the essence of the tragic [*als das eigentlich Tragische*].[21]

Here, of course, the argument is that the overcoming of fate opens in a specific direction. The 'struggle' with fate is no longer mere struggle. 'The moral world order' is no longer triumphant. Fate is positioned – a positioning that is the result of fate's presence as an object of knowledge. An object comprised of a structuring relationship between law, subjectivity and historical time. It is an opening that has already been identified as a *caesura of allowing*.

Finally, it is also the case that the term has an extension within more strictly theological debates. Debates that bring a more traditional conception of the theological into an encounter with philosophy. In part the formulation stages a relation between human laws and the laws of nature.[22] However, as a title – *Die sittliche Weltordnung* – it is deployed to translate a volume of Aquinas' *Summa Theologica*. It appeared as Volume 2 of an edition edited by Bernhart in 1935. While occurring fourteen years after Benjamin's text, the fact that a volume of Aquinas can have this name is relevant; even more so when it recognised that the volume in question orientated a specific account of what Aquinas identifies, in the context of its German translation, as 'Das Wesen der Glückseligkeit' ('The essence of fortune/happiness'). Integral to Aquinas' own response to what this essence would be is the position in which it is argued that:

> *Die letzte und vollkommene Glückruhe kann nur in der Schau der göttlichen Wesenheit bestehen.* (The last and most perfect happiness or peace can only exist in the sight of the divine entity.)[23]

The full force of the claim made by Benjamin is that this position, one in which 'fortune/happiness' depends upon God and in which God's presence becomes a *sine qua non* as the guarantor of its realisation, is not one to which recourse is to be made if *Glück* is understood as naming a modality of destruction whose locus is always already worldly. Moreover, as will be seen in the *Theological-Political Fragment*, argumentation for this position occurs when Benjamin distinguishes between the 'world' and the 'Kingdom of God'. In that particular context, and thus by extension, what is meant by that Kingdom and therefore an imposed 'moral world order', a position that will open towards Augustine's *City of God*, is that none of these 'places' (or senses of place) can have a determining effect on the transformation of human life. None pertains to a possible destruction of the identification of life with guilt and thus with 'mere life'. The contrary is the case. Life has an order that is there to be made. It is not an order therefore that is given to it. Rather, it is an order that exists as a potentiality within life. While it will be essential to return this point it can still be suggested that what might be described as the non-restoration of the moral world means that the moral world is still to be made – the potentiality for which is an already present possibility. Recalled here is of course the centrality of potentiality. In brutal summation, the point is that what has to be maintained is the possibility of a world order to be made (rather than one to come).

To continue to pursue the question of fate as it is being worked through in Benjamin's text, what needs to be noted is his argument that it is the 'judge' who reads in the face of the accused their fate. Equally, the 'judge' acts in relation to 'fate' precisely because the 'judge' perceives its work. What this means of course is that the 'judge' thus construed works within the conflation of 'the order of law' and 'justice'. The conflation constructs an appearance or a semblance that presents justice as bound up with fate and a subject who is then positioned as originally guilty – guilt here defines the subject as subjected to fate. The latter is a setting which appears as normativity, though only as the result of a now effected process of naturalisation. Its having been effected is effaced, or at least this is what is attempted. Effacing naturalisation is undertaken in order to construct that which is at hand as immutable. However, that effacing will not have been complete, a mark will remain. On the one hand, the already present wings on Andrea de Pisano's angel may drive her forward. And on the other, normativity will have been touched by a trace of barbarism. Potentiality and traces endure. What is left open is a possibility, that is, the undoing of semblance (an undoing in which appearance then is able to appear as what it is; this is the counter-realism). That undoing has to be thought in terms of modes of destruction which in the context of both *Fate and Character* and *Towards a Critique of Violence* have to be understood in terms of the possibility that has already been identified as a critique of law in the name of law. Part of this undoing – law's *counter-measure* – involves working with the understanding that, as Benjamin argues, what 'fate' strikes is not the being of being human (a being in which relationality and the 'not-yet-being of the just man' are maintained as potentialities) but rather it strikes 'the mere life in him' (*das bloße Leben in ihm*).[24]

Fundamental here is the process of subject creation. The division within life is an essential component. It is a division that will come to be repeated in the discussion of the 'clairvoyant'. In this regard Benjamin writes that both the fortune-teller and the clairvoyant uncover 'in signs something about a natural life in man [*ein natürliches Leben im Menschen*]'.[25] This is given privilege over the 'genius' as the site of disruption and destruction. Remember here the already noted link between the 'genius' and 'fortune'. The one who listens to the clairvoyant is equally only concerned with that aspect of life 'in him' that is subject to 'fate'. Hence Benjamin writes in this context that 'the man who visits her gives way to the guilty life within himself'.[26] In other words, there is an important aspect of the clairvoyant, one that opens up a defining aspect of time. Namely that the present – which here would be time in which the palm is read etc. – 'can at every moment be made simultaneous with another (not present) [*nicht gegenwärtig*].'[27] The truth that the clairvoyant understands is that continuity can be disrupted. However, despite the clairvoyant's insight, in spite of the possible opening, the clairvoyant does not function as a *counter-measure*. The subject position of guilt continues. There is the continual expression of the 'guilty life'. Nonetheless, the clairvoyant's actions gesture towards the *counter-measure*'s possibility.

After noting the complex positioning of the clairvoyant Benjamin then adds the crucial line, one that needs to be read as forming the basis of the distinction between religion and theology – though it should be noted that neither term is mentioned within it. Relatedly, however, the line also restates the way in which time and subjectivity operate in tandem; and in virtue of a doubled yet irreconcilable presence they reposition the present as a site of the anoriginal complexity that marks the actuality of a politics of time. Benjamin wrote the following:

> The guilt context [*Der Schuldzusammenhang*] is temporal in a totally inauthentic way [*ganz uneigentlich zeitlich*], very different in kind and measure from the time of redemption [*der Zeit der Erlösung*], or of music, or of truth.[28]

What is significant about what is identified as 'the guilt context' is that not only does it provide a reiteration of the already staged interconnection between guilt and fate, it provides in addition the setting in which the related subject position that is defined by that interconnection also takes place. In addition, the temporality proper to that subject position forms an integral part of the 'guilt context'. As a result, history, time and subjectivity are brought into a fundamental connection. This is a connection that defines 'the guilt context'. All the elements cohere 'together' (*zusammen*). This provides the force behind Benjamin's description of these interconnected elements as 'temporal in a totally inauthentic way'. All the elements are marked by this founding inauthenticity. And yet it is vital to underscore the fact that despite the inauthenticity at work here, what coheres together involves a sustained modality of time. To reiterate the point: 'the guilt context' is temporal insofar as 'fate' and the related conception of the subject are temporalised entities. However, the way in which temporality pertains is in terms of its own continual self-replication. Therefore, to restate Benjamin's point in slightly different terms, the argument is that eternal return is an 'inauthentic' form of time because it cannot attribute to itself the moment of its own interruption. As such it stages, once again, the temporality proper to the way Benjamin defines, as has already been noted, the 'cultic' quality of both religion and capitalism.

And yet, the contrast to this setting – the *counter-measure* – has already been provided. It is there in what Benjamin has already identified as 'the time of redemption' (*die Zeit der Erlösung*). This is theology. It is the temporality that occurs within and therefore as part of the process of destruction. What Benjamin defines as 'the time of redemption' is the temporality that marks out the opening of the *caesura of allowing*. As a result it has to be understood as time's other possibility. However, this is not a simple either/or. The important point here is that both conceptions of time pertain at any one moment. Once taken together, they delimit the present while at the time setting the limits for a politics of time. Not only are they a fundamental part of thinking the political philosophically, they provide the form taken by a politics of time, a form that, if the lead provided by Benjamin is maintained, is informed by value.

4

The move to a concern with 'character' is in the first instance staged in relation to freeing the 'concept of character' from its link to the ethical or to the moral. This occurs by trying to understand the nature of the 'error' that is located in such a setting in the first place. This is of course a reiteration of the methodological move that has already occurred in relation to 'fate'. 'Character', because it pertains to single traits or 'qualities' (*Eigenschaften*), some of which have a purportedly moral dimension, can be understood as a consequence as the locus of moral concerns. (Such an understanding constitutes the 'error' in regard to the understanding of 'character'.) As a result, the use of terms such as 'thievish' or 'malicious' to describe given (or certain) characters would appear to fall foul of specific moral principles. And yet for Benjamin this is not the case. Such a claim misunderstands both the nature of the moral and the role of actual characters in literary texts. The relationship between 'character' and the moral is not just reformulated. The relation is severed. For Benjamin, contrary to what would have amounted to the received understanding of the relationship between 'character' and the 'moral', it is 'only actions and not qualities [that] can be morally important'.[29] As such the link between 'character' and the moral, given that the latter is defined in terms of 'qualities', is broken decisively. The truth of this position is evident from the history of 'comedy'. Molière's characters become the examples. In his characters, Benjamin writes, the particularity of 'character'

> develops in them like a sun, in the brilliance of a single trait, which allows no other to remain visible in its proximity.[30]

Singularity as the determining element within character defines both its essential nature, though equally its relevance in relation to both fate and tragedy.

This is the point at which Benjamin stages a fundamentally important part of his argument – it is a position that recalls one of the opening moves in the text in which what might have been taken as the opposition between life and world is undone in terms of what was described as the 'interaction' between subjects and the world. As Benjamin added, 'their spheres of action interpenetrate'. This is the staging of the relationship between human being and the world that is interpreted here as a move towards a conception of subjectivity thought in terms of what has already been identified as *being-in-relation*. It is a repositioning that has already been noted in relation to Benjamin's study of Goethe's *Elective Affinities*. The point that Benjamin makes, as has already been cited, is that 'characters in fiction can never be subject to ethical judgement [*der sittlichen Beurteilung*]'.[31] To define them in these terms involves the refusal to recognise that character in the context of literature is positioned by fated being. Fated being has to be understood within the context of literary texts to recall a formulation that has already been deployed as 'being without potentiality'. Ethical judgements, on the contrary, pertain exclusively to human being and therefore by extension to the 'living'. The ethical (or the moral), in other words, cannot be separated from life. The lives of fictional characters are intrinsically different. The difference is to be found in the location of fictional lives. For Benjamin, again as has been noted, they are 'entirely rooted in nature' (*völlig der Natur verhaftet*).[32] There is a consistency here in Benjamin's argumentation. When, for example, he writes of the 'characters' in the novels of Julien Green he states of them that:

> They stand before the reader in the desperate stereotypicality of all truly fateful moments, like the figures in Dante's *Inferno*, the embodiment of an irrevocable existence after the Last Judgement.[33]

What is described above as 'desperate stereotypicality' is the singularity of character. Characters staged by fate, though equally staging fated lives. The counter here is not the overcoming or sidelining of literature. Rather, it is in understanding what it is that literature does, that what has then to emerge is another conception of life. Here it would be life in its separation from the semblance of life. Thus it is life in its overcoming any identification with so-called 'natural' life. It will be the presence of this equation with 'natural life' that will prompt Benjamin's identification of what might be described as the limit of 'character'. In other words, even though 'character' will appear to disrupt the 'guilt context' that is created by 'fate's' continuity, insofar as character's definition in terms of a single trait as opposed to complexity appears to break the 'knot' that secures the subject within fate, this is not the case. This is a position presented by Benjamin in a long and demanding passage. Prior to drawing any conclusions from having worked through Benjamin's *Fate and Character*, it is essential to trace the actual presentation of this final part of the argument.

Benjamin opens with the claim that recalls the centrality of 'genius'. Earlier 'genius' had appeared in terms of its counter-position to 'demonic fate'. The entire setting for its reappearance is the following:

> To the dogma of the natural guilt of human life, of original guilt [*Urschuld*], the irredeemability [*Unlösbarkeit*] of which constitutes the doctrine, and its occasional redemption [*gelegentliche Lösung*], the cult of paganism, genius opposes a vision [*Vision*] of the natural innocence of man [*der natürlichen Unschuld des Menschen*.[34]

Despite its difficulties, the intricacies of Benjamin's formulation need to be noted. There has already been an evocation of 'redemption'. The 'time of redemption' (*die Zeit der Erlösung*) had been contrasted to an 'inauthentic' conception of time. Present here are two modalities of time defined in terms of authenticity. Within the setting opened by this contrast, the posited presence of both 'natural guilt' and 'original guilt' are positioned in terms of their 'irredeemability (*Unlösbarkeit*). The latter has to be understood in terms of guilt, and therefore as both a modality of time and subjectivity, and does not have the potentiality for its own redemption. Part of what reinforces this description is the use of both 'irredeemability' and 'occasional'. All that guilt encounters is the 'occasional redemption' (*gelegentliche Lösung*). What this means – hence – is that the destruction of guilt demands to be thought of in terms of a *counter-measure*. One name that has already been given to that measure is, as has been argued, *Glück*. 'Genius', understood as that which works against fated presence, cannot enact the *counter-measure*. All 'genius' can do here in relation to character – and it must be remembered that character, in its Benjaminian understanding, involves a single trait or quality and thus the genius is attempting to undo the fated by countering with another single trait – is counter 'natural guilt' with 'natural innocence' (unguilt).

Here is the setting in which limits occur. And yet Benjamin adds in relation to this 'vision' that despite the limits – which are reinforced by the 'vision' remaining 'in the realm of nature' (*im Bezirk der Natur*) – he is still able to make the additional point, in relation to this 'vision', that 'its essence is still close to moral insight' (*moralische Einsichten*).

The 'vision' of character, he then goes on to argue, is both 'liberating' and linked to 'freedom'. He notes that as a vision it 'is liberating in all its forms [*unter allen Formen*].' Both positions, the reference firstly to a sense of liberation and then secondly to freedom, are grounded in the courting of an elimination of complexity in which one trait can be countered by another. And yet despite the gestures towards forms of freedom these singularities are only ever counter-possibilities as opposed to counter-measures. One singularity is countered by another: here this means that 'guilt' is countered by 'innocence'. Again accepting the limit of character in relation to fated presence, Benjamin adds that 'the character trait is not therefore the knot in the net [*im Netz*]'. Here Benjamin is clearly referring back to the position that he has already noted in relation to this 'net'. He argued at an earlier stage in the text that: 'Fortune [*Das Glück*] is rather what releases [*herauslöst*] the fortunate man [*den Glücklichen*] from the embroilment of the Fates and from the net [*aus dem Netz*] of his own fate.'[35] The question to be addressed concerns these two differing evocations of the 'net'. While *Glück* has destructive force, since it is bound up with 'releasing', the 'character trait', while fundamentally different, can only ever gesture to the possibility of release. Whatever redemptive qualities 'the character trait' may have – redemptive because of its link to freedom, restricted because it is merely occasional – it cannot be equated with the destructive force of 'fortune'. And yet tragedy and the comic have a relation. Once they are freed from their fated presence then they both open up possibilities arising with the abeyance of fated presence. Limits still endure. Character is delimited by its relation to 'fortune'. Moreover, 'the fortunate man' (*der Glückliche*) is neither a position within comedy nor one defined by the character trait.

Arising with the destruction of the fated presence of both 'fate' and 'character' is an opening. However, it is more than mere spacing. What has been cleared away has already had an effect. The act of following what might be described as Walter Benjamin's othering of 'fate' and 'character' opens these 'concepts' up. No longer fated, they emerge as implicated within and reinforcing specific positions that are the interarticulation of modalities of historical time and the related subject positions. A different question can be posed. It is this question that is presented as operative continually in Benjamin's work. What is fate's abeyance? A question, the very posing of which can now be seen – once held apart from the presence of mere revolt – to mark an opening in which another life now becomes possible.

Notes

1. This chapter was first given as a lecture in Keeble College, Oxford, on 17 November 2012. I want to thank Professor Anthony Phelan and Dr Ben Morgan for the kind invitation to address their graduate seminar in German philosophy.
2. Benjamin, *Selected Writings* 1, p. 471; *Gesammelte Schriften* IV.1, p. 125. In Andre de Pisano's work, the complexity of the image is defined by the relationship between the hands and the wings.
3. *Selected Writings* 4, p. 392; *Gesammelte Schriften* I.2, p. 702.
4. What is recalled here, moreover, is the analysis by Benjamin of Dürer's *Melancholia*, which occurs in *The Origin of German Tragic Drama*. That there had to be both possibilities at work in that engraving has been argued for in Appendix B.
5. Benjamin, *Selected Writings* 1, p. 472; *Gesammelte Schriften* I.2, pp. 699–70. The claim in the passage from *Central Park* is a complex one insofar as the 'living' here has to be identified with the 'natural' and thus will the attempt to equate life with 'mere life' or 'natural life', a position reinforced by Benjamin's use of the term 'organic' (*das Organische*). It is this set-up that allegory 'destroys'. This is why, moreover, allegory is equally 'the antidote [*das Antidoton*] to myth' (Benjamin, *Selected Writings* 4, p. 179; *Gesammelte Schriften* I.2, p. 677). Allegory ruptures the time of a projected unending continuity. More generally, the importance of the distinction between 'allegory' and symbol' can be given a number of different determinations. The important point for this present concern is that the distinction allows for a reformulation in terms of the mediate in contradistinction to the immediate. The latter, which opens up an identification to semblance, finds its counter in the allegorical. In other words, the distinction brings temporal considerations into play that further the overall project of the work of the *counter-measure*.
6. References to 'awakening', both as a term and as a mode of thought, can be found throughout Benjamin's writings. In the *Arcades Project* the term appears both on its own and in formulations that allow for a distinction to be drawn between the dream and awakening. This occurs in an important passage on Aragon. Benjamin writes in this context that:

   > Whereas Aragon persists within the realm of the dream [*im Traumbereiche beharrt*] here the concern is to find the constellation of awakening [*die Konstellation des Erwachens*] . . . here it is a question of the dissolution of 'mythology' into the 'space of history'. That of course can only happen through the awakening of a not-yet-conscious knowledge of what has been [*durch die Erweckung eines noch nicht bewußten Wissens vom Gewesen*. (*Arcades Project*, p. 458; *Gesammelte Schriften* V.1, pp. 571–2)

   What is significant here is as much the differentiation between the dream and the awakening as it is the evocation of that which is yet to have a presence, that is, there as a potentiality awaiting actualisation. In other words, the evocation of a link between the process of an awakening and what he identifies as occurring *durch . . . eines noch nicht bewußten Wissens vom*

Gewesen ties the 'not yet' to a possibility that is already there within the fabric of existence.

7. Benjamin, *Selected Writings* 3, p. 268; *Gesammelte Schriften* II.2, p. 478.
8. Benjamin, *Selected Writings* 1, p. 200; *Gesammelte Schriften* II.1, p. 172.
9. Aristotle, *Rhetoric*, 1378b. See in addition John Henry Freese's note to his translation of this section of Aristotle's text, which concerns the existence of a law linked to *hubris*. The one acting hubristically – named by Aristotle as ο υβριζων – will lead to the position in which a subject, the object of the hubristic assault, becomes 'dishonoured' and thus becomes what might be described as 'the dishonoured one'. This is the force of the passage from the *Iliad* that Aristotle cites (1378b6) concerning Achilles.
10. Benjamin, *Selected Writings* 1, p. 202; *Gesammelte Schriften* II.1, p. 172.
11. Benjamin, *Selected Writings* 1, p. 203; *Gesammelte Schriften* II.1, p. 174
12. There has been a great deal of recent philosophical literature on Bartleby. For a judicious overview of some of the central concerns see Jessica Whyte, '"I Would Prefer Not To": Giorgio Agamben, Bartleby and the Potentiality of the Law', *Law Critique* 20 (2009), pp. 309–24.
13. Benjamin, *Selected Writings* 1, p. 204; *Gesammelte Schriften* II.1, p. 175.
14. Benjamin, *Selected Writings* 1, p. 307; *Gesammelte Schriften* I.1, p. 138.
15. Benjamin, *Selected Writings* 1, p. 203; *Gesammelte Schriften* II.1, p. 174.
16. Benjamin, *Selected Writings* 1, p. 203; *Gesammelte Schriften* II.1, p. 174.
17. While its detail cannot be pursed, it is worth noting that this evocation of speechlessness and silence needs to be read in relation to the connection between silence and tragedy established by Rosenzweig in *The Star of Redemption*, trans. Barbara E. Galli (Madison: University of Wisconsin Press, 2005), pp. 79–91.
18. Sophocles, *Antigone*, ll. 825–6.
19. Benjamin, *Selected Writings* 1; *Gesammelte Schriften* II.1, p. 175.
20. Johann Gottlieb Fichte, *Fichtes Werke*, Band V (Berlin: Walter de Gruyter, 1971), p. 185.
21. Nietzsche, *The Birth of Tragedy*, trans. Walter Kaufmann (New York: Vintage, 1967), p. 132.
22. See, to this end, Friedrich Traub, *Die sittliche Weltordnung. Eine systematische Untersuchung* (Freiburg im Breisgau: Mohr, 1892).
23. Thomas Aquinas, *Summe der Theologie* 2, p. 30. It is important to note – even if it cannot be pursued – that in this context, when Aquinas translates Aristotle, *Ethics* V11, 13. 1153b16, ἡ δ' εὐδαιμονία τῶν τελείων, this is rendered as *beatitudo est operatio perfecta*. In other words, εὐδαιμονία becomes *beatitudo* in Latin, while in German it becomes *Glück*. It is not difficult to see therefore that what is at work is a conflict – and this conflict can be extended such that it can become a formulation of a politics of time – that occurs through these different modalities of *Glück*. In other words, what these issues, staged in relation to translation, indicate are not matters that can be resolved in relation to questions of fidelity. On the contrary, translation here indicates that with translation's necessary freedom there endures positions whose lack of reconciliation – a lack that is held in place because one sense of *Glück* cannot become another – is the presence of the political. *Glück* as a naming of destruction encounters another that brings 'beatitudo' into play.

24. Benjamin, *Selected Writings* 1, p. 204; *Gesammelte Schriften* II.1, p. 174.
25. Benjamin, *Selected Writings* 1, p. 204; *Gesammelte Schriften* II.1, p. 175.
26. Benjamin, *Selected Writings* 1, p. 204; *Gesammelte Schriften* II.1, p. 175.
27. Benjamin, *Selected Writings* 1, p. 204; *Gesammelte Schriften* II.1, p. 174.
28. Benjamin, *Selected Writings* 1, p. 204; *Gesammelte Schriften* II.1, p. 176.
29. Benjamin, *Selected Writings* 1, p. 205; *Gesammelte Schriften* II.1, p. 177.
30. Benjamin, *Selected Writings* 1, p. 205; *Gesammelte Schriften* II.1, p. 177.
31. Benjamin, *Selected Writings* 1, p. 304; *Gesammelte Schriften* I.1, p. 133.
32. Benjamin, *Selected Writings* 1, p. 304; *Gesammelte Schriften* I.1, p. 133.
33. Benjamin, *Selected Writings* 2, p. 333; *Gesammelte Schriften* II.1, p. 331.
34. Benjamin, *Selected Writings* 1, p. 206; *Gesammelte Schriften* II.1, p. 178.
35. Benjamin, *Selected Writings* 1, p. 203; *Gesammelte Schriften* II.1, p. 174.

Chapter 4

Towards a Critique of Violence

> What matters are never the 'great' but only the dialectical
> contrasts, which often seem indistinguishable from nuances. It
> is nonetheless from them that life is always born anew.
>
> *Walter Benjamin*

1

The project of this chapter is to stage an engagement with Walter
Benjamin's *Towards a Critique of Violence*, a text whose structure is
far more a series of overlapping elements than the presence of sustained
and deliberate argumentation.[1] Hence, *Towards a Critique of Violence*,
were it to be read properly, demands that attention be paid to its own
structuring force and thus its own complex form of argumentation.[2]
Moreover, attending to the text has another exigency here. There has
to be an engagement that is consistent with the constitutive elements of
this overall project, namely, that integral to the recovery of a political
philosophy from Benjamin's writings is the contention that his use of
destruction – either as a named or as a figured presence, and in terms
of specific modes of analysis – is inextricably bound up with a conception
of value that is, contrary to the Kantian heritage, intrinsic to life. The
implicit presupposition, one that aligns Benjamin, if only momentarily,
with an Epicurean or Lucretian impulse within the philosophical, is
that value is not thought in its radical separation from life, a separation
which for Kant is staged in the distinction between the 'sensible' and the
'supersensible'.[3] What this means is that both value and the possibility of
the modes of actualisation linked to it are present as potentialities within
the fabric of existence. In other words, they are not being adduced.
Recovery pertains to an already present possibility. Occasioning their
connection – the connection between destruction and life – is what has

already been identified as the *caesura of allowing*. As will continue to be argued, what this holds open is the possibility of an equation of life with the just life. As such, this position needs to be advanced and developed as the result of an engagement with specific details of the argumentation within *Towards a Critique of Violence*. Detail is vital. Part of the insistence on detail – thereby remaining open to detail's own insistence – will also necessitate the identification of and engagement with what can be described as an almost irreparable tension within Benjamin's argumentation. The tension, as it will emerge, is between, in the first instance, the consequences of the presence of a spacing in which judgement occurs. Here there is a spacing that has to have been marked by the inclusion of a form of mediacy and thus a link between time (which is present here in term of mediacy and thus the passing of time), justice and *Gewalt*. The tension occurs, however, because there is also the projected elimination of that space in the name of a form of immediacy (immediacy countering mediacy, affirming thereby the latter's anoriginality, that is its always already present status). Immediacy in this context is defined in terms of an immediate moment of judgement. There is therefore a radically different relation between time, justice and *Gewalt*. Here time, which had been the temporality of mediacy, becomes the immediacy of the instant. This other relation is clear from one of the examples of 'divine violence' that will emerge as *Towards a Critique of Violence* unfolds, namely God's judgement of the 'company of Khora'. It is a conception of judgement whose immediacy and elimination of activities involving both the passage of time and spacing are to be contrasted – and here the contrast has an inherently emphatic quality – with the necessity of maintaining that spacing's presence within the setting that is announced in the next instance of 'divine violence', namely the form of *Gewalt* linked to education. This latter sense of 'divine violence' introduces both spacing and mediacy and what will be identified as 'mediated immediacy'. As such it identifies a fundamentally different orientation within 'divine violence'. A process, it will be argued, whose presence opens up the tension that marks Benjamin's thinking of this modality of *Gewalt*. There is a fracturing. It takes place, however, within the necessary retention of 'divine violence'. However, prior to an engagement with the text's detail as a whole, a number of preliminary moves are essential.

As a beginning, and almost despite the presence of Benjamin's text when read in English, staging what may be taken to be the unequivocal presence of 'violence', the German term *Gewalt* – though this may be also to announce a commonplace – does not mean violence in any direct let alone unequivocal sense. Indeed, Benjamin's entire text needs to be read as an engagement with different modalities of *Gewalt*. (Difference, and how it is to be understood, is the key question here.) As a result, the text's argumentative force depends upon the way those different configurations take place within the framework of its own self-presentation. It might be better to understand the formulations in which *Gewalt* figures as staging different senses of *operability*, one of which can be described as the presence of actual violence. *Operability*, in terms of some of the ways in which it is used, has a direct affinity, as was suggested in Chapter 1, to what Arendt identifies as 'the structure of power'. To recall the argument, she wrote the following in relation to this structure:

> It (*the structure*) precedes and outlasts all aims, so that power, far from being the means to an end, is actually the very condition enabling a group to think and act in terms of the means-end category.[4]

'Power' then, in Arendt's formulation, is the condition for a means/end relation. The important point here is that 'power' (in the Arendtian sense) is not defined in the terms set by that relation. Moreover, the development of 'power', as it occurs within this context, allows Arendt to position 'power' against what she takes 'violence' to be. In her engagement with 'violence', to recall the passage already cited, it is as though there is a founding antinomy between 'power' and 'violence'.

> Power and violence are opposites: where the one rules absolutely, the other is absent. Violence appears where power is in jeopardy, but left to its own course it ends in power's disappearance.[5]

While this position is not Benjamin's in any direct sense, and indeed it is written in a text published well after Benjamin's, though it can be usefully read in light of the systematic misunderstanding of the range of possibilities held open by the use of the term *Gewalt* in his *Towards a Critique of Violence*, it allows for the recognition that what challenges operability – here named as 'power' – and which would efface the potentiality inherent in the position of the 'not-yet-attained condition of the just man' would be the actualisation of literal violence.[6] Violence is the threat to a sense of operability that is itself articulated within – though equally is the articulation of – a politics of time. Justice will demand a structure of power. Justice qua justice, that is justice in its necessary differentiation from law (to the extent that the latter occurs fatefully), is unthinkable, philosophically, except in relation to a specific conception of operability.[7] Indeed this is a point that Benjamin will make. While a return will need to be made to Benjamin's recognition of *Gewalt*'s necessity, the passage in which it is stated needs to be noted in advance. Benjamin argues that:

Since, however, every conceivable solution [*Lösung*] to human problems, not to speak of redemption [*Erlösung*] from the confines of all the world historical conditions of existence [*weltgeschlichen Daseinslagen*] obtaining hitherto, remains impossible if violence [*Gewalt*] is totally excluded in principle, the question necessarily arises as to other kinds of violence [*andern Arten der Gewalt*] than all those envisaged by legal theory.[8]

The concession here is clear. It has a twofold quality. In the first instance, overcoming the already present setting in which life occurs – named here as 'the world historical conditions of existence' (*weltgeschliche Daseinslagen*) – necessitates *Gewalt*'s ineliminability. However, that ineliminability does not mean that *Gewalt* need be defined by 'legal theory', which is to say that it need not be defined by the already present determinations that are given by the interarticulation of *Gewalt*, fate and guilt. The project of reading *Towards a Critique of Violence* demands understanding what the complexity within *Gewalt*'s ineliminability entails. Hence the question pertains to understanding what is meant by 'other kinds of violence' (*andere Arten der Gewalt*). The already known status of the 'conceivable solution' (*denkbare Lösung*) opens towards a yet-to-be-determined solution named here as 'redemption' (*Erlösung*). There is a transformation in the move from *Lösung* to *Erlösung* despite the similarity of phonic resonance. As a prelude, however, a further return needs to be made to *Gewalt* itself.

In Benjamin's text *Gewalt* – both as a singular term and in compound constructions – as has already been suggested, overflows simplifying and simplistic restrictions that equate it with actual or literal 'violence'. *Staatsgewalt* is the operability of the state. The operable nature of education which is present also involves a modality of *Gewalt* formulated by Benjamin as *erzieherische Gewalt*.[9] Moreover, there are attempts to identify actual violence and argue for the possibility of those acts being distanced in the name of another modality of *Gewalt*. Equally, there are modes of *Gewalt* that will have involved the immediate spilling of blood and others that are characterised as 'bloodless'. Benjamin's text advances its argumentation through an attempt to hold in play these different and radically incommensurable senses of *Gewalt*. In addition – as will continue to be noted – central to the project is the identification of those moments in which 'non-violent [*gewaltlose*] resolutions of conflict became possible'.[10] Here of course the non-violent both is literally non-violent and signals a distancing of law to the extent that law is defined in terms of a necessary operability that stems from both its relation to fate and the construction of subjects as always already 'guilty'. What becomes important in this instance is how this operability without violence is understood. In the end, for Benjamin, as is well known, one of the names that he will give to this position is 'divine violence' (*göttliche Gewalt*). Even though it will be necessary to take up the tensions within the formulation of this modality of *Gewalt*, as a general claim it can still be argued that *Gewalt* here can be understood as violence without 'violence'.[11] In other words, what 'divine violence' holds in place is the possibility of operability without the latter having to be equated with actual or literal violence. While the formulation – violence without 'violence' – may appear to be contradictory, the contention here is that it is not. What the possibility of violence without 'violence' indicates is the emergence of a sense of operability that occurs with and as part of the critique of law. It is what justice, as a possibility, demands. Moreover, it underscores that what is at work in Benjamin's text is the development of a philosophical position in which justice is neither an external regulative ideal nor there as that which is necessarily unconditioned. Justice is defined in terms of the actualisation of a potentiality. The implication of justice within potentiality has important consequences. If what is at stake in Benjamin's work is a critique of law, where that critique and thus law's destruction is present as part of what has to be recovered in order that his work contribute to a philosophical thinking of the political, then the affirmation of a conception of law linked to an allowing that is neither nihilistic nor simply violent will mean that such a possibility needs to be presented in terms of what has already been formulated as a critique of law in the name of law.

In the course of *Towards a Critique of Violence* Benjamin will write of 'the suspension [or depositioning] [*der Entsetzung*] of the law'. Here is the presence of a *counter-measure*. The full context in which this *counter-measure* is situated needs to be noted. A *counter-measure* is of course precisely not a counter-positing. Within the passages as a whole Benjamin argues that:

> On the breaking [*Durchbrechung*] of this cycle maintained by mythical forms of law, on the suspension [or depositioning] [*der Entsetzung*] of law with all the forces on which it depends as they depend on it, finally therefore on the abolition of state power, a new historical epoch is founded.[12]

The 'suspension' (or 'depositioning') (*die Entsetzung*) of activity brings with it a number of differing implications, all of which are inherent in the word *die Entsetzung* itself. They range from *setzen* as positing, and thus to the deposition – a depositioning and again not a counter-positing – of law, to the 'relief' of a siege and the opening that the end of a siege brings with it.[13] What this means is that if there is a form of *Gewalt* – understood now as a mode of operability – that attends Benjamin's project and which extends beyond literal violence, then it is accompanied almost of necessity by interruption and opening and thus by what has already been referred to as a *caesura of allowing*. The latter is not just an opening, nor is it a mere suspension (or depositioning). On the contrary, it is connected to the repositioning of the relation between life and value. To which it should be added, to recall the passage cited above, that what is 'breached' is described by Benjamin, and here a more accurate translation is necessary, as that which 'circulates under the spell [*im Banne*] of mythic forms of law'. There is therefore a form of enchantment and thus the undoing of the enchanted. There would have been (and indeed there remains) a constancy of circulation – an economy – that because of the spell that has been cast has not been perceived as what it is. Hence, once again, there is the double register that links the language of spells, dreams and the generalised strategy of awakening.[14] Undoing that circulation and the hold of an economy of activity occurs as an interruption that is the eruption of the political.

Here critique demands a form of destruction named as a mode of 'breaking' (*Durchbrechung*) in which what is broken is, as noted above, the 'cycle circulating under the spell of mythic forms of law'.[15] While there is an allusion to time as a form of 'eternal recurrence', in which what is impossible to enact – impossible by definition – is a 'break' within this form of circularity, and thus a break *with* it, it remains the case that the conception of 'law' to which direct reference is made in Benjamin's text is one located within the temporality of fate and which yields a subject position defined in terms of guilt. Here, of course, the destruction named both as a 'breaking' and as a 'suspending' is also a form of inauguration. While the question of how the inauguration of 'a new historical epoch' is to be understood endures, it should be clear that what is at work here is the relationship between destruction and inauguration, present in terms of a *caesura of allowing*. What is allowed will be the presentation of a conception of law that is inaugurated with (and as) the *othering* of the law. What this means in this context refers to the possibility of a law that follows from the 'suspension' (or depositioning) of mythic law and as a result is a conception of law that proceeds from justice. It is only this sense of law that has operability while refusing a sense of operability in which it is identified with the actuality of violence – an identification that would itself equate, for example, justice and revenge; an equation that is at the heart of law's presence within what Benjamin will identify as 'mythic violence'. Two points in addition. Firstly, it is the 'suspension' (or depositioning) of the mythic that holds open the space created by the infinite deferral of the Last Judgement, a position that, as has been seen, is integral to the argumentation of *The Meaning of Time in the Moral World*. As will be seen, it also occurs in the *Theological Political Fragment*.[16] Secondly, to the extent that revenge and justice come to be equated, or to the extent that a call for justice amounts to a call for revenge, what can be taken to endure – and thus to have endured – is this mythic structure of law. The mythic continues therefore as that which haunts the contemporary. There is a direct consequence to this form of presence, a consequence that should temper claims about the accomplishment of the modern. The consequence is that the contemporary is not yet done with the mythic. Thereby opening up as both a political but also a philosophical question of what is at stake in doing without the mythic.[17]

Within this setting the threat of actual violence constructs the domain of law (law as the work of fate fashioning its own form of 'revolt') and 'mere life'. As already argued, their destruction allows for a domain of operability that occasions the possibility of the just life. The just life must have its own form of sovereignty and thus operability. This is after all the point that Benjamin makes in the very last line of the text. Even though that line and the conception of 'sovereignty' that it brings into play will need to be taken up in greater detail, it is still worth noting here:

> Divine violence, which is the sign and seal but never the means of sacred execution [*heiliger Vollstreckung*], may be called operable sovereignty [or 'sovereign operability'] [*mag die waltende heißen*].[18]

The *heilige Vollstreckung* is the 'holy enforcement of law'. Equally, it is the 'holy execution'. Created by this formulation is the locus in which the just life will be that life that is indeed – and in deed – just 'a little bit different'. If there is an additional opening point that needs to be made it is the claim that one neither precedes nor causes the other: again, this is the undoing or destruction of a mode of thinking defined by the move from an *arché* to a *telos*. There has to be another understanding of what causality would be in such a context. Part of the answer to the question of a possible reworked presence of causality lies, of course, in the relationship between potentiality, destruction and allowing. The language of causality and sequence – as traditionally understood – has to have been precluded. There has to be another account of inauguration. The latter is demanded, as is the excision of causality, if what is a stake is a complex present that is itself the site of a politics of time. As has already been argued, integral to such a conception of the political is that it has to be thought in terms of a founding irreducibility; again, it is this possibility that historicism and fate (as modes of time and subjectification) seek to refuse. The time of fate/historicism (noting here a meld between them) is a time that generates the forms of continuity in which there is the concurrent attempt to efface what it is that sustains such a conception of continuity. These are not mere events. They need to be understood as the eruption of genuine moments of the political. What would have been effaced by the unchallenged work of fate and the accompanying naturalisation of historicism – or rather this would have been the attempt – is the anoriginality of a founding irreducibility. Again, it should be stressed that this is not Benjamin's language. Nonetheless, it remains a possible expression of what is essential to a politics of time to the extent that the latter is thought within the confines of his work. In addition, it is the position that emerges once, for example, allegory defines what is – the being of what is – as opposed to either beauty or the symbol, both of which presuppose unity and unity's appearance: *Schein* as *Schein* – i.e. appearance as semblance. Allegory is there as the 'antidote to myth'.[19] As has already been outlined in the context of the interpretation of *The Meaning of Time in the Moral World*, what defines the world when it is no longer the world as the merely given is that it has the potentiality to be other. The claim here is a specific one. Namely, that the world is not caused to be other due the action upon it by a form of externality. The event of othering is not defined therefore in terms of a relation between the external and a consequently remade form of internality. The claim is far more emphatic and brings a fundamental shift in position into place. The claim is that the world's othering is in fact a possibility for the world. (As will be taken up, the process of othering is also staged by Benjamin – and this time quite directly – in relation to another modality of 'work' within *Towards a Critique of Violence*.) The world is such that it can be othered. This is a potentiality that exists within a present that refuses just such a possibility. Taken together, these two positions form the basis of critique by having delimited the structure of a politics of time. Given these opening remarks, the project is an engagement with the text's detail. Despite the complexity of argumentation such an approach is essential if the actual force of Benjamin's argumentation and philosophical project is to be recovered and the tensions that emerge within it also to be taken into consideration.

2

At the outset the text's actual title needs to be noted: *Zur Kritik der Gewalt* (*Towards a Critique of Violence*). Not only does attention need to be paid to the centrality of 'critique', it is equally the case that both the cautious and exploratory nature of the text needs to be acknowledged.

The text begins a 'critique of violence'. A beginning in which what in the text's opening words was named initially as a 'critique' is then repositioned as a 'task'. Benjamin writes:

> The task of a critique of violence [*Die Aufgabe einer Kritik der Gewalt*] can be summarised as the presentation [*als die Darstellung*] of its relation to law and justice. For a cause [*Ursache*], however effective, becomes violent, in the precise sense of the word, only when it bears on moral relations.[20]

The presence here of the word 'task' opens a relation to another of Benjamin's texts in which the same word provides part of the title. In addition, its retained presence within that particular text also orientates essential parts of its overall argumentation.

In *The Task of the Translator* (*Die Aufgabe des Übersetzers*), a few lines before his long citation from Pannwitz, Benjamin concludes the simile structured by the relationship between the tangent and the circle it 'touches' (*berührt*) with the suggestion that translation must 'touch' the original (the source text)

> at the infinitely small point of the sense of the original, thereupon pursuing its course according to the laws of fidelity and in the freedom of linguistic flux [*nach dem Gesetze der Treue in der Freiheit der Sprachbewegung*].[21]

The position advanced in this passage needs to be read in relation to Pannwitz's argument that in a translation the translator should 'let his language be powerfully affected by the foreign tongue' (*sie durch die fremde Sprache gewaltig bewegen lassen*).[22] To the extent that this is done, the 'infinitely small point' as marking the co-presence of determination and indetermination – though this takes the present argument beyond the strict confines of Benjamin's text – can itself be understood in terms of the relationship between destruction and the *caesura of allowing*. This 'point', perhaps because 'touch' needs to be thought in terms of a specific modality of destruction, brings connection and disassociation into contention. 'Touch' here names a relationship that is not structured by questions of fidelity or correspondence; moreover, it connects translation to that which enables translation to occur. Namely, it connects translation to 'translatability'. Translation, as Benjamin notes, depends upon the 'translatability of the original' and not on the possibility of equivalences and correspondences.[23] The 'task' is therefore to work within the opening staged by the co-presence of indetermination and determination. As such, the task involves the necessity of discontinuity and continuity where continuity cannot be thought except in relation to 'translatability', the latter marking the ineliminable presence of potentiality. To reformulate this position: the 'task' is there within the opening occasioned by the *caesura of allowing* and which depends upon destruction (what has been destroyed is a conception of law other than one that sought to guarantee a relation between languages, namely 'the law of fidelity'). This is a setting, of course, which in holding to the centrality of 'translatability' – a term that must be added in order to underscore the task's possibility – is only explicable in terms of the already present quality of potentiality. Moreover, the relationship between 'freedom' and the 'law', in which the latter is retained within the continuity of its radical transformation – the retention of the law becomes the indetermination of the preceding sense of law, and yet law endures as transformed – becomes another instance in which a point of origination is present as an *anarché*; though it could equally be recast as an instance of what a critique of law in the name of law may in fact mean.[24]

These are the concerns that determine how the link between the 'task of a critique of violence' and the presentation of violence's relation to both 'law' and 'justice' is to occur once the usual determinations of 'law' and 'justice' no longer determine this 'presentation'. This means that the presentation must be thought in terms of the relationship between continuity and discontinuity. Given such a setting it now becomes possible to address the question of what is at stake when 'the task' (*die Aufgabe*) presented is then defined in relation to 'a critique of violence' (*eine Kritik der Gewalt*). Integral to the answer to that question is that the question itself has to be understood as situated within an opening in which the complex relations between *Gewalt*, *Recht* and *Gerechtigkeit* can be presented again, and where the presence of that set of relations that is then enacted is mediated by potentiality. The claim, perhaps a claim that founds their reiteration within another space, is that, in those relations being presented again, *Gewalt* then pertains as a possibility almost uniquely within 'moral relations'. To which Benjamin adds that the 'sphere' of these relations is itself defined by 'the concepts of law and justice'. (These relations occur therefore within a setting in which the 'suspension' (or 'depositioning') of the law and the processes of othering, when taken together, have an effect.) Their combination works to link potentiality to a form of reality. (Again, the presence of a counter-realism.)

Benjamin's text opens with an undoing of the concepts of law and judgement as they have been traditionally understood. In a sense, such an opening repeats the initial argumentation of *Fate and Character* insofar as what is important is finding the correct way to ask the question of the nature of 'law' and 'justice'. Only this question, once asked correctly, will indicate how the operability of 'law' and 'justice' is then to be understood. Here, again, detail is necessary. What matters is the question posed by Benjamin of what, in this context, will count as a 'critique'. Benjamin's opening move is to note that the relation between 'law' and ' justice' – both in terms of their connection as well as in terms of their separation – has been set by their assumed incorporation into a setting determined by the effective co-presence of 'ends' and 'means'. Given that setting, the presence of their connection then also takes on the quality of an assumption.

Once the presence of a 'legal system' (*Rechtsordnung*) is assumed to be the setting of law, then law comes to be defined in terms of ends/ means relations. There is a reason for noting that the link to law is provided by its reiteration within a 'legal system'. It sets up the site in relation to which a *counter-measure* comes to be deployed. Within a 'legal system', the presence of ends/means relations are integral to law's definition. Identifying this interconnection – and relation of dependency – provides a way to understand what is at work, and therefore what will be othered, as a result of the 'suspension' (or depositioning) of the law. In addition, it locates the specific modalities of *Gewalt* that are present within this definition. In the move from 'ends' to 'means', *Gewalt* only pertains to 'means'. If 'violence' were a 'means' then its presence would seem to be germane to a 'critique of violence'. 'Critique', if this opening were followed, would be linked to the possibility of 'just ends'. However, there is a problematic element at the heart of these possibilities, one than renders such relations merely apparent. Benjamin argues:

> What such a system, assuming it to be secure against all doubt, would contain is not a criterion for violence itself as a principle [*als eines Prinzips*], but, rather, the criterion for cases of its use. The question would remain open whether violence, as a principle, could be a moral means even to just ends. To resolve this question a more exact criterion is needed [*eines näheren Kriteriums*], which would discriminate within the sphere of means themselves, without regard for the ends they serve.[25]

The important point here is the emergence – even if it is only provisional – of a principle that defines *Gewalt* on the one hand and instances of its enactment on the other. The failure to use a critical approach – that is an approach that will form part of a 'critique of violence' – is also at work in the argumentative formulation of 'natural law' theory. Natural law fails to problematise the use of *Gewalt*. The same lack is also at work in 'positive law'. Hence there is the position advanced by Benjamin that locates both their limits as well as their complementarity.

> This thesis of natural law that regards violence as a natural datum is dia-
> metrically opposed to that of positive law, which sees violence as a product

of history. If natural law can judge all existing law only in criticizing its ends, so positive law can judge all evolving law only in criticizing its means. If justice is the criterion of ends, legality is that of means. Notwithstanding this antithesis, however, both schools meet in their common basic dogma: just ends can be attained by justified means, justified means used for just ends.[26]

The first point to note here is that, despite the positing of a real difference between 'natural' and 'positive' law, in regard to the development of a critical relation to the law there is the emergence of a position in which, qua objects of critique, there cannot be an effective separation. They remain caught in a dynamic created by a continual set of interrelations in which the question of law's relation to *Gewalt* remains unposed. There is therefore a need to break what Benjamin identifies as a 'circular argument'. Again the latter needs to be understood as setting an economy of activity that cannot be resolved but which must be undone. The undoing of that 'circularity' is his next move.

In order to do this Benjamin takes up what is identified as the 'question of the justification of certain means that constitute violence'.[27] Where and in what does the justification of and for *Gewalt* reside? As a beginning the position is that 'natural law', when taken as a self-defined and thus also a self-justifying set of concerns, cannot respond to this question. However, 'positive law' can, precisely because 'positive law' assumes the presence, prior to any form of application, of 'different kinds of violence' (*Arten der Gewalt*).[28] This opens an investigation of the distinction between *Gewalt* as 'justified' as opposed to *Gewalt* as 'unjustified'. As a result, the investigative question posed by Benjamin concerns what can be learned about 'the essence of violence' (*das Wesen der Gewalt*) from the fact that this 'distinction' – the one between the 'justified' and 'unjustified' – can be applied to it.[29] In order for the critique to emerge as a critique, the criteria set in place by positive law to evaluate the 'legality of *Gewalt*' has to be understood as occurring in relation to its 'meaning' and, given this position, the sphere of its application has to be engaged with critically in terms of its 'value'. Again there is an apparent impasse. For Benjamin this gives rise to the need to reposition the place of critique. The limits of definitions and emergence of interrelated positions, when taken together, necessitate another setting. Hence he argues:

> [For] this critique a standpoint outside positive [*den Standpunkt außerhalb*] legal philosophy but also outside [*außerhalb*] natural law must be found. The extent to which it can only be furnished by a historico-philosophical view of law will emerge.[30]

The interpretive question that has to be addressed is: what is meant by 'a historico-philosophical view of law' such that it is possible to allow for an 'outside'? The force of the question resides in the possible provision of that which occurs on the 'outside'. This possibility entails constituting the appearance of law's law-like quality as an object of knowledge. In addition, it implicates the epistemological with the process of critique. As a consequence, both are involved in breaking the circularity within which the relationship between natural and positive law has become entrapped.

While this is a position that will continue to be clarified as the general explication of this text unfolds, what should be noted in advance is that what is held open is a definition of the 'historico-philosophical' where part of its definition is the presence of that which takes place 'outside' the 'law', and note here that it will be a positioning of the law as 'the order of law'; moreover, it is 'law' identified by fate and as demanding a subject position which is itself defined in terms of 'guilt'. What is meant by the 'historico-philosophical' is itself therefore connected to a process that would result in the law's 'suspension' (or depositioning). Here it should be added that what comes after this line in the text needs to be understood as the presentation of modes of argumentation and the advancing of positions that are themselves defined by the possibility of the adequacy of an account that is based on the 'historico-philosophical'. Leaving to one side at the moment the question of the success of that project, it should still be clear that what is in question is the possibility that the project of the 'historico-philosophical' and 'critique' are for Benjamin inherently interarticulated.

3

The next part of the argument developed in Benjamin's text and which will be worked through here concerns what is revealed about the 'nature of violence' by the fact that the terms 'sanctioned' and 'unsanctioned' can be applied to it. The position is not abstract. In its formulation Benjamin has recourse to a specific example located in the Western European context, i.e. the 'strike'. As a prelude to his first engagement with the 'strike', he begins to trace some of the complexities built into questions pertaining to the link between ends and *Gewalt*. The first point is the position in which he claims that the state is constrained to oppose those 'natural ends' that could be pursued by individuals and which involve the use of *Gewalt*. It sets up 'legal ends' that can only be realised by (and as) *Rechtsgewalt*.[31] 'Legal ends' will always curtail 'natural ends', if the latter involve *Gewalt*. To which there would seem to be the attached position that it would look as though positions that linked *Gewalt* to 'natural ends' stand as the greatest threat to 'legal ends'. Rights grounded in 'nature' would, if this context were able to prevail, have precedence over the ends of the state. There is, however, much more involved than a simple clash of ends. Hence what is at work within such a conflict has to be reworked. The usual 'dogma' governing the way such a clash is understood needs to be put to one side. It is thus that Benjamin goes on to make the further point that:

> To counter it one might perhaps consider the surprising possibility that the law's interest in a monopoly of violence [*Monopolisierung der Gewalt*] vis-à-vis individuals is explained not by the intention of preserving legal ends but, rather, by that of preserving the law itself; that violence, when not in the hands of the law, threatens it not by the ends that it may pursue but by its mere existence outside the law [*ihr bloßes Dasein außerhalb des Rechts*].[32]

There is an important point being made in the development of this position. Namely that the presentation of the law – its presence within and as the continuity of its own self-presentation – is threatened not by specific actions but by the existence of that which is, from within this setting, taken to be 'outside' the law. To which it might be added that the presence of that which has the potential to be outside the law may have the same effect. Hence there is the need for the policing of this potentiality. The presence, even as a realisable potentiality of this 'outside', marks the possibility of the law's 'suspension' (or depositioning). (There would be, again, the associated need to restrict exactly that possibility. It must remain a potentiality that cannot be actualised.) This means that the law's interest in operability – and thus with the necessity that it remain operable – is bound up with the continuity of that position, that is the continuity of the law's operability. That continuity – and continuity already brings both the domain of fate and its related subject positions into play – is threatened the moment it becomes possible to argue for the possible presence of what may be discontinuous with the law. A position that becomes more emphatic when that possibility occurs as the result of a right granted by the state. These are the concerns that become manifest in relation to the strike and, more, exactly in what can be identified as the right to strike. The latter links a right to the possibility of a law which occasions the law's own outside.

The text's opening treatment of the strike is introduced in terms of the way in which 'organised labour' is 'the only legal subject entitled to exercise *Gewalt*'.[33] This positions 'organised labour', as a result of the right to strike, in a direct and necessary confrontation with the State. Here is an opposition on the level of *Gewalt*. While there is the view that 'non-action' may be understood as 'non-violent' – a positioning of the strike that will begin to fray – it is this precise setting that opens up the possibility for *Staatsgewalt* to allow, if only initially, for strikes. What this means is that *Staatsgewalt* can only allow for inoperable operability. (Recalled here is of course what has already been described as the passive nihilism of Bartleby.)

Labour – understood in this context as the figure of 'organised labour' – can, however, use 'force' (*Gewalt*). What 'organised labour' has been granted – and this is Benjamin's point – is the legal right to act in relation to a position that the state has granted to it and which 'organised labour' then maintains as its own. The reason why 'organised labour' presents such a challenge is that it is positioned outside the state. The 'right to strike' introduces a fundamental distinction between differing modalities of *Gewalt*. It will be in terms of these modalities that Benjamin will rework the position already alluded to in terms of the difference between 'law-preserving violence' and 'law-making violence'. The point of departure here is of course the very possibility of this distinction. Even though Benjamin has already conceded that there is a sense of the 'strike' as involving a type of 'non-violence', here the absence of operability is explicable in terms of 'non-action' – what might be interpreted as a politics of withdrawal. A withdrawal whose passivity maintains what is already there and thus functions as de facto law preserving. What challenges the repetition of *Statsgewalt*, a repetition that is the operability of the state, and thus what the state 'fears', is a form of action or set of actions – 'violence' and thus modes of operability – that are not 'law-preserving' but more emphatically gesture towards what will be 'law-making'. The latter – the form of operability defined by its relation to possible 'law-making' – begins to mark the space of a form of law existing 'outside' the law. (Again, as will emerge, the contradiction is an appearance.) Within this setting 'strikers' are present *als Gewalttätige*, which is to say they are present as the enactors of *Gewalt*. They act it out. Their actions are 'violent'. The complexity of this setting is staged by Benjamin in the following terms:

> For in a strike the state fears [*fürchtet*] above all else that function of violence which it is the object of this study to identify as the only secure foundation of its critique. For if violence were, as first appears, merely the means to secure directly whatever happens to be sought, it could fulfill its end as predatory violence. It would be entirely unsuitable as a basis for, or a modification to, relatively stable conditions. The strike shows, however, that it can be so, that it is able to found and modify legal conditions, however offended the sense of justice may find itself thereby.[34]

The strike, in other words, begins to bring into play ways to understand the possibility of undoing stable conditions. The limit of the strike, in terms of its presentation at this stage in the text's overall development, is that it is defined in terms of a relationship between means and already determined ends. The strike as a mode of interruption will come to be transformed in relation to a move from an already present determination to the yet-to-be-determined. Determination cedes its place, again, to indetermination. To recall the already noted formulation of Benjamin's translation paper, indetermination occurs at the moment at which there is an encounter between 'law' and 'freedom'. Not only will there be a concomitant transformation in how ends are to be understood, the transformation will pertain to both form and content (perhaps by dissolving this distinction) insofar as the presence of what occurs after that moment cannot have been structured by the law that is incorporated into the domain of 'freedom'. This is a position that will recur in Benjamin's argument that 'language' (*Sprache*) is the only sphere that resists the incorporation of that modality of *Gewalt* whose operability is defined in terms of the already determined.

The next stage in the development of his overall position is to show that the capacity of the strike, present here as an instance of *Gewalt* and thus able both to found and to modify legal conditions, is not a result that occurs by chance. It is the potentiality within *Gewalt*. This argument is advanced through a consideration of 'military law'. The excision of chance writes a project into law. As will be seen, that project becomes law's self-preservation. The importance of noting the development of this equation of law's presence with forms of continuity is clear. It is only in terms of a precise understanding of the nature of law – and this involves undoing the identification of law with either 'positive law' or 'natural law' by insisting on law's relation to its own self-preservation and the use of *Gewalt* to that end – that it will then be possible to argue for the presence of a *counter-measure* and to identify with increasingly greater degrees of accuracy what is being countered and thus what is entailed by the presence of such a measure.

4

In regard to 'military law' there is a specific structure at work. It repeats in part what has already been noted in relation to the 'strike': the sanctioning of a form of *Gewalt* – here identified as *die Kriegsgewalt* – the justification of which is 'natural'. The 'end' is 'natural'. Hence there is always present the possibility of a conflict between the 'natural end' of those implementing this end and the 'ends' that they take to be their own. 'Military force' is 'predatory violence'. Within 'war' the necessity of the 'peace ceremony' has to be understood, Benjamin argues, in terms of the sanctioning of the presence of a 'new "law"' (*neues 'Recht'*).[35] It is this link between a form of *Gewalt* and the creation of law that for Benjamin locates that which forms one of the defining elements of 'military violence' (*Militärgewalt*).

> If, therefore, conclusions can be drawn from military violence [*kriegerischen Gewalt*], as being primordial and paradigmatic of all violence used for natural ends [*als einer ursprünglichen und urbildlichen für jede Gewalt zu Naturzwecken*], there is inherent in all such violence a law-making character.[36]

What is fundamental here is the identification of a mode of *Gewalt* with 'a law-making character' (*ein rechtsetzender Charakter*). However, while this is an essential if not defining aspect of *Gewalt* here, which can be inferred from the presence of 'military violence' (*kriegerische Gewalt*), and even though it can be seen as having a certain paradigmatic quality, there are two additional aspects whose presence underscores the centrality of what is at play here.

The first is that there is a justification of 'law-making' in terms of its having an end, the viability of which is established by recourse to the natural. The second is the creation of specific subject positions. The creation of law and subjectification have, as should be clear, a necessary and founding reciprocity. These positions, while created and thus marked by that process, nonetheless still have their own form of necessity. In regard to *kriegerische Gewalt* these will be present in terms of 'conscription'. Noting the connection between law and subjectification is essential once the question of what will count as a *counter-measure* is given a form of priority. Indeed, Benjamin himself is aware of this issue. Evidence for which is that he begins his response to the presence of the twofold quality of *kriegerische Gewalt* with the argument that 'pacifism', and the force of pacifism as a philosophical position will pertain independently of any merit that can be attributed to its presence in this context, cannot function as an effective *counter-measure* to the reciprocity between law-preserving violence and the conception of subject that this modality of *Gewalt* entails. This is precisely because it does not have the measure of what it seeks to counter. (As an aside, there is an important point to be noted here with regard to the already noted connection between epistemology and critique, insofar as the latter depends upon the former.)

Benjamin develops the relationship between the creation of law and the creation of subject position via the identification of two specific modalities of subjectification, namely, those demanded by 'conscription' on the one hand and the 'death penalty' on the other. After having developed the way in which the processes of subjectification are at work in relation both to law-creating *Gewalt* and then 'fate', Benjamin moves to the decisive analysis of the police and of policing. Policing has complex senses of *Gewalt*. Policing is a process that need not depend upon the actual presence of the police. It is this that allows Benjamin to argue in regard to policing that 'its power is formless' (*seine Gewalt ist gestaltlos*).[37] While a return will need to be made to this actual formulation and thus to the question of how the 'formless' nature of this modality of *Gewalt* is to be understood, what will have to be developed as part of that project is the way in which what he describes as the 'ghostly' presence of the police follows from the relationship between law creation and the position of subjects on the one hand, and then, on the other, from the way policing is the 'spectral' presence demanded by that relationship.

Within the setting that will lead from a treatment of 'military violence' to a concern with policing, an important point of departure is provided by the identification of 'conscription' as an instance of 'law-preserving violence'. There is a significant opening here as a 'critique' of 'law-preserving violence', for Benjamin, is a critique of all 'legal violence' precisely because the object of the law is *not* an outcome that is marked by a sense of justice. Rather, the law seeks to preserve itself. This is law's essential quality. Nonetheless, despite the identification of this quality, the critique of 'law-preserving violence' has to be held apart from what Benjamin describes as a 'childish anarchism' on the one hand and the moralism of the 'categorical imperative' on the other. The enforced libertarian nature that such a position yields is premised upon – while also enjoining – what he calls the absence of any 'reflection on the moral-historical sphere'. What is also occluded 'is the possibility of understanding actions having any meaning' – the meaning that would come from understanding their worldly and historical presence. Moreover, the 'categorical imperative' does not sustain the quality of an effective *counter-measure*. While the latter – the 'categorical imperative' – promotes abstract humanity, it does so by locating it in 'each individual'. What is misunderstood is the conception of historicality or historical time that accompanies, and in a way that underwrites, such a conception of the individual. The individual can never be the locus. As Benjamin makes clear, individuals are only ever produced. Any evocation of the categorical imperative fails to address what is at stake. In Benjaminian terms this is 'an order imposed by fate'. With a defence of the individual that 'order' is itself defended. A position to be repeated at the end of the text in terms of critical engagement with arguments pertaining to the so-called 'sanctity' of life and thus to the 'sanctity' of the individual. Moreover, criticism of individual laws leaves the 'order of law' (*Rechtsordnung*) untouched.

What the references to spectres, ghosts and spirits – all of which will play a decisive role in the engagement with the 'death penalty' and 'the police' – introduce is not that which complicates a politics of time; that possibility is already being thought in the use by Benjamin of the language of 'breaching', 'suspension' (or depositioning), etc. Rather what has emerged is the necessity to think the relationship between the politics of time and the presence of ghosts, insofar as the latter is already there in the ways the mythic continues to haunt the contemporary. The force of the reference to conscription emerges at this precise point. The problem of the opposition to conscription is that such an opposition failed to note that the specificity of conscription was that it had both a universalising tendency and a law to which everyone (almost fatefully) is subject, while at the same time it functioned as an instance of that which was true of law in general, namely what was defined in terms of its necessity – and perhaps its capacity – for self-preservation. What mattered therefore was how the *counter-measure* to such a set-up is to be understood. There had to be more than a simple op-position to a conception of law that continues to preserve itself. In other words, a conception of law – and here an interpretive claim will be made – that had the structure of both fate and religion. What is meant by this claim is precise. Namely, here is a conception of law that within the very terms in which it is given – i.e. as self-preserving – can see no end point and thus cannot be understood in terms of its being other. Again it is vital to recall the line that Benjamin used to define this position, that is, 'in the exercise of violence over life and death more than in any other legal act, law reaffirms itself' (*bekräftigt sich selbst*). What is essential here is the act, perhaps the power, of law to re-enact itself. This is a claim about law *tout court* and not a claim about particular statutes or legal decisions. This position is reinforced by the move from 'conscription' to 'capital punishment'. Again it is the question of what form opposition takes – remembering that while there is an affinity between opposition and deposition it is the difference between them that matters. In other words, what will be seen in the death penalty – which is understood as the power over life and death, a power that is posed in terms of *Gewalt* – is the problematic status of its suspension (or depositioning). Brought into consideration by the death penalty is the question of whether or not it is possible to argue for the presence of a counter to that specific modality of sovereignty. Remembering of course that the constitution of a counter-measure is the othering of sovereignty (the othering of sovereignty as an already given determination). It is to this problem that a turn must be made.

5

The 'death penalty' is not defined by the presence of a single law or statute. Rather, centrality needs to be attributed to the conception of sovereignty that is inscribed within it. Expressed more emphatically, it can be argued that fundamental to the death penalty is the conception of sovereignty and thus the conception of life that it demands. Identifying both is essential if the death penalty is to emerge as a concept within knowledge. That emergence is the condition enabling the development – conceptually and politically – of an actual *counter-measure*. There is an important affinity between the conception of the death penalty, as it is developed by Benjamin, and elements central to Derrida's work in this area. The affinity is to be thought in relation to sovereignty. If there is a question that draws them into a productive constellation, then it hinges on the possibility of a *counter-measure*. It is by tracing the points of connection and separation between Derrida and Benjamin that the way death penalty defined by sovereignty, rather than death penalty defined by an instance of legislation, as able to figure within the philosophical, will emerge.

A start will be made with the way that Benjamin presents the death penalty. What matters is its presence. Of significance is the way the penalty stages a certain conception of the law. In this regard Benjamin writes of capital punishment that a critique of capital punishment is a critique of law in its 'origin'. To which he then adds:

> If violence, violence crowned by fate, is the origin of law, then it may be readily supposed that where the highest violence, that over life and death, occurs in the legal system the origins of law jut manifestly and fearsomely into existence. In agreement with this is the fact that the death penalty in primitive legal systems is imposed even for such crimes as offenses against property, to which it seems quite out of 'proportion'. Its purpose is not to punish the infringement of law but to establish new law. For in the exercise of violence over life and death more than in any other legal act, law reaffirms itself. But in this very violence something rotten [*etwas Morsches*] in law is revealed, above all to a finer sensibility, because the latter knows itself to be infinitely remote from conditions in which fate might imperiously have shown itself in such a sentence.[38]

The twofold nature of the death penalty emerges with this description. In the first instance it displays the original determination of law's sovereignty while exposing the relation between law, *Gewalt* and fate. Equally, it also reveals the presence of 'something rotten' (*etwas Morsches*) as already there within the law. The *Gewalt* proper to the presence of the death penalty reveals the presence of the 'rotten'. The evocation of the 'rotten' recalls Hamlet. What it recalls, however, is the line spoken by Marcellus, which in the Schlegel/Tieck translation reads: *Etwas ist faul im Staate Dänemarks.*[39] What matters in both instances is not the consistency of terminology in regard to the rotten (Benjamin's *Morches* compared to Schlegel/Tieck's *faul*) but the continuity of the presence of a 'something' that is in this state. An *etwas* as the present but unnamed 'thing'. The important point here has two elements. In the first instance there is a claim that, despite appearances, there is 'something rotten'. Hence there is a consistency in terms of that which in being at hand cannot be identified with the reality of either the law or the state. The reality is the 'something rotten'. The second element is that what is 'rotten' is not named. There is 'something'. It will not necessarily undo either law or the state. What it will demand, however, is an increasingly more violent defence of either the state or the law (or both the state and the law). This evokes the hold of the 'law-preserving' but does so in ways that indicate that the defence of law is far from having an inbuilt and axiomatic justification in which a form of value would have been attributed to law in virtue of its being law. It becomes increasingly clear that attempts to secure the law and thus to hold to the law – a holding that takes on the quality, now spurious, of a defence of law – are trapped in a spiral of violence occurring in order to preserve the law. As a consequence, acts whose sole object is law's preservation move further and further away from the possibility of justice or of being understood in terms of the reiteration of just acts. The 'something rotten' yields – and thus is marked by – continual reinforcement of a means/ends relation in which law's preservation, as an end, will legitimate any means in order that law be in fact preserved.

If Benjamin's position can be generalised, then it can be argued that the death penalty enacts a hold over life and death and thus becomes, once literalised, the most dramatic form of legal violence. However, were it not to be taken literally – thereby complicating yet again what a *counter-measure* to the death penalty involves – what it reveals is the capacity of law, when understood in terms of law-preserving violence, to have a completely pervasive ubiquity. Reiterated here is the structure of fate as that which determines all subjects and which is erected with a type of immediacy. The attendant subject position – in Benjaminian terms – is 'mere life'. This reinforces the argument that overcoming the equation of life with 'mere life' – a position that the death penalty necessitates – is integral to the actualisation of the just life. The immediacy of fate that is at work in aspects of Greek tragedy is now present in terms of its apparently pervasive hold. The totality of being subject to the law poses at its most insistent the question of what the law's 'suspension' (or depositioning) involves. What needs to be thought through is the possible overcoming of the 'something' that is 'rotten' within the law. A process that would bring with it the possibility of stemming both the hold of fate and the process of subjectification that it demands: winning life back from the always attendant possibility of its reduction to 'mere life'. This is the question that returns with Derrida.

Derrida has taken up the death penalty on a number of important occasions. Here reference will be made to its presence in *De quoi demain* and *Peine de mort.*[40] In the first of these texts he has linked the presence of the death penalty to what is described as the 'theological-political'. Indeed Derrida argues that the way into a sustained thinking of what he calls in *De quoi demain* the 'onto-theological-political' has to begin with the death penalty.[41] There is therefore an important coalescence of concerns insofar as both Derrida and Benjamin can be read as suggesting that the death penalty cannot be taken simply as an end itself (which does not of course obviate the need pragmatically to argue for its repeal as a specific piece of legislation). And thus, in the case of Benjamin, what emerges with the death penalty is the way it stages at its most exacting the relation between 'legal violence' and sovereignty. With the death penalty law, for Benjamin, as noted, 'reaffirms itself'. For Derrida it is not as though the stakes, at this stage, are necessarily different. He locates in the death penalty the means to think what is fundamental to the 'onto-theological-political'. This formulation does not deploy the 'theological' as it appears in Benjamin's work, in which the theological can be said to strike the 'left-handed blow'. However, what the term does designate is what can be described as the fateful character of the political. As such it is closer to the way that Benjamin understands religion. What has to be brought to bear on what Derrida identifies as the 'onto-theological-political' is the possibility of its own cessation. The question that emerges can be formulated thus: is it possible that what Derrida identifies as the 'onto-theological-political', understood in terms of a connection between fate and religion, allows for its own suspension (or depositioning)? In other words, is there a possible *Entsetzung* of this conception of the 'onto-theological-political'? On one level Derrida, in *Peine de mort*, can be read as having addressed this precise question. He writes:

> even when it (the death penalty) will have been abolished, the death penalty will survive [*survivra*]. It will have other lives before it and other lives with which to occupy itself.[42]

What is the claim of this passage? Answering this question must start with the contention established by the earlier position, namely, that the death penalty is not a singular act but exemplifies that conception of sovereignty that is the interarticulation of the 'onto-theological-political', law and life. Taken in this context, the passage cited above needs to be read as suggesting that, even if the death penalty as a particular piece of legislation were repealed, and the relation between law, sovereignty and life no longer deployed the death penalty, it would remain the case that as an unnamed and thus as a spectral presence – a presence that, as shall be noted in a moment, recalls Benjamin's discussion of the police and of *Polizeigewalt* – its function would remain. A position confirmed by Derrida, having added that even with it having been abolished the death penalty 'will survive'.[43] It would, for example, be extended, as Derrida suggests, to the right to kill those deemed to be enemies of the state. The function now names what within the framework of Benjamin's argument would need to be thought in terms of the relationship between law and the totality of life. The repeal of acts of law would not halt law's capacity to be 'the exercise of violence over life and death'. Hence, the death penalty for Derrida, as a modality of sovereignty, may have a capacity to live on despite its absence as a named presence. The philosophical question, a question that will have acquired acuity, concerns the thinking of its cessation or deposition.

What is problematic in Derrida's presentation of the death penalty is the following. It may be possible to argue for the presence of the 'mythic', where the latter is understood as that which haunts the contemporary, without there being the additional argument that it determines the contemporary in every instance. In other words, the possibility of equating, for example, justice and revenge endures as a possibility without it defining justice *tout court*. Indeed, it might be suggested that the inherently contestable quality of any attempt to identify justice and revenge would be evidence of the now complex positioning of such a conception of the relationship between law and *Gewalt*. While this does not entail that with this move there is the othering of the conception of sovereignty at work within the death penalty, at the very least it allows for the recognition of a limit and thus the possibility of posing as a question the possible *Entsetzung* of the death penalty (where the latter is present both as a specific act and as a generalised condition). What has to be left as an open question is whether or not Derrida's position identifies the complex sense in which the death penalty is present at the present. An inherent part of that complexity is the possibility of the death penalty's 'suspension' (or depositioning).

The 'suspension' (or depositioning) of the death penalty is an opening towards another conception both of *Gewalt* and subjectivity, since the othering of both law and of the subject would stem from a different sense of operability while also introducing it. What is absent from Derrida's formulation of the positioning of sovereignty is the necessity of the link between *Gewalt* and subjectification, and the possibility of staging a depositioning of the death penalty that is concomitant with the othering of *Gewalt*, a position which can be enacted precisely because *Gewalt* is not monolithic and thus names a possibility that is the *counter-measure* to the 'onto-theological-political'. (As will be seen, this is inherent to the distinction between 'mythic violence' and 'divine violence', though it also accounts for those aspects of this distinction that have a problematic quality.) Finally, if, as Benjamin has suggested, within the death penalty 'the exercise of violence over life and death, more than in any other legal act, law reaffirms itself [*bekräftigt sich selbst*]', then what Derrida's deconstruction would seem to have left to one side is how to think the destruction, suspension or depositioning of that reaffirmation. After all, this reaffirmation is a quality of *Gewalt*. Hence its suspension (or depositioning) demands another modality of *Gewalt*: a measure that is indeed a *counter-measure*. In other words, it is not simply a question of a deconstruction of the death penalty but the identification of the death penalty as deconstructable – assuming here a type of affinity between a deconstruction and a 'deposition'. These possibilities have an exacting exigency because, as Derrida argues, what is involved is nothing less than a relation between a 'religious message' and 'the sovereignty of a state'.[44] The question that returns concerns the survival of the death penalty. This must be understood as a philosophical question insofar as what is at stake is the possible impossibility of doing without the death penalty and thus its ineliminability. What would it mean to argue both that the death penalty survives and thus that it can be subject to a form of deconstruction? This must be the question to which Derrida's mode of argumentation would need to respond.

A similar set of issues – and thus a similar set of interpretive problems – are raised by Benjamin's treatment of the 'police'. With the introduction of the 'police' there is a reformulation of the question of what a 'depositioning' would mean and, in addition, to what extent – and how – policing opens itself up to the process of othering. Marked out in advance by such questioning is the possibility for another modality of policing, if by policing what is intended is not a claim about literal presence but rather a sense of measure that is linked to another form of operability. The end position is going to have to involve a relationship between othering and measure's ubiquity. This will need to be the case even though it might be contra aspects of Benjamin's argument. Nonetheless, it will be the development of a position that is itself wholly in keeping with the overall development of the argumentation of the text as a whole.

The police introduce an important aspect of Benjamin's position in which policing – understood now as both a named presence and an identifiable force within the state – is a new configuration of the distinction between the form of *Gewalt* that brings both 'law-preserving' and 'law-making' *Gewalt* into play. What is significant in regard to the police is a mode of presence. Benjamin's identification of that presence is precise. He writes that:

> In a far more unnatural combination than in the death penalty, in a kind of spectral mixture [*gespenstischen Vermischung*], these two forms of violence [law-preserving and law-making] are present in another institution of the modern state, the police.[45]

Benjamin notes that in regard to 'police violence' (*Polizeigewalt*) the difference between 'law-making and law-preserving violence is itself suspended [*aufgehoben*]'.

> Unlike law, which acknowledges in the 'decision' determined by place and time a metaphysical category that gives it a claim to critical evaluation, a consideration of the police institution encounters nothing essential at all [*nichts Wesenhaftes*]. Its power is formless [*Seine Gewalt ist gestaltlos*], like its nowhere tangible, all-pervasive, ghostly presence [*gespenstische Erscheinung*] in the life of civilised states.[46]

Benjamin will go on to identify what he describes as the 'spirit' (*Geist*) of the police. What this means is that their place is not defined by actual presence. Hence the identification of the mode of *Gewalt* proper to the police and policing not only brings the presence of the 'formless', the 'spectral' and 'spirits', etc., into play, it identifies the need – one that has both a philosophical and a political register – to engage with the presence of ghosts. If there is the need for a philosophical hauntology then it can be located in the link established by Benjamin between *Gewalt* and policing. There is an additional point made by Benjamin in this regard that also needs to be noted. He argues that, while the ghostly quality of the police and policing occurs within an identification of state power with the 'absolute monarch', the presence of the 'spirit' (*Geist*) of the police within democracies has an entirely different register. Its presence, he argues, 'bears witness to the greatest conceivable degeneration of violence [*die denkbar größte Entartung der Gewalt*].'[47] The unavoidable question here is: how is this 'degeneration of violence' to be understood? Answering it will necessitate leaving to one side aspects of the text insofar as the description can be linked precisely both to Benjamin's critical comments made in relation to 'parliamentarianism' and then to his description of the intrusion of 'legal violence' into language – in regard to 'fraud' – as involving language being in a 'process of decay'.

Again detail is essential. What attends this discussion of this section of the text is the possibility of a 'non-violent resolution of conflict'. The importance of the question is that answers often yield positions that come to be secured by law and thus *Rechtsgewalt*. Hence the 'non-violent' becomes an impossibility if *Gewalt* in this context is equated with law. What needs to be taken up, given this context, is the connection between 'decay' and 'degeneration'. The problem within the parliamentary which introduces a concern with 'decay' arises when the consciousness of the 'latent presence of violence [*Gewalt*]' within the parliamentary disappears. With its disappearance, for Benjamin, the institution 'falls into decay [*so verfällt es*]'. When law pervades language and understanding this is the mark of a *Verfallsprozess*. Policing within democracy is *Gewalt*'s 'degeneration'. What is at stake here needs to be worked out.

Of parliament Benjamin's writes the following. The position involves a critique of the current forms of the institution of democracy rather than a critique of democracy. (Benjamin is not Schmitt.) Benjamin writes, parliamentary democracies

> offer the familiar, woeful spectacle because they have not remained conscious of the revolutionary forces [*der revolutionären Kräfte*] to which they owe their existence. Accordingly, in Germany in particular, the last manifestation of such forces [*Gewalten*] bore no fruit for parliaments. They lack the sense that they represent a lawmaking violence [*die rechtsetzende Gewalt*]; no wonder that they cannot achieve decrees worthy of this violence, but cultivate in compromise a supposedly nonviolent [*eine vermeintlich gewaltlose*] manner of dealing with political affairs.[48]

What marks a democracy therefore is that it is the result of a form of interruption – what could be identified as a *caesura of allowing* – however, once that positioning occurs then there is a loss of that sense of origination. Another way of making this point would be to argue that what was once an *anarché* and thus positioned within the discontinuous continuity of the yet-to-be-determined (or that which endures as the always-to-be-determined) is repositioned such that the origin now appears within the relationship between an *arché* and a *telos*. The *telos* is the continuity and thus the self-preservation of the system. (A system that with regard to democracy effaces the *anarché* in the name of the *arché/telos* relation.) As a consequence, the capacity to be law-creating becomes no more than law-preserving. Within it the 'non-violent' is the violence of the continuity of law's preservation. (Parenthetically, this explains why Benjamin uses the formulation 'a supposedly nonviolent [*eine vermeintlich gewaltlose*] manner'.) The continuity within which parliament is then located inscribes law-preserving violence into the temporality of fate. It is thus that Benjamin is able to conclude that what 'parliament achieves in vital affairs can only be those legal decrees that in their origin and outcome are attended by violence.'[49]

There is a clear analogy here with what is meant by the 'degeneration of violence'. Once it is recalled that what is at work within *Gewalt* – taken as an abstract term – is operability, then the presence of the police as 'spectral' is the undoing of any sense of *Gewalt* that could be linked to the articulation of what might be described as *Demokratiegewalt*. Operability, which a democracy would necessitate, is undone by the spectral once the latter is linked to a form of *Gewalt* within which the distinction between law-preserving and law-making no longer obtains and thus what emerges is de facto law-preserving. Hence, if the argumentation could be reversed, engaging with that which haunts the contemporary, here the spectral presence of policing would be undertaken in the name of *Demokratiegewalt* – a term that signals the necessity that were there to be the democratic then its operativity would be an essential part of its presence. Finally there is the all-important link to language and understanding. Again their importance needs to be limited to the general question of the presence of the 'non-violent'. The 'non-violent' here attends what might be described as techniques of civil agreement. It is in this context that Benjamin then adds that:

> For in it not only is nonviolent agreement possible, but also the exclusion of violence in principle is quite explicitly demonstrable by one significant factor: there is no sanction for lying. Probably no legislation on earth originally stipulated such a sanction. This makes clear that there is a sphere of human agreement that is nonviolent to the extent that it is wholly inaccessible to violence: the proper sphere of 'understanding', language [*Sprache*]. Only late and in a peculiar process of decay has it been penetrated by legal violence in the penalty on fraud.[50]

The complication here is twofold. Firstly, what in this precise context does *Gewalt* mean? And secondly, how are the terms 'understanding' and 'language' being used? *Sprache* is the proper sphere of *Verstehen*. Answering this latter question has to bring with it the recognition that at work here is a specific modality of *Gewalt*. A way in has already been presented by the earlier treatment of translation. It was not as though translation – and here translation has to be considered in relation to a philosophical thinking of freedom – has a non-relation to law. There was a form of determination that operated within the realm of freedom. In other words, within the process of translation – and thereby underscoring 'the task of translation' – there is the co-presence of determination and indetermination. Hence to claim that what this context provides is 'a sphere of human agreement that is non-violent' has to be read as arguing that what counts as 'agreement' within this context is not determined by the law. The expression 'a process of decay' needs to be understood therefore as the intrusion of determination in a way that works to eliminate the effectivity of the indeterminate. However, even with that indetermination there are obligations and consequences that arise. Both are to be explicated in non-legal ways. There is therefore, despite the absence of law as a determining presence, a modality of operability at work. Hence 'there can be is no sanction for lying'.[51]

What can be learnt from this complex of concerns is the difficulty of positioning that which occurs as having the quality of an 'outside' or of that which is other. (There are a number of analogous formulations that can be used here.) If there is a way of addressing this complex state of affairs, it resides in the evocation of the 'pure' (*rein*). Benjamin's use of this term, more exactly the philosophical thinking that accompanies its use, allows for a way into understanding both othering and that which it positions, or which positions itself, outside the law. The 'pure' cannot be understood as the Kantian 'a priori'. Rather, the 'pure' starts from the recognition that, within modernity, that which provides experiences with its conditions of possibility are not simply external to the subject; they operate as 'fate' or 'law' and in so doing yield the positions occupied by subjects. The 'pure' is only linked to an a priori condition to the extent that experience itself is understood in terms of this modern 'transcendental aesthetic'. If there is a way into the 'pure' as it occurs in Benjamin's writings and which draws on the points noted above concerning the presence of an a priori quality then it can be found in the following line:

> We can therefore only point to pure means [*reinen Mittel*] in politics as analogous to those which govern peaceful intercourse between private persons.[52]

Two points need to be remembered here. The first is that this process occurs not within the law (*die Rechtsordnung*) – which is to say that it is not within a setting defined by the law (*die Rechtsordnung*) but on the law's other side. The second is that this form of agreement necessitates what Benjamin describes in an almost untranslatable formulation as *die Kultur des Herzens des Menschen*. Such a formulation, while clearly enveloping civility, links it to the 'heart' and such that the move from *das Herz* to *Herzenshöflichkeit* (courtesy) is not difficult to make. Such a setting is then connected to a domain that involves the variable, the decision, and in the end to 'pure/indirect solutions' (*mittelbare Lösungen*). 'Pure means' are never 'immediate' (*unmittelbar*). While this positioning is further complicated by a distinction between the realm of human relations as opposed to one that concerns 'goods', what emerges as important is the link between the 'pure' and the 'mediate'. Both of these points indicate the processes and positions leading to an understanding of what is involved in the 'depositioning' of the law.

6

In order to understand what is at work in the formulation noted above, in which 'pure means' emerge as integral to a 'deposition' of the law, further consideration needs to be given to the 'pure' as it occurs in Benjamin's writings. The term 'pure' (*rein*) has a specific currency in his work. For example, in a long and complex passage in *The Task of the Translator*, 'pure language' (*reine Sprache*) emerges in the following terms.

> In all language and linguistic creations there remains in addition to what can be conveyed something that cannot be communicated [*ein Nicht-Mitteilbares*]; depending on the context in which it appears, it is something that symbolises or something symbolised. It is the former only in the finite products of languages [*in den endlichen Gebilden der Sprachen*], the latter in the becoming [*Werden*] of languages themselves. And that which seeks to represent, indeed to produce itself in the becoming of languages, is that *very core of pure language*; yet though this core remains present in life [*gegenwärtig im Leben*] as that which is symbolised itself, albeit hidden and fragmentary, it persists in linguistic creations only in its symbolising capacity. Whereas in various tongues, that ultimate essence, *the pure language*, is tied only to linguistic elements and their changes, in linguistic creations it is weighted with a heavy alien meaning. To relieve it of this, to turn the symbolising into the symbolised, to regain the pure language fully formed in the flow of language [*Sprachbewegung*], is the tremendous and single capacity of translation [*das gewaltige und einzige Vermögen der Übersetzung*]. In *this pure language* – which no longer means or expresses anything but is, as expressionless and creative word, that which is meant in all languages – all information, all sense and all intention finally encounter a stratum in which they are bound to be extinguished. (Emphasis added)[53]

The key elements in the formulation of 'pure language' that are germane here are, firstly, the attribution to it of a capacity. 'Pure language' therefore needs to be understood as bound up with the generative or at least the productive. The second is its identification as 'expressionless and creative word'. 'Pure language' persists without expression. Present as that which 'cannot be communicated'. While persisting in this way, its field of operation is language. As a result, 'pure language' does not point beyond language. However, it is neither reducible to any one natural language nor is it simply linguistic. Resisting these reductions – reductions which would be its naturalisation on the one hand or equation with a putative formalism on the other – is what allows 'pure language' to figure within language. The nature of the separation involves neither mere distance nor an eventual form of connection. The separation is an allowing to be thought in terms of production and, even if it is not stated explicitly as such, also in relation to a reworked conception of potentiality. If there is access to 'pure language' then it occurs not as access to an original language, let alone to a final language of reconciliation, but to its having been regained in the act of translation.

What is regained is what allows language's work. It allows for that work. It is part of what happens – it is the condition of language's happening – even though 'pure language' remains 'expressionless'. If the translator, in Benjamin's words, liberates 'the language imprisoned in a work in his recreation of that work', what this entails is that 'pure language' is only ever present as that possibility and thus as an original potentiality. Pure language does not figure. Not having content, it provides content's continual reforming at the point where potentiality and the actual act of translation interconnect. The point at which that occurs is the already identified 'infinitely small point'. That interconnection is the expression of the next translation, a form of repetition whose possibility is of necessity expressionless but which emerges as the interplay of determination and indetermination. A setting that potentiality allows. Thus there is a position demanding that the *caesura of allowing* be understood as the moment where destruction and potentiality occasion.

'Pure language', which stands counter to what Benjamin identifies as the 'bourgeois' conception of language, is the mark of the refusal of the reduction of language to the work of signs and thus to utility. This is not to say, however, that 'pure language' is an 'uninterpretable manifestation'. Not only should the term 'manifestation' be used with care, the question of interpretation has been distanced such that the 'pure' can be rethought in terms of a potentiality and therefore should not be thought within the purview defined by a relation between the interpretable and the uninterpretable. If further evidence is necessary, it is clear from Benjamin's own argument in the passage cited above that 'pure language', while both 'hidden' and 'fragmentary', still 'remains present in life'. Present in a way such that potentiality, both in its differentiation from its presence as actualised, but also with its figuring within actualisation, makes the question – how, in this context, is the presence of potentiality to be understood? – all the more difficult to answer. And yet, intimations of an answer are already present. They can be located, occurring initially in the contrast between that which takes place, on the one hand, as the 'finite products of language' and, on the other, 'the becoming of languages'. The latter is not a reference to the simple evolution of language, as though all that is being identified in Benjamin's formulation is the historical development of languages. There is a different register at work. The contrast is between finitude – the pragmatic determinations of language of which a given translation would be an exemplary instance – and language understood as a process of becoming. The work of language consists of a complex relation between acts of presentation and the process of language's own self-realisation. Translation is defined in relation to that which allows it – translation – to occur. That allowing, a process signalled by a presence that is both 'expressionless' and 'creative', is what occasions translation, indeed it becomes what could be described as the occasioning of translation. As such it marks the impossibility of an outside.[54] With regard to the work of language, the 'pure' signals as much this impossibility as it locates a form of presence that is defined in relation to a conception of potentiality. The 'pure' not only functions as an account of translation's possibility, it is also the case that the work of language is defined both in relation, and only in relation, to the continual and productive interconnection between potentiality and actuality. There is a further point that needs to be added, namely that central to Benjamin's argument is the refusal to sanction any identification of the 'pure' and the pragmatic instance. The latter is of course the locus of communication and reference and is therefore defined by utility and means/ends relations. There needs to be a sustained and clearly delineated distinction between pragmatic instances and that which is identified as 'pure language'; what has been identified remains operative in terms of the continuity of potentiality. The nature of this distinction is decisive for any attempt to understand both law and the nature of the separation of 'justice' and law.

If the relationship between 'pure language' and the pragmatic instance can be understood in terms of the interplay between potentiality and the actual then what has to be taken up is the way this distinction yields an explication of the already noted claim made by Benjamin that 'divine violence is pure violence over all life for the sake of the living [*reine Gewalt über alles Leben um des Lebendigen willen*]'. (This passage will continue to recur.) Here the 'pure' has an extension. Its significance can be found in its providing a definition of *reine Gewalt* in which the conception of operability that it identifies cannot be understood either as immediate in the sense of gratuitous violence or as linked to a form voluntarism. As a result, *Gewalt* will be able to be held apart from any direct, let alone inevitable relation to literal violence. This reworking of *Gewalt* opens up the question of life.

In *The Task of the Translator* Benjamin clarifies the concept of life in the following terms:

> The concept of life is given its due only if everything that has a history of its own, and is not merely the setting for history, is credited with life. In the final analysis, the range of life must be determined by history rather than by nature, least of all by such tenuous factors as sensation and soul. The philosopher's task consists in comprehending all of natural life through the more encompassing life of history.[55]

Moreover, again to recall the formulation in *Fate and Character*, there is another important moment in which character emerges in the overcoming of the interplay of fate and guilt:

> The vision of character . . . is liberating in all its forms; it is linked to freedom . . . by way of affinity to logic. The character trait is not therefore the knot in the net. It is the sun of individuality in the colourless (anonymous) sky of man, which casts the shadow of comic actions.[56]

What passages of this type establish is the setting that 'mythic violence' repeats and 'divine violence' interrupts. Within that setting life is equated with natural history. And yet life will always need to overcome any attempt to equate it with 'organic corporeality'. ('Mythic violence' turns the complex of life, living, into 'mere life', that is into biological life.) Within that overcoming and thus as integral to ending the hold of 'mythic violence', life becomes determined by history. Were the 'soul' and 'feeling' to be taken as ends in themselves they would have been allowed to resist their incorporation into history. That incorporation, however, must eschew any attempt to equate history with the naturalisation of time in which the process of naturalisation is then recast as either history (historicism) or nature. If history is introduced, then it needs to be a conception of history in which both history and life are configured, more likely reconfigured, such that they name loci of value. It will be the same sense of value that allowed Benjamin to argue that 'there is no document of culture which is not at the same time a document of barbarism'.[57] The 'pure' is the term that allows this to be thought. The 'pure' marks the possibility of thinking operability in its radical differentiation from the already determined, where the latter can be defined in terms of 'direct solutions' that incorporate the law defined by its mediated immediacy.

7

At this point in the overall development of the text, the strike returns. The setting in which it occurs is 'class struggle'. There are two forms of strike: namely, the strike defined by its relation to a specific goal and what Benjamin refers to as the 'proletarian general strike'. Benjamin defines their difference by arguing that they are 'antithetical in their relation to violence' (*in der Beziehung auf die Gewalt ein Gegensatz*).[58] And yet the proletarian general strike is non-violent despite its 'single task' being described as 'the annihilation of state power' (*die Vernichtung der Staatsgewalt*).[59] However, the political strike is violent because it is defined in terms of means. On the other hand, 'the proletarian general strike' is 'non-violent'. Here both the claim to and the definition of 'non-violence' is specific. It is 'non-violent' because it is determined 'only to resume a wholly othered work no longer enforced by the state' (*nur eine gänzlich veränderte Arbeit, eine nicht staatlich erzwungene*). Clearly the key here is what is meant by the expression 'a wholly othered work' (*eine gänzlich veränderte Arbeit*). What this question recalls – and indeed its answer will depend upon – is the sense of 'othering' initially developed in the context of Chapter 2. Here othering involves both 'destruction' – named here as *die Vernichtung* – and inauguration, namely work's continuity as othered. Part of the answer to the question of the othering of work lies both in the relation of this now othered sense of work to the state and in the transformation of the relations constituting work. Those relations too will have been othered. The othering of work is the outcome of this 'non-violence'.

The question of work, however, is usually positioned against unemployment. The latter linked to forms of production, even forms that are fundamentally exploitative because of the inherent production of surplus value. What this provides is a setting in which unemployment is counterposed to work having been withdrawn. Unemployment is not the strike. Benjamin's reference to unemployment occurred in the context of his commentary on Anna Segher's novel *Die Rettung*. Almost as a prelude to that commentary he writes that:

> One of the many blessings of working is that toil alone makes perceptible the bliss of doing nothing. Kant calls the weariness at the end of the working day one of the supreme pleasures of the senses. But idleness without work is a torment. This is yet one more deprivation amid the many that the unemployed have to suffer. They are subjected to the passage of time like an incubus [*Sie unterliegen dem Zeitlauf als einem Inkubus*] that impregnates them against their will. They do not give birth, but they have the eccentric desires of a pregnant woman.[60]

The full force of the position occurs with the evocation of the 'incubus'. The incubus works while its victims sleep. The unemployed are therefore unable to exercise a relation to time. They are subject to it. Moreover, they are subject to actions that defy their will. They are worked on. Time works them over. They are fated. The actions of the unemployed are presented as worked upon and thus arising within a form of sleep. The question of what an awakening from unemployment involves is not as straightforward as it seems. The move from unemployment to employment, what would far too quickly be described as the move to work, needs to note the problem of mimicry that Benjamin identifies. There is an important play of mimicry that is evident within the problematic of sleep, and thus the awoken, and then in the move to work. Benjamin writes that:

> The Third Reich mimics socialism [*So äfft das dritte Reich den Sozialismus nach*]. Unemployment comes to an end because forced labour is made legal.[61]

There is therefore a type of imitation or copying in which a similarity of end necessitates its own destruction. It should be noted, of course, that this mimicry is inextricably bound up with the introduction of a fated position. This is a state of being 'subjected to the passage of time'. As a result, as a possible point of the presence of a *counter-measure*, there needs to be a logic that resists the type of imitation identified in this passage and equally works in relation to the law. The interruption of this mimicry involves another form of awakening. More precisely, because it cannot involve the simple evocation of work, what has to be demanded is the reiteration of work within, and as, its othering.

When Benjamin argues that the two forms of strike are 'antithetical in their relation to violence', what is stake in such a formulation is the possibility of linking the strike to what has already been identified as the *caesura of allowing*. Which is the productive capacity of the 'non-violent', remembering that non-violence is linked to another form of operability and therefore to the recovery of earlier forms of relationality that deploy 'means of non-violent agreement' (*Mittel gewaltloser Übereinkunft*).[62]

The 'non-violence' that defines the strike is itself defined, for example, in relation to the othering of work. Is only non-violent within a setting in which violence is defined by the continuity of the state, namely 'violence' as *Staatsgewalt*. In refusing that measure, its counter-measure becomes non-violent. It is non-violent in the strict sense that it is not operable within that system. And yet non-operable non-violence is not pure passivity. The consequence of its not being operable is that it is, at the same time, bound up with another form of operability. The operability, once again, that is named within the process of othering. Equally, it is this mode – operability – that is named as 'non-violent agreement'. It is non-violent in the precise sense that it refuses the determination of law. It is not envisaged by law. It is nonetheless a form of agreement, and as an agreement it has to be thought as operable. Hence the question of the mode of operability that is defined by the law's distancing. This is, after all, the force of the already noted possibility of 'other kinds of violence [*andern Arten der Gewalt*] than all those envisaged by legal theory'.[63]

At this point in the text, and from here until the end, Benjamin's argumentation is at its most demanding. Not only do already noted themes reappear, there is also a sustained attempt to clarify what is involved in the thinking of destruction and its relation to differing modalities of *Gewalt*. Even though it is a passage that occurs just after the discussion of Niobe, it is worth noting one of Benjamin's most striking formulations of destruction. It is a passage whose complications cannot be avoided. Benjamin writes that:

> This very task [*Aufgabe*] of destruction [*Vernichtung*] poses again, in the last resort, the question of a pure immediate violence that might be able to call a halt to mythical violence. Just as in all spheres God [*Gott*] opposes myth, mythical violence is confronted by the divine [*göttliche*]. And the latter constitutes its antithesis in all respects.[64]

Fate-imposed violence decides on 'the justification of means', while God decides on the 'justness of ends'. This is a way of announcing the absolute separation of law and the 'justness of ends'. At this stage it announces simply that. However, what it names in the process is 'God'. The question that has to be addressed and will be central in what follows is: what does God name? This is the first time that God is named in the text. It is the presence of this name that will come to be renamed within the move from God to 'Godly Violence'. What is at stake here is not the presence of God per se. Rather, what is important is what it is that is named by the term God. Hence the question: 'what here does God name?' On one level the answer is straightforward. God names that which calls a halt to 'mythic violence'. What awaits is of course God's translation.

8

In order to stage the distinction between 'mythic violence' and 'divine violence', Benjamin situates them. The first is presented in relation to the story of Niobe from Greek and Roman mythology. (While the story is there in Homer, her most exacting presentation occurs in Book 6 of Ovid's *Metamorphoses*.) The second is in relation to the treatment of the 'company of Khora' that occurs in the *Torah* in *Bəmidbar* (*Numbers*). While Benjamin does not specify the passage it is clear that he is referring to *Numbers* 16: 28–30.[65] Each of these 'instances' needs to be taken in turn.

Niobe boasted to Leto of her fecundity. In response Leto sent her children Artemis and Apollo to kill Niobe's. Of this set of events Benjamin writes that:

> Niobe's arrogance calls down fate upon itself not because her arrogance offends against the law but because it challenges fate – to a fight in which fate must triumph, and can bring to light a law only in its triumph.[66]

It is already clear that at stake here is more than the breaking of a law. Law here is the after-effect of fate and thus it marks the presence of the 'culpable life'. These actions occur within the domain of fate, that is, actions that presuppose a subject as already guilty. In this context it should be remembered that Benjamin has argued that 'fate is the nexus of guilt among the living'.[67] It would be a mistake to see Niobe challenging law, because that would misunderstand the nature of law.[68] What is a challenge to law is de facto that which challenges law's fateful nature. If there is to be an overcoming of fate then it will involve a form of destruction that occurs in the name of life.

The response to Niobe, her subjugation to fate and the process of her becoming fate's subject involves a modality of *Gewalt* that for Benjamin is 'not authentically destructive' (*nicht eigentlich zerstörend*).[69] The lack of authenticity does not reside in the presence of literal violence. There are three reasons. Firstly, it is driven by fate. The second reason is that it fails to be expiatory and then finally becomes law-making. Law here is created after fate. This conception of law making ties it to the modality of *Gewalt* that founded it. It cannot free itself from that founding form. As such law-making will in the end become law-preserving. As such the cycle is condemned to continue. Breaking that cycle involves both an act of destruction and the presence of a potentiality within the cycle itself. The potentiality for othering – being othered – is the only possibility to stem the cycle of eternal return. The third consequence is that within this particular set-up there cannot be a link between law and justice, precisely because it would be the 'dismissal' of that founding form of *Gewalt* that is the opening to justice. (Indeed, it is the necessary precondition for that opening.) Justice therefore takes as its precondition that separation. A separation to be announced as the result of 'divine violence'. That is why for Benjamin justice 'is the principle of all divine end making [*alle göttliche Zwecksetzung*]'.[70]

It is the evocation of the 'authentic destruction' that brings the next important element of the argument into play. Once it can be concluded that 'mythic violence' is 'identical with legal violence' – in other words, qua the modality of *Gewalt* they are identical – a state of affairs which follows both from the relationship between law and fate on the hand and the impossibility of such a conception of law-making freeing itself from the mythic (where the latter is its source) on the other, what then has to be the case is the emergence of the possibility of that which calls 'a halt to mythic violence'. This is the 'task [*Aufgabe*] of destruction'. A task taken on, as has been noted, by 'God' (*Gott*). The argumentation quickly moves at this point from *Gott* ('God') to *göttliche Gewalt* ('divine violence'). God's presence is incorporated. It names a mode of *Gewalt*. That mode is linked to the expiatory, the bloodless and to the 'law destroying'. In other words, it is linked to the *caesura of allowing*. It is at this point that Benjamin introduces the example of the 'company of Khora'. Despite its length, the passage in which this 'contrast' is established and this 'example' (*Exempel*) introduced needs to be noted.

> The legend of Niobe may be confronted, as an example of this violence, with God's judgement on the company of Korah. It strikes privileged Levites, strikes them without warning, without threat, and does not stop short of annihilation. But in annihilating it also expiates, and a deep connection between the lack of bloodshed and the expiatory character of this violence is unmistakable. For blood is the symbol of mere life [*des bloßen Lebens*]. The dissolution of legal violence stems, as cannot be shown in detail here, from the guilt of more natural life, which consigns the living, innocent and unhappy, to a retribution that 'expiates' the guilt of mere life [*dem bloßen Leben*] – and doubtless also purifies the guilty, not of guilt, however, but of law. For with mere life the rule of law over the living ceases. Mythical violence is bloody power over mere life [*das bloße Leben*] for its own sake, divine violence pure power over all life for the sake of the living [*um des Lebendigen willen*]. The first demands. It is. The second accepts it [*die zweite nimmt sie an*].[71]

Prior to taking up the immediacy of the act, what endures as a central element within the passage is the continual evocation of 'mere life'. As has been consistently argued, 'mere life' in Benjamin's work refers to the subject position within fate. It is 'natural' life. It is the life that assumes fate and denies a link between life and activity; the latter is the life in which human activity and the world are always already intertwined. There are, however, three questions to be addressed. Why is the act of destruction – this bloodless violence – 'expiatory'? What is meant by 'divine violence' 'occurring for the sake of the living'? Finally, there is

the question of 'sacrifice': what does it means to say that 'divine violence' accepts it (*nimmt sie an*)? Answering these questions will involve
a slight degree of reiteration of some of the preceding argumentation. As
this is an essential passage within the text as a whole it is vital to take
up the challenge.

The third question is the most demanding since what it brings to the
fore is the relationship between politics and sacrifice. For Benjamin
'mythic violence' requires or demands 'sacrifice'. It is necessary to this
modality of *Gewalt*. Moreover, what is at stake here is a particular
economy of activity. There is no alternative to the imposition and
the operative presence of a logic of sacrifice. (*Gewalt* here is a logic
of sacrifice.) The formulation with regard to 'divine violence' is more
complicated. What does it mean to say that 'sacrifice' is accepted?
This first point to note is not the absence of necessity or obligation.
(*Annehmen* is not *fordern*.) While this still leaves open the non-necessity
of sacrifice, what is clear is that there is no link between 'divine violence' and sacrifice. To suggest that sacrifice is 'accepted' is to argue
that the actualisation of the potentiality for the just life is not without
consequences. However, those consequences are not dependent upon
sacrifice. A different logic is in force. This position is reinforced when
the second question is addressed. It should be clear that the claim that
'mythic violence' occurs for its own sake identifies it as the modality of
Gewalt that is inextricably bound up with law's self-preservation and
thus its eternal recurrence. The destruction of the continuity of preserva-
tions and therefore the destruction of that economy is the articulation
of a politics of time. (It should be remembered that the term 'economy'
cannot be generalised; economies are merely self-regulating systems.)
The contrast is 'divine violence'. Here is a modality of *Gewalt* that is
not defined by its being law-preserving or law-creating. It is defined by
an economy that is both determined by *Rechtsgewalt* and therefore it
does not demand a subject position defined by 'guilt'. The contrast is
captured in the formulation of the description of 'divine violence' understood as 'occurring for the sake of the living'. However, 'the living' has
to be thought in its radical differentiation from 'mere life'. Whatever it
is that can be understood by 'the living' cannot be equated with 'mere
life' (or 'natural life'), nor can it be equated with any of the aspects of
life that would hold were life to be equated with 'mere life'. In other
words, 'the living' identifies a conception of human being that is defined
by guilt and thus by fate – 'guilt' as naming the position of having been
fated. (Even though the term 'the living' will come to mean the subject
positions created within the potentiality for the just life, the argument
for that conclusion is yet to be made by Benjamin.)

The answer to the first question posed above emerges once it is clear that 'divine violence' brings 'the living' into play rather than a subject defined both by guilt and the absence of *Glück*. The problematic aspects of the 'example' – the company of Khora – is not to be found in the answers to the questions posed above, nor is it due to the reiterated presence of the 'strike' (*Schlag*). Rather the problem is the 'without warning' and 'without threat'. God's actions appear unprecedented. In a sense, however, this is the point that Benjamin is after. What is necessary is a form of interruption that defies an already present economy. It is, moreover, a set of actions that would have transformed the way in which law was understood (and thus lived out). Rather than assuming law was there either to be obeyed or to be defied (Oedipus), there needs to be what might be described as a coming to the law. What is problematic therefore is that God's actions – as presented by Benjamin – may have transformed the law, but what was excluded was the educative process staged by a coming to the law. It is not surprising in this context that in relation to the law – indeed in the transformation of *Gesetz* to *Gebot* (law to commandment) – Franz Rosenzweig will write of a 'seeking and being on the way'.[72] Once there is a coming to the law, then this will involve law's transformation insofar as what will have been transformed is the relationship between law and life. While Benjamin would have been – most probably – unaware of the existence of this passage in the *Babylonian Talmud* (Tractate Baba BathraTractate Folio 74a), it would have confirmed both the bloodless nature of the act and equally the recognition that what was at stake was law.

> He said unto me: 'Come, I will show you the men of Korah that were swallowed up.' I saw two cracks that emitted smoke. I took a piece of clipped wool, dipped it in water, attached it to the point of a spear and let it in there. And when I took it out it was singed. [Thereupon] he said unto me: 'Listen attentively [to] what you [are about to] hear.' And I heard them say: 'Moses and his Torah are truth and we are liars.' He said unto me: 'Every thirty days Gehenna causes them to turn back here as [one turns] flesh in a pot and they say thus: 'Moses and his law are truth and we are liars.'[73]

It is important to note that in his exchange with Buber concerning the nature of the 'law' Rosenzweig – as will Benjamin – turns to education. Rosenzweig's concern is specifically Jewish education. Nonetheless his point is relevant here. He notes that:

> We can reach both the teachings and the Law only by realising that we are still on the first lap of the way, and by taking every step upon it, ourselves.[74]

What is problematic in Rosenzweig's position is that it is assumed that the educative act is additive and incremental. (Thus structured by an accumulative economy.) And thus that the awareness or even the awakening that education harbours or affords will just occur within such a structure. While Benjamin will retain the centrality of the educative in his philosophical thinking, it becomes a modality not just of *Gewalt* but also of 'divine violence'. Education has the capacity to be destructive.

> This divine violence is attested not only by religious tradition but is also found in present-day life in at least one sanctioned manifestation. The educative power, which in its perfected form stands outside the law [*außerhalb des Rechts steht*], is one of its manifestations.[75]

However, if there is an 'educative *Gewalt*', then while it cannot be automatically assimilated to what Rosenzweig understands by a coming to the law, precisely because the interplay of destruction and inauguration are absent, the significant point is that it does not have the same sense of immediacy that defines God's action in regard to the company of Khora. There is, as was suggested, an irreparable tension between God's actions and the process of education. To the extent that there can be an educative *Gewalt*, then the immediacy of the interruption that it stages needs to be recast as a process. If immediacy has two senses, one is the immediacy of the moment and the other as 'without mediation', then it is only the latter that pertains in regards to educative *Gewalt*. The problematic element and thus the creation of an irreparable tension between God's action and education occur because of Benjamin's conflation of these two senses of immediacy. However, what brings them together is their relation to the law, a position signalled by Benjamin's use of the expression 'stands outside the law' (*außerhalb des Rechts steht*) to describe this modality of *Gewalt*.

In order to clarify what is meant by the positioning of modes of *Gewalt* that are defined by 'the absence of all law-making' (*die Abwesenheit jeder Rechtsetzung*), the next move in the argument is to counter the supposition that the presence of such a position would lead necessarily to a justification of 'lethal violence' (*die letale Gewalt*).[76] The important point to note, at the beginning, is that 'lethal violence' (*die letale Gewalt*) is a mode of *Gewalt*. The emergence of the question is taken up by Benjamin in terms of the 'commandment' (*Gebot*), 'Thou shalt not kill'. There is an important point here insofar as, while it is not argued directly by Benjamin, what is at stake in the engagement with the 'commandment' is both the subject position to which it gives rise and then the conception of law or commandment that accompanies it. For Benjamin the 'commandment' has neither the status of that which interdicts – as such it does not have the status of law structured by fate – equally it does not provide what he refers to as a 'criterion of judgement'. While he gives a specific rendering of the term – a historicisation that is not essential here – his position is that the commandment has the status of a 'guideline' (*Richtschnur*).[77] Indeed, it can be argued that the ensuing discussion of the imperative – 'Thou shalt not kill' – and this can be understood as what a critique of law would be like when it is undertaken in the name of law (another law, law after the *othering* of the law), involves a transformation of a fateful imperative into 'a guideline'. While the 'guideline' is not pursued, what could have been taken up is the way in which there is a fundamentally different relationship between the 'guideline' and life (where the latter is no longer understood as fated). Indeed, it would be the presence of the 'guideline' that defers the hold of fate and introduces a subject as engaged with the world – the subject identified in *Fate and Character* as 'the active person'.[78] This position is reinforced by the claim that the taking of life – if the latter is equated with 'killing' as opposed to self-defence – cannot be justified on the ground that it leads to justice. This is to locate the act within the context of the possibility of a just life. Life as the overcoming of the equation of life with either 'mere life' or 'natural life'.

Consistent with the need to rework the subject position within the othering fate – a subject position that will continue to appear within the emphatic clarification of life that occurs at the end of the text – Benjamin clarifies the impossibility of equating life with natural life. Indeed, part of the argument is that what underpins claims about that sanctity of life is the presence of life within the mythic. Benjamin begins to work out this position via a critical engagement with the position he attributes to Kurt Hiller. For Benjamin the latter argues that the position of *Dasein* (understood as 'existence') is 'higher' – and perhaps more original – than any positioning of subjectivity that takes either *Glück* or *Gerechtigkeit* as the defining terms. As a form of conclusion, Benjamin goes on and describes as 'ignoble' that position of *Dasein* as higher than *gerechtes Dasein*,

> if existence [*Dasein*] is to mean nothing other than mere life [*bloßes Leben*] – and it has this meaning in the argument referred to. It contains a mighty truth [*Eine gewaltige Wahrheit*], however, if existence [*Dasein*], or, better, life [*Leben*] (words whose ambiguity is readily dispelled, analogously to that of freedom, when they are referred to two distinct spheres), means the irreducible, total condition that is 'man'; if the proposition is intended to mean that the nonexistence of man [*das Nichtsein des Menschen*] is something more terrible than the (admittedly subordinate) not-yet-attained condition of the just man [*Nochnichtsein des rechtes Menschen*].[79]

After which is added the next essential move:

> Man cannot, at any price, be said to coincide with the mere life in him [*mit dem bloßen Leben in ihm*], no more than with any other of his conditions and qualities [*Eigenschaften*], not even with the uniqueness of his bodily person [*ja nicht einmal mit der Einzigkeit seiner leiblichen Person*].[80]

Despite the difficulties inherent in the positions identified in both these passages, they are to be understood here as opening a fundamental distinction between 'life' and 'mere life'. The former cannot be said to 'coincide' with the latter. The body is not the locus of that which is proper to human being. It is worth insisting on Benjamin's actual formulation in the second of the passages noted above. He writes that the human being cannot be equated 'with the mere life in him' (*mit dem bloßen Leben in ihm*). To which it should be added that this is the position determined by both fate and guilt. The words 'in him' not only point to a fundamental divide within the subject, what they indicate in addition is that, while subjects are always able to be repositioned by fate and guilt, this is a position that is no longer inevitable. In other words, as a position its occurrence is no longer fated. Fate therefore has lost its necessity. Hence, while there has been a destruction of fate, it remains the case that it is possible for both positions – fate and guilt – to return. This position has already been noted in terms of the way in which the mythic haunts modernity. However, what has been opened up is the possibility of an engagement with this presence. That engagement continues to locate a politics of time.

The force of the position held within these lines is to be found in the continuity of a distinction between 'mere life' and the just life. The latter is held open as a possibility. To read what is inherent in Benjamin's position, it can be argued that claims about the sacredness of life become no more than the attempt to make the subject position within fate and guilt into a sacred position. It is not difficult to see that such a sense of the sacred is inextricably bound up with the history of religion. Moreover, it links the necessity of sacrifice to this particular conception of the sacred. The Crucifixion as the actuality of sacrifice, for example, is of fundamental importance within this setting. Here, of course, is the point of radical difference between the Crucifixion as that which took place and the conception of 'sacrifice' within 'divine violence'. God is present as complicit in the first form of sacrifice. Hence this is the mythic violence that occurs, presumably, with God's blessing. It is the sacrifice that is 'demanded'. Here actuality is what is necessary. The contrast here is Abraham and Isaac; God acts to halt the actuality of sacrifice. There is therefore a depositioning of the law. The interruption, while immediate, is mediated insofar as Abraham's discovery of the animal caught in the thicket takes place over time. While what is opened up here is the problem of substitution, it remains the case that at work here is mediated immediacy. This is the sacrifice that would have been accepted but which is not necessary. In sum, what is at stake here is a separation between sacrifice, the mythic and 'bare life' on the one hand, while on the other hand there is mediated immediacy, 'guidelines' and the potentiality for justice.[81]

Having come this far, it is now possible to return to the pivotal passage that has played such a decisive role both here and in the preceding chapters.

> On the breaking [*Durchbrechung*] of this cycle maintained by mythical forms of law, on the suspension (or depositioning) [*Entsetzung*] of law with all the forces on which it depends as they depend on it, finally therefore on the abolition of state power [*Staatsgewalt*], a new historical epoch [*ein neues geschichtliches Zeitalter*] is founded.[82]

Here there are three interrelated elements that need to be identified. In the first instance there is the staging of the suspending or deposition of the modalities of *Gewalt* that sustain the law. (Law as fate.) Secondly, were that suspension to occur, it would then be linked to the destruction of *Staatsgewalt*. Finally, when these two elements are taken together they provide the basis on which to found 'a new historical epoch' (*ein neues geschichtliches Zeitalter*). Once again this links the language of destruction to the *caesura of allowing*. Moreover, it indicates that this caesura is now articulated within a conception of value whose most significant consequence is that the possibility of the move to justice cannot be effectively separated from its presence. The caesura's presence is therefore effective. There is an identification of that possibility's actualisation and 'a new historical epoch'. This is the epoch that will be a 'little bit different'. It will be one that has not abandoned law in the name of a putative lawlessness. Rather, it will be the epoch premised on the critique of law in the name of law. Enacted here is a specific conception of sovereignty. It is the conception implicated in the destruction of 'myth bastardised with law' and equally the undoing of the 'pernicious' 'law-preserving, administrative violence' (*die verwaltetet Gewalt*) that serves it. [83] Sovereignty, as named in the text's last line, is staged by (and as) 'divine violence'. This is the 'sovereign operability'. This is the modality of *Gewalt* that can both destroy and inaugurate. Both occasion life. The other life that in displacing 'bare life' becomes the inaugurating moment of the just life.

Notes

1. The project of this chapter is nothing other than an interpretation of *Towards a Critique of Violence*. Judgements, decisions, excisions and additions drive the project. The literature on *Towards a Critique of Violence* is extensive. Much like the text itself it is impossible to provide a simple overview of that literature. Many texts have involved attempts to establish different sets of relations between Benjamin and Schmitt. Others seek to locate his work solely in a Jewish tradition. Yet others have tried to develop that aspect of his work that touches on questions of life. The approach adopted here takes 'life' as one of the text's predominating concerns. Works that have been useful in the writing of this chapter include the ones noted below. It should be added that, as the project has been to develop an interpretation of the text that is consistent with the argument of this book, and as the difficulty of *Towards a Critique of Violence* demands constant engagement – and even here that engagement has had to have been curtailed at certain points – there has been little sustained discussion with these texts as a whole. It should be added that if there is one commentator on Benjamin – a commentator who is equally a thinker in his own right – and whose work stands out, then it is Werner Hamacher. Despite disagreements or differences of formulation that may have emerged both in this chapter and implicitly elsewhere, his work still stands as the crowning achievement of philosophically orientated scholarship on Benjamin. See Samir Haddad, 'A Genealogy of Violence: From Light to the Autoimmune', *Diacritics* 38.1–2 (Spring/Summer 2006), pp. 121–42; Sigrid Weigel, 'The Martyr and the Sovereign: Scenes from a Contemporary Tragic Drama, Read through Walter Benjamin and Carl Schmitt', *CR: The New Centennial Review* (Winter 2004), pp. 109–23; Kam Shapiro, 'Politics Is a Mushroom: Worldly Sources of Rule and Exception in Carl Schmitt and Walter Benjamin', *Diacritics* 37.2–3 (Summer–Fall 2007), pp. 121–34; Udi E. Greenberg, 'Orthodox Violence: "Critique of Violence" and Walter Benjamin's Jewish Political Theology', *History of European Ideas* 34 (2008), pp. 324–33; Martin Blumenthal-Barby, 'Pernicious Bastardizations: Benjamin's Ethics of Pure Violence', *MLN* 124.3 (April 2009), pp. 728–51; Tracy McNulty, 'The Commandment Against the Law Writing and Divine Justice in Walter Benjamin's "Critique of Violence"', *Diacritics* 37.2–3 (Summer–Fall 2007), pp. 34–60; Massimilano Tomba, 'Another Kind of *Gewalt*: Beyond Law Re-Reading Walter Benjamin', *Historical Materialism* 17.1 (2009), pp. 122–44; Jacques Derrida, *Force de loi* (Paris: Galilée, 1994); and Uwe Steiner, 'The True Politician: Walter Benjamin's Concept of the Political', *New German Critique* 83 (Spring–Summer 2001), pp. 43–88.

2. The image of the 'mosaic' is used by Benjamin in *The Origin of German Tragic Drama* to provide the means by which to understand both a mode of presentation and form of coherence: *Origin of German Tragic Drama*, p. 29; *Gesammelte Schriften* I, p. 208. The usual expectation of philosophical argument – the strategy, for example, of Kant's three Critiques – is absent from Benjamin's work. The 'mosaic' takes its place. Two points need to be made in relation to this state of affairs. The first is that if there is a distancing from the concerns of the traditions of philosophy then that

distancing must appear. The second is that what then appears is another form of the presentation of the philosophical. There should be no surprise here. From Plato's use of dialogue to Cicero's use of the dream and then to the continual engagements with presentation within contemporary German and French philosophy – from Adorno's *Minima Moralia* to Derrida's *Glas* – the renewal of the philosophical has always involved an engagement with its presentation. Philosophy cannot escape the question of its own presentation. This is all a paraphrase of the opening lines of Benjamin's *The Origin of German Tragic Drama*.

3. While this is not a point that can be pursued here, it is important to note that the position against which Kant writes with greatest commitment in the *Critique of Practical Reason* is the one he associates with Epicurus. In the case of Epicurus there is the position of *Glück* (happiness/fortune) not as a mere after-effect of the recognition of moral worth but as an end in itself. Benjamin's own engagement with *Glück* can be seen as an attempt to locate it as a possibility within life. However, it cannot be viewed as a mere end – and thinkable therefore in terms of the giveness of means/ends relations; as a result, the movement towards *Glück* has to incorporate the potentiality inherent in the move from 'life' to the 'just life'. With regard to Lucretius, the famous opening treatment of the 'serve' (*declinare/clinamen*) in *De Rerum Natura* – Book II, pp. 250–92 – links this movement to free will; of equal importance is that the possibility of the 'new' is bound up within an overcoming of 'fate'. What has emerged is that determinism, which can be equated with 'fate', demands that in order that something else occur, and thus a form of freedom be instantiated, there needs to be a discontinuity. What is important to note is that for Benjamin an inauguration demands a modality of 'destruction'. Hence the difference between both Epicurus and Lucretius read *à la lettre* and the modernity of Benjamin's thinking. Hence while *ataraxia* and *apatheia* may be taken as end points to which Epicurean thought might wish to move, from a Benjaminian perspective it would have to be argued that it is simply too early for 'tranquility'. To think that it is possible is not simply an inopportune gesture, it identifies political agency with the individual subject. This reinforces the claim already made in relation to Bartleby.

4. Hannah Arendt, *On Violence* (New York: Harcourt, Brace & World, 1970), p. 51. See in addition the discussion of 'power' in Hannah Arendt, *The Human Condition* (Chicago: University of Chicago Press, 1958), pp. 199–207.

5. Arendt, *On Violence*, p. 56. For a sustained development of Arendt's writings on violence see Peg Birmingham, 'Arendt and Hobbes: Glory, Sacrificial Violence, and the Political Imagination', *Research in Phenomenology* 41 (2011), pp. 1–22.

6. I have taken up the problem of the effect of the actualisation of this dimension of violence in my, 'Imagining Violence', *Filigrane* 14 (2011), <http://revues.mshparisnord.org/filigrane/index.php>.

7. Moreover, this is the precise point at which an engagement with Derrida's conception of justice would need to occur. While it cannot be pursued, the difficulty of defining justice in relation to the 'unconditional' is not that it refuses the possibility of justice as an actual state of affairs, but that it

fails to locate the question of justice in relation to its having a potentiality. The construal of the relationship between actuality and potentiality that is being suggested here distances the 'all or nothing' set-up demanded by the opposition between the conditional and the unconditional. This aspect of Derrida's work has been the subject of sustained reflection. Derrida's concerns with justice as the unconditional appear in a range of different texts. In regard to this aspect of Derrida's work see, *inter alia*: Jacques Derrida, *Spectres de Marx* (Paris: Galilée, 1993); *Force de loi* (Paris: Galilée, 1994); and *Voyous: Deux essais sur la raison* (Paris: Galilée, 2003). For an interpretation of the relationship between Derrida and Benjamin on questions pertaining to justice see: Roberto Buonamano, 'The Economy of Violence: Derrida on Law and Justice', *Ratio Juris* 11.2 (June 1998), pp. 168–79.

8. Benjamin, *Selected Writings* 1, p. 247; *Gesammelte Schriften* II.1, p. 196.

9. There will always be a difficulty in holding education apart from the law; by extension, the demands of the state (*Staatsgewalt*) should not detract from the possibility that such a separation is in principle thinkable. Part of what this means involves beginning to rethink the relationship between education and democracy while recognising at the same time that such an undertaking will demand a radical rethinking of democracy itself. While not argued for in Benjaminian terms, an important contribution to the development of this position can be found in Wendy Brown, 'The End of Educated Democracy', *Representations* 116.1 (Fall, 2011), pp. 19–41. Equally as important in this regard is Jacques Derrida, *L'université sans conditions* (Paris: Editions Galilée, 2001).

10. Benjamin, *Selected Writings* 1, p. 244; *Gesammelte Schriften* II.1, p. 191.

11. This formulation has also been used by Gérard Bensussan in his work on *Towards a Critique of Violence*. See his 'Deus sive Justitia: Note sur "Critique de la violence"', *Les Cahiers Philosophiques de Strasbourg* 27 (Premier Semestre, 2010), pp. 15–22 ; in this instance, p. 21.

12. The reference here is to *Selected Writings* 1, pp. 251–2; *Gesammelte Schriften* II.1, p. 202. However, it should be noted that while its formulation is importantly different, Benjamin locates a similar disruptive effect in Brecht. Writing of the *Threepenny Novel*, he notes that 'Brecht strips naked the conditions in which we live, removing the drapery of legal concepts [*Rechtsbegriffe*]'; Benjamin, *Selected Writings* 3, p. 9; *Gesammelte Schriften* II.2, p. 448.

13. While a number of commentators have noted the complex presence of this suspension of the law – a move that already evokes the Pauline suspension of the Jewish law – for an important account, see Christoph Menke, 'Law and Violence', *Law and Literature* 22.2 (Spring, 2010), pp. 1–17. The importance of Menke's interpretation is his recognition that the suspension of the law does not entail the 'abolition of law', rather it requires a different way of 'enacting law'. This is the argument to be advanced here, namely that a critique of law occurs in the name of law (pp. 13–14).

14. It is not difficult to see that what Benjamin will go and develop in terms of 'phantasmagoria' needs to be accounted for in precisely these terms. See Benjamin, 'Materials for the exposé of 1935', in *Arcades Project*.

15. Benjamin, *Selected Writings* 1, p. 251; *Gesammelte Schriften* II.1, p. 202.

16. An interpretive analysis set within the context of this overall project of the *Theological Political Fragment* will occur in Chapter 6.

17. There is an important repositioning of the language of haunting that comes from Derrida's engagement with Marx. See to that end his *Spectres de Marx*. For an overview of this issue raised by this book see Guy Petitdemange, 'De La Hantise: Le Marx de Derrida', *Cités* 30 (2007), pp. 17–29. The problem of haunting, however, is not only the identification of that which endures as a possibility but also what is thus entailed by the suspension of that possibility.

18. Benjamin, *Selected Writings* 1, p. 252; *Gesammelte Schriften* II.1, p. 203.

19. Benjamin, *Selected Writings* 4, p. 179; *Gesammelte Schriften* I.2, p. 677

20. Benjamin, *Selected Writings* 1, p. 236; *Gesammelte Schriften* II.1, p. 179.

21. Benjamin, *Selected Writings* 1, p. 261; *Gesammelte Schriften* IV.1, p. 20.

22. Benjamin, *Selected Writings* 1, p. 261; *Gesammelte Schriften* IV.1, p. 20.

23. Benjamin, *Selected Writings* 1, p. 262; *Gesammelte Schriften* IV.1, p. 21.

24. While the space to develop it adequately is not present, it should be noted, nonetheless, that at work here is a specific conception of freedom. It involves three elements. The first is the presence of a conception of law that is outside the law. This is of course the reiteration both of measure's ubiquity and the possibility of reworking measure. The second is that this conception of law leads to forms of inauguration that have to be understood in terms of the prevalence of indetermination rather than the already determined. Thirdly, location is given but its presence is always informal. It is the presence of informality that allows a transformation of location. Moreover, indetermined transformations will themselves impact upon locations.

25. Benjamin, *Selected Writings* 1, p. 236; *Gesammelte Schriften* II.1, p. 179.

26. Benjamin, *Selected Writings* 1, p. 237; *Gesammelte Schriften* II.1, p. 180.

27. Benjamin, *Selected Writings* 1, p. 236; *Gesammelte Schriften* II.1, p. 179.

28. Benjamin, *Selected Writings* 1, p. 237; *Gesammelte Schriften* II.1, p. 180.

29. Benjamin, *Selected Writings* 1, p. 238; *Gesammelte Schriften* II.1, p. 181.

30. Benjamin, *Selected Writings* 1, p. 238; *Gesammelte Schriften* II.1, pp. 181–2.

31. Benjamin, *Selected Writings* 1, p. 238; *Gesammelte Schriften* II.1, p. 182.

32. Benjamin, *Selected Writings* 1, p. 239; *Gesammelte Schriften* II.1, p. 183.

33. Benjamin, *Selected Writings* 1, p. 239; *Gesammelte Schriften* II.1, p. 183.

34. Benjamin, *Selected Writings* 1, p. 240; *Gesammelte Schriften* II.1, p. 186.

35. Benjamin, *Selected Writings* 1, p. 240; *Gesammelte Schriften* II.1, p. 186.

36. Benjamin, *Selected Writings* 1, p. 240; *Gesammelte Schriften* II.1, p. 186.

37. Benjamin, *Selected Writings* 1, p. 240; *Gesammelte Schriften* II.1, p. 186.

38. Benjamin, *Selected Writings* 1, p. 242; *Gesammelte Schriften* II.1, p. 189.

39. Shakespeare, *Shakespeare's dramatische Werke* 6, trans. A. W. Schlegel and Ludwig Tieck (Berlin: Berlag von Georg Reimer, 1869), p. 42.

40. The interpretation advanced here owes a great deal to the important work undertaken by Elizabeth Rottenberg on this aspect of Derrida's philosophical thinking. See Rottenberg, 'Cruelty and Its Vicissitudes: Jacques Derrida and the Future of Psychoanalysis', *Southern Journal of Philosophy* 50 (Spindel Supplement, 2012), pp. 143–59.

41. Derrida, *De quoi demain*, p. 233.

42. Derrida, *La peine de mort* 1, p. 380. A passage also discussed by Rottenberg in 'Cruelty and its Vicissitudes', pp. 143–59.
43. Derrida, *La peine de mort* 1, p. 11.
44. Derrida, *De quoi demain*, p. 233.
45. Benjamin, *Selected Writings* 1, p. 242; *Gesammelte Schriften* II.1, p. 189.
46. Benjamin, *Selected Writings* 1, p. 243; *Gesammelte Schriften* II.1, p. 189.
47. Benjamin, *Selected Writings* 1, p. 244; *Gesammelte Schriften* II.1, p. 190.
48. Benjamin, *Selected Writings* 1, p. 244; *Gesammelte Schriften* II.1, p. 190.
49. Benjamin, *Selected Writings* 1, p. 244; *Gesammelte Schriften* II.1, p. 190.
50. Benjamin, *Selected Writings* 1, pp. 244–5; *Gesammelte Schriften* II.1, p. 192.
51. Benjamin, *Selected Writings* 1, p. 244; *Gesammelte Schriften* II.1, p. 190.
52. Benjamin, *Selected Writings* 1, p. 245; *Gesammelte Schriften* II.1, p. 193.
53. Benjamin, *Selected Writings* 1, p. 261; *Gesammelte Schriften* IV.1, p. 19.
54. I have discussed the concept of the 'expressionless' in my *Philosophy's Literature* (Manchester: Clinamen Press, 2001). The most sustained engagement with the term is to be found in Winfried Menninghaus, 'Das Ausdruckslose: Walter Benjamins Metamorphosen der Biderlosigkeit', in I. and K. Scheuermann (eds), *Für Walter Benjamin: Dokumente, Essays und ein Entwurf* (Frankfurt am Main: Suhrkamp, 1992), pp. 170–82. The significance here is that the 'expressionless' provides the possibility for expression. This is a possibility that presupposes, within the argument presented here, an already present potentiality.
55. Benjamin, *Selected Writings* 1, pp. 254–5; *Gesammelte Schriften* IV.1, p. 11
56. Benjamin, *Selected Writings* 1, p. 206; *Gesammelte Schriften* II.1, p. 175.
57. Benjamin, *Selected Writings* 4, p. 392; *Gesammelte Schriften* I.2, p. 696.
58. Benjamin, *Selected Writings* 1, p. 245; *Gesammelte Schriften* II.1, p. 193.
59. Benjamin, *Selected Writings* 1, p. 246; *Gesammelte Schriften* II.1, p. 194.
60. Benjamin, *Selected Writings* 4, pp. 127–8; *Gesammelte Schriften* III, p. 532.
61. Benjamin, *Selected Writings* 4, p. 130; *Gesammelte Schriften* III, p. 350.
62. Benjamin, *Selected Writings* 1, p. 247; *Gesammelte Schriften* II.1, p. 195.
63. Benjamin, *Selected Writings* 1, p. 247; *Gesammelte Schriften* II.1, p. 197.
64. Benjamin, *Selected Writings* 1, p. 249; *Gesammelte Schriften* II.1, p. 199.
65. The entire passage from *Numbers* reads as follows:

> Then Moses said, 'This is how you will know that God has sent me to do all these things and that it was not my idea: If these men die a natural death and suffer the fate of all mankind, then God has not sent me. But if God brings about something totally new, and the earth opens its mouth and swallows them, with everything that belongs to them, and they go down alive into the realm of the dead, then you will know that these men have treated God with contempt.'

The line that is of central importance here is *vaim briyah yibrah adonai*. Integral to the overall argument is the interpretation of God's creating. This is God's intervention. While Benjamin does not cite the passage from the Torah, his interpretation depends upon the literal force of God's creating a

creation. The verb used in this passage is the same as the one in *Genesis* 1:
1. In other words, it restages the singularity of God's creative act.

66. Benjamin, *Selected Writings* 1, p. 294; *Gesammelte Schriften* II.1,
    p. 197.
67. Benjamin, *Selected Writings* 1, p. 307; *Gesammelte Schriften* I.1,
    p. 138.
68. For a discussion of the position of Niobe in Homer see Dean Hammer,
    'The Iliad as Ethical Thinking: Politics, Pity, and the Operation of Esteem',
    Arethusa 35.2 (Spring, 2002), pp. 203–35.
69. Benjamin, *Selected Writings* 1, p. 248; *Gesammelte Schriften* II.1, p. 197.
70. Benjamin, *Selected Writings* 1, p. 248; *Gesammelte Schriften* II.1, p. 197.
71. With regard to the question of sacrifice it is important to note here the
    argument advanced in Marc de Wilde, 'Meeting Opposites: The Political
    Theologies of Walter Benjamin and Carl Schmitt', *Philosophy and Rhetoric*
    44.2 (2011), pp. 363–81; in particular, that for Benjamin 'divine violence
    will reduce to accept the sacrifice of life itself it is enforced under the law,
    it will accept those sacrifices that originate in a responsibility before the
    law' (p. 370). Part of the argument presented in what follows resists this
    interpretation. While its detail cannot be pursued with the care it demands,
    what is raised as the overall philosophical problem here is the possibility
    of a thinking of the political that is not ground in sacrifice. What a politics
    would be like that suspends the sacrificial is the question that must continue
    to be addressed here. The distancing of 'sacrifice' is the project named by
    the *Entsetzung* and by *othering*. Benjamin's project, as being suggested, is
    non-sacrificial politics.
72. Franz Rosenzweig, *On Jewish Learning*, ed. N. N. Glatzer (Madison:
    University of Wisconsin Press, 2002), p. 83. For a more sustained account
    of this philosophical encounter see Friedman, 'Dialogue, Speech, Nature
    and Creation: Franz Rozenzweig's Critique of Buber's I and Thou', *Modern
    Judaism* 13.2 (1993), pp. 109–18; and Richard A. Cohen, *Elevations: The
    Height of the Good in Rosenzweig and Levinas* (Chicago: University of
    Chicago Press, 1994), pp. 28–39.
73. Babylonian Talmud, Tractate Baba BathraTractate Folio 74a.
74. Rosenzweig, *On Jewish Learning*, p. 80.
75. Benjamin, *Selected Writings* 1, p. 250; *Gesammelte Schriften* II.1, p. 200.
76. Benjamin, *Selected Writings* 1, p. 250; *Gesammelte Schriften* II.1, p. 200.
77. Benjamin, *Selected Writings* 1, p. 250; *Gesammelte Schriften* II.1, p. 200.
78. Benjamin, *Selected Writings* 1, p. 202; *Gesammelte Schriften* II.1, p. 173.
79. Benjamin, *Selected Writings* 1, p. 251; *Gesammelte Schriften* II.1, p. 201.
80. Benjamin, *Selected Writings* 1, p. 251; *Gesammelte Schriften* II.1, p. 201.
81. In his text on Naples, Benjamin describes porosity as the 'law of life'
    (*Gesetz dieses Lebens*) (*Selected Writings* 1, p. 417; *Gesammelte Schriften*
    IV.1, 311). This is not fate's law. It is a law whose province is defined by
    its presence as 'inexhaustible' (*unerschöpflich*) (*Selected Writings* 1, p. 417;
    Gesammelte Schriften IV.1, p. 311).
82. Benjamin, *Selected Writings* 1, p. 251; *Gesammelte Schriften* II.1, p. 202.
    In a text that has set the measure for all writing on Benjamin's *Towards
    a Critique of Violence*, Werner Hamacher has argued in relation to the
    Entsetzung that:

Deposing must be an event, but not an event whose content or object could be positively determined. It is directed against something, but also against anything that has the character of a positing, an institution, a representation, or a programme. (Hamacher, 'Afformative Strike: Benjamin's Critique of Violence', trans. Dana Hollander, in Andrew Benjamin and Peter Osborne (eds), *Walter Benjamin's Philosophy: Destruction and Experience* (London: Routledge, 1994), pp. 115–16)

The force of Hamacher's position is clear. However, what needs to be added is the recognition that, while it is true to argue that a 'depositioning' is not a counter-positing and thus it is not directed in advance, a position that recalls the absence of an already determined and directing form of 'destruction', a position staged by Benjamin in *The Destructive Character* and to which reference was made in Chapter 1, it remains the case that that 'deposition', which here is linked to law, involves a relation both to life and to the potentiality within it for the just life. It is the inscription at the heart of Benjamin's argument of an unannounced conception of value that has to be thought in terms of the relationship between depositioning and othering – a set-up that announces the co-presence of creating and inaugurating – as central to Benjamin's project. It is within the possibilities staged by that co-presence that the world might become 'slightly different'.

83. Benjamin, *Selected Writings* 1, p. 252; *Gesammelte Schriften* II.1, p. 203.

Chapter 5

Theological-Political Fragment

In the great drama of the passing way of nature,
the resurrection of nature repeats itself as an act.

Walter Benjamin

1

The title – *Theological-Political Fragment* – to the extent that titles are intended to name, will have always been a problem. Its provenance endures as a question. Nonetheless, it can still be argued that what this particular title stages is far from problematic. The title harbours a twofold demand. In the first instance it repeats the overriding claim that accompanies the project of recovery, namely that the theological has to be understood in terms of its radical differentiation from religion. In the second, there is the project of understanding the political within the space created by that separation. That space is the theological-political. The recovery of a political philosophy from Benjamin's writings occurs within that particular context. It is a context created by what could be described as the 'destruction' of religion (where the latter is understood both as a modality of time and its related subject position). Once again, it has to be noted that this possibility is not based on the rejection of religion to the extent that the latter is understood as a personal and therefore private belief. (Within the context of this argument this is the religious: the presence of a private, non-generalisable belief pertains to the religious.) Rather, for Benjamin, that destruction will stem from the 'blow' struck by theology. Moreover, it is with that destruction and thus the related distancing of religion that it becomes possible to pose the question of how a fragment that presents the theological-political is to be understood. As a form of emphatic summation, Walter Benjamin's *Theological-Political Fragment* identifies nature with the messianic. This occurs as a result of the deployed presence of a term that has already been attributed a destructive force, that is, *Glück*. This appears in the following formulation:

> The rhythm of messianic nature is happiness [*der Rhythmus der messianis-chen Natur ist Glück*]. For nature is messianic by reason of its eternal and total passing away.[1]

The interpretive question, one with its own genuine philosophical force, concerns both the comprehension as well as the consequences of this identification, a final identification that brings the fragment to an end.

Walter Benjamin's *Theological-Political Fragment* demands an opening in which its concerns can be situated.[2] Even though the actual title of the text and date of writing remain the subject of debate, what endures at the opening of the text is the figure of the Messiah. Prior then to any concern with an opening to the text itself, prior, moreover, to an engagement with the text's own complex formulations, there is this figure. The Messiah figures within Walter Benjamin's writings. Understanding that figure depends upon grasping its work. Two questions: What does the Messiah figure? What figures with the Messiah? What returns here is what was identified in the preceding chapter concerning the name 'God' (*Gott*). In that context it emerged that the 'name' cannot be separated from its presence within 'divine violence' (*die göttliche Gewalt*). In other words, *Gott* became *die göttliche Gewalt*. Therefore, it is not as though questions concerning the presence and the work of the Messiah are posed here for the first time. Nonetheless, their exigency lies as much in the figure of the Messiah as it does in attributing to that figure a specific project. As has already been intimated, the Messiah does not involve the incorporation of religion into Benjamin's concerns. Indeed, the opposite is the case. The reiteration of the 'Messiah' and the 'Messianic', both present as figures having an operative presence, always needs to be understood as marking the separation of religion and theology, a separation in which religion, through its identification with both the logic as well as the temporality of capitalism, needs to be understood as the reiteration of the always the same.[3] As has become clear, the understanding of religion in Benjamin's work has necessitated showing the way in which religion, fate and 'mythic violence' are the articulation of importantly similar positions; therefore, it has to be argued that what is essential both generally and specifically in the context of this 'Fragment' is that theology provides one of the means in terms of which to think both their cessation and the opening(s) to which such a form of destruction gives rise.[4] The double movement that is defined by the co-presence of an ending and a multitude of possible openings, in other words the co-presence of destruction and inauguration, becomes a restatement of the *caesura of allowing*. The Messiah – as a named figure within the *Theological-Political Fragment* – figures therefore as always already implicated in the process that is the *caesura of allowing*. This is the setting that opens up the Messianic.

While there are a number of different ways of establishing this position, two will be attributed centrality here. The first involves the important claim made by Benjamin in his analysis of the Baroque in *The Origin of German Tragic Drama*. The second is to be found in a line from one of the numbered paragraphs that comprise *On the Concept of History*. A line in which what is staged occurs in relation to the consequences, and they are consequences with an important generality, of the Jews having been forbidden to look into the future (in fact the interdiction pertains to having an image of the future). At work here is the interconnection of the political and a form of iconoclasm. The latter allows Benjamin to indicate the conception of the present that emerges from such a position, and it should be recalled that it is a position in relation to a future which is delimited by the possibility of its arrival. A possibility presented in terms of 'every second' being the temporal moment present as 'the small gateway, through which the Messiah might enter'.[5] Set within the context of the overall argument concerning othering, what this line locates is the potentiality that holds at every moment for what *is* to be *other than it is*. This potentiality is the possibility of the political once the latter is recast as the theological-political.

Destruction and inauguration, the movement that is the work of the figure of the Messiah, has a specific locus. Time is not a simple abstraction. The locus in question is the operation of historical time – an operation in which it then comes to be equated with either natural time, or fate or capitalism. The emergence of the theological-political has to be understood therefore as the structured presence of a politics of time. As has already been argued, what characterises each of these terms – natural time, fate, capitalism – is that they are from the start a reiteration of similar conceptions of historical time. Moreover, what defines their presence is that they do not bring with them, or at least this is the intention, their own capacity for self-transformation. The possibility of transformation is excluded from their own self-conception. Fate brooks no other. Fate, as a philosophical term and a specific register of activity, cannot be separated from the presence of historical time in which its continuity is given as inevitable. (Hence Benjamin describes capitalism, for example, as being 'a cultic religion' and that which distinguishes it as 'the permanent duration of the cult' (*die permanente*

Dauer des Kultus).[6] Moreover, what it stages is lived out. This pertains equally to fate as a descriptor as well as to what is evoked by Benjamin to account for what is at work in the operation of *Trauerspiel*.[7] Integral to the living out of what is presented as continuity's inevitability is the presence of a potentially radical division between the time in which that living occurs and the way that time is configured within the place and play of its being lived out. (The configuring is of course what establishes time as a site of contestation.) In addition, fate provides the setting in which the particularity of melancholia – where the latter is understood as a relationship between historical time and subjectivity – and its formation within *Trauerspiel* takes place. It should not be overlooked, however, that Benjamin concludes his treatment of melancholia within the context of *Trauerspiel* with an assessment of the latter in which its limit is presented. In this regard Benjamin writes that:

> The German Trauerspiel was never able to inspire itself to a new life; it was never able to awaken [*erwecken*] within itself the clear light of self-awareness [*den Silberblick der Selbstbesinnung*]. It remained astonishingly obscure to itself, and was able to portray the melancholic only in the crude and washed-out colours of the mediaeval complexion books.[8]

This passage identifies a potentiality within the Baroque. Precisely because it is only a potentiality, it could not have been realised within the framework of the Baroque. The failure to 'awaken' within itself what was already there as a potentiality marks out that which is proper to *Trauerspiel*. What this passage indicates is that *Trauerspiel* is caught within its own dream, and thus what could not emerge was the interruption that would have enabled the occurrence of another life, a life at the end of *Trauerspiel*: an afterlife. The *Trauerspiel* lacks self-inspiration and therefore self-awareness: in sum an 'awakening'. It calls out therefore for its own awakening: an awakening to its own potentiality. What this means is that *Trauerspiel* occurs within the work of fate. As such fate, and thus *Trauerspiel*, is explicable in terms of the reiteration of the temporality of myth. It becomes self-enclosed. An enclosure that is necessitated because, for Benjamin, 'there is no Baroque eschatology' (*es gibt keine barocke Eschatologie*).[9] This is the setting that demands interruption, since taken on its own terms it would then be condemned to its own repetition. Once again there is a cycle to be broken. The response to the absence of the eschatological – what in the end has to have become a putative absence – is not located in a pure externality. Rather, that which comes from without does so on the condition that there is a potentiality for transformation. In other words there has to be what can be identified as the anoriginal potentiality for othering.

Remembering that the latter is a process, and not just a pure singularity defined in terms of pure singular immediacy. The presence of a process means that what has to be at work here is what has already emerged as mediated immediacy.

What emerges as a question, therefore, is how the moment of interruption is to be understood. The first element in any answer is the attribution to the Baroque of a potentiality. While it remains the case that what was there as a possibility was unknown to the Baroque itself, and that will be true even if there were intimations of such an eventuality within Dürer's *Melancholia II*, what can be recognised retrospectively is that at every moment within the Baroque there was the potentiality for radical transformation. Even though the Baroque may not have had an eschatology in terms of its having been inscribed within its own self-conception, it remains the case for Benjamin that every moment was still charged with the possibility of its own self-overcoming. This is, of course, exactly what Benjamin means by the formulation advanced in *On the Concept of History*, namely that 'every second was the narrow gate, through which the Messiah could enter'.[10] What is clear therefore is that the Messiah is yet to arrive, and thus the Messianic endures as a potentiality.

Two elements are central here. The first is that the future does not have a predetermined image. Thus the interruption allows. It creates an opening and thus the setting for a possibility that is not determined in advance. The possibility is allowed. Its realisation entails the presence of specific forms of activity. Practices which are in accord with the allowing. The second is that while there is an interruption it is itself a possibility that was always already present. Hence, what has been identified as a *caesura of allowing* presupposes that the potentiality for such an eventuality is itself already present. It is precisely the complex relationship between potentiality, interruption and allowing that structures Benjamin's 'Fragment' while locating the Messiah within it. As the figure of the Messiah, in this context, works in relation to nature, an opening to nature needs to be identified.

2

In general terms nature would seem to have only ever been presented within a series of oppositions or divisions. The identification of nature as that which stands opposed is the result of a form of construction. For nature to be other, for nature to reappear, and thus for nature to have another possibility, such a set-up could only occur with and as the denaturing of nature. The identification of a process means that the recovery of nature needs to work through the already naturalised presence of nature. What this means is that nature would emerge through an undoing of the processing of its creation. Working through and recovering in which there is the possible presentation of another position; nature emerging through the process of its being other than that which had already been given within its own construction. That process has to be understood as the othering of nature. As has already emerged, othering is a form of overcoming. The destruction of nature allows for nature. Othering is the movement that incorporates the *caesura of allowing*. Othering as a conceptual term underscores that what is other – other in the sense that it runs counter to a historical temporality delimited by occurrences and their presence within modes of continuity – is not simply an event. Its occasion transforms and in so doing allows for the possibility of a radical revision of continuity. Othering assumes, as will be suggested, a complex relation between internality and externality as the condition of existence for any form of continuity. This is a set-up that is importantly different from the one provided by the positing of a purely external event. Complex forms of relationality preclude the structure within which an event is thought as inherently singular. At stake here is the other of nature. It will always be possible to describe the project of Walter Benjamin's *Theological-Political Fragment* as the othering of nature.

Beginning necessitates a project. Rather than define that project by its end, a start can be made here with a supposition, the continual revision of which creates the occasion for a form of development. In this context the supposition is the following: *There is a time in which history happens and thus external to that time, the time of the happening of history, there is a conception of that which is other.* Within such a setting, alterity is the staging of a form of transformation. Prior to any attempt to take up that other by naming it, or to delimit what is meant by transformation and as such to pose the inescapable question of how the relation between the continuity of the same and that which is other is to be understood, it is essential to begin to identify the structure in which alterity occurs, occurring as a potentiality. However, rather than positing what is other, as though positing established existence, transformation needs to be understood as involving a process with its own inherent sense of activity. Transformation, once it includes the interruption named as the *caesura of allowing*, of which the Messiah becomes an exemplary figure, is the process of othering.

Working with the supposition noted above is, as has been indicated, to introduce the possibility that othering pertains, in part, to what is other than the equation of history with that which happens and thus to history as the history of occurrences. Equally, the supposition opens up the possibility that othering and thus the contestation inherent to a politics of time occurs within this setting. The significant point therefore is not the juxtaposition of the temporality of historicism with that which is other, but the more complex questions of relationality and agency. The critique of historicism, historicism understood as the position in which history is equated with the continuity of occurrences, is central to the philosophical structure of modernity. As such it has become a commonplace. Moreover, it misses what is at stake within the critique. Equally, the concept of an event that introduces the possibility of a relation of non-relation, as though this obviated the need to pose the question of relationality and agency, fails to understand the complex problem posed by *othering*. Othering, once understood as a process rather than a transformative singularity defined in terms of pure externality, necessitates a return to relationality and agency.

3

The text – Benjamin's *Theological-Political Fragment* – is defined by a set of interrelated concerns that includes relationality and agency. They are deployed in order to present a number of possibilities that are the result of strategies of differentiation. Hence the text will be approached in terms of an attempt to work through what had been schematically noted above as othering and thus the form that its occurrence entails in this context. However, the setting of the text cannot be too quickly dismissed from this attempt to reconfigure what is at work within it. As a work it already involves the concerns of a complex relation to Judaism, one in which the latter gets to be reconfigured in the name of theology, where theology is understood as the cessation of religion. This connection, thus the presence of theology itself, cannot just be noted. It demands constant attention. All of these issues are posed emphatically by the text's opening lines:

> First the Messiah himself completes all historical occurrences [*alles historische Geschehen*] in the sense that he himself redeems, completes and creates its relation to the Messianic.[11]

The figure of the Messiah both ends and redeems. The Messiah creates history's relation to the Messianic. On one level this is a clear reference to a conception of *tikkun*: the breaking and restoration of the vessels.

What Benjamin may have been deploying throughout the Fragment is a conception of *tikkun* that stems from Lurianic Kabbalah and within which human agency plays a vital role in the final redemption and putting together of a broken world. In this regard, Scholem writes:

> The crucial point in the various Lurianic discussions of these developments is that although the *tikkun* of the broken vessels has almost been completed by the supernal lights and the process stemming from their activity, certain concluding actions have been reserved for man. These are the ultimate aim of creation, and the completion of *tikkun* which is synonymous with the redemption depends upon man performing them.[12]

What *tikkun* understood in this sense introduces is the role of human action within a process of redemption. However, that definition and position of human agency within redemption depends upon a conception of externality. While the Messiah may be external, there is a dependence on human activity. (The insistence of relationality as a question needs to be noted in passing here.) Moreover, externality will cause a division within the internal as the domain of human activity. In the conventional terms of religion, the distinction is between good and evil. The structure has been adopted, thus adapted, by Benjamin. What has not been included are the terms 'good' and 'evil', let alone the moral exigency linked to them. (If there is a distancing of the domain of religion from the presence of *tikkun* as it occurs as terms within Kabbalah then it will mirror the already noted problems inherent in the wholescale adoption of the conception of *tikkun olam*.[13]) As will be suggested, the division within internality is complex. On the one hand it is between the possibility of interruption and the willed continuity of the always the same. On the other it involves a conception of agency that links 'happiness' (*Glück*) to the individual and thus locates radical transformation (though only present as an unfulfillable possibility) within the life of the individual rather than within what could be described as the life of the world. The latter is of course an already present thinking of life that is no longer secured within anthropocentrism (either as an abstraction or as that which would arise from taking the lives of exemplary individuals as the locus of value). In general terms, therefore, there are two important elements here. In the first place the presence of the internal/external distinction. The second is the introduction of a founding antagonism as marking the composition of that internality.

The division between the external and the internal has clear consequences. They are introduced in the Fragment's next line, which notes that 'nothing historical can refer itself, from out of itself, to the Messianic.' From which it is then stated that the 'Kingdom of God is not the *telos* of the historical dynamic, it cannot be posited as its goal.'[14] The interpretive question here is what is meant by the term 'historical'. What the question alludes to is the inherently disjunctive relation between history as the temporality of occurrences – history as the happening of events – and that which in being external will transform internality: that is, the world. It should be noted that what this depends upon is the potentiality of the internal to be transformed. (Internality, rather than existing as consisting of elements of a similar quality, needs to be understood, as will be sketched below, in terms of a complex play of forces: the interplay of continuity and potentiality.) The presence of this potentiality, indeed its necessity, is the first element that exists within what has been described as relationality. Historical time contains a capacity for self-transformation even if that capacity remains unacknowledged. (This is, of course, precisely what occurred, for Benjamin, within the Baroque.)[15] Within such a setting it would endure as overlooked. This positioning is reinforced by the argument that what is referred to as the 'Kingdom of God' is not the *telos* of a 'historical dynamic'. That kingdom is an 'end'. What is significant here is not just the distinction between a *telos* and an 'end'. It is also the assumption that if there were a historical dynamic then it would not be teleological. The world, once reconfigured as the 'profane', contains within it the possibility for its own self-overcoming. The location of a potentiality within history and the necessity for externality both figure within the possibility of othering.

At this point in the text Benjamin introduces the 'profane', a term that demands careful attention. He writes that 'the order of the profane [*die Ordnung des Profanen*] cannot be built on the thought of the Kingdom of God'.[16] Before taking up the question of the 'profane', what needs to be noted is the nature of the distinction within which it is introduced. Benjamin distinguishes between an 'order' and a 'thought'. There is no sense of the latter's actuality. Indeed, what has actuality is the 'order of the profane'. The actuality in question is not present in terms of a pure separation. The separation and the relation have a more nuanced connection. What is actual, and here the question of recognition plays an important role within the identification of the actual, is that which will occasion its own self-transformation. Occasioning that movement is both a potentiality within the actual and equally a relation of separation to the external. There must be both.

While Benjamin writes of the 'order of the profane' as though it is to be established, nonetheless it should be understood as the world that is at hand. The separation between that world and the 'Kingdom of God' has to be understood as a refusal of the possibility that the City of God could have a determining effect on the organisation of human life, or, more accurately, on life that may always become no more than worldly, namely life condemned to its own repetition.[17] However, and this is a point of fundamental importance, that life is always positioned within a sense of continuity that is held in place by the coterminous continuity of policing. A life, in other words, that is continually subject to what he identifies as the 'order of law'. That 'order', as has become clear, is always contrasted with 'justice'.[18] There is no life other than that which would be given within this sense of subjectification. On the other side of the law, law as defined by continuity and policing, there is justice. However, it is not justice as given within a distinction between law and justice. On the contrary, the possibility of justice – understood as that which emerges with the overcoming of the continual equation of law with statute, an equation that may make a claim to justice, though it is no more than a claim and thus the justice in question would be merely putative – is there as a potentiality within life itself. Justice is there, as a potentiality, in the fabric of life. The recovery of justice needs the law's suspension. However, this is not the suspension of the regulative or even of a sense of normativity. The suspension pertains to the meld or confluence of justice with law and then law with statute. What has to be suspended is that interrelation. Its suspension, and thus that which would emerge from the process of othering, is the recovery of justice. There is therefore a pervasive sense of potentiality, a potentiality that necessitates, if not demands, a reformulation of what counts as agency. The question – one whose answer is still not present – is: what does it mean to act in the name of justice? This is the question that arises from Benjamin's text. It is, however, yet to be posed directly within it.

The interplay between two different conceptions of subjectification within the world is paralleled by the position in which continuity and potentiality are constitutive of worldly life; the use of the term 'profane' and the capacity of the Fragment to draw on the position that actions in the world, human actions, are an essential element in indicating what is at stake in the world's redemption. There is no necessity to choose between these positions. They parallel each other. The division within the world which constitutes the 'profane' is given explicit detail in Benjamin's following claim that the 'idea of happiness' should provide the basis of the 'order of the profane'. Note the term in play here is the 'profane', thus underscoring the necessity to take seriously the distinction between the 'world' and the 'profane'. A number of questions arise here. Why does Benjamin not write simply of 'happiness'? Given that what is at stake is the 'idea', what does the 'idea' mean in this context?

Rather than its being able to provide a direct answer to this question, a hint is given in Benjamin's doctoral dissertation. As part of the detailed analysis of the conception of art in the work of German Romanticism as well as in the writings of Goethe, Benjamin was concerned with what he takes the 'idea of art' to be. In this analysis the term gets to be reformulated. What emerges in the end is that the 'idea of art is the idea of form'.[19] While 'happiness' is held apart from any concern with 'art', the affinity lies in the separation of the 'idea' from simple particularity (the idea/particular relation at work in Plato) or from the possibility of its complete instantiation in a particular. Within such a setting, the 'idea of art' would come to be identified with content. The 'idea' in its identification with the idea of form refuses the possibility that the individual work could search for the form appropriate to the idea and in its search seek to realise it. The relationship between form and content is far more complex. What emerges, in contradistinction to these possibilities, is the presence of the artwork as the site in which there is forming. The art work is not the goal envisaged by the idea, and thus the work is not the idea's realisation. The process of forming – and with forming there is the presence of the work of particularity – can be thought neither in terms of a relationship between universal and particular, nor between idea and instantiation. Form as idea allows the question of forming and the identification of the particularity of the particular to arise as a question. While there is an obvious distinction between 'happiness' and 'art', it can nonetheless be argued that this is the conception of idea that is at work within 'happiness'. Relatedly, therefore, 'happiness' cannot be incorporated into forms of activity in which it is taken either as a particular instance or as a goal. As a term it is a field of activity. Thus it is not the exemplification or expression of an essential nature. What is involved in the formulation of the 'idea of happiness' needs to be pursued. Part of that undertaking necessitates taking up the question of the relationship between the Messianic and the 'order of the profane'. As the Fragment continues, the relationship between the Messianic, the profane and happiness becomes more exacting. What needs to be noted in the following is the reiteration of a language of force. (Hence the use of the term othering as that which captures force.)

The initial image used by Benjamin to develop this complex play of forces is the 'arrow'. Movement which is referred to in the text, in part, as 'striving', a term that will become decisive as the Fragment's argumentation unfolds, involves the following. There is a movement towards a specific 'goal'. It is that towards which a 'profane dynamic' moves. The object is the 'happiness seeking of a free humanity'. (And it is decisive that it is 'happiness seeking' as opposed to 'happiness'.) This movement is at the same time towards a specific goal and away from that towards which 'Messianic intensity' is directed. They run counter to each other. The 'profane' understood as a 'force', and despite its directionality, 'augments' 'the coming of the Messianic Kingdom'. The latter, the 'Messianic Kingdom' is that which is other. Its promotion, the augmentation of its arriving, occurs within the domain of the profane (it occurs within while constituting the profane as the profane). Within the profane therefore – the profane as site and thus as a place – what endures is the continual potential for it to be other. Othering is of course the relationship between externality as other and actions within the profane that run counter to the 'pursuit of happiness' but which can be defined, nonetheless, in relation to it. As such there is, as will be noted in more detail, a complex doubling of happiness. In sum, it is present as a distinction between the 'pursuit of happiness' and 'happiness'.[20] (The incorporation of both occurs within the 'idea of happiness'.) This distinction is only thinkable in terms of agency and what can be described as modalities of action. A division occurs within the latter between that which is explicable in terms of teleology and that which occurs or takes place, a happening therefore, though one which is not determined in the same way. (A happening beyond the hold of the teleological.) A position that can be reformulated in terms of a distinction between immediacy and mediacy and which will allow what emerged as central to the argumentation of *Towards a Critique of Violence*, namely mediate immediacy, to re-emerge.

4

The 'arrow' defines movement. Just as significantly, it locates the 'profane dynamic' as a search by an individual for 'happiness'. In other words, and this is the important point, the search is defined by internality. It remains internal to the profane. It therefore runs counter to the direction of Messianic intensity. And yet, precisely because with the profane there is a striving after happiness, and despite this involving both a misconception of the locus of happiness and in addition the conception of agency proper to its realisation, such an undertaking nonetheless 'promotes the coming of the Messianic Kingdom'.[21] Its impossibility augments the possibility of happiness's actuality. The next three lines of the Fragment are some of its most complex. They can be approached, initially, in terms of internal relationality. Relationality as it occurs within and as the 'profane'. Benjamin argues that the 'profane' is not a category of the 'Kingdom of God' but pertains to its approach and thus to its coming nearer. He continues: 'For in happiness all that is earthly [*alles Irdische*] seeks its downfall [*Untergang*] and only in happiness is its downfall destined to find it.'[22] What is the 'downfall' of the earthly? And who or what is 'the earthly'? Beginning to answer the second of these questions necessitates establishing a distinction between the 'profane' and the 'earthly'. Benjamin had already referred to the 'profane' as a category. As a category, what the term identifies can be reformulated in terms of the possibility of a form of transformation integrated into activity which is itself connected to the already present possibility afforded by potentiality. The 'earthly' is a term that reiterates what is elsewhere named the 'creaturely', the subject position that necessitates subjectification as that which is determined as much by fate as by law. There will be a link therefore between the 'earthly' and 'mere life'. In this context what is meant by 'downfall' (*Untergang*) is defined in relation to a specific subject position. The 'downfall' is a form of ruination which is equally a type of passage. 'Downfall' needs to be understood as the misplaced aspiration for self-overcoming. That subject 'strives' for what is taken to be an end, namely 'happiness'. The striving is therefore for a 'downfall' which is a form of overcoming. The overcoming pertains as much to the one – the 'free individual' – as it does to a generalised 'they', that is, to those who seek 'happiness'.

The 'seeking of happiness', a pursuit defined in terms of an individual aspiration, results in 'unhappiness' (*Unglück*). This is the result of the 'immediate messianic intensity'. Thereby opening up, almost as a matter of necessity, a disjunctive relation between the immediate and unhappiness, on one side, and the mediate and happiness, on the other. That both have a relation to the Messianic underscores the importance of seeing the potentiality for redemption within the striving and thus within the 'pursuit', though this is true only once it has been stripped of its relation to the earthly and thus to the immediate determinations of fate and law. Only once this has taken place is it then possible for 'happiness' to be defined in relation to a potentiality within earthly life – a life that inheres as a potentiality in the fabric of existence – rather than to the subject position that equates life with guilt and thus with fate's inexorable continuity.

Within the Fragment, the next move, the one that will presage this possibility, occurs in a return both to redemption and its opening up another nature. Nature's return occurs within and as the process of othering. The precision of Benjamin's formulation needs to be noted.

> The spiritual *restitutio in integrum*, which introduces immortality, corresponds to a worldiness that leads to an eternity of downfall, and the rhythm of this eternal passing away in its totality, in its spatial and its temporal totality, the rhythm of messianic nature, is happiness. For nature is messianic due to its eternal and total passing away.[23]

The question to be addressed initially is how the structure of correspondence within this passage is to be understood. The sense of return and recovery, a sense of movement that involves a form of completion and which is captured by the legal maxim *restitutio in integrum*, which is said to correspond to a continuity of 'downfall'. It may be that the 'spiritual *restitutio in integrum*' marks the possibility of a form of redemption that is no more than spiritual. In its worldly form what is at work is the 'eternity of downfall', which has its own specific rhythm. The rhythm is identified with nature and named as 'happiness'. While 'happiness' is a term that Benjamin uses on many occasions, the already noted formulation in *Fate and Character* remains decisive for these current concerns.

> Happiness [*Das Glück*] is what releases [*herauslöst*] the fortunate man [*den Glücklichen*] from the chains of the fates and the nets of his own fate.[24]

It should be recalled that in the line noted above the 'profane order' is erected on 'the idea of happiness'.[25] The 'profane order', therefore, an order that identifies the limit of the 'earthly', only emerges within a process of 'release', a process that works as a modality of destruction and which also can be thought in terms of the process of othering. In other words, the continuity of its own 'downfall' writes into the world what could be described as a possibility which while it can be overlooked cannot be excised, that is, the possibility for its own redemption – and thus its own being other. This is potentiality, a process whose actualisation is the movement of othering. Happiness became another name for the moment of interruption within othering. Happiness as an act, therefore, becomes the *caesura of allowing*.

Nature is not an outside that seeks expression through human action. Nature could be contrasted to the worldly. Nature is the world imbued with a capacity for transformation. And yet, it is not just imbued with it. It is possible to go further. Nature names the locus of the possibility, continual possibility, hence the eternality of 'transience'. However, what of the penultimate moment of the Fragment, the one with which a beginning was made?

> The rhythm of messianic nature is happiness. For nature is messianic by reason of its eternal and total passing away.[26]

Nature taken either as a given or as present in its opposition to culture or history is attributed the temporality of continuity and sequences. Nature becomes, *inter alia*, the locus of fate. What then occurs is that historical time then becomes naturalised. Not only is it given the temporality of sequence, it also acquires the attributes of guilt. Guilt pertains as if by nature. Standing opposed to such a conception of nature is 'messianic nature'. Nature thus construed comes to have an affinity with the conception of historical time in which human life is articulated due to the inscription within it of the interruption, endings, beginnings and the refusal of guilt. What needs to be recalled here is Benjamin's argument in his essay on Goethe's *Elective Affinities* in which 'fate' was identified with 'guilt'. His concluding position in the text is that fate 'is the nexus of guilt among the living'.[27] What is significant here is that not only is nature repositioned, it is equally the case that the opposition between natural life and human life will have been overcome in the name of 'life'. Life named here as 'the living'. The argument in the *The Task of the Translator*, as has already been noted, clarifies precisely this conception of life, by linking life to history and breaking its identification with 'mere life' (*bloßes Leben*).

> The concept of life is given its due only if everything that has a history of its own, and is not merely the setting for history, is credited with life. In the final analysis, the range of life must be determined by history rather than by nature, least of all by such tenuous factors as sensation and soul. The philosopher's task consists in comprehending all of natural life through the more encompassing life of history.[28]

Overcoming nature in the name of nature, an overcoming that allows for the interarticulation of nature, history and life, is the process that is the othering of nature. If there is an important shift in emphasis, then what occurs is that the othering of nature locates a sense of agency within human life that acts in accord with this larger sense of life. This gives rise to actions that work to redefine justice, since justice will then be linked to the 'living' rather than to human being (where the latter then becomes a simple abstraction that is able to identify life with the so-called 'sanctity of life', or human being with an ahistorical humanism). Both are positions located within the temporality of the mythic and thus their reiteration is the operative presence of 'mythic violence'. Within this context, 'happiness' becomes the counter-measure taking on the operability of 'divine violence'.

Nature is messianic once its opposition to history is overcome in the name of life. Life is not the creaturely, let alone 'mere life'. Life as it arises within the setting of the Fragment is that which emerges from the othering of life's subordination to fate and guilt. Moreover, a concern with nature is only possible once nature is won back from the settings in which it is usually presented. The recovery of nature, its return within othering, demands the interruption of the settings that held it.

An interruption that occasioned. And thus what is present here is what has already been identified as a *caesura of allowing*. Throughout the Fragment the interruption has a number of names. It is as much the Messiah as it is 'happiness'. The form of argumentation is continued in the Fragment's last line. While the messianic demands figures of interruption, it also necessitates action. The actions that are necessary are identified here as a form of 'striving' that, in refusing the agency of the individual, the sense of agency that locates happiness as the subject of a search, comes to be renamed as politics. Moreover, *othering*, if it can be identified with the process of 'striving', is not simply identified with politics, it becomes more emphatically its 'task' (*Aufgabe*). The 'method' for such a project, the project in which nature both figures and is able to be reconfigured, is not determined in advance. And yet, what is there in advance of any action is the possibility for self-transformation. Potentiality permits a transformative relationship between internality and externality. Another way of naming that dynamic set of relations would be 'messianic nature'.

Notes

1. *Selected Writings* 3, p. 305; *Gesammelte Schriften* II.1, p. 203. The problem of translating *Glück* remains. What the term stages can be discerned from the detail of the discussion that has occurred in earlier chapters. In this context, if only for it to coincide with the established translations, it has been rendered consistently by 'happiness'.
2. There are a great many commentaries on Benjamin's text. One of the most useful, and in terms of the analysis presented here one of the most influential, both for its analysis as well as its provision of the context in which Benjamin's writing of the text occurs, is Eric Jacobsen, *Metaphysics of the Profane: The Political Theology of Walter Benjamin and Gershom Scholem* (New York: Columbia University Press, 2003). See in addition, Werner Hamacher, 'Das Theologisch-politische Fragment', in Burkhardt Linder (ed.), *Benjamin Handbuch* (Stuttgart: J. B. Metzler, 2011), pp. 175–92. While a beginning is made with the text's final moment, this chapter can be read as a line-by-line commentary on the Fragment itself. At all moments what is central is the Messiah as a figure of destruction, which is integral to the recovery of a Benjaminian political philosophy. A political philosophy that enacts a very specific sense of the theological-political.
3. Recalled here is the position developed in *Capitalism as Religion*, in *Selected Writings* 1, pp. 288–91; *Gesammelte Schriften* VI.1, pp. 100–3. Indeed, it is possible to go further and note that for Benjamin capitalism has developed as 'parasitic' upon Christianity. To which Benjamin adds: 'Christianity's history is essentially that of its parasite – that is to say, of capitalism' (*Selected Writings* 1, p. 289; *Gesammelte Schriften* VI.1, p. 102).

4. Benjamin, *Selected Writings* 1, pp. 236–52; *Gesammelte Schriften* II, pp. 179–203). The project of 'destruction' (*Vernichtung*) in *Towards a Critique of Violence* becomes the 'task' in relation to the possible cessation of mythic violence (*Selected Writings* 1, p. 249; *Gesammelte Schriften* II.1, p. 199). This position has of course already been discussed in considerable detail in the previous chapter.

5. Benjamin, *Selected Writings* 4, p. 397; *Gesammelte Schriften* I.1, p. 102. This 'gate' – an image of which is there in Domenico di Michelino's portrait of Dante – will be taken up in greater detail in Chapter 6.

6. Benjamin, *Selected Writings* 1, p. 288; *Gesammelte Schriften* VI.1, p. 100. There needs to be a link drawn here to Benjamin's own engagement with Bergson. Benjamin takes up Bergson at a number of definitive moments. Two are worth noting in this context. The first occurs in *On Some Motifs in Baudelaire* (*Selected Writings* 4, p. 315; *Gesammelte Schriften* I.2). The second takes place in *The Arcades Project*, pp. 205–6; *Gesammelte Schriften* V.1, p. 272. The significant element in both is that Bergson is not a thinker of destruction. As such he becomes a thinker of acquiescence. It is in this regard that Benjamin notes in *On Some Motifs in Baudelaire* that Bergson 'leads us to believe that turning to the contemplative realisation of the stream of life is a matter of free choice' (*Selected Writings* 4, p. 315; *Gesammelte Schriften* I.2, p. 609). What is unavailable to a Bergsonian conception of time is the possibility of the actual impermanence of what appears permanent. The latter is enforced and hence the former has to be enacted. Choice as 'free' – and here freedom is no more than appearance – is premised on the effacing of the necessity of the link between inauguration and destruction. Hence it is a politics that is premised on effacing the very condition of the political.

7. I have developed a detailed analysis of the temporality of *Trauerspiel* in 'Benjamin and the Baroque: Posing the Question of Historical Time'; see Appendix B.

8. Benjamin, *The Origin of German Tragic Drama*, p. 158; *Gesammelte Schriften* I.1, p. 335

9. Benjamin, *The Origin of German Tragic Drama*, p. 66; *Gesammelte Schriften* I.1, p. 246.

10. Benjamin, *Selected Writings* 4, p. 397; *Gesammelte Schriften* I.1, p. 102.

11. Benjamin, *Selected Writings* 3, p. 305; *Gesammelte Schriften* II.1, p. 203.

12. Scholem, Gershom, *Kabbalah* (Jerusalem: Keter Publishing House, 1974), p. 142.

13. See the discussion of *tikkun olam* in Chapter 3.

14. Benjamin, *Selected Writings* 3, p. 305; *Gesammelte Schriften* II.1, p. 203.

15. The clear implication within both the study of the Baroque and those studies that define the 'present' as though the latter had the status of the given – a status in which the empirical takes on the quality of the immutable! – is that, despite the specificity of each, both remain caught within a setting in which the capacity for radical self-transformation is resisted on an ongoing basis. This accounts for the need for 'destruction'.

16. Benjamin, *Selected Writings* 3, p. 305; *Gesammelte Schriften* II.1, p. 203.

17. This is the point that has already been noted in relation to Benjamin's use of the 'the moral world order' in *Fate and Character*. That 'order' which

can be understood in the terms set by religion – i.e. in the writings of both Augustine and Aquinas and thus a setting that repositions utopian visions of the city as an inherent part of the theory of religion – is distanced here with this reworking of the 'profane'.

18. It is clear that what is recalled here is the distinction developed in *Fate and Character* between 'the order of law' and 'justice'.
19. Benjamin, *Selected Writings* 1, p. 183; *Gesammelte Schriften* I, p. 117.
20. A point also noted by Jacobsen in his commentary on the fragment. Jacobsen, *Metaphysics of the Profane*, p. 32.
21. Benjamin, *Selected Writings* 3, p. 305; *Gesammelte Schriften* II.1, p. 203.
22. Benjamin, *Selected Writings* 3, p. 306; *Gesammelte Schriften* II.1, p. 204.
23. Benjamin, *Selected Writings* 3, pp. 305–6; *Gesammelte Schriften* II.1, p. 204.
24. Benjamin, *Selected Writings* 1, p. 203; *Gesammelte Schriften* II.1, p. 174.
25. Benjamin, *Selected Writings* 3, p. 305; *Gesammelte Schriften* II.1, p. 203.
26. Benjamin, *Selected Writings* 3, p. 306; *Gesammelte Schriften* II.1, p. 204.
27. Benjamin, *Selected Writings* 1, p. 307; *Gesammelte Schriften* I.1, p. 138.
28. Benjamin, *Selected Writings* 1, p. 254; *Gesammelte Schriften* IV.1, p. 11.

Chapter 6

On the Concept of History

It is characteristic of philosophical writing that it must
continually confront the question of representation

Walter Benjamin

Even if it were possible to claim that Benjamin's *On the Concept of
History* is simply a text to be read and understood, it will still be the
case that it is a text whose presence will have complicated the demands
of most strategies positioned within theories of reading.[1] Hence the
question: what is it to read a disjointed text? For some, in attempting to
answer that question the usual equivocations about Benjamin's relation
to philosophy will be raised. As though there was an already determined
sense of what comprised philosophy's presentation. Benjamin's texts
present – for philosophy, from within philosophy – a set of problems
similar to those that arise from engagements with texts as divergent as
Heraclitus' 'Fragments' and Pascal's *Pensées*.[2] In addition to its relation
to the history of fragmented texts, it is also true to argue that the structure of *On the Concept of History* registers an important formal as well
as ideational relation to the 'complete' *One-Way Street*.

The text – *On the Concept of History* – consists of a number of
'fragments'. There are different versions of the text. Indeed, there is a
version that Benjamin wrote in French and which exhibits minor though
important differences from the German.[3] Each of the fragments of
which the overall text is comprised is either numbered or identified by
letters. Nonetheless, despite this attempted ordering, it is still not possible to read *On the Concept of History* as a simple sequence. In other
words, the fragments cannot be read as though they staged a progressive
or teleological development. They are not present as if they moved from
beginning to end. If there is a concern that brings them together, then in
this context it can be located in the way the fragments both recall and
develop some of the dominant themes that are already at work in the

texts that have already been subject to differing forms of analysis in the preceding chapters. What continues to guide the approach to Benjamin taken here can be located in the projected recovery of a more generalisable philosophical undertaking. What is recovered will continue to be defined by the way the relationship between destruction and value serves as the basis of a political philosophy, where the latter will continue to be recast as the theological-political. Emphasis needs to be placed, therefore, on those elements of the text that contribute to the recovery of a political philosophy. Present in the fragments, presented by them, is therefore a philosophical position with this precise inflection.

Even accepting the already present philosophical status of this work, caution is still needed. The desire for simplistic forms of summation continues. Avoiding that trap here means that writing on the fragments that comprise *On the Concept of History* will not involve an attempt to synthesise their project. The fragments will be allowed to supplement each other. Consequently, while a number of the fragments will be taken in turn, two groups of fragments – that is, X–XIII and XIV–XVI, A – evince a strong sense of unity and as such will be addressed together. Finally, a number of fragments will only be noted in passing.[4] What matters at each and every moment, as stated above, is the fragments' place within the project of recovering a political philosophy from Benjamin's work. The fragments continue to be at work. Hence Benjamin's *On the Concept of History* has an afterlife. As a result the text brings its own sense of inexhaustibility into play.[5] Part of that inexhaustibility is the limitation of each fragment. They are delimited by endlessness, which their form stages but which their content does not seek to enact. As fragments they may attract the encyclopaedic impulse, but this only occurs because of the inherent impossibility of presenting it. This poses the curious strategic question of what counts as an adequate encounter with each fragment, particularly because all such encounters cannot be grouped under the heading of a general account of adequation. What would a tradition that defined truth in terms of *adequatio rei et intellectus* demand of writing on fragments? When to stop writing on each fragment is therefore a genuine question.

I

The first fragment begins as though it is telling a story, one that will go on to stage a type of analogy.[6] The analogy is set up in terms of an 'automaton' or a 'puppet' that plays chess. The latter should always win at chess. Benjamin is explicit: 'The puppet . . . ought to win all the time' (*Gewinnen soll immer die Puppe*). As the fragment progresses, this 'puppet' is provided with another name. However, that renaming will have to wait. Rather, what should be noted at this stage is that the introduction of the problematic of 'winning' opens a set of concerns that continues throughout the fragments as a whole. Within the game of chess, every move made by the automaton (equally a puppet) is not just a simple response; these moves also take the form of what is described more generally as a 'counter-move' (*Gegenzug*). The latter – these counter-moves – will be understood in this context in terms of the already developed notion of the *counter-measure*. What needs to be noted in addition is that the response that constructs the 'counter-move' looks as though it is structured in the same way as the initial move. While accepting the same rules, it looks as if what is being played out is what those rules will have already dictated. It would be as though nothing else is in play. However, the 'automaton' was being directed by a chess master – one that could not be seen. The chess master is hidden. In addition, were it not for its hidden presence then victory would have been either impossible or simply serendipitous. At this stage in the fragment's development Benjamin adds that there is a 'philosophical counterpart' to this position.

Two points need to be noted here. The first is that what Benjamin claims to be developing is a philosophical position. In other words, he locates and defines his position as philosophical: a philosophical presentation as the counter-move. The second is that the position developed by Benjamin concerns both the nature and the structure of this counter-move. Essential to the project is, therefore, both its operability and what enables that move to be possible. This will involve naming the 'puppet'. The 'counter-move', repositioned as the *counter-measure*, is neither spontaneous nor is it merely calculated. The renamed 'puppet', now present as 'historical materialism', cannot win on its own. In this regard Benjamin's position is once again clear. What is needed is what will make the *counter-measure* possible. It has conditions of possibility. The last lines of the fragment bring all the elements noted above into play.

> One can imagine a philosophic counterpart to this apparatus. The puppet, called 'historical materialism,' is to win all the time. It can easily be a match for anyone if it enlists the services of theology, which today, as we know, is small and ugly and has to be kept out of sight.

'Historical materialism' would not just seem to need theology in order to win. Theology grounds the effective nature of the *counter-measure*. The presence of that measure is secured through the work of that particular addition. This is a positioning that will allow the 'Messiah' to take on the quality of a 'victor' (*Überwinder*). The victor is the 'winner'. At this point, however, the interpretive question concerns what is at stake in the claim that links theology to winning, a link in which the former is the precondition for the latter. Any attempt to answer the question – what would it mean for 'historical materialism' to call on the service of 'theology'? – has to begin with the way theology and religion have been both disassociated and connected throughout the preceding chapters. As such, it is here that the force of this distinction between religion and theology has to be assumed as the point of departure. It should not be forgotten that in *The Arcades Project* Benjamin provides his own formulation of the relationship between theology and what he identifies as his 'thinking':

> My thinking [*Mein Denken*] is related to theology as blotting pad is related to ink. It is saturated with it. Were one to go by the blotter, however, nothing of what is written would remain.[7]

Theology, however, has more than mere presence. Theology becomes the theological-political as a result of having effected a constitutive separation from religion. The question to be addressed is the meaning of 'theology' within the context of this fragment, namely theology as the result of that separation. What 'theology' names is of course that which already plays the decisive role in the 'depositioning' of fate, law and the temporality within which they are articulated. Theology therefore is a term that identifies a position within a politics of time. However, here 'theology' is present as that which is necessary were 'historical materialism' to 'win'. What has to be taken up, therefore, is the necessity of that relationship. How is theology's necessity to be understood? Again: what is it that is necessary here? Necessity involves a relation. Theology, as the term has been used in the preceding chapters, came to be identified with 'divine violence'. To the extent that *Gewalt* is taken to be operable, then 'divine violence' names a specific modality of *Gewalt*. As such, the only relation that theology has to religion is marked by the process of the latter's 'depositioning' to the extent that religion is understood as a modality of time with its own attendant subject position. Theology becomes the theological-political which is then repositioned in terms of the operability of 'divine violence'. The relation to 'historical materialism' links what a politics of time demands, namely its incorporation into the domain of the practical. 'Historical materialism' names the incorporation of the theological-political into the domain of action, yielding actions that stage the already present relation between destruction and value. Historical materialism allows the theological to be determined by ends that are themselves determined by actuality (actual concerns determined by identifiable concerns). Those ends, however, need to stand in relation to the 'pure'. That standing is the way in which the pure is maintained in relation to enactment.

II

Introduced in Fragment II, though as will be noted this introduction is a type of reintroduction, is the central figure of 'happiness' (*Glück*). It is now expressed in terms of 'the image of happiness' (*das Bild von Glück*). What does it mean to write of the 'the image of happiness'? As a beginning, the question that has to be addressed from the start concerns how this form of the 'image' is to be understood. As will be noted in relation to Fragment V, for Benjamin there are different modalities of the image, modalities that incorporate the differences that yield what he will describe as the 'true image' as opposed to 'historicism's image'. Here the suggestion is going to be that the conception of the image that is at stake in this specific context can best be explicated in terms of the way that Benjamin distinguishes between the image within painting and the cinematic image – the question of the viability of the distinction within the strict terms within which it is presented will be left to one side.[8] Of importance here is how the distinction is thought. Essential, therefore, to understanding the 'image' is how the differences between these two senses of image are to be maintained and developed. What is significant is that, for Benjamin, after cinema – that is, since the production of images in the 'era of mechanical reproducibility' – there is another conception of the image. Benjamin writes of the latter that it 'is piecemeal, its manifold parts being assembled according to a new law [*nach einem neuen Gesetze*].'[9] In other words, there is an important connection here between this conception of the image and Benjamin's concern with the disruption and the disruptive force of allegory. The introduction of a 'new law', and it should be noted that law is retained within its own self-transformation, needs to be understood as the othering of the image. (The prompt occasioning it here is a shift in the image's production.)

It should be added that, as Benjamin makes clear, this 'image' could not be thought outside its relation to differing determinations of time: both the time that is given and the conception of time that brings with it the possibility that what is could have been other. Within the framework of Fragment II this is the time of the present. There could have been other events. This concession is the direct recognition that there remain other possibilities. A position captured in the claim that 'the idea of happiness is indissolubly bound up with the idea of redemption'. Despite the unrelenting nature of time's passing, the passing of time which needs to be equated here with the naturalisation of the work of time within historicism, time is not so determined that it has to preclude, by definition, that which could have been other. While it may not have been named, what is central is the always present possibility of what has already been referred to as othering. It is precisely that possibility, the possibility of othering – though in the context of this fragment it now needs it be understood as a type of potentiality – which means that the quality of the future need not have been determined by the past if the past is understood as an inexorable sequence. Hence Benjamin writes in this regard that 'the past carries with it a secret index by which it is referred to redemption.' The question is of course what this 'secret index' takes as its referent. The question demanding an answer hinges on the 'secret' and what a secret actually involves. Remembering, of course, that the term 'secret' recurs at a number of important moments in this set of fragments.

The fragment evokes a link to the 'past'. And yet, there is still some distance to be covered in order to understand what is meant by the 'past' once the time of sequential development is put to one side. This link involves what is described as 'a secret agreement between genera-tions'. Again, the language of the 'secret' is fundamental here. What is at work is not at hand. As a way of explaining that 'secret' there is the famous if nonetheless enigmatic claim that, 'like every generation that preceded us, we have been endowed with a *weak* messianic power, a power on which the past has a claim.' That past, as he writes, has a 'claim' on this 'weak messianic power'. What this means is that the past only has a future if the future is understood in terms of both the mes-sianic and redemption in the context of the fragment means that 'power' is bound up with a form of discontinuous presence with (and within) the present. The possibility of that discontinuity has to be there with the 'past'. (This should be read almost as an ontological claim about time, i.e. that time brings with it its own potential for discontinuous relations. Again the relationship between potentiality and 'weakness' needs to be noted.) The reference to 'redemption' and the connection to modes of time are best understood as a reiteration of the two modes of time that have already been noted in *Fate and Character*. In that context he wrote that:

> The guilt context is temporal in a totally inauthentic way [*ganz uneigentlich zeitlich*], very different in kind and measure from the time of redemption [*der Zeit der Erlösung*], or of music, or of truth.[10]

What is brought into play by the passage from *Fate and Character* is a series of connections in which time takes on a quality allowing it to have a mode of authenticity. Hence the additional claim that the 'historical materialist' is aware of divisions and connections within time. Divisions, as has been said, bring the language of authenticity into play. Authenticity is of course tied to a particular modality of time. Moreover, it is in terms of this conception of authenticity that the temporality of 'fate' – and thus the associated subject position, one constructed by the posited presence of an original form of guilt – then comes to be understood as inauthentic.

What remains complex is the formulation pertaining to the 'weak messianic power'. The language of weakness needs to be linked in part to the presence of the 'secret'. Its 'weakness' lies in the nature of its actuality, and then both in the fact of its not being present as well in the related sense of its contingency. Weakness therefore has a twofold designation. It names both the presence of potentiality rather than the immediacy of actuality as well as the recognition that actualisations involve activity. The presence of the need for activity links the messianic to an inescapable 'weakness'. Weakness therefore names the interplay of finitude and contingency. The evocation of the 'past' in the confines of the fragment – though the past still has a problematic presence – begins to link potentiality to a complex relation between the past and the present. The 'past', as the term is deployed here, identifies that which gives the present its quality of having the possibility to be other. And yet it cannot be the past within historicism. The question of what can be described as the *pastness* of the past has therefore even greater acuity. Part of what is at stake here concerns the 'image'. What continues as a demanding question is what an 'image of happiness' would look like. Or more exactly, there is the question of how an image that corresponded to the authentic within time would appear. Part of the answer resides in Benjamin's citation of Hofmannsthal and the comment that he then makes on it.

'Read what was never written' runs a line from Hofmannsthal. The reader one would think of here is the true historian [*der wahre Historiker*].[11]

In other words, rather than taking that which is at hand – the already given – as setting the measure, there needs to be a form of construction. That construction has to be thought as an inauguration premised on destruction. In other words, on a generalised level it is that which occurs with (and as) the *caesura of allowing*. Equally, its presence can be described – and here there is a reversion to particularity – as a form of 'translation'. 'Reading', as it appears here in this passage, has to be an act of creation in which what is created is the event to be read. As an act of creation it can be neither mere repetition nor posited invention. Hence the necessity to hold to modes of reference that have to be thought within a structure of indetermination.

At this point, however, a return needs to be made to the 'secret' – where the 'secret' is both a word and also the staging of a specific problem within the domain of presentation and appearance. In other words, the presence of the 'secret' is not a term staged within concerns delimited purely by meaning. The 'secret' is a form of presence. Hence the question: what is the presentation of a secret? The line in which the 'secret' occurs should be recalled again: 'The past carries with it a secret index by which it is referred to redemption.' The 'index' is known as a secret, though more accurately is known to be a secret. Here the secret resists that relation to knowledge in which knowledge would have to be defined as the uncovering of the secret's secret. (Recalled here is the identification of the 'veil' in his work on Goethe, in which he writes that the 'task of art criticism' is 'not to lift the veil' but the constitution of the veil as an object of knowledge.[12]) Here, the 'secret' as known is that which is remembered. This will be the possibility that will come to be announced in Fragment B in which the experience of the past occurs 'in remembrance' (*im Eingedenken*). Remembering takes the place of knowing. However, what is remembered – thus the project of remembrance – is not linked to the lost. Remembrance works against the lost in the name of a specific form of recovery. Remembrance unsettles. It breaks the links that hold that which was past as the past and which would demand reciprocally that the remembered be understood in terms of that pastness. As a result of this transformation of remembering, 'remembrance', as it figures here, becomes a form of destruction. And thus it instantiates a modality of destruction – remembering breaks links – and thus it becomes an instance of one of the dominant motifs of destruction both within Benjamin's overall project as well as in this text in particular.

Remembering is integral to the staging of the secret. It is precisely because the secret is not resolved that it has an additional power. The reference to a 'secret index' within the past can be understood therefore as a reference to the past having that capacity for remembrance in which the process of remembrance – remembrance as act – has to be thought in terms of an act of destruction and thus an allowing. Remembrance therefore is another name for the *caesura of allowing*, and thus is there as a destructive act because it breaks open the interarticulation of remembering, the past and temporal continuity. As a result it undoes the hold of a historicist conception of time. The power that enables this to take place is the power referred to in the text in terms of a 'generation' being endowed with a '*weak* messianic power' (*eine schwache messianische Kraft*). Every 'generation' is the same. Every generation will have had this 'power'. The project of the present is to actualise it. The other project, the project defined by fate and held in place by, for example, 'law-preserving violence' is, of course, to maintain the present as it is. The co-presence of these two possibilities is the politics of time.

It is possible to take this analysis of the implications of the secret a stage further and argue that, to the extent that remembrance becomes a form of transmission, its precondition is the endurance of the secret as the secret. Hence the reference to 'redemption' must be secret. Were this not to be the case then the secret would have been given up in its transmission. The afterlife of the past therefore takes the retention of the secret as its condition of possibility. It would be these conditions – as will be noted – that would be undone if the Rankean conception of history were maintained – a conception announced in the opening of Fragment VI in terms of the presentation of the past in terms of 'the way it authentically (or really) was' (*wie es denn eigentlich gewesen ist*). What comes to be repeated throughout the fragments that comprise *On the Concept of History* is a concern with what the 'authentic' (*eigentlich*) image of the past actually is. Where what 'it' is, is not 'it' as it appears. Hence what is at stake are questions that take as a central concern what the 'authentic' actually is and thus what an actualisation of the 'authentic' entails. It should be noted, if only in passing, that the 'image' (*Bild*) cannot be thought independently of the conception of time in which it is articulated. It is not the case that images are timed directly, though it will always be possible to account for the way an image qua image engages with the question of time, even though it will of course only ever be image*s* and time*s*. It is rather that there is a foundational relation between modalities of image and modalities of historical time. And here the sense of disjunctive plurality also works in the other direction, such that there are also differing modalities of the image. In both instances the already present relation between images and time is constitutive of the nature of the image. Opened as a domain of investigation, even if left unresolved within the strict confines of the fragment, it nevertheless remains a domain that has been staged in relation to the image. The image, which in turn is grounded by the question of the connection between, in the first instance, what has already been identified in terms of the organisational logic of an image and, in the second, the temporal register that image's 'law' deploys and demands.[13]

III

The 'chronicler' (*Der Chronist*), Benjamin writes, narrates the 'all', and in so doing does not distinguish between 'small' and 'large' events. Nonetheless, there is in the realisation of that project, a project which because of its commitment to the 'all' ignores the quality of the events, a residual truth, namely that 'nothing that has even been an event should be regarded as lost to history'.[14] The 'chronicler' does not understand what could be described as the quality of events, and thus the possibility of events having fundamentally different modes of being, yet even without this capacity for discrimination and evaluation it can still be argued that the 'chronicler' has acted in an exemplary way. There will not have been an event that could have been lost. This is the setting in which Benjamin makes a fundamentally important addition; it is an addition that has a significant impact on the subject/object relation within acts of both interpretation and understanding. He adds:

> Of course only a redeemed mankind [*der erlösten Menschenheit*] is granted the fullness of its past – which is to say, only for a redeemed mankind has its past become citable in all its moments.

The introduction of the expression 'redeemed mankind' introduces both a significant complication and a way forward. The complexity is that the expression 'redeemed mankind' would seem to involve a conception of agency that is linked to a form of totality. However, to insist on the presence of a potential totality would miss the central point. Centrality pertains to the potentiality and not the totality. As a consequence, the most instructive way of understanding this formulation is in terms of the possibility of there being a future. The future and its concerns must cede their place to the future's possibility. Potentiality has to be the point of orientation given the non-necessary actualisation of a conception of the future defined by othering. Actualisation is marked by contingency; hence the 'weak' messianic power. What is directly significant in the fragment itself is the way that it connects 'redemption' to the future of the past. That 'fullness' is not plenitude without value. Indeed it is the opposite. It is what will allow distinctions within history to emerge. This creates the setting in which to give the last two lines of the fragment the close attention they demand.

> Each moment it has lived becomes a *citation à l'ordre du jour*. And that day is Judgement Day.

What is involved here is 'redeemed mankind', that is, the conception of human being that lives in relation to what has already been identified as the 'not-yet-attained condition of the just man'.[15] Whether this means that justice is at hand or that there is the recognition of this as an actual potentiality – that is, one that arises as a consequence of the *caesura of allowing* and thus which will come to be a possibility – remains an open question. This is the continual tension within an expression such as a 'redeemed mankind'. What needs to be noted, however, is that what is being claimed is that justice is a possibility. Furthermore, it is now possible to understand that justice is not to be identified as following the law or even obeying the law. As should have already become clear, from a Benjaminian perspective justice would not be a concern with the police but with the interarticulated presence of justice and life. Given the necessity for this as the locus that brings justice and life into relation, what this opens up is the position that has already been noted, namely the possibility of both a critique of law in the name of justice – where justice cannot be disassociated from life, this is after all the project of *Towards a Critique of Violence* – and, more significantly, the possibility of a conception of law that took the actuality of justice as its point of departure. It should be added straightway that this would be a radically different conception of justice. It would be the othering of justice. The latter is the position that has already been formulated in terms of a critique of law in the name of law.

The possibility of a 'redeemed mankind' takes the presence of 'food and clothing', where both can be taken as signs of the just life as that which preceded whatever it is that may occur with the Last Judgement. At the beginning of Fragment IV Benjamin cites Hegel to further the position that the 'granting' of the 'Kingdom of God' presupposes the presence of the just life. Hence, a 'redeemed mankind', the subject position that is demanded by the just life, is 'granted' – and the similarity of expression in the passage from Hegel and Benjamin's own formulation in Fragment III needs to be noted here – the 'fullness of the past'. In other words, the past is no longer simply the past. Rather, it has become a past with a sense of actuality that depends upon processes of destruction that have as much a political force as they orientate the practices of the historian.

IV

Fragment IV opens with the evocation of 'class struggle' (*der Klassenkampf*). What is announced by 'class struggle' names a specific form taken by what can more generally be understood as the pervasive 'disequilibria of power'. That much is clear. Equally, there is the definition of the struggle as driven by the need to obtain what is necessary for life. (Again there will be the interarticulation of 'historical materialism' and theology.) After which there is the presence of that which is named in the fragment as the 'refined' or the 'spiritual'.[16] The formulations of the way they are present is of fundamental importance here. Benjamin adds:

> These latter things, which are present in class struggle, are not present as a vision of spoils that fall to the victor. They are alive in this struggle as confidence, courage, humor, cunning, and fortitude, and have effects that reach far back into the past.

What needs to be noted here is the absence or refusal to see the 'struggle' in terms of a relationship between means and ends. (The project of the undoing of the effective presence of the opposition between means/ends which characterised the project of *Towards a Critique of Violence* is recapitulated in this statement.) It is taken a step further by the refusal to see what would count as victory as the obtaining of a state of affairs that did not in some sense already exist. However, the already present – here 'confidence, courage, humor, cunning, and fortitude' – are not there as a form of naturalised continuity. On the contrary, they are present as the unnamed and thus as the marginal. Part of the point here is that undoing the history of the victors and thereby interrupting the history that occurs within the temporality of fate reveals forms of continuity that may have been there within 'confidence, courage, humor, cunning, and fortitude'. Another history, if only ever as a possibility, was harboured within what was already taking place. This is why Benjamin can add that 'they constantly call into question every victory, past and present, of the rulers.' They do so by introducing another history. This other history will be one that depends upon the undoing of the normalisation or naturalisation of a conception of time that would have excluded what terms such as 'confidence, courage, humor, cunning, and fortitude' actually name. It would be a subterranean history, a history written within a shift in orientation. It would be the history – to recall Benjamin's discussion with Bloch – of that which was always the same, even though it has become unmistakably 'a little bit different'. This accounts for how the historian may be 'the herald who invites the separated [*die Abgeschiedenen*] to the table'.[17]

It should be added here that in *Towards a Critique of Violence* Benjamin identified a similar range of affective states that allowed for forms of relationality but did so outside the law. It is important to recognise that the introduction of 'confidence, courage, humor, cunning, and fortitude' needs to be understood as the identification of modes of relationality that do not depend upon the law. These modes have a history that is different from the history of the law. Indeed, their history – perhaps a history of emotions or affects – would be the counter-possibility to a history that took both law and fate as the necessary centre of all history. What is important therefore is that 'what has been' does not become historical through the assumption of the past as historical in virtue of its having occurred. Rather there is a dynamic process in which what has been 'strives' to be remembered. A striving in which what is remembered is othered in the process of its coming to be remembered.

V

In Fragment V the 'image' returns. Now, however, it is no longer defined in terms of an abstraction in which the image is merely that which is given to be seen. The image has to come to be seen. It is only in terms of the latter that it is possible to identify what is described as 'the true image' (*das wahre Bild*). The Fragment as a whole sets this constellation of concerns in play.

> The true image [*Das wahre Bild*] of the past flits by. The past can be seized only as an image that flashes up at the moment of its recognisability [*Erkennbarkeit*], and is never seen again – 'The truth will not run away from us': this statement by Gottfried Keller indicates exactly that point in historicism's image of history where the image is pierced [*durchschlagen*] by historical materialism. For it is an irretrievable image of the past [*ein wiederbringliches Bild der Vergangenheit*] which threatens to disappear in any present that does not recognise itself as intended in that image.[18]

In the French version of the fragment – a version in which there are a number of differences of formulation – the fragment ends with a complex addition. The last line of the French version with the addition reads as follows:

> *C'est une image unique, irremplaçable du passé qui s'évanouit avec chaque présent qui n'a pas su se reconnaître visé par elle.*
>
> # *Il s'appuie bien plutôt sur le vers du Dante qui dit . . .*[19]

The reference to Dante appears in Benjamin's own hand. Not only is it hard to know what it is that is based on a verse of Dante, it is even more difficult identifying the verse to which he is referring. Before turning to the additional lines that appear in the French version – lines that refer to Dante without stating the actual reference – it is essential to take the formulation within the fragment which, it could be argued, defines the fragment's own project. Namely, the project that resides in the claim that the 'image' can only be seized 'as an image' 'at the moment of its recognisability' (*im Augenblick seiner Erkennbarkeit*). The term 'recognisability' (*Erkennbarkeit*) plays an important role in Benjamin's work.[20] What is important in this instance, however, is that the 'recognisability' occurs as a 'moment'. A moment in which what may have never returned (or may have been lost) is present. However, the return in question is not the image's continual or eternal recurrence. Rather, the image's presence is a result of the 'blow' struck in the name of 'historical materialism'. (Here is of course the return of the 'left-handed blow'.) 'Recognisability' has a twofold quality. In the first instance 'recognisability' involves seeing within destruction. In the second seeing is also a form of destruction. Hence the presence of a link that connects recognising and remembering, insofar as both can be understood as modalities of destruction. There is a sense of the 'now' captured in the force of the 'moment' that positions 'recognisability'. This 'moment' is of fundamental importance. Its presence and thus the presence it stages are to be contrasted with both 'myth' and 'eternal recurrence'. Hence Benjamin's remarkable formulation in New Theses C:

> The basic conception in myth is a world of punishment [*die Welt als Strafe*] – punishment which actually engenders those to whom punishment is due. Eternal recurrence [*Die ewige Wiederkehr*] is the punishment of being held back at school projected in the cosmic sphere: humanity has to copy out its text in endless repetitions [*in unzähligen Wiederholungen*].[21]

Myth, as both a modality of time and the creation of subject positions – the positioned subject as originally guilty – is a setting whose truth is revealed and whose insistence is undone in this 'moment'. At work here is an undoing of a set of power relations whose positioned presence is deposed through the recognition – a recognition afforded by the moment of 'recognisability' in which it is 'seen' that these relations are not natural and thus not naturally enduring.

The retrieval of the 'true image', a term that in the French version comes to be named *une image unique*, involves a relationship between the present and the past. Moreover, that image is given the temporality of the moment. In *The Divine Comedy*, specifically in *Paradiso* Canto XXVIII, 1–19, Dante wrote of the relationship between an image defined in relation to truth and its presentation in terms of the intensity of the moment. After the extraordinary description of Beatrice as the one who *imparadisa la mia mente* ('imparadised my soul'), truth begins to take hold. The verses stage a relationship between the intensity of light, time and a form of recognition.

> When she who makes my mind imparadised
> Had told me of the truth that goes against
> The present life of miserable mortals –
>
> As someone who can notice in a mirror
> A candle's flame when it is lit behind him
> Before he has a sight or thought of it,
>
> And turns around to see if what the mirror
> Tells him is true, and sees that it agrees
> With it as notes with their measure –
>
> Even so I acted, as I well remember,
> While gazing into the bright eyes of beauty
> With which Love wove the cord to capture me.
>
> And when I turned, my eyes were greeted with
> What shines within that whirling sphere whenever
> Someone intently stares into its spiral:
>
> I saw a Point that radiated light
> So sharply that the eyelids which it flares on
> Must close because of its intensity.
>
> Whatever star looks smallest from the earth
> Would look more like a moon if placed beside it,
> As star is set next to another star.[22]

There can be no claim here that these are the verses to which Benjamin referred.[23] Benjamin's *Dante qui dit: . . .* must continue to retain their enigmatic hold. Nonetheless, there is an important element within what they present that draws these lines into Benjamin's concerns. As the verses unfold, not only is there the possibility of truth that is linked to a conception of human being and thus human life that cannot be identified with the 'present life of miserable mortals', there is also the extraordinary evocation of a moment of seeing, a moment that will have had a revelatory quality and thus a quality that would have only been there for a moment. Time, truth and recognition are staged together, a staging which is defined by the moment. What has been provided therefore is the setting for a form of passing intensity, an accord of light that is held, and, moreover, what is seen, while drenched in the possibility of 'love', has a force that only allows the light to be sustained for a moment. Eyes must 'close because of its intensity'. Here there is an emphatic instant. There is in Dante's verse a connection between truth and the instant. There is therefore an intrinsic distancing of a link between truth and the eternal image as that which gives itself continuously; there is equally a distancing of the presence of the interplay between light and truth as the 'natural light' that will come to exert a hold on philosophy from Descartes onwards.[24] The natural light becomes a forerunner of the positing of the a priori universality of reason. A positing that necessarily fails to allow for an already present interconnection between the philosophical as a mode of thought and the ineliminability of a politics of time.

The truth beyond mere life appears in both Dante and Benjamin in *une image unique*. Equally, of course, it 'flashes up at the moment of its recognisability' (*Erkennbarkeit*). There is a form of synchronicity in play. Opened up here therefore is the effect of this moment of intensity. Recalled is the position advanced in *The Aracdes Project*, namely that: 'Every present day [*Jede Gegenwart*] is determined by the images that are synchronic with it: each now [*jedes Jetzt*] is the now of a particular recognisability.' The emphatic moment of recognition is also present in Fragment VII, in which there is an important contrast between positions that incorporate both 'empathy' and *acedia*, and as such would have as a consequence a despairing approach to the question of the truth of the image. Despite their presence as possibilities, there is the need to open what is defined in that context as the 'genuine historical moment as it briefly flashes up'.[25] The 'flash', the brevity of its passing, is the 'light' whose specular presence, a presence that is equally delimited by the moment, is staged by Dante. For Benjamin the truth of the image is linked to an appearance that is both passing and yet transforming. This becomes a way of articulating on the level of experience what has already been designated the *caesura of allowing*. This moment occurs again in a later fragment when time is described as coming to 'a standstill'.[26] The 'standstill', however, is not an end. Occurring at this moment is what presages. This would be mysticism or a version of voluntarism if that moment and the possibility of its opening up – presaging – did not occur in the name of another thinking of life.

VI

Fragment VI has a well-known opening. Its evocation of a Rankean conception of historical time and the events occurring within it are meant to encapsulate the project of historicism.[27] What returns with this opening is of course the language of recognition and knowledge. Hence Benjamin begins: 'articulating the past historically does not mean recognizing it "the way it really was."' As is clear from Fragment V, what this means is that there has to be other forms of recognition. What is recalled therefore is that the distancing of Ranke, which is the distancing of a certain conception of the relationship between the event and historical time – a relationship marked by its own necessary reciprocity – is that which can only emerge in the 'moment of its recognisability'. That moment is the result of a form of destruction – recalling, again, the connection between the 'pierced' (*durchschlagen*) and destruction. Now, in the context of this particular fragment, there is a link between this moment of recognition and 'a memory' (*eine Erinnerung*). In the context of Fragment VI, therefore, there would seem to be an unresolved tension between the use of the term 'memory' and the term 'image'. In one instance it is a 'memory' that is 'appropriated'. In the next, it is 'an image' to which historical materialism wishes to 'hold fast' (*festzuhalten*). This image appears. However, it appears both in a manner that is 'unexpected' (*unversehens*) (though equally unforeseen and thus unseen) and at a 'moment of danger' (*im Augenblick der Gefahr*). Reiterated here is the 'moment' – recalling of course the 'moment of recognisability' from Fragment V. What needs to be added is that once 'recognisability' is linked to 'danger', then what is recalled is the distinction that has already been noted in Marx between 'interpretation' and 'othering'. 'Interpretation' as the term appears in the last of the *Theses on the Philosophy of Feuerbach* left the world untouched, insofar as mere interpretation resists by definition that move in which the world is othered in the process of its being known or understood. Othering, by definition, assumed the world can be othered in the act of becoming comprehensible.

The recall therefore is precise. To reiterate the point that has already been made, 'interpretation' leaves both the subject and the object untouched and, as such, always assumes a lack of danger. Danger works to stage the disequilibria of power that structure the present. However, there is more involved, since 'danger' here has a doubled quality which points towards the world as a site of possible self-transformation. It is in terms of this possibility that the world can become dangerous. As such there is the continual potentiality for the world to take on this other quality of danger. It is thus that danger could always engender the response that would seek to maintain the disequilibria through its subsequent normalisation (or naturalisation), or through that danger's repositioning within a temporality of progress. The latter is a position that would amount to the overcoming of danger in the name of a gradual process of amelioration. Progress and perfectibility in working seem to link value and time. Both, however, assume a setting in which perfection – thus the temporality of perfectibility – assumes a founding imperfection. A setting in which imperfection and guilt would become exchangeable descriptions. It is at this point that Benjamin writes, with the recognition of what it at stake, that the consequence of this ambivalence within 'danger' is that:

> Every age must strive anew to win tradition back [*die Überlieferung abzugewinnen*] from the conformism that is working to overpower it [*sie zu überwältigen*].

The 'conformism that is working to overpower it' is the enforcing of a form of continuity. Working against it would be the continuity of othering. Othering names a process. Equally, othering, if the language of 'overpowering' is maintained – a maintaining that is held in place by the structure of Benjamin's sentence – must be thought as involving another modality of *Gewalt*. This other form is the winning back of 'tradition' from its having been subdued by what Benjamin identifies as 'conformism'. The latter is that which has to stem the possibility of a link between 'danger' and destruction. As a consequence, therefore, there is a link between danger and the retrieval or rescue of that which would have been lost. The process of winning back – which must be understood as a modality of destruction which takes as its condition of possibility what he names as 'the spark of hope in the past', which is itself a formulation that names the ineliminability of potentiality within Benjamin's philosophical thinking – is given a figured presence in this particular fragment as the Messiah. Of this figure Benjamin writes: 'The Messiah comes not only as the redeemer; he comes as the victor [*Überwinder*] over the Antichrist.' This is why, as has been argued in relation to the *Theological-Political Fragment*, the figure of the Messiah figures the *caesura of allowing*. The victor becomes the winner who will have won back that which otherwise would have been lost. Winning back occurs in the site maintained by destruction and allowing. The link between 'danger' and what was noted above as 'winning back' links the Messiah as a figure to the interplay between 'danger' and rescue that also appears in Hölderlin. In *Patmos* it occurs at the poem's opening:

Wo aber Gefahr ist, wächst
Das Rettende auch.

(But where Danger is,
The saving power grows.)[28]

This is not to suggest that Hölderlin is a thinker of the Messianic in a way that would allow a direct similarity to be drawn with the figure of the Messiah that occurs in Benjamin. Rather, the point is that the link between danger and redemption or rescue as a mode of thought is also evident, at least at the outset, in Hölderlin. What would need to be taken up in addition is whether or not, in Hölderlin, there is a sense that 'danger' may have been emptied of possibility and as such would then have slipped into boredom. In order for boredom to become dangerous – and this for Benjamin is a genuine possibility – it will have to involve the transformation of boredom, in which it is reactivated as dangerous precisely because it presages transformation.[29] Transformation and rescue – understood as a modality of the *caesura of allowing* – would need to be thought together. The link between 'danger' and 'rescue/redemption' is clear. The problem is an activation of danger. It should not be forgotten that Benjamin writes of a 'moment of danger' (*Augenblick der Gefahr*). In other words, time would have to play a determining role in any thinking of the role of 'danger' in Benjamin's work.[30]

VII

The fragment in its opening lines introduces a distancing of 'empathy' (*Einfühlung*). That distancing is to be understood here as the means by which the past becomes historical; moreover, the becoming historical necessitates that 'empathy' is that with which 'historical materialism' 'has broken' (*gebrochen hat*).[31] This distancing has a clear result. Benjamin reaches it by asking a simple yet dramatic question: 'With whom does historicism authentically empathise [*eigentlich einfühlt*]?' The answer is equally as emphatic: 'with the winner [*in den Sieger*]'. The fragment continues identifying what is at stake in this positioning of the demands of historicism. What is behind and what accounts for the impossibility of a link between 'empathy' and the truth of history – what already emerged as the true image of history – has to do, in this instance, with what for Benjamin is presupposed in claims concerning empathy. There is a twofold assumption at work here. In the first instance it pertains to both the universality and thus the apparent neutrality of the subject position that such a setting demands. And then in the second, the subject with which empathy is felt is itself marked by an enforced form of neutrality, and therefore that object emerges as a type of singularity. It is of course a spurious conception of both neutrality and singularity insofar as both are produced. Appearance becomes semblance. The singularity in question is held in place by the posited absence of any founding internal relations. As a consequence, empathy as given within a subject/object relation is constrained to distance both the structuring force and the felt presence of founding disequilibria of power. To the extent that this presence is founding, what it means is that the singularity which empathy takes as its object is premised on the effacing of anoriginal relationality. What is effaced in addition is the ground of politics. This occurs of course in the name of another politics. The refusal of the structural presence of the politics of time becomes a form of its affirmation.

The fragment continues, 'rulers are the heirs of prior conquerors'. The spoils of this process become cultural treasures. This positioning of the work of 'culture' gives rise to the important claim that, precisely because of the interarticulation of 'cultural objects' and 'rules', it follows that, once it can be argued that 'a document is never free of barbarism [*nicht frei ist von Barbarei*]', it would then follow that 'barbarism taints the manner in which it was transmitted from one hand to another.'[32] There is a clear sense in which this is literally true. The presence of barbarism is also present in another of Benjamin's texts, *Experience and Poverty*. In that context he wrote of the impoverishment of experience that occurs once subjectivity is defined by 'guilt' and historical time takes the form of 'fate':

> This poverty of experience is not only poverty on the personal level, but also poverty of human experience in general. Hence a new kind of barbarism [*eine Art von neuem Barbarentum*].[33]

There is a specific response to 'barbarism', a response that takes the form of a 'task'. The relationship between destruction and allowing – a relationship that is defined in the fragments – will describe the 'task' of the 'historical materialist'. What the latter takes on as a 'task' is 'to brush [*zu bürsten*] history against the grain'. Barbarism is not a moral term. It points, for Benjamin, to another beginning and thus to an interruption in which poverty becomes the prompt. This other form of barbarism accords – an accord located within a general dialectical tension – with the more emphatic claim that all 'documents of culture' are marked by the inescapability of a form of barbarism.

Barbarism therefore is a term that draws the historicity of subjectivity into an understating of works of art – cultural productions – that refuses art the capacity to endure as edifying. (As with tranquility, it is simply too early for consolation.) It is not difficult to see that, even in the most 'beautiful' works, conceptions of, for example, gender or race are present in ways that need not be noticed in order that 'beauty' be held as an immediate quality of a work. The impossibility of this immediacy is to note that works always stage positions that are themselves the presence of the ineliminability of the disequilibria of power. Brushing history against the grain is to insist as much on the impossibility of immediacy as on the anoriginal presence of power as integral to cultural presentation.

VIII

This fragment more than any other sets in play the complex relationship between Benjamin and Carl Schmitt. While there may be biographical anecdotes that draw them together, what matters is the possibility of a philosophical accord. Schmitt's work is evoked and distanced in the language of the opening lines of this fragment:

> The tradition of the oppressed teaches us that the 'state of emergency' in which we live is not the exception but the rule. We must attain to a conception of history that accords with this insight. Then we will clearly see that it is our task to bring about a real state of emergency, and this will improve our position in the struggle against fascism.

However, rather than rework that vexed relation in detail, it is what Benjamin means by the 'real state of emergency' and the movement towards a conception of 'amazement' that may in fact be philosophical – where philosophy is at work within a thinking of the political – that will be of central concern. Moreover, it should be added that Schmitt's concerns might be described as limited to questions that are defined by the centrality of the constitution (as a positive or negative presence).[34] The decision and the exception are linked to the constitution. Within such a setting it would be difficult to sustain a genuine difference between sovereignty and 'law-preserving violence', even though the latter would be the suspending of the law to preserve the law. This accounts for why it was essential for Benjamin to overcome any possible oscillation between 'law-preserving' and 'law-making violence'. What mattered for Benjamin, it was argued in the context of Chapter 5, was a critique of law in the name of law, where the latter was always enacted in the name of the relationship between life and justice. This is not Schmitt's project. With regard to the connection between Benjamin and Schmitt, the contention here is that Beatrice Hanssen is right when she argues that:

> If Benjamin, despite his admiration for Schmitt, managed to keep the jurist's proto-fascist program at bay, it is because he did not share his political anthropology, which remained anchored in a celebration of a primordially belligerent human nature.[35]

What counts with Benjamin is the possibility of another conception of the being of being human – what Hanssen identifies as a 'political anthropology' – which, to follow the argument staged in the preceding chapters, has to be understood in terms of both the 'not-yet-attained condition of the just man' and the complex interplay between destruction, value and life. The situation, therefore, is far more complex than Agamben claims in his positioning of their relationship in which it appears almost as an either/or. Agamben argues that:

> While Schmitt attempts every time to reinscribe violence within a juridical context, Benjamin responds to this gesture by seeking every time to assure it – as pure violence – an existence outside the law.[36]

To which it could be added that this 'outside' is given within the 'depositioning' of the law. Hence, what is at stake within Benjamin's work is a critique of law that provides not law's abandoning but its critique as the opening to justice.

While the importance of the fragment is in part tied to an implicit critique of Schmitt, it can be argued that what actually matters is the argument that it is the presence – and thus the recognised presence – of the disequilibria of relations of power, the latter named by Benjamin as the 'tradition of the oppressed', that enables and sustains the interrelated work of law and the police in which the 'state of emergency' is present as 'the rule' (*die Regel*). In order to preserve that set-up, 'law-preserving violence' and its policed presence have to have been naturalised. 'Law-preserving violence' therefore becomes normativity. Given this recognition it becomes necessary – a necessity given by the inscribed potentiality for the just life that is already there in the fabric of existence – to bring about that 'state of emergency' in which there will be both the exposure and undoing of the process of naturalisation. This is the project of 'divine violence', a project undertaken, as is now known, 'for the sake of the living'.

The last lines of the fragment bring the question of the experience of the actual as open to critique.

> The current amazement that the things we are experiencing are 'still' [*noch*] possible in the twentieth century is *not* philosophical. This amazement is not the beginning of knowledge – unless it is the knowledge that the view of history which gives rise to it is untenable.[37]

To have been 'amazed' by the present is to have assumed that barbarism and the continuity of oppression are somehow incompatible with modernity. This is evidence of a naive belief in 'progress'. That they are 'still' present is not just incompatible with a commitment to the equation of time with progress and gradual amelioration, more significantly, their presence indicates that it is precisely these conceptions of time that maintains them. Amazement therefore counts for little unless it includes this recognition. In other words, affect and knowledge have to be tied together. There cannot be a politics of pure affect. Nor can there be one that fails to incorporate experience. The deadening of experience or its dissipation through 'distraction' demand both a philosophical thinking as well as a cultural politics in which there is the already present inter-articulation of affect and knowledge. Moreover, once knowledge and affect are taken together, not only does this demand an understanding of subjectivity, it also indicates the creation of subject positions that are divided between a subject linked to recognition on the one hand, and one which remains merely 'amazed' on the other. The latter is given over to progress. In addition, it is the subject that cannot separate itself from a founding structure of guilt, because any possibility of othering will have been already nullified in advance by the eternal presence of progress.

IX

The evocation of Klee's *Angelus Novus* is the 'image' (*Bild*) that continues to be associated with Benjamin. The movement of the fragment is complex and demanding. This is the 'angel of history'. This is how it is seen. The angel is turned to the past. What appears to 'us' is a set of events. For the angel there is only 'a single catastrophe'. The angel therefore sees a type of connection between events, that is the continuity of the catastrophic. 'Wreckage' appears at the angel's feet. The angel's response is to want to mend what has been broken, while simultaneously wanting to 'wake the dead'. In other words, the angel wants to intervene and stop the catastrophe. Stem the increase of wreckage and thus put the world to right. However, this is not possible. The angel cannot act. The angel is held by the 'storm' from 'Paradise'. Its wind drives the angel forward. In other words, neither repair nor redemption is the province of the angel. What drives the angel on – and thus what drives history from within this conception of the historical – is the storm moving the angel forward. The angel cannot act in relation to the increasing pile of debris that accrues at his feet. The final line of the fragment brings the complex relation between the angel and history into sharp focus. Benjamin writes: 'What we call progress is this storm' (*Das, was wir den Fortschritt nennen, ist dieser Sturm*).

'Progress' is linked therefore to an inability to intervene both within what is occurring and equally within what has occurred. To which it should be added that progress couldn't remember. (Remembrance is destructive.) This needs to be linked to the angel's inability to act. That inability comes to define the angel. His wings cannot be closed. He is subject to progress and as such becomes progress's subject. The act that interrupts the work of progress and which would then undo the subjugating hold of the storm from paradise is that act that has already been located in that which defines the Last Judgement. In one of the drafts of *On the Concept of History*, Benamin cites the following passage from Kafka: 'The Last Judgement is a kind of summary justice' (*das jüngste Gericht ist ein Standrecht*). The value here of this reference to Kafka is that the movement – and it needs to be noted that progress is an inexorable movement – continues to subject and to subjugate.[38] The Last Judgement cannot be the end. As an end it must be deferred. The only way out of this set-up is announced by Benjamin in Fragment XV in his evocation of the 'revolutionary classes'. There needs to be another project, namely 'to make the continuum of history explode'.[39]

To the extent that Klee's angel is the angel of history, then, this is only true if history is progress. The angel is the setting of the ineffectual response to such a conception of historical time. The angel's failure to awaken the dead or even to act to stem the continuity of the disaster is telling. The storm has to be brought to an end. *Glück* both depends upon it while naming the possibility of its occurrence. Opposed to the angel there is the 'historical materialist'. Hence Benjamin writes:

> The historical materialist cannot do without the notion of a present which is not a transition, but in which time takes a stand [*einsteht*] and has come to a standstill.[40]

Taking a stand and time at a standstill recall the 'moment of recognisability' and hence the latter's destructive, thus creative effect. Equally, there is another evocation of wind blowing in which there is a fundamental – and as will be seen decisive – shift in orientation. In *The Arcades Project*, as part of the process of locating and defining the task that pertains either to the 'historical materialist' or the 'dialectician' – where both positions need to be understood in terms of the staging of the *caesura of allowing* – Benjamin defines a conception of the philosophical task that involves a sense of action. What is central is the way that the conception and action are articulated together. What matters, and this recalls the interarticulated presence of affect and knowledge in Fragment VII, is the way in which knowledge is necessary to action. Benjamin writes that:

> Being a dialectician means having the wind of world history [*den Wind der Weltgeschichte*] in one's sails. Thinking means for him: setting the sails. What

is important is *how* they are set. Words are his sails. The way they are set makes them into concepts.[41]

The contrast is between the 'angel' and the 'dialectician'. The former is blown forward, unable to act. What is not at the angel's disposal is a modality of *Gewalt* that is linked to working with the interplay of destruction and value. The angel is disconnected as much from life as it is from life's concerns. The angel stands apart from redemption. For the angel the catastrophe is continual. Its continuity brooks no end. Redemption on the other hand, for Benjamin, 'depends upon the tiny fissures [*an den kleinen Sprung*] in the continuous catastrophe'.[42] Redemption depends upon a potentiality. Equally, it demands those acts that fissure and thus come to be present as openings that allow. The latter demands use of 'words' and the creation of 'concepts'. With both there is another 'wind'. Acts take the place of passivity. The angel's limit is its endless silence before both the question and the possibility of 'redemption'.

X, XI, XII, XIII

There is a real sense in which these fragments can be read as necessarily interrelated.[43] It is not just because they are directly connected to political events, which would have had their own exigency at the time that Benjamin wrote this text.[44] It is also because what is staged by them is a philosophical thinking of the political that is mediated by and which mediates the acuity of the actual.

The first of the fragments (Fragment X) notes that the themes given to 'friars' that allowed them to meditate had the obvious effect of enabling them to turn from 'the world' (*die Welt*). It is possible to read Benjamin, though only at the beginning of the fragment, as claiming that his work is intended to have the same effect. This turning, however, is a turning from the world in order that the world would return within another form. That return would be the world that appeared within the 'true image'. The 'world' of both conventional politics and conventional politicians fails to recognise the world as it is. There is a need, therefore, to break with what is taken to be the world in order that another world becomes possible. The break, the turning, is othering. For Benjamin, contemporary politics and thus contemporary politicians are trapped in (and by) a 'stubborn faith in progress' and then a 'confidence in their "base in the masses"'. These elements cohere to create a world from which it is necessary to turn. Benjamin concludes his evaluation of the world created by 'politicians' by noting the consequence of traditional modes of political thinking and thus the failure to turn to the world. This has to be understood as

> the high price our customary mode of thought [*unser gewohntes Denken*] will have to pay for a conception of history that avoids any complicity with the concept of history to which those politicians still adhere.

In other words, a turn to the world – and in this turn the already present evocation of the world in both Benjamin and Marx is recalled – demands the incorporation of another sense of the historical. The latter should be regarded as a shorthand for a move away from the politics of habit and towards a politics of time. What this means in addition is that, throughout Fragments X–XIII, the critique of parliament that was noted in *Towards a Critique of Violence* is also at work.

The rest of the fragments in this section are concerned ostensibly with the Social Democratic Party, which over the period 1870 to 1930 had become a political organisation that for Benjamin had become identified with 'progress' and thus the project of intended amelioration. The latter appear in Fragment XIII in terms of the following three characteristics:

> Progress pictured in the minds of the Social Democrats was, first of all, progress of humankind itself (and not just advance in human ability and knowledge). Second, it was something boundless (in keeping with an infinite perfectibility of humanity). Third, it was considered inevitable – something that automatically pursued a straight or spiral course.[45]

As should be clear, while there may be a political disagreement with these commitments, for Benjamin what is at stake is the incorporation of a conception of historical time and its related conception of subjectivity that is not simply false; its deployment within the realm of the practical, because it is premised on the effacing of relations of power, works to maintain those relations. They are maintained as a result of their disavowal. The form that disavowal may take will include, for example, a commitment to the 'infinite perfectibility of humanity' or 'the progress of humankind itself'. While this may appear to be a claim that would extend across the range of all social democratic political parties, what is significant in this instance is the basis of Benjamin's engagement. The argument is simply that holding to progress and perfectibility is a political move that results in the failure to think the political. The latter necessitates developing an understanding of the politics of time. That is the limit of the philosophical. Indeed, the philosophical is delimited by it. The move from the political as a domain of practical activity has for

Benjamin led to 'historical materialism'. Whether that is the only form to be taken by the politics of time, if posed as a philosophical one, has to remain open.

In an extraordinary passage, in which Benjamin is at his most polemical in his engagement with the effect of the Social Democrats on the 'working class', he writes that they undo their power by identifying the working class with a politics of the future. However, as has already been argued, consistent with Benjamin's overall philosophical position, the future is only ever a condition of the present. To define the political in terms of the future is to neglect the present and thus to neglect the task that it would then demand. Benjamin's position becomes one in which the present acquires philosophical insistence. The political form that this insistence then acquires will always be a separate but related question. Benjamin goes on to argue that if the 'working class' are indoctrinated into a politics of the future, rather than one structured by the present, then such a set-up would make it

> forget both its hatred and its spirit of sacrifice [*den Opferwillen*], for both are nourished by the image of enslaved ancestors not by the ideal of liberated grandchildren.[46]

The claim about 'ancestors' is a claim about the form of the historical object and a claim about the redemption of the past. Forgetting the past means forgetting 'the spirit of sacrifice'. The latter recalls the position already noted concerning the connection between 'divine violence' and sacrifice. Sacrifice in that context was linked to a relationship between justice and life. It was the sacrifice that, while not necessary, would have been accepted. Its denial is the denial of the capacity for othering. The move from the present to the future – and thus a concern with 'the ideal of liberated grandchildren' assumes the forgetting of the 'enslaved ancestors' – robs the present of the agency of othering.

There is another moment in this group of fragments that underscores the elimination of othering as the basis of a philosophical critique of the politics of the Social Democrats. It occurs in Fragment XI and concerns the question of work. Here it needs to be remembered that Benjamin has already staged the possibility of a critique of the practices of work resulting in the othering of work. This was the position that emerged in *Towards a Critique of Violence*. The continuity of work is occasioned by its being discontinuous with the already present nature of work. This is the conception of work that resulted from what in that context was the 'proletarian general strike', but which can also be understood more broadly as the mode of work (and thus activity) that is allowed by a modality of destruction that operates outside any oscillation between means and ends. In other words, the strike is present as the *caesura of allowing*. The position advanced by Benjamin concerns a critique of the position that technological development, and thus what could be described as technological progress, involves actual transformations of conditions and thus of work in general. After making this point – a point that has to be interpreted as part of the systematic critique of progress – Benjamin adds that, once this position is accepted:

> It was but a step to the illusion [*der Illusion*] that the factory work ostensibly furthering technological progress constituted a political achievement. The old Protestant work ethic was resurrected among German workers in secularised form.[47]

Apart from the important claim that the secular is not a departure from religion, when both are understood as modalities of time incorporating subject positions, what is being suggested is that 'technological progress' is not an 'achievement' (*Leistung*) on the level of the political. Except insofar as technological progress, in constructing no more than the appearance of progress, maintains work as it is. As such, what is left open is the question of what would in fact count as the othering of work. This is of course the question that the conception of historical time and agency that is at work within Social Democracy is unable to pose.

XIV–XVI, A

It is possible to group these fragments together insofar as what they stage is a continuous concern with winning history, and thus a historical consciousness, back from progress and the universality of the subject positions that progress demands, for example a subject position whose agent may respond empathetically.[48] What is opened up is another exigency, one operating as much in terms of affect as it does time. The fragments both rework and restate a number of essential points that have already emerged. For this reason, a specific path will be taken. Centrality will be accorded to the way in which potentiality is inscribed within the present. It takes the form of 'now-time', the 'monad' or 'splinters of messianic time'. It appears as 'a revolutionary chance' (*eine revolutionäre Chance*).[49] All of these terms – admittedly there are different gradations of force – are attempts to formulate a conception of the present as defined by the potentiality for it to be other.

Of the many ways in which the topos of potentiality is introduced by this group of fragments, one of the most significant is summarised by the opening lines of Fragment XIV, namely: 'History is the subject of a construction whose site is not homogeneous, empty time, but time filled full by now-time [*Jetztzeit*].'[50] The introduction of a conception of time as both 'homogeneous' and 'empty' is a description of historical time as a 'place' without potentiality. In other words, it is a place that is condemned to be always the same as itself. As has already been argued, sameness within such a setting either refuses difference or reduces it to variety. Within the context of XIV, what fractures homogeneity is not mere plurality. On the contrary, the plurality in question involves relations of power. The recognition of such a setting involves a 'leap' (*Sprung*) that brings the past and the present together in a moment of intensity. This 'leap' can also be thought as the *caesura of allowing*. It is a 'leap' that demands the modality of *Gewalt* that is equated with 'divine violence'. For Benjamin it is the movement that Marx 'understood as revolution'.[51]

While the move from 'divine violence' to 'revolution' has a certain inevitability attached to it, what is more important is that what Benjamin continues to take up is the necessity of othering that is intrinsic to a politics of time. The refusal of 'homogeneous time' is to recognise the political as the 'place' of irreducible differences. (What emerges here with that recognition is, of course, another thinking of 'place'.) A position effaced in any evocation of the interplay of progress and time as homogeneous. Moreover, if 'now-time' is the precondition for othering, then what 'now-time' names is the potentiality for othering that is already present within time. Hence, when Benjamin argues in Fragment XIV that to 'Robespierre ancient Rome was a past charged with now-time, a past which he blasted out [*heraussprengte*] of the continuum of history', what is at stake in such a description is a twofold reiteration of that potentiality.[52] In the first instance it is a claim about the relationship between the past and the present and thus a reconfiguration of what it means for an event to become historical. In the second it links blasting and springing to the already noted 'blows' in its evocation of the relationship between destruction and allowing as the result of an actualisation of a potentiality. A position reiterated in Fragment XVII in which the 'historical materialist' is described as taking 'cognisance of it [the present] in order to blast a specific era out of the homogeneous course of history'.[53] The present has always contained the potentiality for it to be other. (Such a claim not only underscores the centrality of time within the political, to the extent that such a claim involves a specific ontology of the present, but it also grounds the possibility of politics in both time and ontology.) That is why, for Benjamin, there is a fundamental difference between historicism as a conception of historical time, with its related sense of place, and what is named in *On the Concept of History* as 'historical materialism'. The former can only offer that which is both empty and unchanging, and thus an 'eternal image' (*das 'ewige' Bild*), while the latter inscribes time within experience.[54]

The significant point here is that the so-called 'eternal image' can never be the 'the true image' (Fragment V). Their difference is not just there on the level of the image. It pertains to the temporality of recognition, but equally to the way in which the intensity of the moment – which yields an image given in the 'moment of its recognisability' – comes to define a site in which the contrary of the homogenous is not the heterogeneous, but in which the opposition (if indeed that is the correct term) is to be thought in terms of the presence and absence of potentiality. Fragment XVII defines the relationship between singularity and potentiality in the following terms:

> Thinking involves not only the movement of thoughts, but their arrest as well. Where thinking suddenly comes to a stop in a constellation saturated with tensions, it gives that constellation a shock, by which thinking is crystallised as a monad.[55]

Thinking is clearly the 'movement of thought'. To that extent thinking becomes a way of proceeding, that is, its concretisation would take the form of a continuous narrative (the narrating of the continuous). Thought as movement, however, contains the capacity for a form of cessation or interruption. It is as though the language of the caesura is at work. Thought interrupts itself. There is the counter-rhythmic possibility. That moment is pure. The moment of interruption is the cessation of movement – a cessation that will seek its own form of presentation. For Benjamin that presentation appears, in the context of Fragment XVII, as a 'monad'. While Benjamin uses the language of Leibniz, what is important in the reference to Leibniz is that the monad is a site of potentiality. The substance of the moment is 'force'. Moreover, change within the monad is the result of what Leibniz describes as 'the action of an internal principle'.[56] And finally, the monad is a multiplicity. Where Benjamin is constrained to depart from Leibniz has to do with the nature of change. Change cannot occur simply as a matter of 'degree'. For Leibniz 'all natural changes take place [*se faisant*] by degree'.[57] This cannot be Benjamin's position. Hence, while what is maintained in his thinking is a commitment to potentiality, there is a related commitment to the monad being a site that sustains a capacity of radical interruption, presented in terms of discontinuity.

The monad becomes the way in which a moment charged with possibilities is formulated. It occurs within a process of arrest. A position that appears at the end of Fragment A in terms of 'a conception of the present [*der Gegenwart*] as now-time shot through with splinters of messianic time'.[58] Here is the monad as a site of a founding irreducibility. However, what is significant here is that not only does this irreducibility signal the precondition for a politics of time, it also inscribes the messianic within the present. In other words, the present will always have the potentiality to be other. However, it needs to be remembered that these positions are not mere empty abstractions concerning time. They involve the relationship between destruction and value. In the context of Fragment XVII, it is presented in terms of the relationship between the 'historical materialist' and the 'historical object', where the latter takes the form of a 'monad'. In this structure 'he recognises the sign of a messianic arrest of happening, or (to put it differently) a revolutionary chance in the fight for the oppressed past.'[59] The monad allows for an undoing of the conception of the present in which the events leading up to it were no more 'the beads of a rosary' moving from the past to the present. What arises in its place is another conception of the historical object. With that emergence, the monad, 'now-time' and this reconfiguration of the present are tied together. The project of history occurs with the undoing of the chain thereby permitting the historian who 'grasps the constellation into which his own era has entered, along with a very specific earlier one.'[60] At work here is a sense of the historical which becomes a version of 'remembrance' linked to 'destruction'. Articulated together, the project of history like that of remembrance is defined by the continual interplay of destruction and value.

The monad as an organising term also appears in New Thesis H, where it is positioned against conceptions of universal history in which the instance – the historical event – is simply the actualisation of that which at once organises and defines the identity of actuality and particularity. Benjamin's position is the following:

> Universal histories are not inevitably reactionary. But a universal history *without* a structural [*konstruktiv*] principle is reactionary. The structural principle of universal history allows it to be represented in partial histories. It is, in other words, a monadological principle. It exists within salvation history [*in der Heilsgeschich*].[61]

The distancing of universal history has to occur, even though such a conception of the historical as universal history may introduce a tension between an external presence that comes to be actualised and one whose actualisation comprises history, because there may be important differences between specific forms of actualisation. This is not the conception of tension that occurs with the monad. The latter results from a 'shock' and becomes as a consequence a 'constellation'. (Benjamin describes this 'constellation' as 'saturated with tensions'.[62]) For Benjamin, moreover, the link between historicism and universal history is clear. (Fragment XVII begins: 'Historicism rightly culminates in universal history'.[63]) The point here, however, is that universal history is neither the history of the continual actualisation of forms of externality nor the progressive, and in the end teleological, development of 'progress'. On the contrary, universality is a structuring principle in which structure pertains to the continual presence of a set-up occurring in a present defined as 'now-time shot through with splinters of messianic time'.[64] The related conception of the historical object is a locus of potentiality. A moment whose potentiality is there in both the inherently strategic and thus the particular nature of the object and therefore in the way it positions the relation between past and present. This is what is identified above as 'the structural principle' that has universality. All partial histories are monadic, and only in being monadic are the presentations of historicism undone – as a general philosophical claim – and only then do specific regional histories become possible. Only the latter will indeed work 'against the grain'.[65]

As has been suggested, there is a real sense in which an engagement with the fragments that comprise *On the Concept of History* is a potentially endless task. This is a position that could be extended to Benjamin's work as a whole. Texts and fragments continue to make demands. This chapter, along with all the others that make up this entire project, is orientated around the recovery of a political philosophy from a select number of Benjamin's wittings. Given this setting it is therefore appropriate to conclude both the chapter and the project as a whole with a final engagement. In this instance, Fragment B of *On the Concept of History* contains a number of elements that will allow – as a strategic measure – a repositioning of one of the terms that has played a central role in the preceding, namely 'life'. Fragment B contains the following extraordinary formulation that brings a concern with life into an engagement with history, time and the present. It is a passage that also evokes the Messiah as the named presence of the messianic. The lines that are central here are the following:

> We know that the Jews were prohibited from inquiring into the future: the Torah and the prayers instructed them in remembrance. This disenchanted the future, which holds sway over all those who turn to soothsayers for enlightenment. This does not imply, however, that for the Jews the future became homogeneous, empty time. For every second was the small gateway [*die kleine Pforte*] through which the Messiah might enter.[66]

It is as though the 'destructive character' has returned. The lines begin with a reiteration of the refusal to create an image of the future. Instead of the image of the future there is the practice of remembrance. The destructive force of remembrance is linked both to maintaining the present a site defined by tensions created by its own complex temporality and to the need to undo the hold of fate which is captured here in the reiterated presence of the 'soothsayer'. The fragment creates a question, one stemming from the problem of accounting for the future if its accompanying image is displaced. How is the move away from the continual threat of 'homogeneous, empty time' to be understood? The complexity of this question suggests that a beginning should be made with the well-known 'small gateway'.

As most commentators point out, the reference here is to Luther's translation of Matthew 7: 13–14. However, it is not the 'gate' per se that is of interest. It is rather that in the context of the Christian Bible the gate leads 'to life'. Indeed this is the key moment of Matthew 7: 14; the original is unequivocal. The gate leads εἰς τὴν Ζωὴν, which becomes in Luther's translation '*zum Leben*'. If there is a moment from the history of art that will stage the concerns of the 'little gate' and, more importantly, that gate's relation to life, then it can be found in Domenico di Michelino's portrait of Dante in the Duomo in Florence.[67] Not only does this painting present the threefold division of the world, where the latter is understood as having a full range and thus a discussion between the earth, purgatory and heaven, it does so by capturing the latter in the image of an eternal city. (This cannot be the true image of history. There will not have been any danger.) 'Paradise' therefore, as it appears in Domenico di Michelino's work, could be understood as the 'moral world order' (*die 'sittliche Weltordnung'*). Not only is this positioning important, what is also of fundamental significance is that it is only after having gone through the gate that life commences. A position that in Luther's translation is expressed in the following terms: '*Und die Pforte ist eng, und der Weg ist schmal, der zum Leben führt; und wenige sind ihrer, die ihn finden*'[68] (For the gate is small and the way is narrow that leads to life, and there are few who find it).

Two points are essential here. The first pertains to the description of the 'way' as 'narrow'. As such it becomes clear that what is being staged by Benjamin is the world opened by Matthew in its having been refracted through Luther. The second point is that an integral part of this world – and this is the world at which Benjamin's conception of destruction or othering is aimed – is captured in the word 'few' (*wenige*). By definition, therefore, the 'gate' will be closed to any sense of totality. The 'few' are necessarily differentiated from what Benjamin refers to as a 'redeemed mankind'. What is meant by the latter is the totality that has already been named as 'the living'. Within Luther's translation something else will have occurred. In that setting, it is only in having passed through the gate – the 'few' who in fact pass through it – that life is possible. The gate leads to 'life'. (Dante points to the gate announcing thereby his entry into the life that his *Commedia* will have staged.) Having passed through the gate – and only in passing through it – could it be argued that real life occurs. Everything else that involved life prior to the gate – to having passed through it – is a mere preparation and thus in that precise sense could only ever be mere life. Note that this sense of life is not yet Benjamin's conception of 'mere life'. The latter is the life and thus the subject position over which 'fate' seeks to exercise control. 'Mere life', when the term is used by Benjamin, assumes the subject as always already guilty. The subject within Benjaminian 'mere life' is indebted to fate. Here is the opening to a link. In Matthew and thus within Luther's translation what has been identified as 'mere life' is indeed fated life, but the overcoming of that fated life can only be there in the anticipation of the life to come, the life after having walked through the 'straight gate', the life that is only there for the 'few'. This is the possibility at which Dante gestures. The latter, within the world of religion – and, as should be clear, it is religion in its opposition to theology – is life itself. What this means is that Benjamin's suggestion that 'every second was the small gateway [*die kleine Pforte*] through which the Messiah might enter' has to be understood as the destruction of what is staged in Domenico di Michelino's portrait of Dante and equally what is there in both Luther and Mark. The object of destruction is religion to the extent that religion is understood as the interarticulated presence of fate and guilt. That destruction is the opening to life. No longer is there life for the 'few'. On the contrary, the entry through the gate by the Messiah becomes a staging of the cessation of guilt and fate. It does not occur in the name of a life to come that is restricted to the few and is predicated upon the Last Judgement. Rather, the life to come is the life occurring with the transformation of the world. This is the life within the othering of the world – a life only possible because of destruction. In other words, it is the life that is allowed and which allows. The worldly life to come, a life of which there are already present intimations inherent within the fabric of existence, a life therefore for which there is an already present potentiality, is the just life. Once potentiality and the just life can be linked philosophically in a sustained way, and it can be argued that this is the project central to Benjamin's work, then it is not difficult to conclude that the means allowing for their presence is the work of recovery. It is a recovery whose extrapolation is the presentation of Benjamin's work as a contribution to political philosophy.

Notes

1. There already exists a number of exceptional commentaries on this text. See, for example, Michael Löwy, *Fire Alarm: Reading Walter Benjamin's 'On the Concept of History'*, trans. Chris Turner (London: Verso, 2005). Important recent articles that make a significant contribution to its interpretation include: Howard Caygill, 'Walter Benjamin's Concept of Cultural History', in David Ferris (ed.), *The Cambridge Companion to Walter Benjamin* (Cambridge: Cambridge University Press, 2004), pp. 73–96; Rolf Tiedemann, 'Historical Materialism or Political Messianism? An Interpretation of the Theses "On the Concept of History"', in Gary Smith (ed.), *Walter Benjamin – Philosophy, Aesthetics, History* (Chicago: University of Chicago Press, 1989), pp. 175–209; Irving Wohlfarth, 'On the Messianic Structure of Benjamin's Last Reflections', *Glyph* 3 (1978), pp. 148–212. Rather than take a critical distance from these works, the project here is to try and integrate the interpretation of Benjamin advanced in the earlier chapters into a detailed treatment of this text.

2. For a discussion of the complex question of what comprises the text in the case of Heraclitus – a question to which there is no one response – see Catherine Osborne, *Rethinking Early Greek Philosophy* (London: Duckworth, 1987), and the Introductions to both Charles Kahn, *The Art and Thought of Heraclitus* (Cambridge: Cambridge University Press, 1979) and Jean Bollack and Heinz Wismann, *Héraclite ou la séparation* (Paris: Editions de Minuit, 1972). Moreover, it can be argued that Louis Marin's interpretation of the relationship between Arnauld and Nicole's 'Logique de port-royal' and Pascal's *Pensées* are in part dependent on the fragmented nature of the latter's work. See Louis Marin, *La critique du discours* (Paris: Editions de Minuit, 1975).

3. The new edition of Benjamin's works, *Werke und Nachlaß. Kritische Gesamtausgabe*, published by Suhrkamp, has collected all the versions, including facsimiles of both the German and French versions, in its volume devoted to just this text. It is the outstanding critical version of this text. See Walter Benjamin, *Über den Begriff der Geschichte*, in Benjamin, *Werke und Nachlaß. Kritische Gesamtausgabe*, Band 19, ed. Gérard Raulet (Berlin: Suhrkamp, 2010).

4. The numbering scheme used in this chapter will refer directly to each of the fragments that comprise the text. To replicate the ordering in both the English, German and French editions, Roman numerals will be used. Again it needs to be noted that, rather than rehearse the history of existing interpretations of the overall text and the fragments within it, priority continues to be given to the continuation of what has already been designated as the project of 'recovery'.

5. Adorno's attempt to respond to the advent of the new deploys the language of inexhaustibility, defining it in relation to 'freedom'. The significance of Berg's March from the Three Pieces for Orchestra Opus 6 is, for Adorno,

present as technique within later 'experiments in music'. He defines that significance as 'the complete freedom [*die volle Freiheit*] of the ear to integrate combined musical sources'; Theodor W. Adorno, *Quasi una Fantasia*: *Essays on Modern Music*, trans. Rodney Livingstone (London: Verso, 1998), p. 194; German reference is to Theodor W. Adorno, *Gesammelte Schriften*, Band 16 (Frankfurt am Main: Suhrkamp Verlag, 1978), p. 427. After which he adds a long and important reflection:

> This freedom is intimately connected to the quality which, when I reflect upon it after all these years, originally attracted me to Berg, as well as to Benjamin's philosophy. This was the quality of inexhaustibility, of a profusion of ideas which constantly regenerates itself and flows in superabundance. In a real world in which matter-of-factness (which was fully justified as a critique of false plenitude) has degenerated into a state of bankruptcy, a kind of spiritual meanness, the need for compositional freedom converges with the need for this sense of the inexhaustible. The sterility for functionality is a mere surrogate for the rigour of the work of art. The happiness [*Glück*] of the latter lies [*liegt*] in the qualitative variety which is not terrorised from outside, by the lie [*die Lüge*] of purity and the pure. (Adorno, *Quasi una Fantasia*, pp. 194–5; Adorno, *Gesammelte Schriften*, Band 16, p. 427)

Part of what Adorno identifies in Benjamin (though equally in Berg) is the body of work that cannot be defined simply in terms of utility. His work, whatever limits it may be possible to establish, stands opposed to 'spiritual meanness'. It is this opening that keeps causing the question of what is at stake in working with Benjamin – and here working is defined in terms of the project of recovery – to continue to be reposed.

6. For an important discussion of the 'hunchback' and its significance within the Fragment see Dimitris Vardoulakis, *The Doppelgänger: Literature's Philosophy* (New York: Fordham University Press, 2010), pp. 144–6.
7. Benjamin, *Arcades Project*, p. 471; Benjamin, *Gesammelte Schriften* V.1, p. 588 [N7a,7],
8. I have taken up the way Benjamin engages with painting and drawing in my 'Framing Pictures, Transcending Marks: Walter Benjamin's "Paintings, or Signs and Marks"', in Andrew Benjamin and Charles Rice (eds), *Walter Benjamin and the Architecture of Modernity* (Melbourne: Re:press Books, 2009), pp. 129–46.
9. Benjamin, *Selected Writings* 4, p. 264; *Gesammelte Schriften* I.2, p. 496.
10. Benjamin, *Selected Writings* 1, p. 204; *Gesammelte Schriften* II.1, p. 176.
11. Benjamin, *Selected Writings* 4, p. 405; *Gesammelte Schriften* I.1, p. 1238.
12. See Benjamin, *Selected Writings* 1, p. 351; *Gesammelte Schriften* I.1, p. 195.
13. There is an interesting link here to the relationship between the secret – an idea that is being developed here – and both responsibility and the decision. See, to this end, the comment made by Hamacher:

> Responsibility strikes me as an initiative but – and there's the rub – it is an initiative in a matter that is already very sensibly sometimes pressingly

and even hauntingly there, and yet which lacks determination, address or form. (Werner Hamacher, 'To Leave the Word to Someone Else', in Julian Wolfreys (ed.), *Thinking Difference: Critics in Conversation* (New York: Fordham University Press, 2004), p. 172)

It is this latter element that locates the secret as the ground of responsibility, a ground that always remains indeterminate rather than determining. Hence it is on the side of contingency. In others words, it is mediate rather than immediate.

14. Benjamin, *Selected Writings* 4, p. 390; *Gesammelte Schriften* I.2, p. 694.
15. While the context is different, the formulation of the 'not yet' is also evident in *The Arcades Project*. In Konvolut N1, 9, it is deployed in the context of a discussion of 'a constellation of awakening'. In this regard he writes that a possible 'dissolution of "mythology" into history . . . can only happen through the awakening of a not-yet-conscious knowledge of what has been [*durch die Erweckung eines noch nicht bewußten Wissens vom Gewesen*].' (Benjamin, *Arcades Project*, p. 458; *Gesammelte Schriften* V.1, p. 572).
16. See the important discussion of this point in Kam Shapiro, 'Politics is a Mushroom: Worldly Sources of Rule and Exception in Carl Schmitt and Walter Benjamin', *Diacritics*, 37.2–3 (Summer–Fall 2007), p. 132.
17. Benjamin, *Arcades Project*, p. 481; *Gesammelte Schriften* V.1, p. 603 [N15,2].
18. Benjamin, *Selected Writings* 4, pp. 390–1; *Gesammelte Schriften* V.1, p. 695. The same quotation from Keller also appears in Benjamin, *Arcades Project*, p. 463; *Gesammelte Schriften* V.1, p. 579 [N3a,1].
19. Benjamin, *Über den Begriffe der Geschichte, Werke und Nachlaß. Kritische Gesamtausgabe*, Band 19, ed. Gérard Raulet (Berlin: Suhrkamp Verlag, 2010), p. 62, facsimile p. 50.
20. See the discussion of the term in Samuel Weber's invaluable *Benjamin's -abilities* (Cambridge, MA: Harvard University Press, 2008), pp. 48–50, 168–9, 350 fn. 4.
21. Benjamin, *Selected Writings* 4, p. 403; *Gesammelte Schriften* I.3, p. 1234. While Benjamin's relation to Nietzsche is too complex to be entered into here, it should still be noted that Konvolute D of *The Arcades Project* is in part devoted to an engagement with 'eternal return'. See Benjamin, *Arcades Project*, pp. 116–19; *Gesammelte Schriften* V.1, pp. 174–8.
22. The English text, presented here in a slightly altered form, is accessible from <http://www.italianstudies.org/>. The Italian text is noted below:

> Poscia che 'ncontro a la vita presente
> d'i miseri mortali aperse 'l vero
> quella che 'mparadisa la mia mente,
> come in lo specchio fiamma di doppiero
> vede colui che se n'alluma retro,
> prima che l'abbia in vista o in pensiero,
> e sé rivolge per veder se 'l vetro
> li dice il vero, e vede ch'el s'accorda
> con esso come nota con suo metro;
> così la mia memoria si ricorda

ch'io feci riguardando ne' belli occhi
onde a pigliarmi fece Amor la corda.
E com'io mi rivolsi e furon tocchi
li miei da ciò che pare in quel volume,
quandunque nel suo giro ben s'adocchi,
un punto vidi che raggiava lume

acuto sì, che 'l viso ch'elli affoca
chiuder conviensi per lo forte acume;
e quale stella par quinci più poca,
parrebbe luna, locata con esso
come stella con stella si collòca.

23. There is little written on the relationship between Benjamin and Dante. What texts there are concentrate on the question of allegory. See, for example, Jeremy Tambling, 'Dante and Benjamin: Melancholy and Allegory', *Exemplaria*, 4 (1992), pp. 342–62. There is an important reference to Dante in *The Arcades Project* [X 7a,3]. As the translators of the English edition indicate, Benjamin is most probably referring to *Inferno* Canto III. 9. It will be important to return to this reference in the discussion of Fragment A.

24. For a discussion of this term – 'natural light' – in the context of Descartes' philosophical work, see John Morris, 'Descartes' Natural Light', *Journal of the History of Philosophy*, 11.2 (April 1973), pp. 169–87.

25. Benjamin, *Selected Writings* 4, p. 391; *Gesammelte Schriften* I.2, p. 696.

26. Benjamin, *Selected Writings* 4, p. 396; *Gesammelte Schriften* I.2, p. 702.

27. The same line that is intended to capture the Rankean position is also used in *The Arcades Project*; see Benjamin, *Arcades Project*, p. 463; *Gesammelte Schriften* V.1, p. 578 [N3,4].

28. Friedrich Hölderlin, *Sämtlich Werke*, Band 1, ed. D. E. Sattler (München: Luchterland Literaturverlag, 2004), p. 379. The link between 'danger' and 'rescue' as a theme in Hölderlin that is taken over by Benjamin is not surprising given Benjamin's knowledge of Hölderlin. This evocation of Hölderlin on 'danger' also occurs in a recent paper by Gerhard Richter, 'Can Anything be Rescued by Defending It? Benjamin with Adorno', *Differences*, 23.3 (2010), p. 35. Richter's text is essential for an understanding of the issues raised by strategies of rescue and redemption.

29. See Appendix B.

30. The question that emerges here would concern the role of time, or rather the perception of time, in Hölderlin. While this question cannot be pursued here, it is nonetheless worth recalling that in the much remarked-upon line from 'Germanien' (*Sämtliche Werke*, Band 10) in which the Gods are described as having 'fled', not only is there an important absence of lament, it is also as though the present, no longer being defined by the Gods, opens up a different relation. Of these Gods Hölderlin wrote *ihr hattet eure Zeiten* ('they had their time'); it is now past. Hence the question of the time of the 'now' is another time. The question concerns not just how that difference would then be thought; of equal importance is the possibility of its being experienced.

31. While the reference to 'empathy' (*Einfühlung*) has its most direct link to the work of Theodor Lipps (and in the context of Benjamin this will also include Ludwig Klages) it is also likely that what he names in the process is Bergson's conception of 'intuition' and 'duration'. For the latter see Henri Bergson, *L'énergie Spirituelle* (Paris: Payot, 2012), and Foucault, *Essai sur les données immédiate de la conscience* (Paris: PUF, 2007). Assumed in all these positions – and this despite their differences – is a neutrality within experience and thus a neutrality and universality in regard to subjectivity. Duration, therefore, constructs as much a theory of the subject as it does a conception of time. Both inscribe difference as variety and thus both fail to provide the means to think difference as having anoriginal presence and thus as *ab initio* irreducible. Lipps and Bergson's conception of time and subjectivity – from the perspective of Benjamin's philosophical project – assume the continuity of the victory of conformism in the name of the naturalisation of both psychology and history. For a sustained treatment of the topics of *Einfühlung* in German philosophical thinking, see Robin Curtis and Gertrud Koch (eds), *Einfühlung. Zu Geschichte und Gegenwart eines ästhetischen Konzepts* (Berlin: Fink, 2008). For an analysis of Benjamin's complex relation to Bergson in terms of those aspects which are subject by him to critique and those which are reworked such that an accommodation can be reached, see Claire Blencoe, 'Destroying Duration: The Critical Situation of Bergsonism in Benjamin's Analysis of Modern Experience', *Theory, Culture and Society* 25.4 (July 2008), pp. 139–58. An important study of the Benjaminian estimation of Bergson's work within the broader context of Benjamin's political philosophy has also been undertaken in Uwe Steiner, 'The True Politician: Walter Benjamin's Concept of the Political', *New German Critique* 83 (Spring–Summer, 2001), pp. 43–88. Despite the excellence of the work noted above, there is an important project on Benjamin and Bergson that is still to be undertaken.
32. Benjamin, *Selected Writings* 4, p. 39; *Gesammelte Schriften* 1.2, p. 696. See in addition *The Arcades Project*, pp. 467; *Gesammelte Schriften* V.1, p. 584 [N5a,7].
33. Benjamin, *Selected Writings* 2, p. 732; *Gesammelte Schriften* II.1, p. 215.
34. See Carl Schmitt, *Political Theology. Four Chapters on the Concept of Sovereignty*, trans. George Schwab (Chicago: University of Chicago Press, 1985), pp. 5–16.
35. Beatrice Hanssen, 'On the Politics of Pure Means: Benjamin, Arendt, Foucault', in Hent de Vries and Samuel Weber (eds), *Violence, Identity and Self-Determination* (Stanford: Stanford University Press, 1997), p. 245.
36. Giorgio Agamben, *State of Exception*, trans. Kevin Attell (Chicago: University of Chicago Press, 2005), p. 59.
37. Benjamin, *Selected Writings* 4, p. 392; *Gesammelte Schriften* I.2, p. 697.
38. Benjamin's short comment here is that what is at work in Kafka is the proposition that 'the Day of Judgement according to this saying would not be distinguished from other days' (*Selected Writings* 4, p. 407; *Gesammelte Schriften* I.3, p. 1245). The line from Kafka's unpublished notes equates the Last Judgement with a conception of law that falls outside the concerns that would be opened by a repositioning of law, where the latter would have occurred as the result of the already noted 'depositioning' of the law.

Benjamin's addition indicates that to the extent that the Day of Judgement cannot be distinguished from any other days, it has the twofold effect of defining subjectivity and law in terms of guilt and fate while refusing the possibility of there being a day in which what determined every other day did not apply.

39. Benjamin, *Selected Writings 4*; *Gesammelte Schriften* I.2, p. 701.
40. Benjamin, *Selected Writings 4*, p. 396; *Gesammelte Schriften* I.2, p. 702.
41. Benjamin, *The Arcades Project* [N9,6], p. 473; *Gesammelte Schriften* V.1, p. 591.
42. Benjamin, *Selected Writings 4*, p.185; *Gesammelte Schriften* I.2, p. 683.
43. Moreover, it is possible to suggest that swapping VIII and IX would create a better order. A real affinity exists between VIII and then X, XI, XII and XIII, which is slightly and unproductively interrupted by the current ordering (recognising that this is the ordering of the original manuscript).
44. David Renton, 'On Benjamin's *Theses*, or the Utility of the Concept of Historical Time', *European Journal of Political Theory* 11.4 (2012), p. 380.
45. Benjamin, *Selected Writings 4*, p. 394; *Gesammelte Schriften* I.2, p. 700.
46. Benjamin, *Selected Writings 4*, p. 394; *Gesammelte Schriften* I.2, p. 700.
47. Benjamin, *Selected Writings 4*, p. 393; *Gesammelte Schriften* I.2, p. 699.
48. While the literature on Benjamin's understanding of history is considerable, for papers that emphasise the importance of Benjamin's work within the development of a philosophical thinking of history, see the collection by Andrew Benjamin (ed.), *Walter Benjamin and History* (London: Continuum Books, 2005).
49. Benjamin, *Selected Writings 4*, p. 396; *Gesammelte Schriften* I.2, p. 703.
50. Benjamin, *Selected Writings 4*, p. 395; *Gesammelte Schriften* I.2, p. 701. I have written a commentary on this particular fragment. See my 'The Time of Fashion: A Commentary on Thesis XIV in Walter Benjamin's "On the Concept of History"', in A. Benjamin, *Style and Time. Essays on the Politics of Appearance* (Evanston: Northwestern University Press, 2006), pp. 25–38.
51. Benjamin, *Selected Writings 4*, p. 395; *Gesammelte Schriften* I.2, p. 701.
52. Benjamin, *Selected Writings 4*, p. 395; *Gesammelte Schriften* I.2, p. 701.
53. Benjamin, *Selected Writings 4*, p. 396; *Gesammelte Schriften* I.2, p. 702.
54. Benjamin, *Selected Writings 4*, p. 396; *Gesammelte Schriften* I.2, p. 702.
55. Benjamin, *Selected Writings 4*, p. 396; *Gesammelte Schriften* I.2, p. 703.
56. G. W. Leibniz, *Oeuvres Philosophiques* 2, ed. Paul Janet (Paris: Libraire Philosophiques de Ladrange, 1866), p. 596.
57. Ibid.
58. Benjamin, *Selected Writings 4*, p. 397; *Gesammelte Schriften* I.2, p. 704.
59. Benjamin, *Selected Writings 4*, p. 396; *Gesammelte Schriften* I.2, p. 703.
60. Benjamin, *Selected Writings 4*, p. 397; *Gesammelte Schriften* I.2, p. 704.
61. Benjamin, *Selected Writings 4*, p. 404; *Gesammelte Schriften* I.3, p. 1234.
62. Benjamin, *Selected Writings 4*, p. 396; *Gesammelte Schriften* I.2, p. 702.
63. Benjamin, *Selected Writings 4*, p. 396; *Gesammelte Schriften* I.2, p. 702.
64. Benjamin, *Selected Writings 4*, p. 397; *Gesammelte Schriften* I.2, p. 704.
65. Benjamin, *Selected Writings 4*, p. 393; *Gesammelte Schriften* I.2, p. 697.
66. Benjamin, *Selected Writings 4*, p. 397; *Gesammelte Schriften* I.2, p. 704.

67. This painting is reproduced on the front cover. For a detailed discussion of the work – a discussion that occurs independently of any reference to Walter Benjamin – see Rudolph Altrocchi, 'Michelino's Dante', *Speculum* 6.1 (January 1931), pp. 15–59.
68. Die Bibel, *Schulausgabe: Lutherübersetzung mit Apokryphen* (Stuttgart: Deutsche Bibelgesellschaft, 1984).

Boredom and Distraction: The Moods of Modernity

Opening

History, once freed from the hold of dates, involves bodily presence. The presence of those bodies is positioned within a nexus of operations. If that nexus can be named then it is the locus of moods. Moods are lived out; equally, however, they are lived through. Implicit in the writings of Walter Benjamin is a conception of historical subjectivity presented in terms of moods. The project here is the formulation of that implicit presence. This necessitates not just the recovery of this direction of thought, but the attempt to plot possible interconnections of historical time and the complexity of lived experience. What is essential is that their occurrence be understood as integral to the formulation of modernity. Subjectivity cannot be simply assumed. Its modern configuration is essential.

History, in Benjamin's writings, is not a distant concern. While the late work 'On the Concept of History' is a short text – a set of theses – in it Benjamin began to give systematic expression to the final development of a philosophy of history. The theses or notes contain certain allusions to subjectivity. And yet, subjectivity is not incorporated as a condition of history. Precluding a concern with subjectivity would seem to leave out an important element through which experience and hence the subject's being in the world takes place. This condition does not pertain to the psychic dimension of subjectivity. The organisation of experience – experience as organised – takes place in terms of moods. Boredom and distraction, to cite but two, are not conditions of a subject. On the contrary, they are conditions of the world. And yet they are neither arbitrary conditions nor are they historically random. Moods, it will be contended, are inextricably bound up with the modern. This occurs both in terms of what would count as a conception of the modern and equally in terms of what will be described as modernity's self-theorisation. It should be added immediately that any one instance of this self-theorisation is not assumed to be true; indeed this could not be the case given fundamental distinctions in how terms such as 'boredom' are conceived.[1] Rather, part of what marks out the modern is the presence of this self-theorisation, a process bound up with the inevitability of a form of conflict. Conflict can be defined, at the outset, as designating differing and incompatible constructions of the present – constructions that enjoin specific tasks – that occur at the same point in chronological time.[2] This is the context within which a conception of mood needs to be located.

Highlighting the centrality of moods has to be seen as a way of thinking through a relationship between bodily presence and the operation of historical time. (An operation thought beyond any conflation, let alone identification of historical time with chronology.) To the extent that boredom functions as a mode determining experience, there will be an important distinction between the factual boredom of a given individual and the world that continues to present itself as boring. In the second instance, boredom will have a greater scope precisely because it is not subject dependent. (This form of boredom is not more authentic. Rather it identifies a different locus of intervention and thus enjoins a different politics.) However, there is the subject's boredom. There is the subject's distraction; distracted by the world though distracted nonetheless. If there is a critique of experience that takes as its object an overcoming of the hold of Kant's 'Transcendental Aesthetic' as the organisation of experience's possibility then, it will be conjectured, it takes place not just through the addition of moods but in relation to the complexity of subjectivity that the interconnection of moods and historical time creates.[3] The 'transcendental aesthetic' need not refuse the hold of history per se; what it refuses is a conception of history in which the detail of the 'now' of its happening demands specific attention. Moreover, it will be the identification of that 'now' that allows for the advent of inventions and innovations enjoining their own philosophical and political response. Interruption and innovation demand more than simple incorporation. They allow for forms of transformation. This is an argument advanced by Benjamin in relation to the interruption within the presence and the practice of art brought about by the emergence of reproducibility. (Clearly reproducibility, while central to Benjamin's position, can be read as a transformative figure. In other words, reproducibility need not be literalised since more is at work. Not only therefore can it be retained as a mark of interruption, in this context it will also be the case that interruption as a potentiality need not be identified with reproduction *tout court*.)

Positioning the importance of moods necessitates noting the way the techniques of art's production are connected to the relationship between the advent of the new and the recognition – thus experience – of the demands made by it. The 'new' is therefore not just a different image, let alone another image. Benjamin argues this point in the following terms:

> It has always been one of the primary tasks of art to create a demand whose full hour of satisfaction has not yet come. The history of every art form has critical periods in which the particular form strains after effects, which can be easily achieved only with a changed technical standard – that is to say, in a new art form.[4]

What has to be read within this formulation is a state of affairs that is more complex than first appears. Complexity arises precisely because the recognition of a demand is a position that can always have been created retrospectively by the advent of a new art form. (Development is neither deterministic nor teleological.) The presence of the new – the identification of the new as the new – can be grounded in the twofold movement of locating limits and then defining their having been overcome. There is an inbuilt fragility to this position, since technological reproduction – reproducibility, if only in this context, being the mark of the new – cannot preclude attempts to explicate its presence within concepts and categories that are inappropriate. (Fragility will re-emerge as an important motif.) However, what counts as appropriate is not defined by the positing of an essential quality to art but rather is present in terms of the particularity of the art form itself. After all, Benjamin's formulation pertained to 'a new form' (*eine neue Kunstform*) and not a new content. Particularity is as much concerned with the medium as it is with the accompanying effect that forms will have on perception. They will make up part of a general conception of the 'what and how' of perception. An example here is photography. The photograph breaks the link between art and what Benjamin calls a work's 'cult value'.

Two points need to be made concerning this break. The first is that it occurs because of the nature of the photograph as opposed to a work whose particularity is located within ritual and thus as part of cult. On the other hand, precisely because what is important is not the photographic content per se but the condition of its production and the implications of those conditions, it will always be possible that a given content will have a greater affinity to cult value than to its break with that value. The presence of the face in a portrait, for example, will bring into play considerations that are already incorporated in the oscillation between a set of 'eternal' values, the essentially human, the soul, etc., and the rearticulation of those values within the ethics and politics of humanism.

While the photograph of the face will allow for such a possibility, the technique resulting in the photograph of the face holds out against it. The presence of these two possibilities, a presence whose ambivalence will be a constitutive part of the work – even though only ever played out on the level of content – marks the need for a form of intervention. The site of intervention is this ambivalence – the cause politics.[5] In addition, though this is the argument to be developed, ambivalence will come to define not just art work but mood itself. The ontology of art work defining the configuration of the moods of modernity. (Hence art will only ever enjoin politics to the extent that both content – understood as a predetermined image structured by a concern with meaning – and instrumentality are displaced in the name of technique.[6])

Rather than assume this position, a specific location in Benjamin's work will provide a point of departure. The moods of *distraction* and *boredom* will be central. Working through these organising moods will demand a consideration of Konvolut D of Benjamin's *The Arcades Project*. (A Konvolut whose title is 'Boredom, Eternal Return'.) A prelude is, of course, necessary. It will be provided by Benjamin's famous engagement with architecture in 'The Work of Art in the Age of Its Mechanical Reproducibility'. That engagement is presented in terms of 'distraction' (*Zerstreuung*). The argument to be developed is that 'distraction' is an organising mood of modernity. Benjamin's concern is to situate the emergence of distraction within the context of art's reception. However, were it to be situated, in addition, in relation to the emergence of art, remembering that Benjamin limits his analysis merely to art's reception, then a further argument would be necessary. What would need to be underlined is that distraction, as a mode of reception, arises because of the unavoidable link between art and secularisation. Art arises because the necessary inscription of objects within ritual has been checked by developments within 'art' itself. These developments are themselves part of the process of secularisation.[7] With the abeyance of ritual differing subject positions arise. In this context, therefore, the link between art and the secular entails the ineliminability of distraction as a mode of reception. Distraction involves fragility. It is never absolute. The subject is drawn across positions. Edges fray. Distraction is a form of ambivalence, one that presages another possibility. (Distraction and ambivalence are signs of the secular.)

Distraction

'I' am distracted, unable to concentrate, hence adrift. Unnoticed, a haze – perhaps *eine Nebelwelt*[8] – overtakes me. Of course, it is a haze through which 'I' see. As the haze settles – perhaps the *brouillard des villes*[9] – its presence as a felt condition has vanished. In the grip of boredom, inured to the situation in which 'I' come to find myself, even my boredom – the imposition, its imposing presence – leaves me unmoved. What little interest there is. The subject, the fetish of a residual humanism, matters little. What matters – precisely because it matters for the subject – is the 'there is'. Hence – *what little interest there is*. How then does this 'there is' provide a way into the mood and thus into the subject's distraction, 'my' being distracted? The question therefore is what happens to the 'my' within the opening up of distraction – in its encounter with the 'there is'? Within the movement, 'I' return to my self. Once 'my' being as me, and 'my' being me, emerge as questions there will be the possibility of their rearticulation within a different framework. Rather than the 'my' having centrality and thus defining distraction, the concern will be with the relationship between what is presented in terms of the mass as opposed to a form of singularity. How this distinction, individual/mass – a distinction rather than a straightforward opposition – is to be understood is one of the questions that have to be addressed. Addressing it will indicate in what way a conception of the interplay of moods and subjectivity can be given a distinctly modern orientation rather than being simply assumed. That orientation will arise from having located the relationship between moods and subjectivity beyond the hold of the opposition defined in terms of the individual as opposed to the mass. 'I' will take another quality. The state of 'my being me' will have acquired a different location.

With 'The Work of Art in the Age of Its Mechanical Reproducibility' distraction has to be situated within the framework of a specific argument arising in the context of a general engagement with art's technical structure. Distraction is a result of a fundamental shift in those structures. Strategically, the term is deployed as part of Benjamin's critique of Duhamel's *Scènes de la vie future*.[10] The strategy of that critique is the attempt to reposition distraction, winning the term back for a different critical project. What Benjamin's critique refuses to accept is Duhamel's argument that the masses 'seek' distraction, as opposed to the singular spectator as the one on whom art makes a demand. This 'commonplace' is insufficient. The inadequacy is not simply philosophical. Its occurrence is linked to the demands made by the medium of film. This medium does not become an end in itself – rather it generates other concepts and categories through which art's work is to be understood. In Benjamin's analysis the distinction between 'distraction' and contemplation is central. He repositions the terms in the following way: 'a man who concentrates before a work of art is absorbed by it . . . In contrast the distracted mass [*die zerstreute Masse*] absorbs the work of art.'[11] The example used to capture the force of this distinction is architecture. 'Architecture', he argues, 'has always offered the prototype of an art work that is received in a state of distraction and through the collective [*das Kollektivum*]'.[12] The unpacking of this position demands careful attention since, among other things, it works to reposition the components of the opposition individual/mass.

A preliminary point needs to be noted prior to proceeding. As was intimated above, what is at play here is the question of what happens to the relationship between the individual and the mass once there is a shift, not just in the production of art work, but with the structure that is then produced. Even though art, both in terms of practice as well as its history, is the continuity of its taking place, the mere presence of continuity, which concedes no more than the possibility of art having a history, does not entail that art has an essential quality. Indeed, art cannot be essentialised since what takes place is the practice and history of discontinuities – the continuity of the discontinuous – which are present both formally and technically. This presence will have differential effects both on subjectivity and relatedly on conditions of reception.

What arises from the centrality attributed to architecture is the possibility, for Benjamin, of distinguishing between two modes of art's reception. The first is the 'tactile' and the second the 'optical'. The first is linked to 'usage' (*Gebrach*). What is important is that within the opposition between the 'tactile' and the 'optical', the position that would be taken up by 'contemplation' and thus individual attention no longer figures. The individual – as opposed to the mass – does not have a position. A transformation has occurred. Indeed, if there is to be a conception of the individual then it will have to be reworked after having taken up this new position. In other words, if the individual is to emerge it will only do so in relation to this reworked conception of the 'mass'. This conception is presented by Benjamin in the opening lines of section XV of the essay, the 'masses are a matrix'. It is in regard to this matrix that 'all habitual behaviour [*alles gewohnte Verhalten*] towards works of art is today emerging newborn'.[13] The question of the habitual (the customary) is central. Art is given again – reborn – because of a reconfiguration of the relationship between subject and object. There is a shift in the comportment towards the art object, a move which, because its occurrence is internal to art, has to be understood as concerning art's mode of formal presentation. The object nature of art comes to be repositioned. (Thereby underlining the proposition that objects only ever have discontinuities as histories.) The disclosure of art therefore does not open beyond itself, precisely because the unity that bears the name 'art' is already the site of divergent activities and histories. Questions of reception and production will always need to have been refracted through this setting.

The mode of reception demarcated by the 'tactile', a mode that will also predominate in relation to the optical – and which defines reception in terms of 'perception' (*Wahrnehmung*) – is structured by 'habit'. That architecture whose concern is with dwelling – *Wohnen* – which should be defined in relation to habit – *Gewohnheit* – is an important opening move, and yet on its own it is not sufficient. What matters is the subject of habit and, as will be noted, habit's implicit temporal structure. Learning to live comes through habit. Within the terms given by this setting the mass becomes the site of distraction. The mass is distracted. The film positions the mass as mass. And yet, the film brings with it a real possibility. Benjamin writes that the film 'makes the cult value recede into the background not only because it encourages an evaluating attitude in the audience, but also because, at the movies, the evaluating attitude requires no "attention" [*Aufmerksamkeit*].'[14] It is, of course, 'attention' that, for Benjamin, is the term that defines art as a relation between an individual and the singular work. The 'evaluating attitude' is a concern neither of the individual nor of the mass (understood as no more than an abstraction ground in the individual). The use of this term therefore announces a distancing of the opposition between the individual and the mass. Moreover, what is distanced in addition is the 'all or nothing' response to the operation of art's work. The distancing means that a type of ambivalence has been introduced. While the film, as with architecture, is received in a state of distraction, film as a medium – film in terms of what Benjamin identifies earlier in the essay in regard to its 'technical structure', not simply in regard to its content – brings with it the capacity to reposition the hold of distraction. This does not occur on the level of the individual as opposed to the mass, nor the mass in opposition to the individual. (The mistake made by Duhamel was not just the retention of the opposition mass/individual as an either/or but the failure to recognise that the technique of reproducibility meant that the terms themselves had to be rethought.)

The adoption of what is described as an 'evaluating attitude' by the mass occurs because of the work's operation. Distraction endures as both subject and object. The state of distraction can become an object without this leading to a position of pure overcoming. The audience is an 'examiner' (*ein Examinator*), even though a distracted one. What this points to is not a critique of ideology, as though truth were simply counter-posed to the ideological. Rather, what is in play is the implicit recognition that countering the hold of distraction is to work with what it was that engendered the determining role of habit. (The examples of film and architecture are the most appropriate in this instance since they indicate ways in which mood and modernity are interconnected.) Undoing habit means deploying what made its recognition possible in the first place. Namely, that habit is lived out within a specific temporal framework. Continuity brings with it the possibility that clings – perhaps on the underside – to ambivalence. There is an important temporality to this structure, one that is also at work in the implications found in the description of the masses as a 'matrix'.

With regard to this conception of temporality what arises is a positioning, defined as much by partiality – partial occurrences, the state of being not quite there, etc. – as it is by the necessity for forms of activity. The truth of the hold exerted by moods is not found either in the mood having been completely overcome or in the refusal of activity. Activity, not voluntarism, needs to be understood as the type of deliberative calculation identified by Benjamin as the 'evaluating attitude'. When Benjamin finishes the essay with the evocation of criticality and distraction, the suggestion should be read as the claim that one arises in the context of the other. Arising, not because of distance, nor from absolute differentiation – a differentiation that would have thought within the posited divide between truth and ideology that his explicit project has already distanced – but arising in the context of what is occasioned by particular art works. Film has ambivalence. However, its technical structure enables that movement in which a type of partiality occurs, a seeing that is neither simple contemplation nor complete absorption, the latter being that absorption in which either the subject or the object would have vanished. The move is from the individual to the mass. The seeing in question is as much a seeing in time as it is a seeing through time in the sense of a seeing without end. Occurring concurrently is a restructuring of time that stems the hold of eternal recurrence – which for Benjamin is the temporality of 'mythic doom' – by the introduction of what he identifies elsewhere as the 'now of recognisability'. However, three questions arise. Who sees? What is the quality of this 'now', and for whom? These questions mark the intersection of moods and time.

The question of identity of the mass needs to be taken further, since the mass is invariably thought of in opposition to the individual. Even the recognition that the mass is not reducible to the sum total of the individuals who comprise it – a lesson presented with exacting concision

in Fritz Lang's film *Fury* – leaves the opposition in play, even if enigmatic.[15] Once the mass is understood as a matrix – thus as a network
– it becomes possible to locate what will henceforth be described as
the *mass individual*.[16] Not the individual that is always the same, nor
a conception of mass as a site of an all encompassing sameness – the
mass as the site of Heidegger's *das Man* (a positioning of the mass still
in terms of a structure of authenticity) – what emerges in their place
is a conception of the mass individual as that which is both dispersed
across though also articulated within this matrix.[17] Presence involves a
network. Equally, central to the construction of the mass individual is
the structure of ambivalence. The co-presence of distraction and criticality are central to that construction. What becomes important therefore
is the extent to which the mass individual becomes a site of conflicting
forces. Positioning is neither absolute nor complete. As will be noted,
Benjamin's account of the construction of subjectivity and intersubjec-
tivity in terms of the move from play to habit is integral to an account of
why ambivalence is constitutive. Only through ambivalence does a cessation of what can be described as *always-the-same* become a possibility. Ambivalence is marked by a potentiality within which interruption
will have conditions of possibility that resist the hold of eternal return.

An additional point needs to be made. Formulations such as 'mass
individual' and the 'mass as a matrix' are not just registers. Both are
inextricably woven within a conception of history in which culture
and barbarism are intertwined. History is the history of victors. This
accounts for why undoing the hold of historicism is, in part, overcoming
'empathy with the victor'. The subjectivity of the mass individual does
not stand opposed to the mass. The site of the mass, as already a locus
of differential relations of complex and incompatible determinations
all balancing the distinct ways in which power operates, means that
the mass individual is neither the one nor the many. As an abstraction,
therefore, the mass individual is the many in one. What then is the mood
of (for) the mass individual? Answering this question will, in the end,
necessitate returning to the relationship between the 'there is' and the
'my'. In the move from 'my boredom' to boredom's 'there is' quality a
different question emerges: who is bored? This is the question addressed
to the mass individual.

Boredom

Konvolut D of Benjamin's *The Arcades Project* – *die Langeweile, ewige
Wiederkehr* (Boredom and Eternal Return) – does not have an intentional

structure. This must necessarily be the case. Nonetheless, the move from the thematic of 'boredom' to Nietzsche takes place via the intermediary of Blanqui. In regard to the latter Benjamin cites specific passages from his *L'Eternité par les asters*, a work that Benjamin will deem to be Nietzschean. Deeming it as such was not based on a clear study of Nietzsche in any straightforward sense, but rather from what he develops using as a basis a citation from Karl Löwith's 1935 study of Nietzsche. A quotation in which the central section of *Die fröhliche Wissenschaft* (*The Gay Science*) concerning 'eternal recurrence' is, indeed, repeated. The whole project therefore is not just selective in terms of the tendentious nature of the quotation, but its selectivity would be compounded if the proper names were allowed to dominate. The Konvolut is about the mood of boredom and the reality of boredom's already present structural location within certain conceptions of historical time. Again, mood meets time. The centrality of that connection provides the way in and, moreover, allows the proper names to be positioned beyond the hold or the accuracy of either citation or interpretation. Viewed is this light, the interpretive question then has to concern the Konvolut's actual project.

Even though the elements of the Konvolut would in the end need to be detailed – a move in which the identification of boredom is caught between the weather, the sameness of grey, somnambulism, etc. – the philosophical dimension of boredom is presented with its greatest acuity in the following:

> We are bored when we don't know what we are waiting for [*worauf wir warten*]. That we do know or think we know is nearly always the expression of our superficiality or inattention. Boredom is the threshold [*die Schwelle*] of great deeds. Now it would be important to know: What is the dialectical antithesis to boredom?[18]

The force of this final question resides in part in the answer not being found in any attempt to identify the content of 'what we are waiting for'. This reinforces the centrality of Benjamin's formalism in the sense that what matters is the structure of an awaiting, rather than filling in that structure with specific images of the future. The project is not to give the future an image or to reduce it to an image. As such, what must be taken up is boredom as a 'threshold'. A threshold is of course as much a line or division as it is the site allowing for equivocation – hence it functions as the locus of ambivalence, par excellence. What this means is that the crossing of a threshold – a crossing in which futurity is introduced as made possible by the present's potentiality – has to be thought beyond a conception of the future that is already pictured. An already present picture would mean that the future had already been given in advance by its conflation with a pre-existing and thus already identifiable image. (There is an important connection here between the possibility of politics – the political as the winning of the future – and a type of iconoclasm.)[19]

The Konvolut opens with an evocation of weather as that which blankets the 'all', leading to a form of sameness. Equally, dust settles on the rooms and is attracted even by the brightest and most intricate of clothes. Dust is the 'stifler of perspective'. Perhaps, dust's potential lies in its capacity to absorb blood. As such, and despite the continuity of its always being the same, dust can absorb the passage of time, part of which is history's continual encounter with barbarism. As with dust so with grey. Countering the grey – a countering presaged by an encounter with grey as a site of potentiality – is not to juxtapose it with colour. Hence Benjamin cites with evident approval de Chirico: 'Only here is it possible to paint. The streets have such gradations of grey.'[20] With this formulation – with the grey, its depth, even depth within the subtle *solche Skalen von Grau* – there is the first intimation of the threshold. The relationship between 'grey' and the 'threshold' will emerge as central.

As is often the case with *The Arcades Project*, it is not just Benjamin's actual writings that are fundamental; equal emphasis should also be given to the nature as well as to the content of his quotations. He cites a long passage from Rodenberg's book on Paris. The passage concerns a visit with a 'millionaire' (Benjamin's term). Entering the house, despite the glitter – understood as the play of surfaces – *Schein* without beauty – Rodenberg notes: 'Something like suppressed boredom lay in the air' (*Etwas wie heimliche Langeweile lag in der Luft*). In the room were a series of brightly coloured parrots. They, for Rodenberg, 'all seemed to suffer from homesickness' (*alle scheinen an Heimweh zu kranken*). While a lot could be made of the repetitive force of terms involving *heim*, what is of significance in the passage lies elsewhere. Namely, that in order to come to an understanding of boredom as a mood it is essential to recognise that it is not undone by the introduction of colour. While the parrots were at a distance, holding to a type of separation, boredom still prevailed. It should be remembered that this is not Benjamin writing but Rodenberg. However, the extract from Rodenberg's text works precisely because it captures the problem of boredom in terms of what was identified earlier as the 'there is' quality of moods. Once 'there is' boredom, then it is not countered by that which seems to stand against its phenomenal presence, hence Benjamin's interest in the dandy, the one who despite colour and due to the insistent presence of a form of singularity compounds boredom. The dandy is, of course, only the individual within a structured opposition between mass and individual. The dandy is not the mass individual. Donning a new garb – history as the play of no more than surfaces – becomes a conception of the new in which its conflation with novelty defines its presence. To utilise another quotation deployed by Benjamin: 'Monotony feeds on the new' (*La monotonie se nourrit de neuf*).[21]

Once therefore the question of the 'new' emerges it can be linked to the 'threshold'. What matters is that the threshold should not be explained in terms of the 'new'. What could be more boring? And yet, the constancy of the new is hardly news. Hence there needs to be another understanding of the temporality of moods. A given mood is not countered by its juxtaposition with its phenomenal opposite. Nor, moreover, is it undone by the mere assertion of the new. (The question of the new and the posited overcoming of boredom through novelty makes it clear why the Konvolut has to deal in the end with the problem of 'eternal return'.) Asserting the new and the positing of boredom's having been overcome has to define both – the new and boredom – in relation to the individual. However, it is essential to be precise: the individual in question is the one given within the opposition individual/mass. What this does is define boredom as the province of the individual. At the same time, therefore, it elides any possible concern with boredom's 'there is' quality. Once that quality is denied then a different politics opens up; rather than the mass individual and thus a commitment to a form of mass action, the political would be defined by the individual's centrality and orchestrated in terms of the happiness or the well-being of the individual. (The political distinction is between a conception of the political linked to individual needs and aspirations – a version of liberalism – and one defined by the ever present possibility of mass action.)[22]

Benjamin provides a way into this formulation of the problem of time – the temporality of moods – in terms of what he describes as the temporality of awaiting. What is the time of awaiting? Benjamin's response to this question necessitates that this awaiting be distinguished from an awaiting in which the image of the future determines both what is to occur as well as its having occurred. What cannot be expected – even though it is too often expected – is victory to come through continuity. This recalls the passage cited earlier in which Benjamin dismisses as a form of binary opposition boredom linked to not knowing what is awaited as one pole, and the superficiality or lack of attention inherent in the claim that we can give a form to that which is awaited as the other. (The latter point is, despite moments of real equivocation, an inherent part of Benjamin's critique of a version of utopian thinking.) Awaiting, transform time. Benjamin writes that the one who waits, 'takes in time and renders it up in altered form [*in veränderter*

Gestalt] – that of expectation.'[23] Expectation and the one awaiting – *die Erwartung* and *der Wartende* – become figures. Equally, this holds open the possibility of another formulation of moods. It may be therefore – though this is still a conjecture – that what counters boredom as a mood is not just action but the possibility of a counter-mood. A mood not just as a disposition but as that which organises experience. Awaiting and expectation – as necessitating the transformation of time – a transformation in which the future becomes a condition of the present, rather than the present being a series of empty moments awaiting a future, would mean that there is another mood. This possibility does more than tie moods and time together. They become linked to a possibility and thus to a form of potentiality.

Potentiality inheres in one of the most striking presentations of the threshold condition. This takes place when boredom is described as a 'warm grey fabric' that has, on its other side, 'lustrous and colourful silk'. For Benjamin 'we' sleep wrapped in this blanket. The sleeper appears 'bored'. On awakening the sleeper wishes to communicate the dream, and yet all that is narrated is this boredom. Overcoming boredom is the narrating of the dream. Doing so, however, necessitates 'at one stroke' (*mit einem Griff*) turning 'the lining of time to the other side [*nach außen zu kehren*]'. This 'other side' – time's other side, a side revealed or turned out in an instant by an action – is the narrating of the dream as the overcoming of boredom. What is significant here is twofold. In the first instance this possibility is already present in the fabric holding boredom in play. In other words, it is present as a potentiality. That is why in the following entry in the Konvolute boredom becomes 'the external surface [*die Außenseite*] of unconscious events'.[24] Crossing the threshold therefore will involve more than simple movement. Secondly, the 'fabric' – one side of which is grey and the other lustrous, two sides holding a threshold in place, a place whose articulation is given as that across which something would occur when one side is turned to another – provides a way into understanding what a 'dialectical antithesis' to boredom would involve. For Benjamin, the dialectical needs to be explicated as a juxtaposition of elements rather than their synthesis. Opposition needs to be shown. It becomes a form of narration whose conditions of possibility are themselves already possible. The possibility lies in the construction of boredom itself. Rather than existing as a discreet and separate entity, it exists as bound up with its opposite. The overcoming of boredom is not the move to the coloured underside. Indeed, it is not even a matter of the simple juxtaposition of grey and colour, as though all that was involved amounted to choice. Benjamin's formulations should not be taken as literal. Rather, narrating the dream that would be the movement across the threshold – the movement on from boredom – needs to be thought in relation to the structure of temporality marked out by awaiting. Moreover, it is a sense of awaiting that depends upon the potential actuality of interruption.

Boredom is an awaiting without an object. This cannot be countered by the presentation of images of the future. Boredom works as a threshold precisely because the move away from boredom is carried by it as a potentiality. The site of potentiality is the present. However, it is not a conception of the present that is reducible to the moment thought within the passage of chronological time. Rather, the present moment is the event happening as the 'now of recognisability'. The coat turning with a rapidity within which both the grey and the colour in an instant – the instant as 'standstill' – become the opening where 'great deeds' will occur. The grey and the lustrous are brought into play. Their juxtaposition will have become an opening. An opening that appears within the repetition of habit, though equally it appears within repetition as habit. (Occurring *within* these settings and not *as* them.) Once again what appears is an occurrence, which, in having to be thought in terms of an interruption eschewing the hold of both novelty on the one hand and, on the other, the repetition of a given content that cannot be represented within the temporality of eternal return, takes on the form of a caesura.[25] Repetition has to be understood in relation to a founding interruption, the interruption that founds. As will be seen, this is the opening up of habit.

In writing about children's toys Benjamin produces one of his most important reflections on habit. While the position arises from within the context of a discussion of play – a context whose importance will be decisive – two other aspects, those providing the very basis of his actual argument, are fundamental. The first is that for Benjamin it is through the rhythms of play that 'we' 'first gain possession of ourselves'. 'We' gain it prior to those other stages – such as love – in which there is an entry 'into the life and often alien rhythm of another human being'.[26] Not only is there a conception of subjectivity announced in this formulation, of equal significance is the related additional aspect, namely, both subjectivity as a construction and then its enactment in the realm of others is articulated in terms of repetition. Play, for Benjamin, is presided over by the 'law of repetition'. Within play there is a necessity for the same thing to be done over again. Both for the child and then for the adult (the adult's version will contain important differences, however) repetition – through, and as, play – allows for what frightens (or has frightened) to be incorporated and therefore mastered. Equally, the reiteration of the disturbing enables it to be lived with. With its repetition what had initially frightened becomes parody. In Benjamin's argument, the adult articulates this position in terms of storytelling, while the child repeats the event in all its details.

> An adult relieves his heart from its terrors and doubles happiness by turning it into a story. A child creates the entire event anew and starts again right from the beginning.[27]

In both instances there is a type of transformation. What is fundamental is its nature. The 'essence' (*Wesen*) of play resides in its being 'the transformation of a shattering experience into habit' (*Verwandlung der erschütterndsten Erfahrung in Gewohnheit*). Play allows an originating event to be accommodated. Living with it becomes the registration of play within habit and thus within dwelling. (This is the link between *Gewohnheit* and *Wohnen*.) Habit, now as the living out of a certain structure of activity, contains within it an element that cannot be mastered even by the demand that habit has to be lived out continually. It harbours that transformative moment that is its own construction. Habit contains therefore not the capacity to revert to play but the fundamental doubling that brings two incompatible elements (inassimilable both as an occurrence and as image) into a type of constellation, a constellation containing both the experience that shatters and its transformation. This complexity has to be run back through the construction of subjectivity, construction as a process of self-possession. What will emerge is that, in terms of their formal presence, one will mirror the other.

Gained in this act of self-possession is a doubled site. Play is the continual encounter with a particular conception of the founding of subjectivity. Founding involves a dislocation that locates. The representation – thus reiteration – of this positioning occurs as habit. The possession that 'we' have of 'ourselves' prior to any encounter with the other is of a site that is not simply doubled but constructed within and as ambivalence. What enters into relations with the other therefore is this doubled entity who can love – and therefore be surprised – because that transformative potential is there from the start. However, precisely because it is given by a founding ambiguity, even love will not transform absolutely. (Love's end is, after all, an insistent possibility.) Nonetheless, love is only possible because of an original ambivalence. However, this original condition is not to be understood as epistemological. Ambivalence is not relativism. Even though within the precise structure of Benjamin's own formulation it may not have been presented in these terms, ambivalence needs to be understood as an ontological condition. As such, it is another description of what has already been identified as the many in one. In other words, the mass individual is the locus of ambivalence; the potentiality of the masses lies therein. The realisation of that potential, however, should not be interpreted as a move from an ideological condition – a state of self-deception – towards truth. Benjamin brings these elements together in the following formulation:

> The sort of distraction that is provided by art represents a covert measure of the extent to which it has become possible to perform new tasks of appercep-tion. Since, moreover, individuals are tempted to evade such tasks, art will tackle the most difficult and important tasks where it is able to mobilise the masses.[28]

Mobilisation, the clear instance of which is in film, occurs as a mobilisa-tion within distraction. Central to the passage therefore is the concep-tion of mass it envisages. Individuals are not transformed into the mass. Rather, the site of transformation is the mass individual. Ambivalence becomes production. For this very reason ambivalence brings with it an inevitable fragility. There is an instability.

Art that 'mobilises the masses' is not a conception of art that trans-forms the life of an individual. The art in question creates the mass. It demands the mass and makes demands of it. The mass individual is the subject of modernity whose potential for collective action and thus acts of solidarity are grounded in the structure of ambivalence. Integral to that structure is the awaiting linked to boredom. Accompanying both is the potentiality for interruption. In general terms, interruption comes about. An interruption that will be an occasioning. Precisely because interruption has to be thought beyond the hold of the temporality of fashion – the positing of the completely new – there will always be fragility. Fragility, however, marks as much the inevitability of contesta-tion as it does its possible recuperation. Subjectivity and historical time mirror each other. The structure in question, however, does not pertain to the individual as such but to the mass individual. This conception of the subject takes on boredom as a condition. But in taking it on, it brings with it, because it recapitulates it, the very set-up that is itself given by boredom's 'there is' quality. Boredom's being overcome – understood as a potentiality rather than the countering of a set of 'dead' images with apparently new and enlivening ones – becomes the moment in which the 'straining after effects' encounter their possibility. In other words, the dialectical antithesis to boredom is experimentation, experimenta-tion both as mood and as act. However, there cannot be any naivety concerning experimentation. It occurs at the time of the commodity. Moreover, its occurrence cannot be disassociated from the temporality of commodity production. Though equally with a complacency in which continuity both as a political process and as a form of production has been naturalised. Experimentation has to be thought in relation to its inherent fragility. Once again, it is that very fragility that demands the affirmation of experimentation – an affirmation in the face of the inescapable possibility of its recuperation. That affirmation is the project of criticism. Equally, it is the project of politics. If images of the future are forbidden, the imaging of the future involves the continual encounter in the present – an encounter that works equally to construct the present – with what 'there is'. Subjectivity's incorporation into the 'there is' gives to the subject a capacity for action. It is, however, not the action of a hero, but the cunning of the mass individual.

Notes

1. Clearly the other important thinker of boredom is Heidegger. While both Heidegger and Benjamin locate boredom as a condition of the modern and thus as one of the mood of modernity, there is a fundamental difference in how the conception of the present and thus the way it determines the philosophical project is understood. For Heidegger's most sustained engagement with boredom see his *The Fundamental Concepts of Metaphysics*, trans. William McNeill and Nicholas Walker (Bloomington: Indiana University Press, 1995).
2. I have tried to give a detailed account of this conception of the present in my *Present Hope* (London: Routledge, 1997).
3. Benjamin's relation to Kant is a topic of research in its own right. In general terms, however, Kant positions Space and Time as providing the conditions of possibility for experience. They are the 'pure forms of sensible intuition' (A39); Immanuel Kant, *Critique of Pure Reason*, trans. Paul Guyer and Allen Wood (Cambridge: Cambridge University Press, 1997), p. 183. While experience is essential in terms of its possibility, what is left untreated – by definition – is the nature of the experience and any strong conception of the experiencing subject other than one refined by pure interiority. Indeed, it is the fact that for Kant space and time are a condition of the subject, which means that while Kant is right to argue that experience has to be accounted for in terms of that which makes it possible, the possibility of experience within modernity involves a relationship between both moods and the subject. Moods have a determining effect on a subject. Moreover, what needs to be added to any thought of mood as having a determination on a subject is their articulation within a structure maintained by disequilibria of power.
4. Benjamin, *Selected Writings* 4, p. 266; *Gesammelte Schriften* I.2, pp. 500–1.
5. Ambivalence as an ontological state rather than one linked to the relativism of epistemology. What this means is that ambivalence is an aspect that is constitutive of subjectivity itself. Within the prevailing presence of ambivalence, knowledge is essential.

6. The heritage in which the technology of art is discussed usually oscillates between two predetermined positions. In the first instance, the term 'technology' assumes a monolithic quality and thus cannot be used effectively to account for different and conflicting practices that stem from the same technological source. While the second technique, as a domain of practice, often adopts a humanist conception of techné and as such presents it in terms of human skill. The hand works with the machine. As opposed to both of these directions of research, what needs to be pursued is what could be described as the development of an ontology of techniques. This is of course a project to come. However, it is one that can be located within a mode of thinking that begins with Benjamin.

7. I have tried to provide a more sustained version of this argument in my *Disclosing Spaces: On Painting* (Manchester: Clinamen, 2004). See in particular Chapters 1 and 3.

8. Benjamin, *Arcades Project*, p. 103; *Gesammelte Schriften* V.1, p. 158 [D1,4].

9. Benjamin, *Arcades Project*, p. 101; *Gesammelte Schriften* V.1, p. 157 [D1,1].

10. There are other uses of the term 'distraction' in the same period – see, for example, Siegfried Kracauer, *The Mass Ornament*, trans. Thomas Y. Levin (Cambridge, MA: Harvard University Press, 1995). One of Kracauer's formulations opens up the question of who sees and thus the nature of the subject of distraction. Writing of the interior design of the cinema he notes that the 'stimulation of the senses succeed one another with such rapidity that there is no room left between them even for the slightest contemplation' (p. 326). The temporality of this movement – one marked by the elimination of any possible intervention – is implicitly challenged by Benjamin's notion of distraction. The audience's state of absorption retains a partiality precisely because of the ineliminability of the potential for criticality.

11. Benjamin, *Selected Writings* 4, p. 267; *Gesammelte Schriften* I.2, p. 504.

12. Benjamin, *Selected Writings* 4, p. 268; *Gesammelte Schriften* I.2, p. 505.

13. Benjamin, *Selected Writings* 4, p. 267; *Gesammelte Schriften* I.2, p. 504.

14. Benjamin, *Selected Writings* 4, p. 269; *Gesammelte Schriften* I.2, p. 505.

15. For a detailed investigation of the complex politics of *Fury* see Anton Kaes, 'A Stranger in the House: Fritz Lang's Fury and the Cinema of Exile', *New German Critique* 89 (Fall 2003), pp. 33–58.

16. An obvious site in which it would be possible to begin to identify this development is in Sigmund Freud, 'Group Psychology and the Analysis of the Ego', *Standard Edition* XVIII, pp. 65–143. The value of Freud's work is the way it complicates any straightforward distinction between the individual and the group. What is of interest with Benjamin, however, is the possibility of introducing not the constraint of the ego-ideal but a relationship between distraction and criticality that links their presence to a founding ambivalence. The ambivalence means that the critical will have a relation to formal presence rather than the projection of one content as opposed to another. While it cannot be undertaken here, the question of ambivalence as a motif in psychoanalysis would need to be pursued through section II of 'Totem and Taboo'.

17. While its detail cannot be pursued here, the distinction between 'authentic'

and 'inauthentic' self is formulated in *Being and Time* in the following terms: 'The self of everyday Dasein is the they-self which we distinguish from the authentic self – that is from the self which has been taken hold of in its own way. As the they-self, the particular Dasein has been dispersed into the they, and must first find itself' (Martin Heidegger, *Being and Time*, p. 167).

18. Benjamin, *Arcades Project*, p. 105; *Gesammelte Schriften* V.1, p. 161 [D2,7].

19. The iconoclasm involves the need to retain technique and thus abstraction as a site of the political and not to identify the political nature of art with content. As such the image must always be secondary. What matters therefore is not an image but an understanding of techniques within which (and with which) the future is produced. It is in this regard that it becomes possible to link the political in art to abstraction, where the latter is understood as a site of potential.

20. Benjamin, *Arcades Project*, p. 103; *Gesammelte Schriften* V.1, p. 159 [D1a,7].

21. Benjamin, *Arcades Project*, p. 111; *Gesammelte Schriften* V.1, p. 168 [D5,6].

22. See in this regard Werner Hamacher, 'Afformative Strike: Benjamin's Critique of Violence', trans. Dana Hollander, in Andrew Benjamin and Peter Osborne (eds), *Walter Benjamin's Philosophy: Destruction and Experience* (London: Routledge, 1994), pp. 108–37.

23. Benjamin, *Arcades Project*, p. 107; *Gesammelte Schriften* V.1, p. 164 [D3,4].

24. Benjamin, *Arcades Project*, p. 106; *Gesammelte Schriften* V.1, p. 162 [D2a,2]

25. This is of course the point at which the encounter with Nietzsche has to be staged. The section from *The Gay Science* that Benjamin quotes would need to be the site of engagement.

26. Benjamin, *Selected Writings* 2, p. 120; *Gesammelte Schriften* III, p. 131.

27. Benjamin, *Selected Writings* 2, p. 120; *Gesammelte Schriften* III, p. 131.

28. Benjamin, *Selected Writings* 4, pp. 268–9; *Gesammelte Schriften* I.2, p. 505)

Benjamin and the Baroque: Posing the Question of Historical Time

The true picture of the past flits by. The past can be seized only as an image that flashes up at the moment of its recognisability, and is never seen again. 'The truth will not run away from us' – this statement by Gottfried Keller indicates exactly the point in historicism's image of history where the image is perceived by historical materialism. For it is an irretrievable image of the past, which threatens to disappear with every present, which does not recognise itself as intended in that image.

Walter Benjamin

Accounting for the differences, especially those that are taken to comprise historical periods, brings with it questions of beginnings, endings and the articulation and identification of what will be distinct modes of differentiation.[1] Difference is not simply defined by the content of the philosophical, the literary and the art historical. The presupposition is that difference can be neither presupposed nor posited. There is, however, an important additional dimension. Difference also involves the work of a specific conception of historical time. At stake here therefore is the question of difference as a term that can be incorporated into a philosophy of history. More generally, difference only emerges and thus appears as genuine where difference involves limitation and inauguration. Within such a setting, differences would be present in terms of the actually differential and thus *not* in terms of a conception of difference in which difference comes to be identified with variety. In this instance, at work within questions of difference – difference as opposed to variety – is a conception of historical time that is present in relation to breaks and interruptions that have an inaugurating potential. Fundamental to this project therefore is the establishing of limits and points of demarcation. This is a process of identification whose retroactive quality cannot pass unnoticed.

In writing of the distinction between Renaissance and Baroque art Walter Benjamin, in ways that betray a remarkable prescience, defines their difference in the following terms:

> Whereas the painters of the Renaissance know how to keep their skies high, in the paintings of the Baroque the cloud moves, darkly or radiantly, down towards the earth. In contrast to the Baroque the Renaissance does not appear as a godless and heathen period, but as period of lay freedom [*als eine Spanne laienhafter Freiheit*] for the life of the faith, while the Counter-Reformation sees the hierarchical system of the Middle Ages assume authority in a world which was denied direct access to a beyond.[2]

The project of this Appendix will be to pursue the importance of this claim made by Benjamin, as an instance of the identification of the historically distinct. What this necessitates pursuing are the problems set by the relationship between forms of periodisation and the question of historical time as a general concern, and then more particularly the ways in which limits and forms of overcoming figure in the treatment of 'fate' and 'melancholia' within *The Origin of German Tragic Drama*.[3] Of added importance here is that, for Benjamin, 'the problem of subsequent ages is foreign to the Baroque'.[4] Hence the question of retroactive identification. This designation of the Baroque and the necessity for retroactive identification means that any intervention in relation to the Baroque, to the extent that this estimation of Benjamin's is correct, cannot be defined straightforwardly in the terms set by the Baroque. There is an already present need to reveal the Baroque's own self-conception through an engagement with two elements that play a decisive role within Benjamin's text, that is, 'fate' and 'melancholia'. These terms bring into play both the question of historical time and that of historical specificity. Benjamin suggests explicitly that the Baroque was able 'to see the power of the present' within *Trauerspiel*.[5] The 'present' staged within this formulation was its own.[6] What therefore arises as an inescapable question is what a return to the Baroque opens up for another present.

Fate, both as a philosophical term and a specific register of activity, cannot be separated from the presence of historical time. Moreover, what it stages is lived out. This pertains to the term as both a descriptor as well as to what is evoked by Benjamin to account for that which is at work in the operation of *Trauerspiel*. Integral to its being lived out is the presence of a radical division between the time in which that living occurs and the way that time is configured within the place and play of its being lived out. (The configuring is of course what establishes time as a site of contestation.) In addition, fate provides the setting in which the particularity of melancholia and its formation within *Trauerspiel* takes place. It should not be overlooked, however, that Benjamin concludes his treatment of melancholia within the context of *Trauerspiel* with an assessment of the latter in which its limit is clearly established. He writes:

> The German Trauerspiel was never able to inspire itself to a new life; it was never able to awaken [*zu erwecken*] within itself the clear light of self-awareness [*den Silberblick der Selbstbesinnung*]. It remained astonishingly obscure to itself, and was able to portray the melancholic only in the crude and washed-out colours of the mediaeval complexion books.[7]

What this passage indicates is that there is a potentiality in the Baroque that was not, and more significantly could not, have been realised. The failure to 'awaken' within itself what was already there as a potentiality delimits, for Benjamin, *Trauerspiel*. That Benjamin uses the language of 'awakening', a term that will come to play a central role in his later writings, is significant.[8] Indeed, 'awakening' both in its own right and in its link to dreaming becomes an important refrain in *The Arcades Project*. It is as though the *Trauerspiel* was caught within its own dream, and thus what could not emerge was the interruption that would have enabled the occurrence of a new life. The *Trauerspiel* lacks self-inspiration and therefore self-awareness: in sum, an 'awakening'. It calls out therefore for its own awakening: an awakening to its own potentiality. The *Trauerspiel* occurs within the work of fate. As such fate, thus *Trauerspiel*, is explicable in terms of the reiteration of the temporality of myth. It becomes self-enclosed. An enclosure that is necessitated as, for Benjamin, 'there is no Baroque eschatology' (*Es gibt keine barocke Eschatologie*).[9]

Fate constructs what could be described as an operative sense of time, that is, the incorporation of time into what will be the construction of a philosophico-historical, a literary as well as political, position. Benjamin is careful that his initial formulation resists the identification of fate (and thus its temporality) with either 'nature' or 'history'. Indeed, it can be argued that the analysis of fate, an analysis that becomes the positioning of fate, in resisting the opposition nature/history undoes, as a consequence, the hold that such an opposition can exert over historical and philosophical analyses. In so doing, it allows for the introduction of both 'history' and 'nature' construed in radically different ways – indeed, one now depends upon the other.[10] Benjamin's opening move is of central importance. He argues that 'fate is meaningful only as a category of natural history in the spirit of the restoration-theology of the Counter-Reformation.'[11] The 'Counter-Reformation' provides a form of location.[12] And yet, the force of this claim – despite an initial suggestion to the contrary – should not be identified with the straightforward location of the term 'fate' within the history of either religion or theology, as if that location provided it with an exclusive definition. Rather, it attests to the tension within theological positions. That tension has an extension that reaches beyond such positions. What will become clear is that the potential within *Trauerspiel* and thus within the Baroque can be identified with what will emerge, in the first instance, as an original divide within the structure of melancholia and then, in the second, from the suggested possibility of an overcoming of fate due to the inscription of 'grace' within the world of faith. This inscription, however, will register a form of potentiality that nonetheless founders, leading to the eventual impossibility of that overcoming.[13] This impossible possibility is the Baroque's self-limitation. The concern with 'grace' is a theological position; nonetheless, what it indicates is the presence within fate – lived out within a world permeated by faith – of the potentiality for its own interruption. And it is a potentiality whose impossibility is inextricably tied up with melancholia.[14] The presence of 'grace' concedes the possibility of an overcoming in which the potential is internal, even though its actualisation necessitates a form of externally originating interruption. An actualisation that the Baroque cannot itself stage even though the potential is there. The intricacy of this positioning of both fate and 'grace', as has been suggested, will unfold in the ensuing treatment of fate and melancholia.

Benjamin's attempt to differentiate *Trauerspiel* from tragedy involves a sustained engagement with Nietzsche's theory of tragedy. Within that engagement both the importance as well as the limits of Nietzsche are sketched with precision. However, there is another reference to Nietzsche. One that is not announced as such and in which the proper name does not figure. Nevertheless, it is a reference that brings to the fore that which is central to fate. Benjamin writes that fate is 'the true order of eternal recurrence' (*die wahre Ordnung der ewigen Wiederkunft*).[15] The reference to Nietzsche's doctrine of 'eternal return' is clear. In *The Arcades Project* 'eternal return' figures with the 'belief in progress' as that against which a radically different conception of time should be positioned. Both of these conceptions of historical time are in Benjamin's sense of the term 'mythic'.[16] The question to be taken to the Baroque and thus to *Trauerspiel* is the presence of a capacity that would counter the work of fate. Encountering and discovering limits are part of a process of 'awakening', a process that the Baroque could not enact, but which (and despite this identified limitation) is the only means by which there can be an interruption of the temporality of 'eternal return'.

Fate within *Trauerspiel* is not the incorporation of the sequential logic of causality that is then attributed to nature and which is, as a consequence, incorporated into the chain of events within a literary form. Rather, for Benjamin, fate cannot be disassociated from guilt: 'Fate is the entelechy of events within the field of guilt.'[17] What, however, does 'guilt' mean? The obvious reference to an original state of innocence that preceded the Fall and thus allowed post-Lapsarian existence to be understood as guilt must be viewed as incorrect. Guilt cannot be defined in terms of its relation to a subject. Guilt pertains to the acceptance of fate's unavoidability and thus to the naturalisation of fate. The latter is the construction of fate as inevitable. While this leaves open the identification of fate with 'original sin', such an identification would be misplaced. Once guilt is defined in relation to historical time and the inscription of the subject as temporal, this then demythologises 'original sin' and thus strips it of its inevitability. As such, what would have been given as 'sin' would then take on a different quality. Repositioned, it would no longer be original; it would have been imposed on life. Fate and myth position human activity and thus create a conception of subjectivity as the subject of fate. Unlike the work of fate within tragedy in which fate is bound up with 'individual destiny', within *Trauerspiel*, fate is situated and this is effective, for Benjamin, within a community. In addition, it operates through the presence of 'things' within their theatrical staging. This point will be taken up below in relation to the role of the handkerchief in Shakespeare's *Othello*.

At this point, what needs to be developed is the relationship between 'guilt' and subjectivity. What occurs within the relationship is the identification of subjectivity with the subject of fate. This subject position is defined by Benjamin in terms of the 'creaturely'. The creature is not the animal in any direct sense.[18] It is what he identifies elsewhere as 'mere life' (*das bloße Leben*), namely the equation of subjectivity – both in terms of the subject's affective presence as well as its historical presence – as that which is positioned continually by fate's inexorability.[19] In *The Origin of German Tragic Drama* this is formulated in the following terms:

> For once human life has sunk into the merely creaturely [*in den Verband des bloßen kreatürlichen gesunken*], even if the life of apparently dead objects [*der scheinbar toten Dinge*] secures power over it. The effectiveness of the object where guilt has been incurred is a sign of the approach of death. The passionate stirrings of the creaturely life in man – in a word passion itself – bring the fatal property into action [. . .]. In the drama of fate the nature of man which is expressed in blind passion, and the nature of things, which is expressed in blind chance [*Zufall*], are both equally subject to the law of fate [*Gesetz des Schicksals*].[20]

The connection between the 'creaturely' and 'dead objects', which are more generally the domain of 'things', raises the possibility that what is involved in the sinking of 'human life' amounts to the equation of that life with pure animality. But such an identification would misunderstand what is implied by the term 'creaturely'. This point emerges in the following engagement with Shakespeare. While Benjamin locates a great deal of his argument in *The Origin of German Tragic Drama* in an extensive engagement with *Hamlet,* in this chapter it is Shakespeare's *Othello* that allows for an investigation of the relationship between the creaturely and the world of objects (things) to arise.[21]

The handkerchief is the central object that orientates activity within the play from Act III Scene 3 onwards. It works upon what is given from the play's opening as Othello's already predetermined nature: his 'guilt' insofar as he becomes the subject of fate. Before turning to the handkerchief – the object (thing) that 'overpowers' Othello – it is worth noting the connection to the animal. Act II Scene 1 ends with Iago's soliloquy in which he confesses to hating 'the Moor', while raising and then dismissing his own possible jealousy as a reason for undoing him. All this occurs in the context of his plotting what will become Othello's destruction. The destruction in question is linked to Othello's 'nature' and depends on Iago's playing on Othello's own susceptibility in relation to Desdemona.[22] The point to be clarified concerns the relationship between this susceptibility and what Benjamin identifies as 'guilt'. This, of course, is not the guilt that is structured by moral concerns, rather it is the guilt that allows for fate, which within the context of the play is at work within objects, giving them an operative and determining presence both within and as life. The creature – as the subject of fate – creates the moral world: 'The creature is the mirror within whose frame alone the moral world of the Baroque was represented to its eyes.'[23]

Iago announces in advance that that he will 'abuse' Othello's 'ears' with the suggestion that Cassio is 'too familiar with his wife'.[24] Having made this comment he then opens up the link to the animal. It takes place within his estimation of Othello's 'nature'. Iago's use of 'nature' reinforces the fact that what is at work here is an already present condition. An ineliminability that not only brings fate and guilt into a connection, it also ensures that the connection in question is not a posited relation. On the contrary, it has an operative quality, thereby providing that which is integral to the play's economy.

> The Moor is of a free and open nature
> That thinks men honest that but seem to be so;
> And will as tenderly be led by th'nose

As asses are.
I have't! It is engendered. Hell and night
Must bring this monstrous birth to the world's light.[25]

Although there is a suggestion that Othello will be as pliant as an animal (that is, tamed and then led), this is not the point. Indeed the analogy is irrelevant. What matters in the passage is that the identification of Othello's 'nature' will allow for the unfolding of fate. His character is therefore given within the domain of fate and thus not as character in opposition to fate.[26] This is the moment in which the creaturely is actually introduced. It occurs after the analogy – 'As asses are' – and thus after the evocation of animal presence. Animality as part of a simple binary in which the animal is contrasted with the human is precisely not what Benjamin means by 'mere life'. 'Mere life' is the identification of subjectivity with guilt and fate. While the emotions play an important role – Benjamin underscores the 'role of human emotions as the predictable driving mechanism of the creature'[27] – responding emotionally is not animality as opposed to humanity. In this precise context it is the incorporation of the order of fate.

Fate is not external. Othello is not fated in the way in which it can be argued that Oedipus is fated.[28] Othello's fate does not come from an external source. It has neither a divine origin nor does it have historical inevitability. The externality is the incorporation of guilt. Hence Iago's triumphant, 'I have't!': he recognises with exacting precision Othello's predicament, a predicament from which he will conjure the 'monstrous birth'. This will be caused by an object – a handkerchief. The force of the object is clear. To reiterate Benjamin's position, the object 'secures power' over life. The life in question is, however, life as fated. Namely, a life that has become 'mere life', the life of creatures. Moreover, the role of the handkerchief creates and reinforces the logic of the play. Each scene from the moment of the handkerchief's introduction is the result of its presence. The operative is the handkerchief's effective presence. It is not a mere thing. In the final moments, in which the intrigue established by Iago has been revealed, the handkerchief returns. What Iago set in play stemmed from the 'monstrous birth'. That birth was the bringing forth of life – life as constructed subjectivity – to which guilt had always already been adduced. With Iago's revelation the handkerchief has been devalued, its power exhausted as its effects have been realised. Cassio makes it clear that the handkerchief cannot be separated from the work of the play. He reports Iago's own confession – namely that he, Iago, 'dropped it for a special purpose / Which wrought to his desire'.[29] To which Othello responds, 'O fool, fool! fool!'[30] This response, the reiteration of 'fool' as allowing for the position to be performed rather than simply stated, signals both the recognition of the object's hold, while conceding that, even though the handkerchief's force could be acknowledged retrospectively, at the time it did not have a separate existence, it permeated life. Moreover, its hold was insurmountable. Hence Benjamin's claim that central to fate is a conception of guilt that 'however fleeting its appearance, unleashes causality as the instrument of the irresistibly unfolding fatalities'.[31] Guilt and fate are worked out therefore in relation to the object or 'thing'. The handkerchief as a 'thing' created a world and a chain of events. It naturalised the process that then incorporated it as a mere 'thing'. Hence Benjamin's point that fate is not simply causal, as though the cause could stand apart from the effects. It is present as the 'entelechy of events' and as such permeates and structures that which is lived out.

The creaturely, while it may appear to refer to a form of animality, is in fact, as has been intimated, the repositioning of subjectivity within the field of guilt. Fate can be withdrawn from the lives of animals and plants – a position advanced by Benjamin in his essay on Goethe's *Elective Affinities*. Benjamin's point is clear:

> Fate does not affect the life of plants. Nothing is more foreign to it. On the contrary fate unfolds inexorably in the culpable life. Fate is the nexus of guilt among the living.[32]

In this passage, fate and what will become another conception of life are held apart. That life, the life held apart and which is as much the life of plants as it is the life of animals, will take on a different quality once it is positioned beyond the oppositions human/animal and human/plant. Life, the transfiguration of life allowed for by the ineliminable potentiality that life will have always contained, opens up beyond its incorporation within the logic of fate. Hence Benjamin's argument in 'The Task of the Translator':

> The concept of life is given its due only if everything that has a history of its own, and is not merely the setting for history, is credited with life. In the final analysis, the range of life must be determined by history rather than by nature, least of all by such tenuous factors as sensation and soul.[33]

The reference to 'history' in this passage is to a conception of history that is no longer thought in terms of either historicism (progress, chronology, etc.) or 'eternal return'. This means that there is the extension of life to that which has a history, though the reciprocity here should be noted. Having a history includes plants and animals – perhaps even rocks – even though the way history figures in relation to such entities remains an important if unresolved project. In other words, the becoming historical of animals and plants has to be thought beyond the exclusive identification of history with human history, an identification that necessitates, from within such a purview, a link between history and a subsequent avowed recognition of historical existence as that which pertains exclusively to human being. Could history be that which is expressed by the *rhythms* of animal life? While these 'rhythms' are observed as abstraction from a human perspective, on the level of animal life they are lived out. If the lives of animals can be reconsidered as historical, then the question of what counts as history will have to be rethought.

From within the domain of *Trauerspiel* the work of fate creates an enclosure allowing for no obvious departure. The hold of the form is clear. *Trauerspiel* has a formal presence. Moreover, the form itself refuses any real possibility for an interruption of the hold of fate. Hence, what arises in this context as a genuine question is the following: What conditions would need to pertain in order to involve fate's cessation? A condition which would give rise to a mode of existence – life as transformed – such that the life in question would be neither defined nor structured by guilt. The interruption of the work of fate, work as fate's unending reiteration occasioned by fate's naturalisation, cannot come from an internal form of forgiveness. Neither guilt nor fate is moral. There is therefore no moral universe for which amends need to be made and a form of salvation sought. Equally, ending the work of fate cannot have either a source or a prompt that is completely exogenous. Elsewhere in Benjamin's writings the inexorability of fate is positioned as the reiteration of 'mythic violence', the interruption of which is brought about by the caesura that takes the form of 'divine violence'. The latter is the generative cessation of the temporality of myth in the name of an allowing and thus the opening up of a future. However, it is not as though fate and the mythic do not contain that which occasions or more emphatically prompts that interruption. In the 'Critique of Violence' Benjamin is explicit on this point. He argues that 'divine violence is pure violence over all life for the sake of the living' (*reine Gewalt über alles Leben um des Lebendigen willen*).[34] In other words, at the centre of arguments convening life, there is the 'living'. Life as a static abstraction becomes living as a complex of particularities. Acting on their behalf – acting, for example, contra the reiteration of 'barbarism' – occurs from without.[35] However, crucially, exteriority demands a locus of interior potentiality in order that delimitations are staged and openings occur. This is a claim whose location is the present and which identifies a possible politics of the present. Moreover, it announces a political possibility – a possibility with its own enjoining forms of cultural practice – that was not available to the Baroque and thus could not be worked out within the logic of *Trauerspiel*. This identifies the inherent limitation of the Baroque. It emerges in relation to this sense of what is possible and the means by which what is possible could become actual; hence the presence of the disjunction between the logic of *Trauerspiel* and the retrospective identification of the limitations that such a logic stages. As will be suggested, this particular identification brings into play a relationship between history and remembrance.

If it becomes plausible, to argue for overcoming the creaturely should not be thought as being a reversion to a form of humanism. The creature is not the animal. Rather, overcoming the creaturely needs to be understood as a form of intervention. While this comes to be expressed in terms of 'divine violence', in the case of the argumentation of *The Origin of German Tragic Drama* it is announced, albeit negatively, in the formulation, firstly, that the Baroque was denied 'direct access to a beyond', and secondly, that it had not awoken within it 'the clear light of self awareness'.[36] The first of these formulations not only underscores the nature of the difference between the Renaissance and the Baroque, it also incorporates the role of theology. Intimations of a beyond have to do with a commitment to a beyond and thus to a conception of there being another possibility for life – what can be described as an image-free utopian impulse – that was not suffused by 'faith', where faith is understood as the naturalised fateful determination of life, and therefore not constructed in advance, either by the reiteration of historical time as fate or by the identification of subjectivity with the 'creaturely'. What held the Baroque in place and endowed fundamental instances of *Trauerspiel* as well as specific art works with their functional quality was not just the work of fate, but also the operative presence of the structure of melancholia. And yet the presence of that structure, for Benjamin, if only within a possible afterlife and thus as given within remembrance (thus given again, albeit for the first time), also provided the moment of hope.

While melancholia clearly pertains to the individual – Benjamin writes in a clear allusion to Hamlet that 'the prince is the paradigm of the melancholy man'[37] – melancholia is, at the same time and more significantly, a condition of the world. Benjamin begins his extensive treatment of the topic by noting that, within the Baroque, Lutheranism had taken over 'secular life' (*das profane Leben*), with the result that activity in the world, while regimented by a strict moral code, cannot lead to any form of salvation. As Benjamin indicates, drawing on his reading of Luther, 'civic conduct' and 'good works' had, for the Baroque, a

radically different quality.[38] The world was separated fundamentally
from its own possible transcendence. And yet what accompanied this
closure was the link between faith and 'grace'. While the overcoming of
the world was cut off from any action within it, the condition of that
separation, namely the centrality of faith, brought with it that which
would eventually allow the 'soul' to undergo a form of overcoming.
However, there is a limitation. Overcoming would be the province of
the 'soul'. And here the limit arises: in going no further than that which
was sanctioned by Christianity, human beings remained trapped in the
world. Human life was held by what had arisen. As a result, overcoming the hold of the world was marked by forms of impossibility. The
retention of 'grace' therefore has to be understood as a locus of mournful hope within the world. While reducing life to the domain of 'faith',
which seems to allow no way out, it introduced 'grace' as suggesting
precisely that possibility, even if that possibility was in the end limited.
Benjamin suggests that it was this predicament that was productive of
melancholy. Melancholy occurs within a world that has already been
emptied. Existence was traversed by this emptiness, on the one hand,
and by a pervasive sense of the inauthentic, on the other. In response
to this determination of the world and of 'existence' (Benjamin uses the
term *Dasein*), he writes that: 'Life itself protested against this' (*Dagegen
schlug das Leben selbst aus*).[39] While this position is not pursued explicitly, it is, nonetheless, a position that recurs when Benjamin traces the
dialectical structure of both melancholia and Saturn.[40] Nonetheless,
such a formulation underscores the potentiality inherent in life, a
potentiality there once the static notion of life is allowed to contain the
unpredictable presence of the 'living'. Enduring beyond any form of
neutrality, life remains as that which contains an inherent potential for
activity. While it is necessary to return to 'life' as a source of potentiality,
it is vital at this point to develop the relationship already established by
Benjamin between melancholia and the 'empty world'.

Benjamin's work on melancholia is informed by an attempt to recover
a sense of its limitation from his insistence on its dialectical nature.
That insistence is based on an interpretation of both melancholia and
Saturn that attributes primary significance to what he refers to as an
'ancient dialectic' in the way the terms 'melancholia' and 'Saturn'
figured from Aristotle onwards. The limitation has a twofold presence.
In the first instance it delimits a specific philosophico-historical setting.
In the second it uncovers an inherent limitation. The latter is that from
which the Baroque failed to wake. While Benjamin's argument has the
appearance of a claim that is simply specific – that is, determined by the
Baroque – there is far more at stake. From within this purview there are

a number of elements of Benjamin's presentation of melancholia that need to be noted.

A point of departure can be identified in the supposition that melancholia is in part the response to the impossibility of forms of transcendence interarticulated with the position in which there is 'the subjection of man to fate'.[41] Even the sovereign is thus positioned. In Benjamin's terms, the sovereign may be 'the lord of the creatures', but nonetheless 'he remains a creature'.[42] Not only does this connection tie melancholia and fate together, it also indicates that central to that relation is a conception of subjectification that incorporates humanity in its totality. There is therefore a generalised subject for whom the world is dead. Fate deadens. Objects that were thought to have utility have become inoperative. Equally, objects came to be invested with a power that could not be aligned with their utility. The first, the inoperative nature of objects, informs Benjamin's interpretation of the objects that surround the figure of Melancholia in Dürer's engraving *Melencolia 1*, while the second, objects invested with power, accounts for the force of the handkerchief in *Othello*. The deadening of the world, its relation to fate and the connection to a conception of subjectivity, once taken together, need to be placed in the context of what can be described as Benjamin's overall philosophico-historical project. That project is in fact a reconstruction of the history of melancholia.[43] Benjamin's reworking of the history of melancholia and its relation to fate has the effect of denaturalising fate, thus stripping both it and melancholia of their inevitability (inevitability as 'eternal return'); in so doing he locates that inevitability historically (thus ridding it of its inevitability). This is the project of history beyond the hold of fate, and thus beyond the hold of what the Baroque envisaged for itself. As a result a specific delimitation is constructed, which arises at the interplay of destruction and allowing.

Melancholia, Benjamin writes, is 'the most creaturely of creative impulses'.[44] In other words, it is an impulse that is intimately connected to fate and its naturalisation. The emphasis on creativity is essential. Melancholy can be understood as eschewing that relation when it is linked, almost exclusively, to 'madness' (*Wahnsinn*), leading to the interconnection between creativity, genius and madness. While Benjamin does not argue it as such, implicit in his reworking of melancholia is the recognition that this interconnection, in excluding a sense of measure since 'madness' and 'nonsense' are always counter-forces to measure, positioned creativity in relation to what could be described as a dialectic of despair and nonsense. In returning to the 'ancient' formulation, Benjamin begins with a discussion of Aristotle's *Problemata*. In this context, what arises as inevitable within the structure of melancholia is ineliminability of measure. There is, as Benjamin indicates, drawing on Warburg specifically, a close connection between melancholia and astrology and thus to 'stellar influences'. However, once viewed from within the ambit of a philosophy of history rather than as an isolated historical occurrence, the connection becomes a formulation of fate, a formulation giving rise, almost too easily, to its own naturalisation. The relation to inevitability – that which could be understood as the fate of fate – prompts Benjamin's reinterpretation. While there was a relation between melancholia and Saturn in which the planet exerted a determining hold – the hold in which madness and fate would become entwined – there was another possibility. Deploying the insights of Panofsky's and Saxl's interpretation of Dürer's *Melencolia 1*, Benjamin takes up what he describes as a 'dialectical trait in the idea of Saturn'.[45]

What interests Benjamin is the argument that the potential within the presentation of Saturn, coupled with its connection to melancholia – a potential, he argues following Warburg, that was lost in the Middle Ages – was located in a tension, for some a 'contradiction', between Saturn's creating in the soul that which on the one hand becomes 'sloth and dullness' while on the other opens up 'the power of intelligence and contemplation'.[46] This set-up mediates the link between Saturn and the interplay of depression and manic ecstasy. Deploying the work of Panofsky and Saxl, Benjamin reiterates the connection already established between Saturn and the figure of Cronos, the 'god of extremes'. Again there is a similar dialectical tension. He is simultaneously 'mournful' and 'condemned', while also being the one who 'creates' and is 'wise'. In relation to examples of this kind Benjamin writes that the 'history of the problem of melancholy unfolds within the perimeter of this dialectic'.[47] In an argument that takes up the work of Warburg on the Renaissance, Benjamin argues that this tension reappeared in the Renaissance in productive ways, which had a structuring effect on the Baroque. The legacy of that reappearance is that it gave a different impetus to the question of creation. While the Baroque closed down the possibilities that obtained in the Renaissance, the potentiality could be taken to endure. At the very least this is the supposition to be maintained. Benjamin writes that the melancholic posed the question of how it might be possible 'to discover for oneself the spiritual powers of Saturn and escape madness'.[48] Another way of asking this question is to ask how measure can be retained, given the clear link between 'madness' and the absence of measure.

What Cronos figures – namely, melancholy as the locus of a dialectical tension – also occurs within Dürer's *Melencolia 1*. For Benjamin the tension exists, *inter alia*, in the figure of the dog in the engraving.

The spleen of the dog, the site in which melancholia is active, can lead to the dog becoming rabid. And yet, the dog is equally the 'image of the tireless investigator and thinker'.[49] This tension is reinforced within the engraving by the dog's being asleep. Sleep is as much the place of nightmares (stemming from the spleen) as it is that which allows for prophetic dreams. While continually reiterated within Dürer's work, once the tension is incorporated into a Baroque sensibility, it closes down the possibility of overcoming the place in which it is located. Within the Baroque, what cannot be heard is 'the voice of revelation'. Benjamin is clear:

> For all the wisdom of the melancholic is subject to the nether world: it is secured by the immersion in the life of creaturely things, and it hears nothing of the voice of revelation.[50]

The point of departure for any response to this location of the 'melancholic subject' has to begin with the recognition that what is referred to above as the 'life of creaturely things' is not life. Rather, it is the equation of life with guilt. An equation that opens up, as a consequence, the question of what will be involved in the recovery of life, a recovery which has to be interpreted as the overcoming of guilt. Overcoming here is positioned in stark contrast to the continuity of repetition. In other words, the remembering of life as the activation of life's inherent potentiality and thus the incorporation of the move in which life rebels against its own entrapment within guilt. It is vital to note that overcoming is not the disavowal of guilt; on the contrary, it allows for guilt to emerge as that which had been imposed on life. Guilt comes to be recognised, and thus known, through the process of denaturalisation and demythologisation.

In his engagement with *Melencolia 1* Panofsky quotes a version of Dürer's important comment concerning beauty: 'But what Beauty is I know not' (*Was aber die Schönheit sei, das weiß ich nit*).[51] This claim needs to be interpreted in the context created by the influence of Ficino on Agrippa and Melanchthon, and their subsequent influence on Dürer (positions noted by Panofsky and Warburg and thus Benjamin); but, even taken on its own, it provides a genuine insight into the gaze of the figure of Melancholia within the engraving.[52] It would be an understanding of her gaze that drew on what has already been identified as a 'dialectical tension' within melancholia. The tension arises from the necessity for creation (a necessity that is linked to the retention of measure as the ineliminable component within the act of creation) and that which either hinders it – e.g. sloth – or renders it impossible – e.g. madness. The latter is the marker of measure's own impossibility. (If measure is a form of

reference, then 'madness' (*Wahnsinn*) and 'nonsense' (*Unsinn*) would
work in different ways as reference's undoing.)

The commitment to Beauty appears here as a negative presence. What
defines Beauty is not the impossibility of an idea (or ideal) but its impossibility of functioning either as an object of knowledge or as that which
appears. Beauty exists within these latter two senses of the impossible.
Both of these elements are there within the engraving. They are present
– the presentation of the impossibility of presentation – in Melancholia's
gaze. Absence and impossibility figure in her eyes. What is significant
here is that this sense of impossibility is not one that casts doubt on
the viability or even the necessity of there being a realm of ideas that
are external to presentation and which are then at work in accounts of
presentation. It is important to contrast this position with Warburg's
location of the figure and the conception of history within which it takes
place. Warburg argues that:

> Dürer's Melancholy has yet to break quite free of the superstitious terrors of
> antiquity. Her head is garlanded not with bay but with teukrion, the Classical
> herbal remedy for melancholy and she follows Ficino's instructions for
> protecting herself against Saturn's malefic influence with her numerological
> magic square.[53]

What is important in Warburg's description is the identification of the
limit within the array of symbolism. Even allowing for melancholia to
contain a dialectical tension, such a description takes the presentation
of a world that is not just self-enclosing but also a description that
precludes – a preclusion understood as the enactment of a specific philosophico-historical position – the possibility of its own self-overcoming.
Warburg's delimitation of Dürer is simply in terms of the work's historical register and as such misses the present possibility (its possibility
for the present) that is at work in the engraving. Even if a dialectical
tension exists, for Warburg it is maintained within the singularity of
the temporal moment. From within such a purview, history becomes
a form of writing that establishes delimitations that are present, thus
also presented, in terms of the singularity of their having occurred. As
a consequence history cannot open up beyond the identification of such
occurrences. While the Baroque may have had neither an 'eschatology'
nor a conception of 'other times', as Benjamin indicates (a position
that can be incorporated into and thus forms part of the reiteration of
history as historicism), it does not follow from the presence of such a
possibility that the potentiality of the Baroque functioning historically,
albeit within a radically different conception of the historical, is precluded by definition. To the extent that such a conception of history is

real – in contradistinction to the conception of the historical at work in Warburg's description – and that it is bound up with remembrance and thus the presence of what can be called the *always-possible reactualisation* of the past, then that potentiality would always have to have been there.

Returning to *Melencolia 1* necessitates the recognition that there needs to be a way beyond a conception of history as the description of a self-enclosure. This is the construction of a history that juxtaposes that enclosure with potentiality: a positioning that allows for an always-possible potentiality to be actualised, and hence the *always-possible reactualisation* of the past. What this envisages is a juxtaposition that will work as a continual prompt within philosophico-historical analyses. The question that needs to be addressed therefore concerns the recovery of this potential and thus the inscription within the frame of the conditions opening up the possibility for 'life' to rebel. Life takes on the quality of that which resists, even if that resistance is recovered retroactively and as a form of remembrance.

In the first instance *Melencolia 1* presents the retention of a version of the idea or the ideal. The idea/ideal in question is Beauty. It is retained precisely in terms of its impossibility and thus it is that whose loss (not loss as death but loss as the unactualised) is retained in its impossibility. While Benjamin does not argue it explicitly, what can be juxtaposed with this sense of impossibility is the irreconcilable tension that can be located in the relation between Saturn and Jupiter and the figure of the dog as the site of both the rabid (madness and unmeasure) and creativity, and thus of both creation and measure. For Warburg that tension closes in on itself. However, the force of the juxtaposition is not between the latter elements, it is between the figure of Melancholy as the site of Beauty's impossible possibility and those elements. Beauty's impossibility generates a form of lament. What is unknown is felt to be lost. The loss is pervasive. And yet, the sense of impossibility encounters possibility. The encounter is not unfettered creativity; rather it encounters creativity, and thus a form of production within the continuity of its contrast, with that which would restrict, diminish and render it impossible. Possibility and a complex sense of the impossible encounter each other.[54] The encounter does not stage the overcoming. It brings with it two important consequences. In the first instance, it is the necessity of a form of production that cannot be restricted by either the retention of an already predetermined image or its impossibility. That sense of the creative, in working beyond both the already determined and its impossibility, on the one hand, and 'madness', on the other, opens up the second instance. The opening up is a recalling. Within the creative, what cannot be dispelled, and what is therefore also present once the creative works move beyond the hold of impossibility, is life. This is not the life of the creature: not fateful life which on the level of creativity and therefore on the level of the image becomes the reiteration of the already given. Creativity unable to work beyond the structuring hold of 'eternal return' is another life and a different sense of creation.

Melancholia's gaze, therefore, while figuring loss and holding Beauty's impossible possibility in place, in its being unable to stem the potential for creativity, opens up the question of recasting the impossibility of the idea/ideal as the overcoming of idealism. This is an overcoming that would be, at the same time, the refusal to give fate a determining role within the process of creation. The interplay of figures and symbols within Dürer's engraving cannot preclude this eventuality. That it was not available to the Baroque cannot preclude the possibility of its being found, now, to be there.

Accounting for the differences that operate within and as the work of historical time is not just a matter of establishing divisions and conditions of possibility that delimit forms of periodisation in an exact and exacting sense. Equally, assuming that concepts or moments within historical periodisation can be simply decontextualised would be premised on having failed to understand what particularity entailed and thus what establishing actual differences – for example, the difference between the Baroque and Modernity – actually involves. Instead, implicit in Benjamin's treatment of *Trauerspiel* is an argument that is premised on undoing the naturalisation of historical time, which in this context involves the incorporation of time within a particular conception of fate. However, it is only by paying careful attention to that conception that it then becomes possible to note the ways in which fate and melancholia work together. Despite their operative presence, indeed *within* it, there is a possibility, while not available at the time – the time that locates *Trauerspiel* – that cannot be excluded. That possibility, as has been argued, is there as a potentiality. Equally, it is there in the ineliminability of a conception of life in which life is held apart from its subordination to guilt and 'eternal return'. Potentiality allows for the identification of the historical in a way that both identifies and refuses limitations; this identification and refusal is history as remembrance. Life's link to potentiality inheres in the impossibility of the former's equation with the work of fate. Fate is a conception of historical time. The philosophico-historical project overcomes the work of fate only though the scrupulous identification of its operative presence. This is the task of the historian and equally that of the critic. However, there is an opening out: self-enclosed worlds give way. As a result, history, life and potentiality come to be connected to the concept central to Benjamin writings in this period – 'happiness' (*das Glück*): 'Happiness is . . . what releases the fortunate ones [*den Glücklichen*] from the embroilment of the Fates and from the net of their own fate.'[55] History will have become that other possibility already within and as life.

Notes

1. The question of periodisation cannot be divorced from the question of historical time. The latter is subject to philosophical analysis and discussion. Indeed, Benjamin's study of *Trauerspiel* should not be thought of as a work of history, if history is simply historicism. The question of how it functions as a work of history is itself problematic. *The Origin of German Tragic Drama* can be read as a prolegomena towards the writing of history. If there is a prompt that organises then it can be seen retrospectively in a formulation such as the following from 'On the Concept of History': 'Every age must strive anew to wrest tradition away from the conformism that seeks to overwhelm it' (Benjamin, *Selected Works* 4, p. 391; *Gesammelte Schriften* I.2, p. 695).

   What is significant about this formulation is that Benjamin's work on *Trauerspiel* and thus the way periodisation is established, in sum the way the Baroque is constructed, cannot be separated from this formulation of the historical project.
2. Benjamin, *Origin of German Tragic Drama*, p. 79; *Gesammelte Schriften* I.1, p. 238.
3. Of the many important studies of Benjamin's text, that which has focused most forcefully on the concerns taken up in this paper is Max Pensky, *Melancholy Dialectics: Walter Benjamin and the Play of Mourning* (Amherst: University of Massachusetts Press, 1993).
4. Benjamin, *Origin of German Tragic Drama*, p. 92; *Gesammelte Schriften* I.1, p. 270.
5. Benjamin, *Origin of German Tragic Drama*, p. 100; *Gesammelte Schriften* I.1, p. 278. A similar point in relation to the same passage is made by Eva Guelen in her *The End of Art: Readings in a Rumour After Hegel*, trans. James McFarland (Stanford: Stanford University Press, 2006), p. 67.
6. I have tried to develop a detailed account of the way in which the present works as a term that orientates Benjamin's conception of the philosophico-historical task in my *Present Hope: Architecture, Judaism, Philosophy* (London: Routledge, 1997).
7. Benjamin, *Origin of German Tragic Drama*, p. 158; Benjamin, *Gesammelte Schriften* I.1, p. 335.
8. I have discussed Benjamin's use of this term in the context of *The Arcades Project* in 'Boredom and Distraction: The Moods of Modernity', in Andrew Benjamin (ed.), *Walter Benjamin and History* (New York: Continuum Books, 2005).
9. Benjamin, *Origin of German Tragic Drama*, p. 66; *Gesammelte Schriften* I.1, p. 246.

10. This introduces an important methodological point. The possibility of creation and thus of the introduction of that which functions as 'other' – perhaps
even the new – depends upon a form of destruction. The 'new' etc. cannot
be simply posited. That which is other cannot arise from an older system
of thought being 'exhausted'. Destruction becomes a generative allowing;
destruction occasions. While it cannot be pursued here, taking up this point
would necessitate a detailed investigation of Benjamin's text, 'The Destructive
Character' (*Selected Writings* 2, pp. 541–2; *Gesammelte Schriften* VII,
pp. 220–6). For a sustained discussion of the possibility of another form
of destruction, destruction as creation, as it works throughout Benjamin's
oeuvre, see Gérard Raulet, *Le caractère destructeur* (Paris: Aubier, 1997).

11. Benjamin, *Origin of German Tragic Drama*, p. 129; *Gesammelte Schriften*
I.1, p. 308.

12. The link between melancholia, fate and Lutheranism cannot pass unnoticed.
Some of the most important recent commentaries on this connection are to
be found in Jane Newman, 'Enchantment in Times of War: Aby Warburg,
Walter Benjamin, and the Secularization Thesis', *Representations* 105
(2009), pp. 133–67; Newman, 'Periodization, Modernity, Nation: Benjamin
Between Renaissance and Baroque', *Journal of the Northern Renaissance*
1.1 (2009), pp. 27–41; and Newman, '"Hamlet ist auch Saturnkind":
Citationality, Lutheranism, and German Identity in Benjamin's *Ursprung
des Deutschen Trauerspiels*', *Benjamin Studien* 1 (2008), pp. 175–95.
Newman's work positions Benjamin within the history of thought and thus
is able to draw important connections between Benjamin, Warburg and
Weber among others, and she undertakes a detailed analysis of the literary
works on which a great deal of the *Trauerspiel* study is based. She comments on the plays in great detail. While the importance of this work must
be noted, if there is a limit then it emerges in her reluctance to engage with
Benjamin's larger project. The danger of contextualisation, no matter how
rigorous and important, is that the larger project – what is referred to here
as the philosophico-historical project – can be subsumed within it.

13. Benjamin, *Origin of German Tragic Drama*, p. 138; *Gesammelte Schriften*
I.1, p. 317.

14. This impossibility as a mere impossibility as well as the presence of a form
of potentiality is a perception defining the contemporary.

15. Benjamin, *Origin of German Tragic Drama*, p. 135; *Gesammelte Schriften*
I.1, p. 308.

16. Benjamin, *Arcades Project*, p. 119; *Gesammelte Schriften* V.1, p. 178.

17. Benjamin, *Origin of German Tragic Drama*, p. 129; *Gesammelte Schriften*
I.1, p. 308.

18. The reference to the creature and its possible relation to the animal has
been the object of focus in a number of recent studies. Even though
the understanding of the creaturely within it is not straightforwardly
Benjaminian, one of the most significant is Eric Santner, *On Creaturely
Life: Rilke, Benjamin, Sebald* (Chicago: University of Chicago Press, 2006).
In regard to the work of Agamben, I have tried to offer a critical assessment
of his approach to the question of both the creaturely and the animal in
my 'Particularity and Exceptions: On Jews and Animals', *South Atlantic
Quarterly* 107.1 (2008), pp. 71–86.

19. To this end see the discussion of 'mere life' in Benjamin, 'Critique of Violence', *Selected Writings* 1, p. 250; *Gesammelte Schriften* II.1, p. 201.

20. Benjamin, *Origin of German Tragic Drama*, p. 132; *Gesammelte Schriften* I.1, p. 311.

21. All references to *Othello* are to William Shakespeare, *Othello*, ed. Russ McDonald, The Pelican Shakespeare (New York: Penguin Books, 2001). There is a great deal of important contemporary scholarship deploying Benjamin's work in order to interpret Shakespeare. Two important instances of this are: Hugh Grady, 'Hamlet as a Mourning-Play: A Benjaminesque Interpretation', *Shakespeare Studies* 36 (2008), pp. 135–65; and Zenón Luis-Martínez, 'Shakespeare's Historical Drama as Trauerspiel: Richard II – and after', *ELH* 75 (2000), pp. 673–705.

22. After Brabantio has given Desdomona to Othello – 'I here do give thee with all my heart / Which, thou hast already, with all my heart I would keep from thee' (I, iii, 193–4) – he warns him of the possibility of deception (I, iii, 292–3). Having 'deceived her father' she may deceive Othello. The key moment in the passage is 'if thou hast eyes to see'. Othello will see an object whose very ordinariness will undo him. So/hence, he will not have seen. The problem of perception and seeing marks him and mars him from the beginning.

23. Benjamin, *Origin of German Tragic Drama*, p. 91; *Gesammelte Schriften* I.1, p. 270.

24. Shakespeare, *Othello*, II, 1, 388.

25. Shakespeare, *Othello*, II, 1, 391–6.

26. A position developed by Benjamin in his text 'Fate and Character'; *Selected Writings* 1, pp. 201–7; *Gesammelte Schriften* II.1, pp. 171–9.

27. Benjamin, *Origin of German Tragic Drama*, p. 80; *Gesammelte Schriften* I.1, p. 239.

28. In commenting on Gide's discussion of Greek myth, Benjamin writes that Oedipus 'utters speeches in which there can be no room for thought [*Denken*], for reflection [*Besinnung*]'; Benjamin, *Selected Writings* 2, p. 579; *Gesammelte Schriften* II.1, p. 393. This formulation recalls the description of *Trauerspiel* in which the space of reflection is also excised. What matters is that even though there is an affinity, tragedy and thus the operation of fate within Greek tragedy is defined in relation to an external dimension working on the individual; within *Trauerspiel* it concerns the interiorisation of fate. The difference is fundamental.

29. Shakespeare, *Othello*, V, ii, 322–3.

30. Shakespeare, *Othello*, V, ii, 324.

31. Benjamin, *Origin of German Tragic Drama*, p. 129; *Gesammelte Schriften* I.1, p. 308.

32. Benjamin, *Selected Writings* 1, p. 307; *Gesammelte Schriften* I.1, p. 138.

33. Benjamin, *Selected Writings* 1, p. 255; *Gesammelte Schriften* IV.1, p. 14.

34. Benjamin, *Selected Writings* 1, p. 250; *Gesammelte Schriften* II.1, p. 201.

35. Benjamin writes the following in 'Experience and Poverty':

> This poverty of experience is not only poverty on the personal level, but also poverty of human experience in general. Hence a new kind of barbarism. (*Selected Writing* 2, p. 732; *Gesammelte Schriften* II.1, p. 215)

Barbarism is not a moral term. It points, for Benjamin, to another beginning and thus to an interruption in which poverty becomes the prompt. This other form of barbarism accords – an accord located within a general dialectical tension – with the more emphatic claim that all 'documents of culture' are inescapably marked by a form of barbarism. For the latter see Benjamin, *Selected Writings* 4, p. 392; *Gesammalte Schriften* I.2, p. 700.

36. The terminology of 'transcendence', 'overcoming', etc., has been used here to indicate that Benjamin's project needs to be situated in a form of transformation that both retains and transforms at the same time. However, rather than link that project to a form of Hegelianism the idealism of the latter is eschewed. What allows for the process to take place is the interplay between interruption and allowing, an interplay that, as is argued here, depends upon an ineliminable and original sense of potentiality.

37. Benjamin, *Origin of German Tragic Drama*, p. 142; *Gesammelte Schriften* I.1, p. 321.

38. Benjamin, *Origin of German Tragic Drama*, p. 138; *Gesammelte Schriften* I.1, p. 315.

39. Benjamin, *Origin of German Tragic Drama*, p. 139; *Gesammelte Schriften* I.1, p. 317.

40. For a comprehensive examination of the role of Saturn within the structure of European history of ideas – albeit not a study that deploys a concern with the problem of historical time – see Rudolf and Margot Wittkower, *Born under Saturn* (New York: Norton Library, 1969).

41. Benjamin, *Origin of German Tragic Drama*, p. 138; *Gesammelte Schriften* I.1, p. 315.

42. Benjamin, *Origin of German Tragic Drama*, p. 85; *Gesammelte Schriften* I.1, p. 264.

43. Benjamin's argument in this section of *The Origin of German Tragic Drama* draws extensively on the writings of Warbug, Panofsky, Saxl and Giehlow, in order to construct this history. While his use of their work is for the most part acritical, it can be argued that Benjamin should have established the distinctions between the conception of history in his project and the differing though related conceptions that inform theirs. For a detailed investigation of the complex relations between some of these differing art-historical projects see Georges Didi-Huberman, *Devant le temps* (Paris: Les Éditions de Minuit, 2000), pp. 85–159.

44. Benjamin, *Origin of German Tragic Drama*, p. 146; *Gesammelte Schriften* I.1, p. 324.

45. Benjamin, *Origin of German Tragic Drama*, p. 149; *Gesammelte Schriften* I.1, p. 327. For a detailed investigation of the relationship between Benjamin, Panofsky and Warburg in relation to Dürer and the general question of melancholia in Benjamin's work, see Beatrice Hanssen, 'Portrait of Melancholy (Benjamin, Warburg, Panofsky)', *MLN* 114.5 (1999), pp. 991–1013.

46. Benjamin, *Origin of German Tragic Drama*, p. 149; *Gesammelte Schriften* I.1, p. 327.

47. Benjamin, *Origin of German Tragic Drama*, p. 150; *Gesammelte Schriften* I.1, p. 328.

48. Benjamin, *Origin of German Tragic Drama*, p. 151; *Gesammelte Schriften* I.1, p. 329.
49. Benjamin, *Origin of German Tragic Drama*, p. 152; *Gesammelte Schriften* I.1, p. 330.
50. Benjamin, *Origin of German Tragic Drama*, p. 152; *Gesammelte Schriften* I.1, p. 330.
51. Erwin Panofsky, *The Life and Art of Albecht Dürer* (Princeton: Princeton University Press, 1971), p. 171. In citing Dürer, Panofsky does not provide a reference, but a similar position can be located in the passage cited here. The reference in this instance is Albrecht Dürer, *Schriften und Briefe* (Leipzig: ReclamVerlag, 1993), p. 110.
52. Those relations and influences are traced with great care by Panofsky in *The Life and Art of Albrecht Dürer*. For the relationship between Ficino, Saturn and art see André Chastel, *Marsile Ficin et l'art* (Geneva: Droz, 1996), pp. 177–85.
53. Aby Warburg, 'Pagan Antique Prophecy in Words and Images', in *The Renewal of Pagan Antiquity*, trans. David Britt (Los Angeles: Getty Research Institute, 1999), p. 647.
54. See in this regard Michael Ann Holly's insightful discussion of melancholia. Michael Ann Holly, 'The Rhetoric of Remembrance', in *Perspectives on Early Modern and Modern Intellectual History*, ed. Joseph Marino and Melinda Schlitt (Rochester, NY: University of Rochester Press, 2001), p. 326.
55. Benjamin, *Selected Writings 1*, p. 203; *Gesammelte Schriften* II.1, p. 174.

The Illusion of the Future: Notes on Benjamin and Freud

Opening

The future's inevitability makes it a matter of continual concern. (A concern, more significantly, that is played out in divergent ways. A state of affairs already signalled by the interplay of the inevitable and the continuous.) If the future's inevitability works as a continual refrain, what then of the future? What would comprise an account of its presence? What is it to think the future? Allowing for the future, though, not just as a mere event but also as part of a discursive possibility, makes demands. Thinking the future is already to allow time, and consequently both a philosophy as well as a politics of time, to have a direct impact on how thought is constructed. Once it is conceded that the future exists as that which demands to be thought then more is at stake than its simple occurrence. What is of significance is that thought – understood as a practice – is placed. (Place allowing for an intersection of history – understood as the work of time – and geography.) Indeed it is possible to conjecture that thinking is placed even if that state of affairs is not recognised as such. The place of thought is of course the 'now' of its happening: thought occurs at the present (thereby having presence). And yet, inherent in these concerns is the question of whether the future need be envisaged. In other words, the general question is whether thought is always to be accompanied by an image. More specifically, as indicated, what is of concern is the presence of the future within and as an image.

While the history of art and literature provides a divergent range of imagined futures, it is also the case that ritual (and in a certain sense the theological) works to guarantee the content of the future. What this means is that elements of ritual can be understood as linked to an attempt to guide the future's inevitability by providing it with its form. Hence there is an immediate distinction between the future's insistent reality and that reality having one particular determination (and thus image) rather than another. The disjunction between two particular forms of the political can be situated in relation to this distinction. In fact, what is brought into stark contrast are two different conceptions of a politics of time. In the first instance there is one that works in relation to the image. In the second, there is a different conception of the political and with it a different conception of time. Their combination distances the hold of the image by linking the future – not its inevitability but its quality – to an undertaking no longer structured by the image but by action.

Benjamin

If nothing else, these opening reflections prepare the way for one of Walter Benjamin's more emphatic statements concerning the future. In one of the final sections of 'On the Concept of History' he writes the following:

> The soothsayers who found out from time what it had in store certainly did not experience time as either homogeneous or empty. Anyone who keeps this in mind will perhaps get an idea of how past times were experienced in remembrance – namely, in just the same way. We know that the Jews were prohibited from inquiring into the future: the Torah and the prayers instructed them in remembrance. This disenchanted the future, which holds sway over all those who turn to soothsayers for enlightenment. This does not imply, however, that for the Jews the future became homogeneous, empty time. For every second was the small gateway through which the Messiah might enter.[1]

The significance of this passage, in this context, lies in the claim that there was a prohibition on Jews investigating the future. On one level this underscores the centrality of the concept of *zakhor* within Judaism.[2] In this regard Benjamin's position is quite correct. For example, the mitzvah concerning the observation of the Sabbath is formulated in terms of its being remembered ('Remember the Sabbath day and keep it holy'). In addition, though perhaps more problematically, the festival of Purim, it can be argued, is structured around the evocation to remember – *Devarim* 25: 17–19: 'Remember what Amalek did to you on your journey, after you left Egypt.' Nonetheless, the significance of Benjamin's observation is intended to be greater.

If there is a straightforward way of positioning Benjamin's claim then that to which the interdiction refers is not the future per se but the creation of an image of the future. Again, Benjamin would have been familiar with the elements of the synagogue service in which, during the period from Rosh Hashanah to Yom Kippur, the words 'Remember us into life' are introduced. Here there is a sense of remembering that evokes both the present and the future. Allowing for a place in the future is given in relation to the present. Hence there isn't a real sense in which the future is expressly forbidden, except insofar as there is the possible creation of its presence (the presence of the future) in an image. In other words, bound up with Benjamin's position is an iconoclasm in relation to the future. If there is to be a sense of the future – the future given within memory – then it is the future without an image and therefore without an already given and thus present topos. (The relationship between topology and the present is one to which it will be essential to return.)

This interpretation can be reinforced by recognising that Benjamin identifies immediately what may be taken as one of the obvious consequences of the position that he is developing. In sum, the consequence is that if the future has to be imageless then, so the argument would proceed, it would be empty. The response is to argue that the absence of an image does not entail emptiness. The contrary is the case. The image's absence is a precondition for the present to be charged with potentiality. The present's intensity is that which allows for the future. An allowing that would be undone by its being given an already determined image. Indeed, counter-posed to the image of the future is the centrality of potentiality. What a formulation of this nature brings to the fore is the relation of necessity between, on the one hand, potentiality and the future and, on the other, prohibition and the image (where image is understood in terms of the presence of an identified, and therefore already identifiable, topos). The point needs to be made that the necessary connection between the future and the refusal of the image introduces an intrinsic fragility. Actions cultural, artistic and political need to work beyond the hold of the identification of the future with an image precisely because were this not to be the case, and thus were the future to be given an already identifiable content, then the present as a site of intensity is undone. Once the future can be imagined – in the literal sense of being pictured and thus have an image that can be described – then what this constructs is a path towards it (the identified future). Teleology would have taken over, since what is allowed for by the creation of this path is the introduction of the temporality of continuity. Its introduction occurs in the place of a productive sense of discontinuity. (As will emerge, it is the relationship between production and interruption that is fundamental.)

For Benjamin continuity is semblance, a position presented in *The Arcades Project* in regard to a twofold interconnection between continuity and its appearing. It is the nature of the connection between them that establishes a site demanding interruption. Interruption and discontinuity figure in the present in relation to potentiality. Their actualisation is always strategic. (One of the names that this actualisation can take is politics.)

> It may be that the continuity of tradition is mere semblance [*Schein*]. But then precisely the persistence of this semblance provides it with continuity.[3]

The interplay of semblance and continuity is already to position time in terms of repetition. However, the positioning pertains to more than the temporality of continuity. Also implicated as a repetition is its appearing. While it will be essential to return to the presence of repetition – a return in which a particular affinity between Benjamin and Freud will come into play – what can be derived from Benjamin's formulation is that continuity has its image. However, positioned counter to continuity is not the future, let alone an image of the future. The counter-position in question involves a different conception of time than one defined by a relationship between past, present and future articulated in terms of time's simple passage. Continuity is countered not by the future, let alone its imagined presence, but by interruption or discontinuity. (These, *in nuce*, are the two differing politics of time, mentioned above.) In others words, given the centrality of continuity and then its image within appearance, the future would never have been in question. And yet, from a different political position, the contrary is the case. Within it the future should only ever be present as a question (thus as a task rather than an image.)

While this overall argument may be only implicit in Benjamin's engagement with the interdiction concerning the future, it is fundamental to the politics of time that orchestrates his writings. Again, implicitly, there is a more insistent question, one that touches Benjamin's work but which should be central to any engagement with the utopian: why does a concern with the future necessitate recourse to the future as an image? In order to answer this question it needs to be noted that one of the dominant tendencies within the utopian is to conflate the future with space. The result of this conflation is that the future will have an already given topology. In the move to the topological not only is an image a necessity, topology has replaced temporality as the organising concept. That replacement, as has been suggested, incorporates the present within the temporality of continuity – a continuity that exists necessarily once the future has an image – that is the mark of historicism. It is important to note, however, that the history of utopian thinking need not be circumscribed by having to provide images of the future. Indeed, it is possible to trace a path from 'visions' in both Plato and Cicero's Republics (the vision of Er and Scipio's dream) to work in the seventeenth and eighteenth centuries in which there is an important interconnection between vision, fantastic voyages and utopian literature. What is central is that which occurs in another place. Hence place, rather than a posited future, is fundamental to certain conceptions of the utopian. Place would be defined by its existence in the present. Both Bacon and Campanella, for example, link the political projects in regard to the utopian by insisting that the *New Atlantis* and *La Città del Sole* exist in the present. Moreover, the political effect of Cyrano de Bergerac's *L'autre monde* (a seventeenth-century critique of the 'absolutist state') is not due to the location of the 'moon' (the 'other world') in the future.[4] The contrary is the case. The fact that it was possible to voyage to the Moon and back – occurring therefore within the present – provides the text with a critical dimension precisely because it is not merely utopian. Indeed, it is possible to argue that the position that was held at the period was that utopian literature had a political force only if the topos that was then thought as the utopian was positioned in the present and not in the future. In sum, the critical depended upon the co-presence of distance and temporal simultaneity. (Moreover, the link between utopian writing – philosophical as well as literary – and fantastic voyages literature in the same period was also structured by a concern with place rather than chronology.)[5] Hence, even the history of utopian writing cannot be reduced to a concern with an imagined future. What occurs does so at the same point in time though in a radically different place.

Against an image of the future there is what Benjamin calls elsewhere in his writings 'the dialectical image'. While the term is given a number of different presentations, central in this context will be the one provided in Konvolut K of *The Arcades Project*:

> The new, dialectical method of doing history presents itself as the art of experiencing the present as waking world, a world to which that dream we name the past refers in truth. To pass through and carry out *what has been* in remembering the dream! – Therefore: remembering and awakening are most intimately related. Awakening is naming the dialectical, Copernican turn of remembrance.[6]

The theme of awakening needs to be held back from its incorporation into a mere moment (the latter being the instant within chronological time). A theory of experience will always have to be differentiated from the spontaneity of an act. In K1,2 Benjamin argues that there 'is a not-yet-conscious knowledge [*noch-nicht-bewußtes Wissen*] of what has been: its advancement has the structure of awakening [*die Struktur des Erwachens*].'[7] The structure works in relation to potentiality. Therefore the task involves realising the potentiality that defines the 'not-yet'. The way through this task starts from the recognition, to use Benjamin's formulation, that 'remembering and awakening are intimately related'. At this point an intervention into Benjamin's own mode of argumentation needs to be made. While Benjamin does argue for a conception of the present as a locus of infinite possibility, this is not formulated, within the detail of his writings, in terms of the centrality of potentiality. The claim is, however, that this is the term that allows Benjamin's project, as well as other projects stemming from Benjamin's work, to have both precision and actuality.[8] It should be added that such projects might be as much cultural and artistic as they are political. Indeed, it is possible to argue that 'potentiality' opens up the way in which all three can be connected, such that dimensions of one will be refracted through the others. A cultural politics, for example, does not involve giving the cultural a political content. It demands the cultural (or artistic) presence of the 'structure of an awakening'.

With Benjamin what emerges is a conception of the present that is defined in terms of potentiality. What matters therefore is the identification of the present, not as a point in time – a point having its own possible topology – but as a locus of activity. Activity and potentiality define the present as a site of work and therefore a place that *is* – i.e. has the ontological character it has – in its being worked through. Working through the present, construing the present as a network of activities, has a number of important consequences. One of these is the necessity that the present cannot have the quality, in the strict sense of the term 'quality', of that which is complete unto itself. (In other words, within such a formulation the present is not a self-referring singularity.) The opening of the present and its definition in terms of both potentiality and work necessitate that image construction – if this is the project – be bound to the present's work. For Benjamin, the relationship between the past and the present has to be understood in terms of the complex and productive set of interconnections between 'remembering and awakening' (a set of relations that are themselves the site of unending work precisely because it is a field of operations explicable in terms of the continual actualisation of potentialities). The combination of these elements allows for that which is remembered (and this will be the only useful definition of the past) to become a concern in and for the present.

Freud

In general terms, for psychoanalysis the question of the future will have at least two registers. In the first instance it would concern the way in which the analysand has a future. How, within the analytic setting and for the life of the analysand, is the future to be negotiated or even had? In the second instance the future figures within the realm of the social. Freud's writings on 'civilisation', 'war', etc., remain attempts to think through the contribution that psychoanalysis could make to the development of social and political communities. However, there is a more specific formulation, one in which these two more general elements will interconnect. His 1927 text *The Future of an Illusion* (*Die Zukunft einer Illusion*) not only names a concern with the future in its title, it incorporates into the structure of its argumentation a form of iconoclasm that is also implicitly present in Benjamin's text.

For these current concerns, the key moment in Freud's overall argument within this text is formulated in the following terms. It needs to be noted that the argument contains Freud's acknowledgement that the goals of religion – insofar as they concern 'the love of man and the decrease of suffering' – are not simply the same as his own personal beliefs, but accord with a psychoanalytically orientated conception of the social and thus with how individual psychic lives are thought in relation to it.

> Our god Logos will fulfill whichever of these wishes nature allows, but he will do it very gradually [*sehr allmählich*], only in the unforeseeable future [*in unabsehbarer Zukunft*] and for a new generation of men.[9]

The question of the 'gradual' and the description of the future as 'unforeseeable' indicate the way in which a psychoanalytic conception of the future becomes a reconceptualisation – in both temporal as well as topographical terms – of the present. In order to understand the operation of these terms it is vital that they be understood in relation to Freud's key text on the temporality of the psychoanalytic, i.e. 'Remembering, Repeating and Working-Through'.[10] While each of these terms designates areas and procedures that are fundamental to the techniques of analysis, they have greater extension.

Central to the procedure of analysis is repetition. However, the repetition in question concerns the way in which what has been repressed (and thus forgotten) reappears not as a memory but as that which is 'acted out'. After which Freud adds that, in regards to the analysand, 'he *repeats* it, without, of course, knowing that he is repeating it'.[11] This is the structure that, in this instance, defines the analytic encounter.

What has to be brought about within that encounter is an interruption of what Freud calls the 'compulsion to repeat'. However, this cannot be a pure and instantaneous act, as would occur were the analyst to do no more than confront the analysand with the position that, rather than the acting out of the new, all that was occurring was the enacting of repetition. Such a formulation would lead to a form of disavowal. What has to occur is an opening in which the move from repetition to its recognition as repetition and thus the occasioning of remembering can take place. The analysand will have an essential 'resistance' to this possibility. Hence there is the need for an opening. As it pertains to the analytic encounter, which is itself already a form of opening, this space is the 'transference'. Resistance cannot be overcome merely by an act of identification. As Freud argues, giving the resistance a 'name' will not result in its 'immediate cessation' (*unmittelbares Aufhören*).[12] Rather than the structure of the immediate there is a set-up defined by the inherently mediate. The mediate is not the refusal of the given. Rather, the mediate can be defined as the opening created by the impossibility of both singularity (giving a singular name with an intended singular response) and the temporality of the instant (the temporality defining naming and its response). In relation to this limit, Freud redefines the temporality of the setting that will have been opened.

> One must allow the patient time to become more conversant with this resistance with which he has now become acquainted, to *work through* it [*ihn durchzuarbeiten*], to overcome it [*ihn zu überwinden*] by continuing, in defiance of it, the analytic work according to the fundamental rule of analysis.[13]

Allowing time – understood as an opening created and recreated by the nature of the analytic encounter – cannot, for that reason, be an act of pure passivity. The task of 'overcoming' and 'working through' does not involve a simple response. For both analyst and analysand, it is demanding. Freud's formulations are explicit. For the analysand it is an 'arduous task', and for the analyst a 'trial of patience'. Within the space that is opened up, time is inextricably bound up with action. Precisely because what is at work is a process defined by activity – one that has an inherently dissymmetrical structure – any conception of futurity is that which is the consequence of work. The future becomes therefore a quality that inheres not just in the present but also in a conceptualisation of the present as a site of work. Work involves potentiality in the strict sense that once the encounter can be delimited, on the one hand by the transference, and on the other by the role of resistance in structuring the relationship between the conscious and the unconscious, then futurity is continually given by the process of 'working through'. There is a final point to note here. Dissymmetry – itself already a complex set-up in which the unconscious and conscious elements of the analysand and the analyst figure, hence the reference to the centrality of the transference – indicates that potentiality unfolds within a setting that does not lend itself to a final summation. The impossibility of finality is descriptive of the ontological quality of the present. Moreover, it is precisely this quality – one defined by the relationship between potentiality and action that resolves itself into differing and varying projects – that means that the present exists as a site of continual activity. (Again, in regard to the structure of thought, this is the affinity between Benjamin and Freud.) This site of original ontological complexity brings, as will be noted below, its own temporal considerations into play.

When writing of the practice of dream interpretation Freud evokes what could be described as the potential endlessness of interpretation. This should not be understood as a form of interpretive relativism but as the relationship between potentiality and a conception of the present which, to use the formulation that has already been deployed, is not a self-completing singularity.

> There is often a passage in even the most thoroughly interpreted dream which has to be left obscure; this is because we become aware during the work of interpretation that at that point there is a tangle of dream-thoughts which cannot be unraveled and which moreover adds nothing to our knowledge of the content of the dream. This is the dream's navel, the spot where it reaches down into the unknown. The dream-thoughts to which we are led by interpretation cannot, from the nature of things, have any definite endings; they are bound to branch out in every direction into the intricate network of our world of thought.[14]

While Freud concedes that there are further elements of the dream, the recovering of which is not fundamental to the interpretation, what is of greater significance is the claim that dream thoughts are potentially endless.

Within the interpretation the potentiality of the dream is always worked through by other aspects, for example the analysand's recounting of a particular dream at a particular moment within the analysis and the subsequent revision and retelling of the same dream such that what matters is not content per se, but the revisions occurring in its reiteration. These elements are not just given. Their occurrence has to be measured by the necessity that the work of repetition be overcome. Overcoming repetition occurs to the extent that it loses the appearance of novelty and emerges recognised as repetition (a re-emergence as an originating event). This is a process that takes place 'gradually'. (Not a conception of the gradual thought within continuity. The gradual is the opening defined by work. Moreover, working gradually acknowledges the impossibility of complete cessation. The gradual works through the continual possibility of disavowal.) Within the psychoanalytic session it involves what Freud calls the 'handling of the transference'.[15] More generally, it can be understood as linking the future to that which is remembered. However, the remembrance in question is not the completed or completing moment in which an act of memory closes the present by its having provided the future with an image. (The future endures as 'unforeseeable'.) Rather, the act of memory brings to the present (understood as the moment within chronology) an encounter between the remembered and the repeated. An encounter that redefines the moment such that it is no longer reducible to its chronological expression. This occurs within an opening. In psychoanalytic terms that opening is the analytic session. In Benjaminian terms it is the present created by the dialectic image that involves a juxtaposition which works as an interruption that presages – hence the future is only ever a condition of the present – because the past has, through memory, the actuality it would not have had were it to have been assimilated, through the process of continuity, to an image to come.[16]

A productive affinity between Benjamin and Freud occurs at this point. It had already emerged when it was argued that, for Benjamin, not only is it impossible for the future to have an image (and this for reasons that are as much philosophical as they are political), the future cannot have an already defined topos. The future as a topos is to be made. There is, therefore, an insistence on productive forms of practice. To the extent that the future is given an image, that image (either in terms of the image qua image or the image's contents) would then determine action. As such, the present would no longer figure as a concern and the past – not the past of historicism but the past of remembrance – would no longer function as that which informed and formed the present.

Notes

1. Benjamin, *Selected Writings* 4, p. 397; *Gesammelte Schriften* I.2, p. 704.
2. See Yosef H. Yerushalmi, *Zakhor: Jewish History and Jewish Memory* (New York: Schocken Books, 1989).
3. Benjamin, *The Arcades Project*, p. 486 [N19,1].
4. Savinien Cyrano de Bergerac, *L'autre monde* (Paris: Editions Sociales, 1975).
5. In regard to fantastic voyage literature during this period see Paul Cornelius, *Language in Seventeenth and Early Eighteenth-Century Imaginary Voyages* (Geneva: Librairie Droz, 1965). In more general terms, what this means is

that arguments to do with the utopian are best recast in terms of arguments to do with a politics of time.

6. Benjamin, *The Arcades Project*, p. 389 [K1,3].
7. Ibid. p. 389 [K1,2].
8. I have developed this argument in a number of places, most recently in 'Boredom and Distraction. The Moods of Modernity', in A. Benjamin (ed.), *Walter Benjamin and History* (London: Continuum, 2005), pp. 156–70.
9. Freud, 'The Future of an Illusion', in *Standard Edition*, vol. XXI, p. 54.
10. Freud, *Standard Edition*, vol. XII, pp. 145–56.
11. Ibid., p. 150.
12. Ibid., p. 155.
13. Ibid.
14. Freud, *Standard Edition*, vol. V, p. 525.
15. Freud, *Standard Edition*, vol. XII, p. 154.
16. For an informed and critical engagement with Benjamin's conception of the 'dialectical image', see Max Pensky, 'Method and Time: Benjamin's Dialectical Images', in David S. Ferris (ed.), *The Cambridge Companion to Walter Benjamin* (Cambridge: Cambridge University Press, 2004), pp. 177–98.

Bibliography

The bibliography contains all the works either consulted or cited in the writing of this book.

Adorno, Theodor W., *Gesammelte Schriften*, Band 16 (Frankfurt am Main: Suhrkamp Verlag).

Adorno, Theodor W., *Quasi una Fantasia: Essays on Modern Music*, trans. Rodney Livingstone (London: Verso, 1998).

Aeschylus, *Oresteia*, trans. Alan H. Sommerstein (Cambridge, MA: Harvard University Press, 2008).

Agamben, Giorgio, *State of Exception*, trans. Kevin Attell (Chicago: University of Chicago Press, 2005).

Agamben, Giorgio, *The Coming Community*, trans. Michael Hardt (Minneapolis: University of Minnesota Press, 1993).

Altrocchi, Rudolph, 'Michelino's Dante', *Speculum* 6.1 (January 1931): 15–59.

Anidjar, Gil, 'Christians and Money (The Economic Enemy)', *Ethical Perspectives: Journal of the European Ethics Network* 12.4 (2005): 497–519.

Aquinas, Thomas, *Summe der Theologie* 2, ed. Joseph Bernhart (Leipzig: Kröner, 1935).

Arendt, Hannah, *On Violence* (New York: Harcourt, Brace & World, 1970).

Arendt, Hannah, *The Human Condition* (Chicago: University of Chicago Press, 1958).

Aristotle, *The 'Art' of Rhetoric*, trans. John Henry Freese, Loeb Classical Library (Cambridge, MA: Harvard University Press, 1926).

Baessler, Katharina, *Walter Benjamins Thesen über den Begriff der Geschichte* (Grin Verlag, 2010).

Balibar, Etienne, 'Gewalt', in Wolfgang-Fritz Haug (ed.), *Historisch-Kritisches Wörterbuch des Marxismus*, Vol. 5 (Berlin: Hamburg: *Argument*, 2001).

Benjamin, Andrew, 'Boredom and Distraction: The Moods of Modernity', in Andrew Benjamin (ed.), *Walter Benjamin and History* (New York: Continuum Books, 2005).

Benjamin, Andrew, 'Framing Pictures, Transcending Marks: Walter Benjamin's "Paintings, or Signs and Marks"', in Andrew Benjamin and Charles Rice (eds), *Walter Benjamin and the Architecture of Modernity* (Melbourne: Re:press Books, 2009), pp. 129–46.

Benjamin, Andrew, 'Imagining Violence', *Filigrane* 14 (2011), online at: <http://revues.mshparisnord.org/filigrane/index.php>.

Benjamin, Andrew, 'Method and Time: Benjamin's Dialectical Images', in David Ferris (ed.), *Cambridge Companion to Walter Benjamin* (Cambridge, MA: Cambridge University Press, 2004), pp. 177–98.

Benjamin, Andrew, 'Particularity and Exceptions: On Jews and Animals', *South Atlantic Quarterly* 107.1 (2008): 71–86.

Benjamin, Andrew, *Art Mimesis and the Avant-Garde* (London: Routledge, 1991).

Benjamin, Andrew, *Being-in-Relation* (Forthcoming).

Benjamin, Andrew, *Disclosing Spaces: On Painting* (Manchester: Clinamen, 2004).

Benjamin, Andrew, *Leben und Glück* (Forthcoming).

Benjamin, Andrew, *Philosophy's Literature* (Manchester: Clinamen Press, 2001).

Benjamin, Andrew, *Place, Commonality and Judgment: Continental Philosophy and the Ancient Greeks* (London: Continuum, 2010).

Benjamin, Andrew, *Present Hope: Architecture, Judaism, Philosophy* (London: Routledge, 1997)

Benjamin, Andrew, *Style and Time: Essays on the Politics of Appearance* (Evanston: Northwestern University Press, 2006).

Benjamin, Andrew, *The Fabric of Existence: Placed Relationality as the Ground of Ethics* (Forthcoming).

Benjamin, Andrew, *The Plural Event* (London: Routledge, 1997).

Benjamin, Walter, *Gesammelte Schriften*, vols 1–7, ed. Rolf Tiedemann and Herman Schweppengäuser (Frankfurt: Suhrkamp Verlag, 1980).

Benjamin, Walter, *Selected Writings, Volume 1: 1913–1926*, ed. Marcus Bullock and Michael W. Jennings, trans. Rodney Livingstone (Cambridge, MA: Harvard University Press, 1996).

Benjamin, Walter, *Selected Writings, Volume 2: 1927–1934*, ed. Michael W. Jennings, Howard Eiland and Gary Smith (Cambridge, MA: Harvard University Press, 1999).

Benjamin, Walter, *Selected Writings, Volume 3: 1935–1938*, ed. Michael W. Jennings and Howard Eiland (Cambridge, MA: Harvard University Press, 2002).

Benjamin, Walter, *Selected Writings, Volume 4: 1938–1940*, ed. Michael W. Jennings and Howard Eiland (Cambridge, MA: Harvard University Press, 2003).

Benjamin, Walter, *The Arcades Project*, ed. Rolf Tiedemann, trans. Howard Eiland and Kevin McLaughlin (Cambridge, MA: Harvard University Press, 1999).

Benjamin, Walter, *The Origin of German Tragic Drama*, trans. John Osborne, intro. George Steiner (London: Verso, 1998).

Benjamin, Walter, *Über den Begriffe der Geschichte*, in Walter Benjamin, *Werke und Nachlaß. Kritische Gesamtausgabe: Band 19*, ed. Gérard Raulet (Berlin: Suhrkamp, 2010).

Bensussan, Gérard, 'Deus sive Justitia: Note sur "Critique de la violence"', *Les Cahiers Philosophiques de Strasbourg* 27 (Premier Semestre, 2010), pp. 15–22.

Bergson, Henri, *Essai sur les données immédiate de la conscience* (Paris: Paris, 2007).

Bergson, Henri, *L'énergie Spirituelle* (Paris: Payot, 2012).

Birmingham, Peg, 'Arendt and Hobbes: Glory, Sacrificial Violence, and the Political Imagination', *Research in Phenomenology*, 41 (2011): 1–22.

Birnbaum, Antonia, *Bonheur Justice: Walter Benjamin* (Paris: Payot, 2009).

Blencoe, Claire, 'Destroying Duration: The Critical Situation of Bergsonism in Benjamin's Analysis of Modern Experience', *Theory, Culture and Society* 25.4 (July 2008): 139–58.

Blumenthal-Barby, Martin, 'Pernicious Bastardizations: Benjamin's Ethics of Pure Violence', *MLN* 124.3 (April 2009): 728–51.

Bollack, Jean and Heinz Wismann, *Héraclite ou la séparation* (Paris: Editions de Minuit, 1972).

Bourtez, Pierre, *Les Lumières du messianisme* (Paris: Herman éditeurs, 2008).

Britt, Brian, *Walter Benjamin and the Bible* (Lewiston, NY: Edwin Mellen Press, 2003).

Brown, Wendy, 'The End of Educated Democracy', *Representations* 116.1 (Fall 2011): 19–41.

Buonamano, Roberto, 'The Economy of Violence: Derrida on Law and Justice', *Ratio Juris* 11.2 (June 1998): 168–79.

Butler, Judith, *Antigone's Children: Kinship Between Literature and Death* (New York: Columbia University Press, 2000).

Caygill, Howard, 'Walter Benjamin's Concept of Cultural History', in David Ferris (ed.), *The Cambridge Companion to Walter Benjamin* (Cambridge, MA: Cambridge University Press, 2004), pp. 73–96.

Caygill, Howard, *Colour of Experience* (London: Routledge, 1998).

Chanter, Tina, *Whose Antigone? The Tragic Marginalization of Slavery* (Albany, NY: SUNY Press, 2011).

Chastel, André, *Marsile Ficin et l'art* (Geneva: Droz, 1996).

Cohen, Hermann, *Ethik des reinen Willens* [1904], 3rd edn (Berlin: Cassirer, 1921).

Cohen, Richard A., *Elevations: The Height of the Good in Rosenzweig and Levinas* (Chicago: University of Chicago Press, 1994).

Cornelius, Paul, *Language in Seventeenth and Early Eighteenth-Century Imaginary Voyages* (Geneva: Librairie Droz, 1965).

Cottingham, John, *Cartesian Reflections: Essays on Descartes's Philosophy* (Oxford: Oxford University Press, 2008).

Courtine, Jean-François, *Levinas. La trame logique de l'être* (Paris: Hermann, 2012).

Cowan, Bainard, 'Walter Benjamin's Theory of Allegory', *New German Critique* 22 (Winter 1981): 109–22.

Curtis, Robin and Gertrud Koch (eds), *Einfühlung. Zu Geschichte und Gegenwart eines ästhetischen Konzepts* (Berlin: Fink, 2008).

Dante, *Inferno*, trans. Mark Musa (Bloomington: Indiana University Press, 1971).

de Bergerac, Savinien Cyrano, *L'autre monde* (Paris: Editions Sociales, 1975).

de Launay, Marc, 'Messianisme et philologie du Langage', *MLN* 127 (2012): 645–64.

de Wilde, Marc, 'Meeting Opposites: The Political Theologies of Walter Benjamin and Carl Schmitt', *Philosophy and Rhetoric* 44.4 (2011): 363–81.

Derrida, Jacques, *Force de loi* (Paris: Galilée, 1994).

Derrida, Jacques, *L'université sans conditions* (Paris: Galilée, 2001).

Derrida, Jacques, *Parages* (Paris: Galilée, 2003).

Derrida, Jacques, *Séminaire: La peine de mort*, vol. I (1999–2000) (Paris: Galilée, 2012).

Derrida, Jacques, *Spectres de Marx* (Paris: Galilée, 1993).

Derrida, Jacques, *Voyous: Deux essais sur la raison* (Paris: Galilée, 2003).

Derrida, Jacques and Élisabeth Roudinesco, *De quoi demain . . ., entretiens de Jacques Derrida et Élisabeth Roudinesco* (Paris: Flamarrion, 2003).

Descartes, René, *Meditations on First Philosophy*, trans. Michael Moriarty (Oxford: Oxford University Press, 2008).

Descartes, René, *Oeuvres de Descartes*, ed. Charles Adam and Paul Tannery (Paris: Librairie Philosophique J. Vrin, 1996).

Deuber-Mankowsky, Astrid, *Der frühe Walter Benjamin und Herman Cohen. Jüdische Werte, Kritische Philosophie, vergängliche Erfahrung* (Berlin: Verlag Vorwerk, 2000).

Didi-Huberman, Georges, *Devant le temps* (Paris: Les Éditions de Minuit, 2000).

Die Bibel, *Schulausgabe: Lutherübersetzung mit Apokryphen* (Stuttgart: Deutsche Bibelgesellschaft, 1984).

Downing, Eric, 'Divining Benjamin: Reading Fate, Graphology, Gambling', *MLN* 126 (2011): 551–80.

Drutt, Matthew, *Kazimir Malevich: Suprematism* (New York: Guggenheim Museum, 2003).

Dürer, Albrecht, *Schriften und Briefe* (Leipzig: ReclamVerlag, 1993).

Fackenheim, Emil L., *To Mend the World: Foundations of Post-Holocaust Jewish Thought* (Indianapolis: Indiana University Press, 1994).

Ferris, David, 'Politics of the Useless: The Art of Work in Heidegger and Benjamin', in Dimitris Vardoulakis and Andrew Benjamin (eds), *'Sparks will Fly': Benjamin and Heidegger* (New York: SUNY Press, 2014).

Ferris, David, *Walter Benjamin* (Cambridge, MA: Cambridge University Press, 2008).

Fichte, Johann Gottlieb, *Fichtes Werke*, Band V (Berlin: Walter de Gruyter, 1971).

Freud, Sigmund, *The Standard Edition of the Complete Psychological Works of Sigmund Freud*, ed. and trans. J. Strachey, in collaboration with Anna Freud (London: Hogarth Press, 1953–74).

Friedlander, Eli, *Walter Benjamin: A Philosophical Portrait* (Cambridge, MA: Harvard University Press, 2012).

Friedman, Martin, 'Dialogue, Speech, Nature and Creation: Franz Rozenzweig's Critiique of Buber's I and Thou', *Modern Judaism* 13.2 (1993): 109–18.

Gandler, Stefan, *Materialismus und Messianismus: Zu Walter Benjamins Thesen Über den Begriff der Geschichte*, Essay 29 (Aisthesis Verlag, 2008).

Gillespie, Michael Allen, *The Theological Origins of Modernity* (Chicago: University of Chicago Press, 2009).

Gold, Joshua Rober, 'The Dwarf in the Machine: A Theological Figure and Its Sources', *MLN* 121 (2006): 1220–36.

Grady, Hugh, 'Hamlet as a Mourning-Play: A Benjaminesque Interpretation', *Shakespeare Studies* 36 (2008): 135–65.

Greenberg, Udi E., 'Orthodox Violence: "Critique of Violence" and Walter Benjamin's Jewish Political Theology', *History of European Ideas* 34 (2008): 324–33.

Guelen, Eva, *The End of Art: Readings in a Rumour After Hegel*, trans. James McFarland (Stanford: Stanford University Press, 2006).

Haddad, Samir, 'A Genealogy of Violence: From Light to the Autoimmune', *Diacritics* 38.1–2 (Spring–Summer 2006): 121–42.

Hamacher, Werner, 'Afformative Strike: Benjamin's Critique of Violence', trans. Dana Hollander, in Andrew Benjamin and Peter Osborne (eds), *Walter Benjamin's Philosophy: Destruction and Experience* (London: Routledge, 1994), pp. 115–16.

Hamacher, Werner, 'Das Theologisch-politische Fragment', in Burkhardt Linder (ed.), *Benjamin Handbuch* (Stuttgart: J. B. Metzler, 2011), pp. 175–92.

Hamacher, Werner, 'Guilt History: Benjamin's Sketch "Capitalism as Religion"', trans. Kirk Wetters, *Diacritics* 32.3–4 (Fall–Winter 2002): 81–106.

Hamacher, Werner, 'To Leave the Word to Someone Else', in Julian Wolfreys (ed.), *Thinking Difference: Critics in Conversation* (New York: Fordham University Press, 2004).

Hammer, Dean, 'The Iliad as Ethical Thinking: Politics, Pity, and the Operation of Esteem', *Arethusa* 35.2 (Spring 2002): 203–35.

Hanssen, Beatrice, 'On the Politics of Pure Means: Benjamin, Arendt, Foucault', in Hent de Vries and Samuel Weber (eds), *Violence, Identity and Self-Determination* (Stanford: Stanford University Press, 1997), pp. 236–52.

Hanssen, Beatrice, 'Portrait of Melancholy (Benjamin, Warburg, Panofsky)', in *Modern Language Notes* 114.5 (1999): 991–1013.

Hegel, G. W. F, 'Der Geist des Christentums', in G. W. F. Hegel, *Werke*, vol. 1, *Frühe Schriften* (Frankfurt am Main: Suhrkamp, 1986).

Hegel, G. W. F., *Early Theological Writings*, trans. T. M. Knox (Philadelphia: University of Philadelphia Press, 1975).

Heidegger, Martin, *Basic Questions of Philosophy: Selected 'Problems' of 'Logic'*, trans. Richard Rojcewicz and Andre Schuwer (Bloomington: Indiana University Press, 1994).

Heidegger, Martin, *Being and Time*, trans. John Macquarrie and Edward Robinson (Oxford: Basil Blackwell, 1962).

Heidegger, Martin, *Grundfragen der Philosophie* (Frankfurt am Main: Vittorio Klostermann, 1992)

Heidegger, Martin, *The Fundamental Concepts of Metaphysics: World, Finitude, Solitude*, trans. William McNeill and Nicholas Walker (Bloomington: Indiana University Press, 1995).

Hölderlin, Friedrich, *Sämtliche Werke*, Band 1, ed. D. E. Sattler (Munich: Luchterland Literaturverlag, 2004).

Holly, Michael Ann, 'The Rhetoric of Remembrance', in Joseph Marino and Melinda Schlitt (eds), *Perspectives on Early Modern and Modern Intellectual History* (Rochester, NY: University of Rochester Press, 2001), pp. 325–46.

Homer, *Iliad*, trans. A. T. Murray, rev. William F. Wyatt (Cambridge, MA: Harvard University Press, 1999).

Hume, David, *History of England*, vol. 5 (Indianapolis: Liberty Fund Press, 1983).

Jacobson, Eric, *Metaphysics of the Profane: The Political Theology of Walter Benjamin and Gershom Scholem* (New York: Columbia University Press, 2003).

Jennings, Michael, 'Towards Eschatology: The Development of Walter Benjamin's Theological Politics in the Early 1920s', in Carolin Duttlinger, Ben Morgan, Anthony Phelan (eds), *Walter Benjamins anthropologisches Denken* (Freiburg im Breisgau: Rombach Verlag, 2012), pp. 41–58.

Kaes, Anton, 'A Stranger in the House: Fritz Lang's Fury and the Cinema of Exile', *New German Critique* 89 (Fall 2003): 33–58.

Kahn, Charles, *The Art and Thought of Heraclitus* (Cambridge, MA: Cambridge University Press, 1979).

Kambouchner, Denis, *Les Méditations métaphysiques de Descartes* (Paris: PUF, 2005).

Kant, Immanuel, *Critique of Pure Reason*, trans. Paul Guyer and Allen Wood (Cambridge, MA: Cambridge University Press, 1997).

Khatib, Sami, 'Towards a Politics of "Pure Means": Walter Benjamin and the Question of Violence', *Anthropological Materialism*, online at: <anthropologicalmaterialism.hypotheses.org>.

Kracauer, Siegfried, *The Mass Ornament*, trans. Thomas Y. Levin (Cambridge, MA: Harvard University Press, 1995).

Lebovic, Nitzan. 'The Beauty and the Terror of *Lebensphilosophie*: Ludwig Klages, Walter Benjamin and Alfred Bauemular', *South Central Review* 23.1 (Spring 2006): 23–39.

Lehman, Robert S., 'Allegories of Rending: Killing Time with Walter Benjamin', *New Literary History* 39.2 (Spring 2008): 233–50.

Löwy, Michael, *Fire Alarm: Reading Walter Benjamin's 'On the Concept of History'*, trans. Chris Turner (London: Verso, 2005).

Lucretius, *De Rerum Natura*, trans. W. H. D. Rouse, Loeb Classical Library (Cambridge, MA: Harvard University Press, 1992).

Luis-Martínez, Zenón, 'Shakespeare's Historical Drama as Trauerspiel: Richard II – and after', *ELH* 75 (2000): 673–705.

McCracken, Scott, 'The Completion of Old Work: Walter Benjamin and the Everyday', *Cultural Critique* 52, *Everyday Life* (Autumn 2002): 145–66.

McLaughlin, Kevin, 'Benjamin's Barbarism', *Germanic Review* 81.1 (Winter 2006): 14–16.

McLynn, F. J., 'Jacobitism and David Hume: The Ideological Backlash Foiled', *Hume Studies* IX.2 (1983): 171–99.

McNulty, Tracy, 'The Commandment Against the Law Writing and Divine Justice in Walter Benjamin's "Critique of Violence"', *Diacritics* 37.2–3 (Summer–Fall 2007): 34–60.

Marin, Louis, *La critique du discours*, (Paris: Editions de Minuit, 1975).

Martel, James R., 'Taking Benjamin Seriously as a Political Thinker', *Philosophy and Rhetoric* 44.4 (2011): 297–308.

Martel, James R., *Textual Conspiracies: Walter Benjamin, Idolatry and Political Theory* (Ann Arbor: The University of Michigan Press, 2011).

Marx, Karl, 'Theses on Feuerbach' [1845], in *Karl Marx: Selected Writings*, ed. and intro. Lawrence H. Simmon (Indianapolis: Hackett, 1994).

Menke, Christoph, 'Law and Violence', *Law and Literature* 22.2 (Spring 2010): 1–17.

Menninghaus, Winfried, 'Das Ausdruckslose: Walter Benjamins Metamorphosen der Biderlosigkeit', in I. and K. Scheuermann (eds), *Für Walter Benjamin: Dokumente, Essays und ein Entwurf* (Frankfurt am Main: Suhrkamp, 1992), pp. 170–82.

Mertens, Bram, *Dark Images, Secret Hints: Benjamin, Scholem, Molitor and the Jewish Tradition* (Berlin: Peter Lang, 2007).

Morris, John, 'Descartes' Natural Light', *Journal of the History of Philosophy*, 11.2 (April 1973): 169–87.

Moses, Stéphane, *L'ange de l'histoire* (Paris: Editions de Seuil, Paris, 1992).

Newman, Jane, '"Hamlet ist auch Saturnkind": Citationality, Lutheranism, and German Identity in Benjamin's *Ursprung des Deutschen Trauerspiels*', *Benjamin Studien* 1 (2008): 175–95.

Newman, Jane, 'Enchantment in Times of War: Aby Warburg, Walter Benjamin, and the Secularization Thesis', *Representations* 105 (2009): 133–67.

Newman, Jane, 'Periodization, Modernity, Nation: Benjamin Between Renaissance and Baroque', *Journal of the Northern Renaissance* 1.1 (2009): 27–41.

Nietzsche, Friedrich, *The Birth of Tragedy*, trans. Walter Kaufmann (New York: Vintage, 1967).

Nonnos, *Dionysiaca* 1–15, trans. W. H. D. Rouse (Cambridge, MA: Harvard University Press, 1940).

Noor, Ashraf, 'Walter Benjamin: Time and Justice', *Naharaim. Zeitschrift für deutsch-jüdische Literatur und Kulturgeschichte* 1 (2007): 38–74.

Osborne, Catherine, *Rethinking Early Greek Philosophy* (London: Duckworth, 1987).

Osborne, Peter, *The Politics of Time: Modernity and Avant-Garde* (London: Verso, 1995).

Panofsky, Erwin, *The Life and Art of Albecht Dürer* (Princeton: Princeton University Press, 1971).

Pensky, Max, 'Method and Time: Benjamin's Dialectical Images', in David S. Ferris (ed.), *The Cambridge Companion to Walter Benjamin* (Cambridge, MA: Cambridge University Press, 2004), pp. 177–98.

Pensky, Max, *Melancholy Dialectics: Walter Benjamin and the Play of Mourning* (Amherst: University of Massachusetts Press, 1993).

Petitdemange, Guy, 'De La Hantise: Le Marx de Derrida', *Cités* 30 (2007): 17–29.

Popper, Karl, *The Unended Quest* (London: Fontana, 1982).

Raulet, Gérard, *Le caractère destructeur* (Paris: Aubier, 1997).

Renton, David, 'On Benjamin's *Theses*, or the Utility of the Concept of Historical Time', *European Journal of Political Theory*, 11.4 (2012): 380–93.

Richter, Gerhard, 'Can Anything be Rescued by Defending It? Benjamin with Adorno', *Differences*, 23.3 (2010).

Rosenzweig, Franz, *On Jewish Learning* (New York: Schocken Books, 1955).

Rosenzweig, Franz, *The Star of Redemption*, trans. Barbara E. Galli (Madison: University of Wisconsin Press, 2005).

Rottenberg, Elizabeth, 'Cruelty and Its Vicissitudes: Jacques Derrida and the

Future of Psychoanalysis', *Southern Journal of Philosophy* 50 (Spindel Supplement, 2012): 143–59.

Ryder, A. J., *The German Revolution 1918–19* (London: Routledge, 1958).

Salzani, Carlo, 'Quodlibet: Giorgio Agamben's Anti-Utopia', *Utopian Studies* 23.1 (2012): 212–37.

Santner, Eric, *On Creaturely Life: Rilke, Benjamin, Sebald* (Chicago: University of Chicago Press, 2006).

Schmidt, Christopher, 'Zeit und Speil: Gesitergespräche zwischen Walter Benjamin und Carl Schmitt über Ästhetik und Politik', in Jen Mattern, Gabriel Motzkin and Shimon Sandbank (eds), *Jüdisches Denken in einer Welt ohne Gott. Festschrift für Stéphane Mosès* (Berlin: Verlag Vorwek, 2001).

Schmidt, Michael, 'L'allégorie entre écriture et l'instant', in Heinz Wismann and Patricia Lavelle (eds), *Walter Benjamin: Le critique Européen* (Paris: PUS, 2012), pp. 199–213.

Schmitt, Carl, *Political Theology. Four Chapters on the Concept of Sovereignty*, trans. George Schwab (Chicago: University of Chicago Press, 1985).

Scholem, Gershom, *Kabbalah* (Jerusalem: Keter Publishing House, 1974).

Scholem, Gershom, *Tagebücher 1917–23*, ed. Karlfried Grunder, Herbert Kopp-Oberstebrink and Friedrich Niewöhner (Frankfurt am Main: Jüdisher Verlag, 2000).

Schwebel, Paula L. 'Intensive Infinity: Walter Benjamin's Reception of Leibniz and Its Sources', *MLN* 127 (2012): 589–610.

Shakespeare, William, *Othello*, ed. Russ McDonald, The Pelican Shakespeare (New York: Penguin Books, 2001).

Shakespeare, William, *Shakespeare's dramatische Werke 6*, trans. A. W. Schlegel and Ludwig Tieck (Berlin: Berlag von Georg Reimer, 1869).

Shapiro, Kam, 'Politics Is a Mushroom: Worldly Sources of Rule and Exception in Carl Schmitt and Walter Benjamin', *Diacritics* 37.2–3 (Summer–Fall 2007): 121–34.

Sofocle, *Antigone*, trans. Ezio Savino (Milano: Garzanti, 1989).

Sophocles, *Antigone, Woman of Trachis, Philoctetes, Oedipus at Colonus*, ed. and trans. Hugh Lloyd Jones (Cambridge, MA: Harvard University Press, 1994).

Sophocles, *Three Tragedies: Antigone, Oedipus the King, Electra*, trans. Humphrey Davy Findley Kitto (Oxford: Oxford University Press, 1962).

Steiner, Uwe, 'The True Politician: Walter Benjamin's Concept of the Political', *New German Critique* 83 (Spring–Summer 2001): 43–88.

Tambling, Jeremy, 'Dante and Benjamin: Melancholy and Allegory', *Exemplaria* 4 (1992): 342–62.

Tawney, R. H., *Religion and the Rise of Capitalism* (London: Penguin Books, 1969).

Tiedemann, Rolf, 'Historical Materialism or Political Messianism? An Interpretation of the Theses "On the Concept of History"', in Gary Smith (ed.), *Walter Benjamin – Philosophy, Aesthetics, History* (Chicago: University of Chicago Press, 1989), pp. 175–209.

Tobias, Rochelle, 'Irreconcilable: Ethics and Aesthetics for Hermann Cohen and Walter Benjamin', *MLN* 127 (2012): 665–80.

Tomba, Massimilano, 'Another Kind of *Gewalt*: Beyond Law Re-Reading Walter Benjamin', *Historical Materialism* 17.1 (2009): 122–44.

Vardoulakis, Dimitris, *The Doppelgänger: Literature's Philosophy* (New York: Fordham University Press, 2010).

Vatter, Miguel, 'In Odradek's World: Bare Life and Historical Materialism in Agamben and Benjamin', *Diacritics* 38.3 (Fall 2008): 45–70.

Warburg, Aby, 'Pagan Antique Prophecy in Words and Images in *The Renewal of Pagan Antiquity*', trans. David Britt (Los Angeles: Getty Research Institute, 1999).

Weber, Max, *The Protestant Ethic and the Spirit of Capitalism* (Oxford: Oxford University Press, 2010).

Weber, Samuel, *Benjamin's -abilities* (Cambridge, MA: Harvard University Press, 2008).

Weidner, Daniel, 'Thinking Beyond Secularization: Walter Benjamin, the "Religious Turn" and the Poetics of Theory', *New German Critique* 37.3 111 (Fall 2010): 131–48.

Weigel, Sigrid, 'The Martyr and the Sovereign: Scenes from a Contemporary Tragic Drama, Read through Walter Benjamin and Carl Schmitt', *CR: The New Centennial Review* (Winter 2004): 109–23.

Whyte, Jessica, '"I Would Prefer Not To": Giorgio Agamben, Bartleby and the Potentiality of the Law', *Law Critique* 20 (2009): 309–24.

Wittkower, Margot and Rudolf Wittkower, *Born under Saturn* (New York: Norton Library, 1969).

Wohlfarth, Irving, 'No-Man's-Land: On Walter Benjamin's "Destructive Character"', *Diacritics* 8.2 (Summer 1978): 47–65.

Wohlfarth, Irving, 'On the Messianic Structure of Benjamin's Last Reflections', *Glyph* 3 (1978): 148–212.

Yerushalmi, Yosef H., *Zakhor: Jewish History and Jewish Memory* (New York: Schocken Books, 1989).

Index